A NEW THEORY
OF THE EARTH

A NEW THEORY
OF THE EARTH

William Whiston

ARNO PRESS

A New York Times Company

New York / 1978

Editorial Supervision: ANDREA HICKS

⸺··◁◎▷··⸺

Reprint Edition 1978 by Arno Press Inc.

HISTORY OF GEOLOGY
ISBN for complete set: 0-405-10429-4
See last pages of this volume for titles.

Manufactured in the United States of America

⸺··◁◎▷··⸺

Library of Congress Cataloging in Publication Data

Whiston, William, 1667-1752.
    A new theory of the Earth.

    (History of geology)
    Reprint of the 1696 ed. printed by R. Roberts for
B. Tooke, London.
    1. Creation—Early works to 1800. 2. Bible and
science. I. Title. II. Series.
BL224.W5 1977   213   77-6545
ISBN 0-405-10463-4

A NEW
THEORY
OF THE
EARTH

Systema Solare.

Cometa a Sole nuper digressus.   Cometa versus Solem descendens.

Orbita Cometæ   Orbita Cometæ

Sol.

Orbita Mercurij

Orbita Veneris

Luna

Orbita Telluris

Orbita Martis

Orbita Jovis

Orbita Saturni

A NEW
THEORY
OF THE
EARTH,

From its ORIGINAL, to the
CONSUMMATION of all Things.

WHEREIN

The CREATION of the World in Six Days,
The Univerſal DELUGE,
And the General CONFLAGRATION,
𝕬s laid down in the 𝕳oly 𝕾criptures,
Are ſhewn to be perfectly agreeable to
REASON and PHILOSOPHY.

With a large Introductory Diſcourſe concerning the Genuine Nature, Stile, and Extent of the *Moſaick* Hiſtory of
the CREATION.

By *WILLIAM WHISTON*, M. A.
Chaplain to the Right Reverend Father in God,
JOHN Lord Biſhop of *NORWICH,* and
Fellow of *Clare-Hall* in *Cambridge.*

LONDON:

Printed by R. *Roberts,* for *Benj. Tooke* at the
Middle-Temple-Gate in *Fleet-ſtreet.* MDCXCVI.

SUmmo Viro Isaaco Newton, Apud Londinenses Societatis Regalis, Apud Cantabrigienses suos Collegij S. S. Trinitatis Socio Dignissimo ; Matheseωs Professori Lucasiano longè Celeberrimo ; necnon Regio Nummorum Cusorum Præfecto ; Reipublicæ, quoquò patet, Literariæ Ornamento ; Seculi, Gentis, Academiæ egregio Decori ; Orbis Philosophici Delicijs. Qui rem præsertim Mathematicam eousque Excoluit, Adauxit, Dilatavit, ut ipsam Physicam intra pomœria sua complecti, & Mundi Systema, conatu inaudito, ditioni suæ subjicere tandem aliquando audeat. Quem Morum Candor & Modestia ; Quem Sagax animus & penetrans ; Quem assidui Labores, indefessæ Vigiliæ, Industria incredibilis promovendis veræ ac solidæ Sapientiæ studijs unicè dicata ; Quem Rerum Divinarum Humanarumq; hoc est Universæ Philosophiæ,

peritia

peritia planè singularis ; Quem de-
mum PHILOSOPHIÆ NATURA-
LIS PRINCIPIA MATHEMATI-
CA, auro contrà æstimanda, & mor-
talibus vix aut ne vix propalanda te-
merè, Ultimæ posteritati æternùm
Commendabunt.

Exiguum hocce Tentaminis Philosophici Spicilegium, è Messe NEW-
TONIANA primitùs sublectum ;
Subsidijs, Consilijs, Auspicijs potissi-
mùm NEWTONIANIS acceptum,
uti par est, referendum ratus, Totum
hoc, qualecunque sit, NEWTONI
nomini, in omne ævum perennaturo,
Nuncupandum ; &, in Grati Animi
Μνημόσυνον, Consecrandum censuit Gu-
lielmus Whiston. 17. Kal. Jun. A. D.
1696.

A DIS-

A
DISCOURSE
Concerning the
Nature, Stile, and Extent
OF THE
MOSAICK HISTORY
OF THE
CREATION.

 T being no inconfiderable part
of the enfuing Theory, to
account for the Creation of
the World, agreeable to the
defcription thereof in the Book
of *Genefis*, it cannot but be very
neceffary in this place, to dif-
courfe of the nature of that Sacred Hiftory, the
Stile in which it is Writ, and how far it is to be
Extended. The mifunderftanding of which
points has been, I think, the principal occafion of thofe perplexities and contrarieties into
which Men have run with relation to it ; while
fome have adher'd to the common and vulgar,
tho' lefs rational Expofition, without any

B con-

consideration of Nature, Reason, Philosophy, or just *Decorum* in the several parts of it: And others, on the contrary, have been so sensible of the wildnefs and unreasonablenefs of *That*, that they have ventur'd to exclude it from any just fenfe at all; afferting it to be a meer Popular. Parabolick, or Mythological relation; in which the plain Letter is no more to be accounted for or believ'd, than the fabulous reprefentations of *Æfop*, or at beft than the myftical Parables of our Saviour. Of what mifchievous confequence this latter is commonly efteem'd, I need not fay; a late excellent Author, who thought it abfolutely neceffary to be introduc'd, having felt reflections fufficiently fevere, and feen effects fufficiently mifchievous of fuch an Interpretation. And how unworthy of God, how incoherent and abfurd the former Expofition is in it felf, and muft be efteem'd by free and inquifitive Thinkers, 'tis not difficult to make appear to any impartial Man, and fhall in this Difcourfe be particularly attempted. Indeed I cannot but imagine that, as thofe who plead for the Mythological fenfe, do it only becaufe they fuppofe it impoffible to give a commodious and rational fcheme of it on any other Hypothefis; and therefore will eafily and readily embrace any more literal Interpretation which fhall agree to the Divine Attributes, the Reafon of their own Minds, and the true Syftem of the World; fo I think thofe who, notwithftanding its apparent incongruities, adhere to the vulgar Expofition, will have great reafon to encourage, and reft fatisfy'd in fuch an account, as fhall at once keep fufficiently clofe to the Letter of *Mofes*, and yet be far from allowing what contradicts the Divine Wifdom, Common Reafon, or

Philofophick

Philofophick Deductions: to both which therefore, I perfuade my felf this new attempt ought
not to be unacceptable.

But becaufe the principal difficulty is likely to
arife from the prejudices and prepoffeffions of
the latter, and from the vulgar and common notions already fix'd in the Minds of moft Men,
relating to this *Mofaick* Creation ; I fhall in this
place chiefly have a refpect to them, and endeavour to evince, That the notions they have entertain'd of the Nature, Stile, and Extent of the
Creation of the World in fix days, are falfe,
precarious, and no lefs contrary to the Holy
Scriptures themfelves, than to found Reafon and
true Philofophy. The Propofition therefore
which fhall be the fubject of this Differtation, and
includes the whole point before us, fhall be this:
The Mofaick *Creation is not a Nice and Philofophical account of the Origin of All Things; but an
Hiftorical and True Reprefentation of the formation
of our fingle Earth out of a confufed Chaos, and of
the fucceffive and vifible changes thereof each day,
till it became the habitation of Mankind.*

That this Propofition is exactly agreeable to
that Account, which in the following Theory
is given of this Creation, will be evident upon
the perufal thereof ; and that the fame Propofition is alike agreeable to the Defign and Stile of
the Sacred Penman in the firft Chapter of *Genefis,* is what I am now to make appear ; and
that I fhall endeavour to do by the following
Arguments ; which tho' they might have been
diftinguifh'd, and fuited to the feveral branches
of this Affertion, yet for eafe I fhall wave that
nicenefs, and fet them down indifferently in that
order they were put into by my own thoughts,
before I intended to adapt them to the juft form

of the foregoing Propofition ; Strength of Reafoning, more than Exactnefs of Compofure, being the aim of the Author in this whole Theory : And if he be found to go upon folid grounds, he hopes the Reader will never the lefs embrace the Conclufions, becaufe of the inaccuracy of the Stile, or harfhnefs of the Periods ; which wholly to have avoided, he freely owns, would to him have been more tedious and operofe than the Work it felf ; and fo he hopes 'twill not be expected from him by the Inquifitive Reader : Which Apology once for all he defires may be accepted, and call'd to mind whenever (as too frequently it will) there fhall be occafion in the following Pages.

I. The very firft words of *Mofes* plainly imply, that the Production of all the World out of nothing, which we ufually ftile Creation, was precedaneous to the Six days Works, given an account of in the fame chapter. *In the Beginning* Gen. i. 1. *God Created the Heaven and the Earth,* fays the Scripture ; which is, as I take it, a Preface or Introduction to the following account, and may be thus paraphras'd : " Altho' that Hiftory of " the Origin of the World which fhall now be " given you, do not extend any farther, as will " appear prefently, than that Earth we live up- " on, with thofe Bodies which peculiarly be- " long to it ; and fo the reft of the Univerfe be " not at all directly concern'd therein ; and al- " tho' the fame Hiftory will not reach to the " Creation of the matter, but only Production " of the form, and difpofition of the Earth it " felf : Yet, to prevent any mifunderftanding, " and obviate any ill effects of a perfect filence " touching thefe things, I am oblig'd, by the " Divine

" Divine Command, to afiure you, That the
" Original of all Beings whatfoever, was pri-
" marily owing to that fame God of *Ifrael*,
" whofe Works I am going to relate ; and that
" not only this Earth, and all its Bodies, but the
" vaft Frame of Univerfal Nature, was by him
" at firft Created out of Nothing, and dispos'd
" into thofe feveral Syftems which now are ex-
" tant, and make up what in the largeft fenfe
" is ftil'd Heaven and Earth, or the whole
" Word.

This fenfe of the Words is allow'd by our
late Excellent Commentatour, the Right Reverend the Lord Bifhop of *Ely* ; (whofe Sentiments cannot but be juftly valued by all who
are converfant in his Expofitions of the Holy
Scriptures) and is I think clearly confirm'd by
the following words ; *And the Earth was with-* Gen. i. 2.
out Form and Void, and Darknefs was upon the Face
of the Deep, and the Spirit of God moved on the
Face of the Waters. Where 'tis clear, that as foon
as the Holy Writer defcends to the Defcription
of the Chaos, and the commencing of the Six
Days Creation, he mentions not a word of any
Production out of Nothing (before fuppos'd and
afferted to have been paft and done, *In the Be-*
ginning) he omits, and thereby evidently excludes that Heaven, or thofe Superior Syftems
of the World already fpoken of, from any place
therein, and by the whole coherence plainly confines the Narration following to the Earth alone
with its dependencies. *Mofes* does not fay, as
the common Expofitors do, " That juft at the
" commencing of the Six Days Work, the
" Earth, and all the reft of the World was
" originally produc'd ; But that, When God
✶ had (formerly) created all the World, which
B 3 " is

" is ufually diftinguifh'd into the Heaven and
" the Earth, the latter of thefe, (the confide-
" ration whereof was alone pertinent to the
" prefent defign) at the time preceding the
" Six Days Work, was in a Wild, Irregular,
" and Dark condition ; or fuch a perfect Chaos,
" as nothing but the Power of God, and his
" Spirit's moving on, and influencing the fame,
" could ever have reduc'd into a habitable
" World.

This is a very eafie and natural account of
this matter, and I think the moft obvious and
genuine fignification of the words themfelves:
And were not Mens Minds too much prejudic'd
with other apprehenfions, this alone might be
fufficient to limit their thoughts, and prevent
their Enquiries after any Creation of Bodies out
of nothing in the Six Days Work; and their
ftretching the fame beyond the Earth, either
to the whole Syftem of things, as the moft do;
or indeed to the Solar Syftem, with which
others are more modeftly contented in the cafe.
Which two things once granted me, the Propo-
pofition we are now upon would foon be eftablifh d, and little farther labour become neceffary.

But that I may give all poffible fatisfaction,
and lay this Foundation firm, on which my Account of the *Mofaick* Creation is intirely fuperftructed ; I fhall more at large prove the fame
Truths, craving the Pardon of thofe Readers
who are already fatisfy'd in thefe matters, if I
fhall feem to them to infift too long on a plain
cafe ; as perhaps they may (and that I think
very juftly) efteem this to be.

And indeed, The prejudices of Men are here
fo great; their fears of a Philofophical Hypothefis

thefis fo rooted; the attempts hitherto made
have been fo unfuccefsful; and befides, the
Honour of God in his Holy Word is fo much
concern'd; and the ufual Expofitions of this
Hiftory of the Origin of Things is fo poor, fo
jejune, fo unbecoming the Penman, much more
the primary Author of the fame; that a large
and full Difcourfe is but necefary; and tho' it
fhould prove fomewhat prolix, will be. tis hop'd,
not improper; but as well ferviceable to Religion as to Philofophy, by refcuing this Ancient,
Venerable, and Sacred Account of the Origin
of things, from fuch falfe and unwary Gloffes
as have been, and ftill are put upon it; as have
rendred it, in the opinion of too many, an uncouth and incredib e Syftem, nay fomewhat below fome of thofe Θεογονίαι or Κοσμογονίαι, which
the imperfect Tradinons of the Heathen World
enabled them to defcribe. To proceed therefore in the arguments before us, I affirm,

II. That the words here us'd of *Creating* ,
Making , or *framing* of things, on which the
main ftrefs is laid; in the ftile of Scripture are
frequently of no larger importance than the
Propofition we are upon does allow; and figni-
fie no more than the ordering, difpofing, changing, or new modelling thofe Creatures which
exifted already, into a different, and fometimes
perhaps a better, and more ufeful ftate than they
were in before. I do not fay this is the utmoft,
or only importance of thefe words; I have already allow'd, that Creating, in the firft words
of *Genefis,* includes Producing out of nothing;
and I add, that in our common Creed, wherein we profefs our *Faith in God the Father Al-*
mighty, Maker of Heaven and Earth; the words

are,

are, agreeably to the extent of the Divine
Power, and the nature of that profeffion, to be
taken in the fame large and comprehentive fenfe:
and the like is to be faid of many other places
of the Holy Scripture. But then I obferve withal, that the other more narrow and limited fenfe
is very common and familiar in the Holy Writings ; and therefore, where the fubject matter
and coherence requires it, as I think twill be
evident it does in the prefent cafe, thefe words
both may and ought to be taken in the fame
acceptation.

This fignification of the two latter words
Make and *Frame*, will, I fuppofe, be granted
me by all; and that the fame is as true of the
other *Create*, the following Texts will fufficiently evince : and from the promifcuous ufe
of them all, and others of a like importance,
might however be very fairly fuppos'd. *If*, fays
Mofes, *the Lord make a new thing, or Create a*
Creature, and the Earth open her Mouth and fwal-
low them up. Where none can imagine any thing
produc'd out of nothing, but only fuch an unufual and miraculous difpofal of things as would
at once demonftrate God's Vengeance againft
the Wicked, and his abfolute Command over
all Creatures. Thus God himfelf fays, *I form the*
light and create darknefs; I make peace and create evil;
I the Lord do all thefe things : Where the objects
of the Divine Creation being not real and fubftantial Beings, could not be capable of a proper production out of nothing : Which alfo is
the cafe in the verfe immediately following, *Let*
righteoufnefs fpring up together ; I the Lord have
created it. Thus alfo, fays God by the fame
Prophet, *I create new Heavens and a new Earth :*
which, tho' the very cafe before us, yet would
odly

Num. xvi.
30.

Ifa. xlv. 7.

ver. 8.

Cap. lxv.
17.

odly enough be expounded of an annihilation of the World, and a reproduction of it again. But what comes still more home to our purpose is, that in the very History of the Creation it self, the word Create, as well as Make, is us'd in the sense we contend for ; the very same things being ascrib'd to the Creating and Making Power of God, which are also describ'd as the regular offspring of the Earth and Seas : *God created great* Gen. i. 21. *Whales, and every living Creature that moveth ; which the waters brought forth abundantly after their kind. And God said, Let the Earth bring forth* ver. 24, 25. *the living Creature after his kind, Cattel and creeping thing, and Beast of the Earth after his kind ; and it was so : And God made the Beast of the Earth after his kind, and Cattel after their kind, and every thing that creepeth upon the Earth after his kind ; and God saw that it was good.*

So that when the words made use of in the History of the Creation are there, and every where taken promiscuously ; when some of them are, by the confession of all, of no larger importance than the Proposition before us will admit ; and when, lastly, that word, of which the greatest doubt can arise, has been prov'd not only in other Texts of Scripture, but in the very History of which we are treating, to be of no more determinate signification than the rest, and alike capable of the sense we here put upon it ; I think 'tis a clear Case, that if no Argument can be drawn from such words for, yet neither can there justly be any against, that Proposition we are now upon.

III. Those synonymous Phrases, *The World* ; or *the Heavens,* and *the Earth,* under which the Object of the six days Creation is comprehended
every

every where in Scripture, do not always denote the whole Syſtem of Beings; no nor any great and general Portion of them; but are in the Sacred Stile frequently, if not moſtly, to be reſtrained to the terraqueous Globe with its dependances; and conſequently both may, and if the ſubject matter require it, ought to be underſtood in ſuch a reſtrained ſenſe, and no other: That by theſe Phraſes the *Moſaick* Creation, or ſix days work is uſually underſtood, is evident every where in Scripture, as the following Texts will eaſily evince: *God who made the World, and all things therein. The Divine* Λόγος *was in the World, and the World was made by Him, and the World knew Him not.* Hence thoſe frequent expreſſions, *From the Foundation of the World, from the Beginning of the World, from the Creation of the World,* and *before the World was*; which, tho' capable of including more, muſt yet be allow'd to have generally a peculiar, nay ſometimes a ſole regard to the ſix days work, particularly ſtil'd by St. *Mark, The Beginning of the Creation which God created.*

Acts xvii.
24. John
i. 10. Mat.
xiii. 35. &
xxiv. 21.
& xxv. 34.
Luk. xi. 50.
Joh. xvii.
5, 24.
Rom. i. 20.
Eph. i. 4.
Heb. iv. 3.
& ix. 26.
1 Pet. i. 20.
Apoc. xiii.
8. & xvii.
8. Mark
xiii. 19.
Gen. ii. 1.
ver. 4.

Command. 4.

In the ſame manner, and with the like frequency, the other Phraſe Heaven and Earth, denote the ſame ſix days work alſo: *Thus the Heavens and the Earth were finiſhed, and all the Hoſt of them. Theſe are the Generations of the Heavens and of the Earth when they were created, in the day that the Lord God made the Earth and the Heavens. In ſix days the Lord made Heaven and Earth, the Sea, and all that in them is, and reſted the ſeventh day;* which being ſo expreſs, I ſhall not need to look out for any other parallel places.

And that both the *World*; and *Heaven,* and *Earth,* ſignify the terraqueous Globe alone, with its Air or Atmoſphere and other Appurtenances, without including the whole Univerſe, nay, or
Solar

Solar Syftem, alfo, (which yet I do not deny fometimes to be comprehended therein) the following Texts will fufficiently fhew. Our Lord fays of the Woman who poured the Oyntment on him, *Wherefoever this Gofpel fhall be preached in* Mat.xxvi. *the whole World, there fhall alfo this which this Wo-* 13. *man hath done be told for a memorial of her.* His Charge and Commiffion to his Apoftles was, *Go* Mark xvi. *ye into all the World, and preach the Gofpel to every* 15. *Creature. The Tempter came to Jefus, and fhew'd* Mat.iv.8. *him all the Kingdoms of the World, and the Glory of them.* In all which places, no other than the habitable Earth can be underftood: and 'tis ftill fo frequent and natural for Men to ufe this manner of Speech in the fame reftrained Senfe to this very day, that one may the lefs wonder at the Sacred Stile in this Cafe. But this word, *the World*, having not fo much difficulty in it, nor being fo much ftood upon, as thofe which follow, *the Heavens and the Earth*, I fhall no longer infift upon it, but proceed.

And here, when the *World*, as a *totum integrale*, is divided into its two contradiftinct Parts, *the Heavens* and *the Earth*, it will be faid, That by fuch a Phrafe or Enumeration of the Parts of the Univerfe, no lefs can be meant than the whole World in the largeft acceptation; or however, more muft be intended than the bare Earth, which is but one Member or Branch, and fo certainly lefs than that whole of which it is a part.

In anfwer whereto, I freely confefs, That the Heavens and the Earth do not feldom denote the intire Univerfe, an inftance of which the firft words of *Genefis* have already afforded us; but that they always do fo, I have reafon to deny. As the Signification of the *Earth* is known, and capable of no Ambiguity, fo 'tis quite otherwife

wife in the word *Heaven,* which in common ufe,
and the facred Authors, fometimes refers to the
Seat of the Bleffed, or the third Heaven; fometimes to the place of the Sun, Moon, and Stars;
and otherwhiles is no farther to be extended than
the Clouds, or the open *Expanfum* about the
Earth, where the Air, Atmofphere, Meteors,
Clouds, and Volatils, have their abode. Inftances of the two former Significations, were it
pertinent to my prefent purpofe, might eafily
be produc'd; but that not being fo, I fhall wave
the fame, and only prove the third and laft Signification, namely, That by the Heavens is frequently underftood nothing 'more' than the Atmofphere of the Earth, with its appendant or
contained Bodies.

Thus, *God made the Firmament, and divided the*
Waters which were under the Firmament, from the
Waters which were above the Firmament; and it was
fo. And God called the Firmament, Heaven. Which
place is fo exprefs; and in the very Hiftory it
felf, which we are now about alfo, that it ought
to be of peculiar force in the prefent cafe. Thus
alfo the Builders of *Babel* faid, *Go to, Let us build*
us a City, and a Tower, whofe top may reach unto
Heaven. So mention is made of *Cities great and*
fenced up to Heaven. The Clouds pafs by the
name of the *Clouds of Heaven;* nay, they are by
the *Pfalmift,* (agreeably to the Interpofition of
the *Expanfum,* Firmament or Heaven on the fecond day of the Creation between the fuperior
and inferior Waters) made as it were its fartheft
Boundaries and Limits; the Waters contain'd
in them being call'd, *Waters which are above the*
Heavens. The very Fowls, which ftill refide
nearer to the Earth, are ftil'd *the Fowls of Hea-*
ven; and were originally appointed to *fly above the*
                                          Earth

Gen i.7,8.

Cap. xi. 4.

Deut ix.1.
Mat. xxiv.
30.
& xxvi.
64.

Pf. cxlviii.
4.

Mat. viii.
20. & xiii.
32.

Earth in the open Firmament of Heaven. By all which Gen. i. 20.
places 'tis evident, That the word *Heaven* is commonly so far from including the Sun or Planetary *Chorus*, (much less the fix'd Stars, with all
their immense Syſtems) that the Moon, our
attending and neighbour Planet is not taken in :
The utmoſt bounds of our *Atmoſphære*, being so
of this our *Heaven* alſo ; which was the only
Point which remain'd to be clear'd.

But here, before I proceed farther, I muſt
take notice of a conſiderable Objection, which
threatens to wreſt this Argument out of my
hands, and indeed to ſubvert the intire Foundation of the Propoſition before us ; and is, I freely own, the main difficulty in this whole matter ; and 'tis this, That ſuch a Senſe of the words,
World, and *Heaven*, and *Earth*, as has been pleaded for, whatever may be ſaid in other caſes,
will yet by no means fit here, nor take in all the
extent of the *Moſaick* Creation ; becauſe 'tis certain, that neither the Light, by whoſe Revolution Night and Day are diſtinguiſh'd, nor the
Sun, Moon, and Stars, which are ſet in our Firmament, belong to our Atmoſphere, or are contain'd within thoſe Boundaries, within which we
confine the preſent Hiſtory ; and 'tis equally certain that both of them belong to the *Moſaick*
Creation, and are the firſt and fourth days works
therein ; and by conſequence it may be ſaid, the
Subject of the ſix days Creation muſt be the
whole Syſtem of the heavenly Bodies, or at leaſt
that particular one in which the Earth is, and
is ſtil'd the Solar Syſtem.

Now this Objection is in part already taken
off by the Senſe, in which the Production and
Creation of things has been ſhewn to be frequently taken in the Holy Scriptures ; whereby
there

there appears to be no neceſſity of believing theſe
Bodies to have been then brought into being,
when they are firſt mention'd in the *Moſaick*
Creation.

But becauſe this is not meerly the chief, but
only conſiderable Objection againſt the Propoſition we are upon ; becauſe it ſeems to have been
the principal occaſion of men's Miſtakes and
Prejudices about this whole Hiſtory ; and becauſe 'tis the ſingle inſtance wherein this intire
Theory, as far as I know, ſeems to recede from
the obvious Letter of Scripture ; 'twill be but
proper to give it a particular review, and clear
withal, not only this, but ſeveral other like Expreſſions and Paſſages in the Holy Scripture.

Now, in order to the giving what ſatisfaction
I can in this Point ; let it be conſider'd, That
the Light being not ſaid to be *created* by *Moſes*, its
Original were without difficulty to be accounted
for, if the other Point, the making of the Heavenly Bodies were once ſetled, which therefore is
the ſole remaining difficulty in the caſe before us.
And that would be no harder, if the Tranſlation
of the Words of *Moſes* were but amended, and
the Verſes hereto relating, read thus, *And God*
ſaid, Let there be lights in the firmament of the Hea-
ven, to divide the day from the night ; and let them
be for ſigns, and for ſeaſons, and for days and years;
and let them be for lights in the firmament of the
Heaven, to give light upon the Earth, and it was
ſo. And God having (before) *made two great*
lights, the greater light to rule the day, and the leſſer
light to rule the night ; and having (before) *made*
the ſtars alſo, God ſet them in the firmament of Hea-
ven to give light upon the Earth, &c. or which is
all one, *And God had* (before) *made two great*
lights, the greater light to rule the day, and the leſſer
light

Gen. i.14, 15, 16, 17.

light to rule the night; *he had* (before) *made the stars alfo, and God fet them in the firmament,* &c. In which rendring, 'tis only changing the *perfectum* for the *plufquam perfectum*, and every thing is clear and eafy, and the Objection vanifhes of its own accord; the Creation of the heavenly Bodies being hereby affigned to a former time, and the Work of the fourth day no other than the placing them in our Firmament, according as the account hereafter to be given does require.

Now to prove this a fair and juft Interpretation, (to omit the Creation of the Heavens and Heavenly Bodies already related before the fix days work) 'tis only neceffary to obferve that the *Hebrew* Tongue having no *plufquam perfectum*, muft and does exprefs the Senfe of it by the *perfectum*; and that accordingly, the particular circumftances of each place muft alone determine when thereby the time prefent, and when that already paft and gone, is to be underftood. How many knots in the Scripture the omiffion of this Obfervation has left unfolv'd, and which being obferv'd would be immediately untied I fhall not go about to enumerate, there being fo many in the very Hiftory before us, of the Origin of the World that I fhall not go one jot farther for inftances to confirm the before-mention'd Tranflation; and which on the account of their agreement in place, w more forcibly plead for a like agreement in fenfe alfo. *On the feventh* Gen ii. 2. *day God had ended his work which he had made, and he refted on the feventh day from all his work which he had made.* ―――― *He had refted om all his work* ver. 3. *which God had created and made.* ―――― *The Lord* ver. 5, 6. *God had not caufed it to rain on the Earth, and there had not been a man to till the Ground; but there had*

gone

gone up a mist from the Earth, and had water'd the whole face of the ground; and the Lord God had form-
ver. 7.
ver. 8.
ed man of the dust of the ground, and had breathed into his nostrils the breath of life. —————— And the Lord God had planted a Garden eastward in Eden. ——
ver 9.
And out of the ground had the Lord God made to grow every tree that is pleasant to the sight, and good
ver. 19.
for food. ——— And out of the ground the Lord God had formed every beast of the field, and every fowl of the air. ——— In all which places the whole Context is so clear'd by this rendring, and so many strange Absurdities avoided, that there is, I think, all imaginable reason to acquiesce in it.

And tho' the fourth days work is among those other, where no such alteration need be made, in which therefore it may seem hard to allow of a single instance against the use in the precedent and subsequent Context in the first Chapter, yet the circumstances of that day being peculiar; the like mixture of the *perfectum* and *plu. quam perfectum* being in the second Chapter, and in other places of Scripture to be observed; and a distinct work being still hereby preserv'd to that day, the placing the Sun, Moon, and Stars, in our Firmament, which otherwise is after a sort double; do all in good measure, take away the force of such Reasoning, and conspire to allow us that Interpretation before given, and thereby to secure the Proposition before us from that grand Objection which seemed capable of causing so great an obstruction in our course. But if any should be dissatisfied with this Answer, I shall, for their sakes, enter deeper into this matter; and, without any assistance from what has been already said, endeavour to establish the Proposition before us, and take away the foundation of the present difficulty.   And

And here I obferve, That the Scripture all along accommodates its felf to the vulgar Apprehenfions of Men, with relation to fuch Points of Natural Philofophy as they were not able to comprehend; and in particular, with relation to the Site, Diftance, Magnitude, Ufe, and Motions of the Heavenly Bodies. Tho' thefe be really very diftinct, as well as diftant from the Earth, with all its dependances; yet are they rarely, if ever, fo confider'd in the Holy Scriptures. They are all along there reprefented as fiery Luminaries plac'd in our Atmofphere, and as much belonging to, and depending on the Earth as the Clouds. Meteors, or other Aerial *Phænomena*: And fo 'tis no wonder that in the Hiftory before us, they are included among the reft of their Fellows, and come within the verge of the *Mofaick* Creation, notwithftanding its limits be no larger than we here affign thereto. In order to the accounting for which things, I fhall,

(1.) Shew the truth of the Obfervation, in feveral inftances from the Holy Scriptures.

(2.) Shew the rational Original and Occafion of fuch ways of fpeaking.

(3.) Explain what, according to my Notion, muft be meant by the Creation or Production of thefe Heavenly Bodies in the *Mofaick* Hiftory before us, and demonftrate fuch a Conftruction to be agreeable to the Sacred Stile in other places.

(4.) Affign fome Reafons, why, in a Hiftory of the Origin of our Earth, thefe remote and diftant Bodies come to be taken notice of, tho' their own proper Formation did not at all belong to it.

C (1.) I

(1.) I fhall fhew the truth of the Obfervation, in feveral inftances from the Holy Scriptures; namely, that the Heavenly Bodies are no other-wife there defcribed than with relation to our Earth, and as Members and Appurtenances of our Atmofphere. And this Obfervation is con-firm'd by the firft mention that is made of them in this very Hiftory we are upon; all the Cir-cumftances whereof fully atteft the truth of what is here affirm'd of them. When the Light firft difplay'd it felf, notwithftanding thofe number-lefs advantages accruing to the whole World therefrom, none are taken notice of but fuch as refpect our Sublunary World. 'Twas intirely with regard to our *Light and Darknefs,* our *Day and Night,* that all was done, as far as can be collected from the words of *Mofes.* Thus, as foon as the Heavenly Bodies are made, tho' they be univerfally ufeful, they are *plac'd in the Firmament of Heaven,* (a Phrafe us'd in this Hiftory for our Air only) *to divide* our *day from night, to be* to us *for figns and feafons, for days and years; to be for lights in the firmament of heaven to give light upon the earth; to rule over* our *day and night, to divide* our *light from darknefs.* And as to the order of their Introduction, 'tis not that of their proper Greatnefs or Dignity, but that of their refpective Appearance and Ufes here below. All which is far from a full account of the real Original, uni-verfal Intentions, and true Places of thefe Glo-rious Bodies; but on the Suppofition here made ufe of, exactly eafy and natural. Agreeably whereto when our Air is clogg'd with grofs Va-pours, fo as to hide or disfigure their Faces to us, *The Sun is* faid to be *turn'd into darknefs, the Moon into blood;* and when fome Aerial Meteors, call'd by their Names, and for a moment refembling them,

Gen. i. 3, 4. 5.

Verfe 14, 15, 16, 17.

Acts ii, 20.

them, fhoot and drop down in the Air; *the Stars* Mat. xxiv.
are faid to *fall from Heaven.* The Sun and Moon, 29.
as if they were two Globes of Fire and Light
pendulous in our Air, and hanging over certain
places, are order'd to *ftand ftill,* the one *upon Gi-* Jofhua x.
beon, the other *in the Valley of Aijalon.* The Sun 12.
is reprefented as *fet in a Tabernacle, rejoycing as a* Pfalm xix.
Gyant to run his race. His going forth, is faid to be 4, 5, 6.
from the end of Heaven, or the Horizon, *and his*
circuit unto the ends of it. All which Expreffions,
with many others through the whole Bible, plainly Vide Pfal.
fhew, That the Scripture did not intend to teach civ. 1, &c.
men Philofophy, or accommodate it felf to the Ifaiah xl.
true and *Pythagorick* Syftem of the World. The 22.
Holy Writers did not confider the Heavenly Bodies abfolutely, as they are Great and Noble in
themfelves, main and glorious Parts of the Univerfe, very diftinct from our Earth, plac'd at
various and immenfe Diftances from it, and
from one another; defign'd for, and fubfervient
to many, wife, and comprehenfive Ends and
Methods of the Divine Providence; difpos d in
a regular order, in proportionate and harmonious
Periods and Revolutions, and finally endued
with mighty Powers and Influences with refpect
to numerous and vaft Syftems of Beings. Under fuch a confideration we might have expected
another fort of Reprefentation of the Heavenly
Bodies, their Original, Defigns, Courfes, and
Circumftances, than the foregoing Texts, or
their parallels every where afford us. But if we
look on them under the Notion of Neighbour-
Luminaries, which are fituate at the utmoft
bounds of our Atmofphere, and belong, as well
as the Clouds, to our Earth; which are appointed to be our peculiar Attendants, and a part of
our Retinue; ferve our fingle Neceffities, and
every

every day rife and fet on purpofe to provide for our Advantage and Convenience: If I fay, we thus look upon them, (as all Men not otherwife taught by Philofophy do and muft) the Texts above-cited, and the whole current of the Holy Books will eafily accord and correfpond to fuch a Syftem. And I dare appeal to any impartial and competent Judge, to which of the forementioned Schemes the moft obvious and eafy Senfe of the Expreffions of Scripture hereto relating are adapted; and whether it does not ufually fpeak as an honeft and inquifitive Countryman, who no more doubted of the Heavenly Bodies, than of the Clouds appertaining to the Earth; rather than as a new Aftronomer, who knew them to be vaftly diftant from, and to have nothing in a peculiar manner to do with the fame. Which will be lefs wondred at when we confider in the next place,

(2.) The Reafon and Occafion of fuch ways of fpeaking. And here I fhall not content my felf in general to obferve, that the defign of Divine Revelation was of quite another nature, than requir'd a nice Adjuftment and Philofophick Explication of the Natural World; that the Capacities of the People could not bear any fuch things; that the Prophets and Holy Penmen themfelves, unlefs over-rul'd by that Spirit which fpake by them, being feldom or never Philofophers, were not capable of reprefenting thefe things otherwife than they, with the Vulgar, underftood them: That even, ftill, thofe who believe the true Syftem of the World, are forc'd among the Vulgar, and in common Converfation to fpeak as they do, and accommodate their Expreffions to the Notions and Apprehenfions of the generality of Mankind. I fhall not, I fay,

content

content my felf with fuch Obfervations, moft of which are ufually, and with good reafon, infifted on in the prefent cafe; but rather attempt to find out the true Origin and Source of fuch Notions and Expreffions, made ufe of, as by moft other Writers, fo efpecially by the Sacred Ones in the Holy Bible.

God has fo fram'd the Eyes of Men, that when the diftance of Bodies, and their proper Magnitude is very great, they fhall both be imperceptible to us. There is every way from our Eye a fpherical Diftance or Superficies which terminates our diftinct Perception of Objects, and beyond which, all Diftances and Magnitudes, abfolutely confidered, are not by us diftinguifhable. The Clouds, tho', lying parallel to the Horizon, they are (fo far as comes at once within our view) almoft in the fame Plain, yet to us they feem bent into a concave Figure, or kind of Hemifpherical Superficies, equidiftant almoft on every fide from its Center, the Eye of the Spectator, and fo feem every way to touch the Ground at a Mile or two's diftance from him. And this happens by reafon of the Imperfection of our Sight, which diftinguifhing remote Objects but to a certain diftance, beyond which the Clouds are, can have no other Idea of their Situation than fmall and like Objects at that Spherical Superficies would excite. On which Principle 'tis certain, that till Geometrick and Philofophick Principles rectify mens Notions, all Bodies whatfoever beyond the Clouds, fuch as the Cœleftial are, muft needs be efteem'd at the fame equidiftant Superficies with the Clouds, and appear among them; and by confequence 'twould be on this account, as poffible for the Vulgar to be perfuaded that the Clouds were vaftly remote from,

C 3   and

and bear no relation to this Earth, as that the
Sun, Moon, and Stars were fo; and to them as
ftrange to have found no account of the Formation
of them with that of the other vifible World,
as the omiffion of the *Clouds* would have been.
It being impoflible that the Sun, for inftance,
tho' fo many thoufands of Miles diftant, fhould
to us appear above one or two from us; and alike
impoflible that his bignefs, tho' fo many thoufand
Miles in Diameter, fhould appear to be as many
Feet to us on Earth: As all who have any skill in
Opticks very well know.

So that when thefe Heavenly Bodies are and
mult needs be to our Sight and Imagination at
the fame diftance with the Clouds, and confequently, *as to us*, are with them plac'd in our
own Air; when their vifible Magnitude, Situation, Motion, and Habitudes, are all one *with
refpect to us*, as if they really were light and fiery
Balls rowling upon or among the Clouds; when
their apparent Changes, Figures, Colour, Countenance, Effects, and Influences would be (as
far as Senfe and vulgar Obfervation could determine) *on this Earth*, and *to its Inhabitants*, the
very fame as were to be expected from fuch light
and fiery Balls, revolving at the prefumed diftance; when all wife Men, efpecially the Sacred
Penmen, in their Writings defign'd for the Advantage and Inftruction of all, condefcend ftill to
the Apprehenfions and Capacities of Men, and
fpeak of the *Being* of things as they conftantly
Appear; of which the Bible is full of inftances:
All thefe things confider'd, 'tis not to be wonder'd at, that the Heavenly Bodies are accounted Appendages of our Earth, and agreeably
thereto made mention of in the *Mofaick* Creation.

(3.) I

(3.) I shall explain what, according to my Notion, must be meant by the Creation or Production of these Heavenly Bodies in the History before us, and demonstrate such a Construction to be agreeable to the Sacred Stile in other places. Now 'tis easy to tell what is meant by their Creation in the case before us, when it has appear'd that their Production out of nothing was precedaneous to the six days Work, and that they are wholly consider'd as belonging to our Earth, and plac'd in our Air; *viz. their primary being so plac'd ; their first becoming visible to Men on Earth,* or in other words, *their original appearing to be there.* I mean in plain *English*, Light is said then first to *Be*, (for it being an effect of the Heavenly Bodies, not a distinct thing from them, is not by *Moses* said to be *made* or *created*)   Gen. i. 3. when the superior Regions of the Chaos were become so far clear and defecate, that the Rays of the Sun in some degree could penetrate the same, enough to render a sensible Distinction between Night and Day, or that space the Sun was above, and that it was beneath the Horizon. And agreeably, The Sun, Moon, and Stars, are   Verse 14, then said first to *Be*, or to *be made*, when after-   16. wards the Air was rendred so very clear and transparent, that those Luminaries became conspicuous, and their Bodies distinctly visible, as in a clear Day or Night they now appear to us.

That this Exposition is agreeable to the Scripture Stile, is evident by this Observation; That several things are there affirm'd to *Be*, in any certain manner, when only those effects we feel are such as they would be were they so indeed; and 'tis not unusual to assert the *Being* of any Cause, when all those consequences are no other-

wise

wife in the World, and with regard to Men,
than they muft and would be upon its real Exiftence, without any exacter niceneſs as to the
truth of the ſame. Thus God is ſaid ſeveral times
to repeat of ſomewhat he has before done, when
his future Actions are the very ſame as would in
Humane as well as Divine Affairs, be the certain confeqnents of a proper Repentance : Thus
alſo God is ſaid to be *pleas'd* or *angry* with Men,
and that in a very *paſſionate* and *ſenſible* manner,
when he confers ſuch great Mercies, or inflicts
ſuch great Judgments, as, were he really ſo, he
muſt naturally do. Thus alſo *Eyes* and *Ears* are
frequently ſuppos'd of God, becauſe he as certainly is conſcious of all the Actions and Speeches
of Men, as if he really ſaw and heard the ſame. In
a different inſtance, The Sun is ſaid to *ſtand ſtill*
or *move*, tho' in propriety of Speech, as is now
well known, thoſe affections ought to be aſcrib'd
to the Earth, becauſe every thing, as to ſenſible
appearance, is in the ſame condition as from the
Annual and Diurnal Motions of the Sun, were
they real, muſt, and would obtain. The Sun is
ſaid to be *turned into Darkneſs*, and the *Moon
into Blood*, when without any alteration in
themſelves, they appear of a dark or bloody
Countenance to the Inhabitants of the Earth.
Nay, which is moſt of all to our preſent pur-
Apoc. xxi.
5.
Iſaiah lxv.
17. poſe, God is then ſaid to *make all things new*,
and to *create a new Heaven, and a new Earth*,
when he ſo changes the Conſtitution and State
of our Earth, as to render thereby this whole
Sublunary World very different from, and much
excelling that which formerly appear'd. In all
which, and innumerable other inſtances, 'tis
plain and evident, that the Holy Writers do not
conſider merely how things *are* in themſelves, but
                                                how

how they are *to us* ; not what is their proper *nature*, but vifible *appearance* in the World.

But here, left this Doctrine fhould be abus'd,
I muft interpofe this neceffary caution, That
fuch a liberty is neither by other Authors, nor
the Sacred Penmen taken on all occafions, or in
every cafe; but peculiarly when the fublimity
of the Matter, the capacities of the People, the
more eafie inftilling ufeful principles into Men,
or fome other weighty reafon, requires fuch an
accommodation. 'Tis chiefly with regard to the
Spiritual Nature, and fublime way of operation
in God ; or fuch Phyfical and Philofophick
Truths, as relate to diftant, invifible, or inac-
ceffible bodies ; the abfolute Effence or Affections whereof, were not explicable to the vulgar
in a plain and natural manner. In which cafes
this Liberty in the Interpretation of Scripture is,
with the greateft Juftice to be allow'd. But
'twere thence very unreafonable to extend it to
all others, or indeed to any, where the fame, or
as good, reafons were not affignable. He who
fhould argue, that becaufe the Literal fenfe of
Scripture about the Corporeal Members, and
Humane Paffions of the Divine Nature, is not
to be ftrictly urg'd, that therefore when he is
call'd a Spirit, and reprefented as the Rewarder
of Good, and the Punifher of Bad men, thofe
Expreffions are no more to be depended
on ; or he who fhould infer, that becaufe the
Firft and Fourth Days Works, the Origin of
Light, and the making of the Heavenly Bodies,
muft not be ftrictly literal , that therefore neither in the *Mofaick* Creation, ought the other
four to be any more efteemed fo; He, I fay,
that fhould thus argue or infer, would be very
unfair and unreafonable ; becaufe he would af-

fert that in one cafe, without ground, which
on peculiar and weighty ones alone was allow'd
in another. Thus thofe things that are afcrib'd
to God, which evidently agree to his Nature,
and Idea, are furely to be literally underftood;
tho' the other which are repugnant thereto be
not : And in like manner, 'tis but juft to believe, that fo much of the *Mofaick* Creation, as
related directly to the Earth and its appurtenances, and fo came at once within the comprehenfion of the Hiftory, and of the capacities of
the Readers, ought literally to be Interpreted;
tho' fome things extraneous to the Formation
of the Earth, and beyond the notice of the
People, be to be taken in a different acceptation.
Tho' the common ufe of Tropes and Figures
make our Speech very often not to be *literal*,
yet generally we can underftand one another
very well without danger of deception, or of
turning plain Sentences into Allegorical Difcourfes, in our Converfation one with another.

And 'tis evident that the Holy Books ought
not to be tormented or eluded, as to their obvious fenfe, on every occafion, under pretence
that fome particular Texts are to be conftrued
another way. That S A C R E D R U L E ought
for ever R E L I G I O U S L Y to be obferved,
That we never forfake the plain, obvious, eafie and
natural fenfe, unlefs where the nature of the thing it
felf, parallel places, or evident reafon, afford a folid
and fufficient ground for fo doing.

Now this being prefuppos'd; I fhall leave it
to the impartial Reader to judge, after the perufal of this whole difcourfe, whether I have not
fubftantial reafons for the prefent Expofition;
and whether therefore, any one ought to blame
my

my receding from the Letter in this fingle cafe,
or imagine that I give a juft handle thereby to
others, to Allegorize this Hiftory of the Creation, or any other parts of Scripture.

And I muft here own and profefs, That tho'
I think, in cafe the common Tranflation be receiv'd, there is an abfolute neceffity of receding
from the Letter in the point before us, and that
this Venerable and Sacred Κοσμοποιΐα, or hiftory
of the Creation, is otherwife in the higheft degree, ftrange and unaccountable to the free Reafon of Mankind; yet I am fully of opinion,
that generally the difficulties occurring in the
Sacred Books are to be clear'd, not by a greater
receding from, but a clofer adhering to the obvious and moft natural Interpretation of the Periods therein contain'd : And that the general
nature of the Scripture Stile every where duely
obferv'd and confider'd, feveral great fcruples
with relation to the Actions and Providence of
God, and other things contain'd in thofe Books,
would be taken away, if we might be allow'd to
recede a little from the receiv'd opinions of men,
and Placits of Syftematical Authors; on no other
condition than that, for a recompence, we
keep fo much the clofer to the Oracles of God,
and the obvious and literal Interpretation of them;
and explain the Bible no otherwife than the plain
words themfelves would appear moft naturally
to intend to any difinterefted and unconcern'd
Perfon : Of which many inftances might eafily
be given, were this a proper place for it. But I
muft leave this digreffion, and return to what I
before propos'd in the

(4.) Laft place, *viz.* To Affign fome Reafons
why in a Hiftory of the Origin of our Farth,

thefe remote and diftant Bodies come to be taken notice of, tho' their own proper formation
did not at all belong to it. Now tho' many
might eafily be alledg'd for this procedure, yet
I fhall include the main I intend here to infift on
in the two following:

(1.) The Advantage of the *Jews*, or fecuring them from the Adoration of the Hoft of
Heaven, could not otherwife have been provided
for. Now as the foundation of fuch Idolatry is
taken a way by their being included in this Hiftory, which imply'd them to be fuch dependent
and created Beings, as could have no influence
of their own, but what were deriv'd from God;
and confequently were fubject to his difpofal
and government; which affirm'd them to be by
Him plac'd in the Firmament, and there fubjected to fuch Motions, Rules and Laws, by which
they became advantageous and ferviceable to the
World: So had they been taken no notice of,
they would have feem'd exempted Bodies, and
when all Worfhip of Terreftrial things was demonftrated, by this account of their Original,
to be foolifh and abfurd; that of the Celeftial
Bodies would feem thereby to be permitted at
leaft, if not patroniz'd and recommended to
'em.

For when, as we have before obferv'd, 'twas
impoffible for the *Jews* to know the real ftate of
the cafe, and to apprehend that they were vaftly
remote from, and fo no way belonging to this
Earth, or its Formation; there was no other
way to apply a fitting remedy, to that prevailing
cuftom of Worfhiping the Hoft of Heaven, (fo
particularly caution'd by *Mofes*) but to condefcend to the Capacities of the People, and fuppofing them Light and Fiery Globes pendulous
in

Deut. iv.
19. & xvii.
3.

in the Air, and revolving juft beyond or among
the Clouds, to recount their refpective, as well
as the *real* Formation of the other parts of the vifible World, and affign them their proper place,
and diftinct period in the Six days work, as well
as any other more directly concern'd therein.
The Sun, Moon, and Stars were fuch noble and
glorious Bodies, and fo vifible, fo remarkable, fo
ufeful parts of the Word; and the Heathen Nations fo generally doted on the Worfhip of them;
that had they been intirely omitted in this particular account of the Origin of things, there
would have been the moft eminent danger of
this kind of Idolatry among the *Jews*; and the
feeming approbation of that practice, to which
they were fo prone before, from the filence of
their great Lawgiver in his Creation of the
World, might probably have defy'd all diffua-
fions, and been the moft fatal encouragement
to them, to fo vile a Worfhip that were eafie
to be imagin'd. Any particular declaration of
the reafons of fuch omiffion, from the real Diftance, Magnitude, Motions, and Defigns of the
faid Bodies, and how improperly they could be
reduc'd within the faid narration, (the only precaution fuppofable in the cafe) being more likely to difcredit the whole Book, than overcome
their prejudices, than give them a true and juft
Idea of the matter it felf, and fo obviate their
falfe reafonings and practices thereupon in the
foremention'd Idolatry. So that 'twas abfolutely neceffary to include the Heavenly Bodies in
the *Mofaick* Creation, in order to prevent Idolatry among the *Jews*: which feems to have been
a principal aim not only of recording this whole
Narration, but of the intire *Mofaick* Difpenfation:

tion : and therefore was in the firft place by all
means to be confider'd.

(2.) The peculiar Nature and Circumftances
of this Hiftory of the Creation, neceffarily require the mention of the Heavenly Bodies, as well
as of any other parts of the Vifible World. And
'tis this miftake that has hitherto hindred any
rational account thereof ; that men have either
fuppos'd it a Real and Philofophical relation of
the proper Creation of all things; or a meer
Mythological and Myfterious Reduction of the
vifible parts of it to fix periods or divifions, under which mighty Myfteries were fuppos'd to be
hid, and by which the foundation of a feventh-
day Sabbath was to be laid among the *Jews.*
Now tho' fomewhat of truth I believe be contained in each of thefe different notions; yet I
think 'tis undeniable that they are neither of
them to be acquiefced in, and by no means give
a fatisfactory account of the compleat Nature
and Kind of this Hiftory. That alone to which
all its particulars exactly anfwer, and which is
as Literal and Philofophical as the capacities of
the *Jews* could expect or reach, and did require,
is, *An Hiftorical Journal or Diary of the Mutations
of the Chaos, and of the vifible Works of each Day,
fuch an one as an honeft and obferving Spectator on
the Earth would have made, and recorded, may and
believ'd to be in all cafes the truth and reality of the
things themfelves.* Now that this Idea alone fits
this Sacred Hiftory, might eafily be made out
by the confideration of the particulars related,
and of thofe omitted, with all the other circumftances thereof, by no means correfponding to
any other Hypothefis; but moft exactly to this
before us ; without the leaft force offer'd to the
Nature and Syftem of the World, to the Divine
Perfections,

Perfections, or the Free Reafon of Mankind;
and exactly fuitable to the Stile of the Holy
Books, in the mention of the *Phænomena* of the
Natural World in other places. Which being
fuppos'd (and by that time this Differtation is
confider'd throughout, I hope 'twill appear no
precarious fuppofition,) 'tis evident that both
the appearance of Light , and of the Bodies
themfelves, the Sun, Moon and Stars, (the things
we are now enquiring about,) muft as certainly
come within fuch a Journal, and make as remarkable Turns and Changes in the World, as
far as this Spectator could judge, as any other
within the intire fix days could poffibly do. The
appearance of Light to him who never before is
fuppos'd to have feen fuch a thing, and was till
then incompafs'd with the thickeft Darknefs;
and the plain view of the Heavenly Bodies themfelves to him who before had no manner of notion
of 'em, efpecially when he had no poffible means of
diftinguifhing them from Light and Fiery Balls,
fituate with, and pertaining to the Clouds; muft
as certainly have inferr'd a new Creation, and
under fuch a notion have been recorded in their
due place in the Journal before-mention'd, as
any other whatfoever; and their order, pofition,
and ufes would naturally be recounted no otherwife than we now find them in the *Mofaick*
Creation. From which confideration I think
'tis not at all furprizing, that thefe parts of the
Vifible World, how remote and feperate foever
they be from our Earth in themfelves, are yet
included in this Hiftory before us; and have
their diftinct periods in the fix days work; tho'
at the fame time the Κοσμοποιία it felf do properly relate to the formation of the Sublunary
World only.

IV T

IV. I prove that the History before us, extends not beyond the Earth and its Appendages, because that confused Mass, or rude heap of Heterogeneous matter, which we call the Chaos, whence all the several parts were deriv'd, extended no farther. It will here I suppose be allow'd me, that the ancient Chaos, so famous among the old Philosophers, and so evidently refer'd to by *Moses*, was the intire and single source or promptuary of the six days productions ; and that consequently nothing ought to be esteem'd a part of that *Creation*, but what in its Rudiments and Principles was so of the Chaos also ; and this *Postulatum* is so agreeable to *Moses*, as well as all the antient accounts of the *Chaos*, and I think so suitable to the sentiments of most men, that I shall, without farther proof, suppose it granted, and betake my self immediately to the other branch of the argument, and endeavour to evince, that the Chaos was so far from comprehending the intire matter of the Universe, nay or of the Solar System, that it reach'd not so far as the Moon, nor indeed any farther than that Terraqueous Globe we now Inhabit, with such Bodies as are immediately contiguous and appertaining thereto. Which I think the following arguments will sufficiently demonstrate.

(1.) If we Appeal to External Nature, and enquire what confused Masses or Chaos's either at present are, or ever, within the Annals of Time, were extant in the Visible World, we shall discover no footsteps of any such thing, excepting what the Atmosphere of a Comet affords us. If therefore, without the allowance of precarious and fanciful Hypotheses, relying on no known *Phænomena* of Nature ; a Comet's Atmosphere

be

be the fole pretender, if moreover the fame Atmofphere gives a Juft, Adequate, Primitive, and
Scriptural Idea of that ancient Chaos ; if it anfwers its particular *Phnœmena*, recounted by
Sacred or Prophane Hiftory ; if it prove a peculiarly fit Foundation of fuch an Earth as ours is,
and is extraordinarily adapted to fuit, and account
for its prefent and paft *Phænomena* ; all which
shall be prov'd hereafter; I think we may ceafe *Vid.*
our farther enquiries, and with the higheft rea- *Hypoth.* 2.
fon and juftice conclude, That a Comet, or more
peculiarly the Atmofphere thereof, was that very Chaos, from whence that World arofe,
whofe Original is related in the *Mofaick* Hiftory :
And with equal reafon and juftice be fatisfi'd,
(which is but a certain confequent thereof) that
not the innumerable Syftems of the fixt Stars, not
the narrower Syftem of the Sun, nay nor the
Moon her felf, but our Earth alone, was the
proper fubject of the *Mofaick* Creation. Which
conclufion will be farther eftablish'd by the coincidence of the feveral days works recounted by
Mofes, with thofe Natural and Orderly Mutations which, in the Digeftion and Formation
of a Planet from a Comet's Atmofphere, would
Mechanically proceed, as hereafter will appear.

(2.) The Chaos mention'd by *Mofes* is by
him exprefly call'd *The Earth*, in contradiftincti-
on to *The Heavens*, or the other Syftems of the
Univerfe ; and all its parts taken notice of in
the Sacred Hiftory, appear, by the following
Series of the Scriptures, to belong to our Earth
and no other. The words of *Mofes* are, *In the* *Gen.* i. 1.
Beginning God created the heaven and the earth ; 2.
and the earth was without form and void, and
darknefs was upon the face of the deep ; and the

D   *Spirit*

Spirit of God moved upon the face of the waters.
Where I think 'tis plain, as has been already observ'd, that when the Author comes to the Chaos
or Foundation of the six days work, he excludes
the Heavens from any share therein, and calls
the Chaos it self *An Earth, without form and void,*
with Darkness upon the Face of its Abyss ; and
this all ought to grant, these being the very
Words from which 'tis concluded that the Heathen Chaos was no other than what *Moses* deriv'd the World from.

And that the Chaos is here confin'd to *the
Earth,* will be sure put past doubt by the latter
part of this Argument, which observes no other
parts to be mention'd belonging thereto, than
such as the succeeding Series of the Holy Scriptures shews to have afterward belong d to our
Earth and no other, *viz.* An *Abyss* or *Deep,* and
Waters : Both of them frequently mention'd in
the Holy Books, and now actual parts of the
present Globe, as will appear hereafter.

So that when *Moses* calls his Chaos expressly the
Earth ; when by the coherence of his discourse
he excludes the Heavens, taken in a large and
proper sense, from the same ; when, lastly, he
mentions no other parts of this Chaos than such
as afterward, and at this day, are parts of our
Earth ; 'Tis somewhat unaccountable, and like
a kind of fate upon Commentators, that they
should unanimously resolve to make this Chaos
of so extravagant a compass as they too incon-
gruously do ; and that they should agree in it so
universally, tho' without any warrant from,
nay contrary to, the obvious sense of the Text
it self, and the plain drift, coherence and description of *Moses* therein. I know it will be
said the First and Fourth days works, (the Origin

gin of Light, and of the Sun, Moon and Stars)
neceffitated fuch a fuppofition, and gave juft
caufe for the common Expofition. Which as I
believe to have been the true occafions of all
fuch miftaken Gloffes , fo I think them far from
juft and neceffary ones; and if what has been already faid has clear'd thofe difficulties, there can
be no reafon to reject the Cogency of the prefent
Argument, but a great deal to reft fatisfi'd in it ;
and to confefs it no lefs unfcriptural than 'tis
abfurd, to expect from this fingle Chaos, a Sun,
Moon, and Syftems of fix'd Stars, as hitherto
the World has commonly done.

(3.) The *Mofaick* and ancient *Chaos* could not
include the Sun or fix'd Stars, becaufe juft before
the extraction of Light from it, as 'tis ufually explain'd, it was Dark and Caliginous ; which on
fuch a fuppofition is not conceivable. A ftrange
Darknefs this! where more than ninety nine
parts of an hundred (whether we take in the
intire Syftem of the World, or the Solar Syftem
only) appear to be fiery Corpufcles , and the
very fame from whence all the fix'd Stars, or at
leaft the Sun, were conftituted ; and are now the
Fountain of all that Light and Heat which the
World has ever fince enjoy'd. Let every unbiafs'd perfon judge, how Dark that *Chaos* could
be, where the Opake and Obfcure parts were fo
perfectly inconfiderable in comparifon of the
Light, the Active, and the Fiery ones. So that
on this Hypothefis, The ftate of the Chaos muft
have been exceeding Light, Hot, and Fiery, before the firft days work ; when it was on the
contrary, according to all Antiquity, Sacred
and Profane, Dark and Caliginous. 'Tis true,
upon the feparation of the particles of Light (the
bufinefs, in this Hypothefis, of the Firft Day)

*Vid. Lem.
33. infra.*

D 2   the

the Chaos would become Obſcure and Dark enough, at the ſame time that the Sun, or fix'd Stars, were collecting their Maſſes ſo lately extracted, and were growing Splendid and Glorious. But this is to contradict the Hiſtory, according to which the Light, on the Firſt Day, is conſider'd with relation to the Chaos, and its diſtinguiſhing Night and Day *There*, not as it was collecting into Bodies of Light without it (which rather muſt belong to the Fourth Days Work); when by this account 'tis evident, that this day is the peculiar time for the moſt pitchy Darkneſs poſſible. For when all the Light was juſt ſeparated from the Chaos, the moſt Caliginous Night muſt certainly enſue. So that unleſs we can change the Order in *Moſes,* and prove that the Chaos before the Firſt Days Work was all over Light, and on the Firſt Day cover'd with the Thickeſt Darkneſs, we in vain pretend to juſtifie the vulgar opinion, and include the Sun or fix'd Stars among the other Matter of the Chaos.

Beſides, when Heat is the main Inſtrument of Nature in all its ſeparations of Parts, and Productions of Bodies, 'tis ſure a very improper ſeaſon juſt then to extract the Light and Fiery Corpuſcles out of the Chaos, when the Formation of things began, and there was the principal occaſion for their preſence and efficacy, that ever was or could poſſibly be. A ſtrange method of Generation! To take away the Cauſe at the very inſtant when it was to produce its Effects, and to recount the Effects not before, but as ſoon as ever the Cauſe is taken away! But to proceed.

(4.) The now undoubted property of the Univerſal Gravitation of Matter, contradicts and overthrows this fancy of the Heavenly Bodies having
been

been originally included in, and at the Creation extracted from the Chaos of which we are speaking. For on this Hypothesis when once they were mingled with the parts of the Earth, and are since at immense distances from it, they must have fled off every way from their former place, and in a small space of time have thrown themselves to those vastly remote seats which they have ever since possess'd. Now if instead of the *vis centripeta,* a *vis centrifuga*; instead of mutual attraction, a mutual repulse or avoidance were found to be the standing unchang'd Law of Nature, and Property of Matter, this might have look'd like a possible, at least, if not a probable Hypothesis; and the whole Order of Nature ever since need not have been contradicted in this primary formation of things. But when the contrary force, that I mean of mutual tendency, attraction, or gravitation obtains, and that, as far as we have any means of knowing, universally, which Mr. Newton has demonstrated, there is no room or foundation in Nature for such an Imagination.

'Tis by no means impossible that all the Bodies in the Universe should approach to one another, and at last unite in the common Center of Gravity of the intire System: Nay from the universality of the Law of Gravitation, and the finiteness of the World, in length of time, without a miraculous power interpose and prevent it, it must really happen. But by what Law of Nature, or Property of Bodies, they, when once conjoin'd, (as those I now oppose must affirm) should be separated, 'tis hard to conceive.

Which difficulty is increas'd by the prodigious velocity of their motions; when according to the

Phil. Nat. 1. & 2. *Lem.* 11. *&c.*

D 2

the vulgar Hypothesis, but a few hours can be allow'd the Heavenly Bodies to waft them to those immensly , yet variously distant Seats, which they were immediately and for ever after to possess. All which harsh and ungrounded fictions are intirely avoided, and all things represented according to the known Laws of Matter and Motion, in that natural and easie Hypothesis we take, and which therefore is as consonant to, as the other is averse from , the Make and Constitution of the Natural World.

(5.) This fancy, that the Heavenly Bodies proceeded originally from the Terrestrial Chaos, and cast themselves off from it every way, supposes the Earth to be the Center of the World, or of all that System of Bodies, and they plac'd in a kind of circumference every way about it. How well soever such a Notion would agree with the Vulgar or *Ptolemaick* System of the World, I fear the *Pythagorean* , which has forc'd its reception, and is universally receiv'd by Astronomers, will not at all square therewith. In that account which would only include the Planetary or Solar System within the six days Creation, the Sun, its known and undoubted Center, seems the only proper place for such a Chaos as were to be the common source and promptuary of the whole : But in the vulgar account, where all the Stars and Planets of the Universe are to be suppos'd at a Center together, we, who know not the bounds and circumference of the World, cannot be suppos'd able to pitch upon a Center proper for so immense and strange a Chaos. Only one may venture to say, that the Earth, a small moveable Planet, revolving about the Sun, is an ill-chosen one however.

And

And now upon a recollection and view of this whole Argument, I do not queſtion but an unprejudic'd perſon, who knew nothing of the ſentiments of Commentators, or of the opinions of the vulgar, and who had only been converſant in the Works, and Word of God, the Book of External Nature, and the Book of Scripture, would eaſily find the bounds of the *Moſaick* Creation; and on a little conſideration and compariſon of the Sacred and Profane Accounts of the Primitive Chaos, with the preſent Nature and Situation of the Heavenly Bodies, would quickly be convinc'd that our Earth alone were therein concern'd; he could ſcarce be ſuppos'd once to Dream that the Origin of the Sun and Planets, much leſs of innumerable Suns and Planets, and of the intire Univerſe, was there accounted for. Such Notions, how general ſoever, are not the reſult of Nature and Scripture carefully conſider'd and compar'd one with another, but the effects of ignorance of the frame of the World, and of the ſtile of Scripture; of an unacquaintedneſs with the Works, and thence an inability of judging concerning the Word of God relating to them; or indeed commonly of a certain μικροψυχία, or narrowneſs of Soul, which Temper, Education, Converſation, Application to ſome particular Studies and Authors, with a ſtrangeneſs to free and generous Enquiries, ſome or all have been the unhappy occaſions of. In ſhort, 'tis becauſe men are not able to give themſelves or others a ſatisfactory account of ſuch things, that they are forced to fall into a beaten path, and content themſelves with thoſe poor and jejune Schemes, which, when carefully examin'd, prove neither Rational nor Scriptural, but as perfectly contradictory to

found

found Philofophy, as the genuine fenfe of thofe very Texts on which they build their conclufions. Every unbyafs'd Mind would eafily allow, that like Effects had like Caufes; and that Bodies of the fame general Nature, Ufes, and Motions, were to be deriv'd from the fame Originals; and confequently, that the Sun and the fixed Stars had one, as the Earth, and the other Planets another fort of Formation. If therefore any free Confiderer found that one of the latter fort, that Planet which we Inhabit, was deriv'd from a Chaos; by a parity of Reafon he would fuppofe, every one of the other to be fo deriv'd alfo; I mean each from its peculiar Chaos.

Nay truly I might carry this matter ftill higher, and if one Planet muft be made Parent to another, juftly claim the principal place for *Jupiter*, about fixty times as big as our Earth, and the largeft and moft confiderable of all the Sun's *Chorus*; and fo with greater fhew of Probability affert, that from its Chaos any of the other Planets were deriv'd, than himfelf from theirs. Particularly the Earth is fo fmall a Globe, that in point of Dignity or Origination, very many of the Celeftial Bodies may moft fairly claim the precedence of her, and curb her afpiring pretenfions to any fuch mighty Prerogatives above her Fellows. There is in reality no occafion for any fuch childifh reafoning on either fide; and every one of the Planets (efpecially the Moon, fo exactly refembling her Sifter Earth) ought to be deduc'd from a diftinct Chaos of its own, as well as that particular one which Providence has allotted for the Seat of Mankind. And 'tis not to be queftion'd, were we as well acquainted with the Nature, Conftitution, and Ufes of the other Planets, with their various Inhabitants, and the
                                        feveral

several methods of Divine Providence relating to 'em all; we should not be backward to allow 'em every one a proportionable share in the care of Heaven, and a like conduct in their Origins and Periods, as the Earth, on which we dwell, can boast of. We should, 'tis probable, soon understand, that, (bating the stupendious and miraculous dispensation of the Gospel by the *Messias* Θεάνθρωπ-) as well the Moral, as the Natural Histories of these Worlds; those of their first rise out of Chao's, of their several Changes, Revolutions, and Catastrophes, with regard to the inanimate, the animate, and Reasonable Beings, both as to the dignity of the things themselves, and their newness to us, would equally deserve the view and consideration of Inquisitive Minds, with any like Accounts relating to our own Earth; and we should easily satisfy our selves, that the single Chaos, the Seminary of our present Earth, was so far from extending it self to the Sun, or fixt Stars, that not the least secondary Planet in the Solar System could be contain'd therein.

V. The *Mosaick* Creation is confin'd to our Earth, with its Appurtenances, because otherwise the time of the Creation of each Body was so extreamly disproportionate to the Work it self, as is perfectly irreconcileable to the Divine Wisdom of its Creator, and the accounts of the Works themselves as they are set down by *Moses.*

In order to the *Reader's* perceiving and admitting the force of this, and some following Arguments, I must premise some things touching the nature of such Reasonings, and how far they may be made use of without any just Imputation

tion

tion of Boldnefs, Irreverence, or an audacious
Stinting and Determining the Divine Actions.

And here I freely confefs, That 'tis not neceffary in all Cafes that we fhould comprehend the
reafons of the Divine Actions or Providence
before we can be under an Obligation to believe
them. They may be hid from us on feveral accounts, tho' the things themfelves be plain in
Scripture. Under which circumftances, I hear-
tily own the ftricteft Obligation to yield our un-
feigned Affent to what God has clearly reveal'd,
notwithftanding we cannot fee the intire accoun-
tablenefs thereof to our imperfect Underftandings.
But then, 'tis one thing to be *above*, and another to be *repugnant* to our Reafon; 'tis one thing
to be beyond the comprehenfion of, and another
directly contradictory to our Humane Faculties.
Befides, the clearnefs or obfcurity of the Revelation is here very confiderable; the former cafe re-
folves our Affent into the Divine Veracity; but
the latter may only be the miftakes of Humane Deductions, and by confequence, tho' our
fallible reafonings be fuperfeded by the firft, yet
there is room for them in the fecond. I believe,
for inftance, and am oblig'd fo to do, that our
Saviour Chrift is truly Θεάνϑρωπ Θ, God and
Man, becaufe I find it every where plain and
evident that the Stile, Titles, Attributes, Actions, and incommunicable Name of the Eternal
Deity, the God of *Ifrael*, are at leaft as frequently afcrib'd to him the Son, as to the Father
himfelf, through the whole Bible; notwithftanding any inability of comprehending the Nature
of God, and thence of judging of the Unity or
Plurality of Perfons in the Divine Effence. But
I do not think my felf equally oblig'd to believe
the

the Doctrine of abfolute and uncondition'd Reprobation, becaufe the Proofs alledg'd for it are far from being clear, and becaufe 'tis not fo properly above, as contradictory to the moft evident Reafon. And this comes neareft to the prefent cafe; in which, neither can any one juftly affert the plainnefs of the Revelation on the fide of the common Scheme; nor alledge the fublimity of the Subject, on account whereof it might be fairly fuppos'd above the reach of our finite Capacities. The Scripture, as I take it, is evidently for, at leaft muft be own'd not evidently againft this reftrained Senfe of the *Mofaick* Hiftory before us; and the Subject it felf is finite and limited, and fo within our ken, and capable of our comprehenfion : On which accounts fuch Arguments as follow, ought to have their place, and if confiderable, their force and influence on our Faith alfo, and go a great way to determine fuch a Difpute as we are now upon.

And 'tis fure not impoffible, within certain bounds, for a confidering man to determine what is rational, wife and prudent ; what is confonant to the nature of things ; what is fuitable to forecaft and contrivance; what is in moft cafes proper, decent and becoming, even with relation to the Divine Operations in the World. We naturally, in the reflecting on the Syftem of External Nature, obferve many Marks and Tokens of the Wifdom and Art, the Skill and Artifice of the Great Creator ; which fuppofes that we are competent Judges in fuch matters. And indeed, 'tis but changing the Scene, and confidering what we naturally pronounce to be rational and orderly, fit and proportionable among Men ; what will become a Wife General or

Statef-

Statesman , a Skilful Builder and Architect , nay an ordinary Workman or Artificer, in usual and obvious cases : What on the one hand are the Tokens of Foresight and Prudence ; and on the other , of Heedlesness and Folly, in the common Affairs of Life ; and we shall not wholly be to seek what to think of several analogous Actions relating to God himself : Due allowance being every where made for that infinite distance, and different state and management of the Supream Governour of the World, from those of all finite Beings, depending on, and subject to him. Thus we collect our Idea's of the Divine Attributes, by considering what is good, great, valued, and esteemed lovely and venerable among Men, and ascribing every such thing to the Divine Nature ; who being the Origin of them all, must contain 'em within himself in a higher and more eminent manner. By accumulating all things that appear Perfections in Men, or other Creatures, and removing all Imperfections necessarily adhering to them, we arrive at the Notion of an Infinitely Perfect Being ; which is but another name for God ; and whom, on that account, we justly think the proper Object of our Worship and Adoration.

When therefore our very Idea's of the Divine Properties are owing to, and depend on, our consideration of those lesser degrees of the same which we observe in Men; and when the reason why the contrary Properties are not by us ascribed to him, is, because we find that in Men they argue imperfection ; what is a sign or effect of some degree of Perfection in Men , must also be acknowledg'd a sign or effect of a like Perfection in God. And what is a sign or effect of Imperfection in Men, must also be own'd, if it were

sup-

fuppofable, a fign or effect of a like Imperfection
in God. Thus for inftance we certainly gather,
that God cannot be properly pleas'd or delighted
in the mifery and torment of his Creatures, where
yet the Juftice and Wifdom of his Government
require him feverely to punifh 'em; Becaufe we
cannot but efteem it an odious Vice, and bafe
Imperfection in a Judge on Earth, in like cafes,
to be fo affected; and whether we will or no,
we look upon it as an inftance of cruelty and
barbarity of difpofition to rellifh and tafte a
fweetnefs, in the Cries and Groans of condemned
and dying Malefactors. In like manner we juftly
conclude, God cannot *Impofe* on Innocent Creatures, no not by fuch Wiles, Stratagems, or other
methods of Collufion, wherein yet direct and
downright Falfehood were avoided; becaufe we
find a fpontaneous averfion and indignation arifes
in our minds when fuch Tricks and Shams are
difcovered among Men. And by the fame way,
and equal force of reafoning may we collect,
that God cannot, in the formation or difpofition
of things, no more than in other cafes, act ab-
furdly or difagreeably to Reafon; difproportio-
nately or unfuitably to the nature of things;
immethodically without rule and order, or fool-
ifhly without drift and defign, according as an
impartial and confidering Man, who were duly
acquainted with the Syftem of Nature, would
judge and determine in the cafe. And confequently, 'Tis a difhonourable reflection on God,
to afcribe to him thofe things which to the free
Faculties of Mankind would amongft us be look'd
on as marks of unfkilfulnefs, imprudence, or folly, in parallel cafes; and for which meer Men
could not efcape the moft fevere and indecorous
imputations.

Put

Put the cafe that I fhould chance to obferve a certain Mafter-builder in his parcelling out the feveral diftinct Tasks of the Under-workmen, and apportioning the time he would allow to the finifhing of the whole ; and that I perceiv'd 9 parts of 10 were to be done in one day, but the other fingle part had a month's fpace affigned to it; and yet 9 parts of 10 of the intire number of Workmen were to club together for that Work to be done in the month, while only every tenth man were permitted to affift at the days task : Were it poffible to fuppofe fuch a cafe on Earth, I need not inform you what opinion the Spectator would have of the Abilities or Prudence of the Architect. Or, Put the cafe that an ordinary Husbandman, who had two Plots of Ground, the one of a fcore feet in circumference, not very promifing or capable of Cultivation above others, the other of a thoufand Acres of good Land, and very fit for Tillage or Improvement; fhould fpend four or five days every Week about his little fpot of Indifferent Ground, and allot no more than the remaining one or two for the Care and Management of the other fpacious Field : 'Tis eafie to imagine under what Notion and Character the Plowman would pafs in the World. Or laftly, Suppofe one fhould light upon an Hiftorian, who undertook to give a compleat and full Account of fome large and fpacious Country, with the many Noble Kingdoms, Principalities, Lordfhips, and Governments therein contain'd; and upon perufal nothing was to be found mention'd in any particular manner, but a certain little and remote Ifland (fo inconfiderable that the generality of the Inhabitants of the Main Land never heard fo much as its name) which indeed was defcrib'd
                                        carefully

carefully, and its several circumstances diligently accounted for : But as to the rest, there appear'd no more than at the conclusion of a Chapter two or three names of its principal Divisions, and some advantages which one or two of their Maritime Towns afforded this small Island, and then all was concluded. Now he that should take this for a just and adequate History of the whole, and earnestly contend for the Compleatness and Perfection of the Work, would be certainly taken for a *strange* person ; or rather would be thought in Jest, and to design the real exposing of the folly and ridiculousness of the Publisher thereof. These familiar instances amongst Men shew what unbrib'd and untainted Nature instantaneously pronounces in such cases; and thereby directs us what we ought to judge in parallel ones in which God himself is directly interested.

Where the change of the Person is so far from altering, that it exceedingly confirms these dictates of Right Reason, and makes those suppositions which were harsh and incredible with regard to Men, to become intolerable and impious when apply'd to the Deity. Whatsoever bears the characters of Truth, Justice, Order, Wisdom, and Contrivance, which I cannot but expect from good and skilful Men; I undoubtedly require and believe of the Divine Majesty without the least hesitation, in the highest degree and supreamest measure imaginable. But whatsoever looks like Falseness, Injustice, Confusion, Folly, and a Wild Disproportion or Precipitancy among Men, and which I am difficultly induc'd to imagine of a frail and imperfect Creature like my self, I am much more hardly persuaded, or rather find it impossible to believe of God. Those very faculties by which I am enabled to distinguish and

pass

pass a Sentence in thefe matters, are deriv'd from God, and a part of the Divine Image on the Soul of Man; and fhall I fo odly make ufe of them, that what I could not be brought to credit of any one of my Neighbours, it were fo uncouth, abfurd, and prepofterous, I freely admit and contend for when afcrib'd to my Creator? The Mind of Man, if it have leave to reflect freely, can no more acquiefce in any Scheme of the Works of God, where nothing of Forecaft, Order, *Decorum,* and Wifdom is confpicuous; where every period appears puzling, immethodical, difproportionate, and ill difpos'd, (fuch is that of the vulgar Idea of the *Mofaick* Creation, as will be prov'd prefently) than it can believe contradictions, or that God is an Infinitely Wife and Perfect Being indeed, but yet at the fame time acting what, in the common fenfe of Mankind, argues the greateft folly and imperfection; which intirely and with plenary fatisfaction to do, is certainly impoffible. There is fomewhat in the Humane Soul that has too quick a fenfe of the decency and fitnefs of things, and withal too deep a veneration for the Adorable Majefty of God, to be *eafie under,* tho' it may be *overborn with* fuch Notions. It cannot be willing to believe that of its Wife and Glorious Creator, which for another to believe of it felf would be efteem'd as an high indignity.

'Tis true, there is fo great a difference between the compafs of the Divine, and the ftreightnefs of Humane Knowledge; between the State of Creatures and of the Creator, Bleffed for evermore; there may be fuch an incapacity in us to reach, or unfathomable, yet wife, reafons for God to hide fome things from us; not to infift on the Divine Prerogative, which

frees

frees him from the obligation of giving an account of every thing to any of thofe Beings he has made ; That we ought to be very wary of Arguing from Man to God, without due allowance for thefe confiderations; and confequently mighty cautious of affirming or denying whatever is afcrib'd to him from fuch a comparifon. In particular, wherever a clear Revelation interpofes, we are bound to quit our fallible reafonings, and fully to acquiefce in fuch a decifion : It being impoffible for *God* to *Lye*, but by no means fo, that *we* may be *miftaken.*

But then this neceffary prudence and warinefs is chiefly, if not only, concern'd in fublime and myfterious points; concerning the incomprehenfible Nature, or unfearchable Providences of God ; which Doctrines fometimes are fo much above the prefent Scene of things ; fo remote from the notions and affairs of this World ; relate to and depend on fuch other Syftems of Beings or circumftances of the Inviible World ; that we ought not rafhly to pafs our Judgment of them; but wait till our Souls become fo improv'd, and our Underftandings enlightened in a future ftate; till our means of information, and opportunities of looking through the whole Chain and Syftem, be fo many more than now they are, that we may juftly be fuppos'd more competent Judges, and equal Arbitrators, than at prefent the imperfection of our condition will permit us in reafon to pretend to.

But this being again precaution'd, to prevent any mifconftruction or abufe of this reafoning, I cannot but fay, that fince 'twill be hard to prove the cafe before us to be of fo exalted a nature as to tranfcend our faculties ; and perhaps ftill harder to prove the plainnefs of the revelation on

E   the

the fide of the common expofition, I am fully
perfuaded that while the Perfections of God are,
as to our affent, deduc'd from their effects, they
may in good meafure, within certain bounds, as
was before difcours'd, be judg'd of by what is
obfervable among Men. And as whatfoever is
worthy, good, and valuable among our felves, is
rightly own'd as an efflux and gift of God ; fo
whatfoever is prepofterous, abfurd, or diforderly,
whatfoever is unworthy, bafe, or defpicable in
humane affairs, cannot without great indignity
be believed of him ; and where we have no
other ways of determining, fuch reafonings
ought to be perfuafive and decretory.

Now therefore, all this being faid by way of
Introduction to this and fome following Arguments, let us apply it to the cafe before us ; and
fuppofing, (which yet I need not allow) that
the matter were indifferent on all other confiderations, let us fpeak freely whether fuch a method, fuch time, and fuch proportion of the feveral parts as the Ordinary Scheme of the Creation fets before us, be in any degree fo well contriv'd, and fuitably difpos'd, as, I fay not a Divine, but a meer Humane Architect may be fuppos'd the Author of. I need not here give a
particular account of the vulgar expofition of the
firft Chapter of *Genefis*: 'Tis fufficiently known
as to the main parts of it. But the difproportions
I would take notice of in it under this Head are
thefe three ;

(1.) The length of the Day ufually affign'd, is
wholly difproportionate to the bufinefs done upon it.

(2.) When the Works of each of the other
Days are fingle, diftinct, and of a fort, the Third
Day has two quite different, nay incompatible
Works affigned to it. (3.) And

(3.) And Principally the Earth with its furniture, how inconfiderable a Body foever it is, takes up four intire days, at leaft, of thofe fix which were allotted to the whole Creation, when the Sun, Moon and Stars, thofe vaftly greater and more confiderable bodies, are crowded into one fingle day together.

(1.) The Length of the Day ufually affign'd of Twenty four Hours is wholly difproportionate to the bufinefs done upon it. This plainly appears by the Hiftory it felf, where, to omit other inftances, the whole train in the generation or firft production of Animals, has no longer a fpace afforded to it; when yet all experience fhews, that a much longer is neceffarily requir'd, and has obtain'd in all the fubfequent Ages. Now I do not queftion but it will be confefs'd by all, that according to the conftant procefs of Nature, this time is utterly infufficient for this purpofe : But what will be faid is, that a Divine Power immediately interpos'd, and either form'd every thing in its grown and mature ftate ; or at leaft accelerated and haften'd the courfe of Nature, fo as to enable her to perfect each Creature in fo fhort a fpace; and that confequently no ftraitnefs of time ought to be alledg'd on this account. In anfwer whereto I freely grant, that God can produce all things in their moft perfect ftate, in a moment; and if that could be prov'd to have been the method here, this exception were of no validity. But as on fuch a fuppofition 'tis ftrange that fix intire and fucceffive days fhould be requifite to, or pitch'd upon by an Infinite and Unlimited Agent ; when the inftantaneous Creation of the whole appears more agreeable to the Dignity and Power of the Creator; fo I am pretty fecure that this Hypo-

thefis

thesis, how common soever, is repugnant to the *Mosaick* History. The Sacred Penman does there ascribe indeed the Origin of every thing to the Divine Power; yet no otherwise than the like would be, and is done by the Holy Writers afterwards, nay by every body at this day ; when yet the constant method of Generation is exactly observ'd. If any of us were ask'd who made us ? We should soon answer, God; without the least imagination that we were excused from that nine months abode, and gradual growth in our Mothers Womb ; which every one by the general Rule and Method of Nature is oblig'd to undergo. Which appears in the present case to be the intention of the Holy Writer, because he makes these very Animals productions of the Water and Earth , as well as the proper effects of the Divine Power; as has been obferv'd already on another occasion. And those who deny this gradual Generation according to the course of Nature, must without reason recede from the Letter of *Moses,* and that when by so doing they render this Sacred History more difficult and unintelligible than it really is.

But if instead of immediate Creation it be said that 'twas only a supernatural acceleration of natural causes, without any other alteration of the process ; which is I think the only probable evasion, and the fairest supposition of all other ; I reply, That this is *gratis dictum*, without any foundation in the Scripture, and so as easily denied as asserted; it is introduc'd only to salve the shortness of time mention'd in the History, which will be prov'd hereafter to stand in no need of it ; and it overthrows all attempts of accounting for this six days Creation in a rational and natural way; for if a miraculous power be

allow'd

allow'd in a needlefs cafe, we fhall be ever at a lofs how far to extend it, and where mechanical caufes ought to take place. On which confiderations I take this extraordinary acceleration of natural caufes to be, tho' not impoffible, nor (were there any intimation or neceffity of its interpofition from the Sacred Hiftory) very improbable neither, yet in the prefent cafe, groundlefs, unneceffary, perplexing of the caufe, and by no means a fufficient folution in the prefent Affair. Which being therefore thus anfwer'd, the Argument remains in full force, and the length of the days affign'd by the vulgar Hypothefis appears wholly difproportionate to the Works done therein; of which farther notice will be taken hereafter.

(2.) When the Works of each of the other Days are fingle, diftinct, and of a fort, the third Day has two quite different, nay incompatible ones affigned to it. This is plain from the Hiftory, where the divifion of the Waters from the Earth, or the diftinction of the Terraqueous Globe into Seas and dry Land, the firft work on this Day, is fucceeded by that of the production of the intire Vegetable Kingdom; contrary to the perpetual Tenor of the other periods of the Creation How this comes about, or is accountable in the vulgar Scheme, I know not; and I believe the reafon thereof is very little enquir'd into, and lefs underftood. But becaufe this whole difficulty will be urg'd againft the fhortnefs of days in the Vulgar Hypothefis, and clear'd in Ours, at their proper places hereafter, I fhall wave the farther infifting upon it here, and proceed.

(3.) But principally, the Earth with its Furniture, how inconfiderable a body foever it is, takes

E 3

up four intire days, at leaft, of thofe fix which were allotted to the whole Creation ; when the Sun, Moon and Stars, thofe vaftly greater and more confiderable Bodies, are crowded into one fingle day together. Now in order to our paffing a rational judgment in this matter, I fhall take leave to reprefent to the Reader's view a fhort comparifon or parallel between the Earth on one fide and the reft of the World on the other ; and fee what refemblance, correfpondence and proportion there is between the former and the latter, either in its feveral parts, or the whole taken together ; and this fhall be done on fuch certain and undoubted grounds and principles as the late vaft advancement of Natural Knowledge has afforded us ; and will be more at large explain'd in the following Pages.

This Earth then, on which we live, though it be in diameter more than 8000 miles, and fo a vaft Globe, if compar'd with thofe Bodies we daily fee, imagine, and converfe withal, is yet one of the leffer of the primary Planets, and with *Jupiter*, *Mars*, and the other her fellows, revolves round the great Center of our Syftem the *Sun*, in a years time. 'Tis an Opake and Dark Body, as they all are, and in common with them borrows its light and heat from that glorious Body which we juft now obferv'd to obtain the center of their Orbits ; without which it, as well as the intire Chorus of the other Planets, muft be foon reduc'd all to one dark heap of matter, far beyond the defcription of the old caliginous and unprofitable Chaos, and in no capacity of ever emerging out of that horrid and frightful ftate. In dignity, if our Earth expect not to come the laſt, yet is fhe fo exceeded, in all things that might feem Characters thereof, by

feveral

several of the rest, that there can be no manner of claim to the *first* Place. If she have a secondary Planet, the *Moon*, for her attendant (tho in truth she is at least as serviceable to that Planet, as that Planet is to her); *Jupiter* has certainly four; and some good Glasses have discover'd five about *Saturn*; who however is not wholly destitute, as all Astronomers confess. The density and place of the Earth is pretty near the middle of the Planets, and as she exceeds, and is higher than some, so is she exceeded by, and lower than others in those respects. Her own Secondary Planet, the *Moon*, has an Air much more homogeneous, pure, and transparent, than she at present enjoys; and in all probability free from Winds, Clouds, Storms, Tempests, Thunder, Lightning, and such other irregular and pernicious Effects, which render our Atmosphere so contagious and pestilent to the Inhabitants of the Earth. In which circumstances the generality of the other Planets imitate the Moon, and render our miserable Condition the more remarkable and sensible; as appearing thereby almost singular. Our days and nights are longer than those of some, and shorter than those of others of the Planets. The figure of the Earth is nearly sphærical, as is that also of the other Heavenly Bodies; its surface unequal, with Mountains and Valleys, as well as that of the rest, especially the Moon's, appears to be. Only 'tis observable that the last, though much less in bigness, has her Mountains higher than we on Earth. The Sea and Land, Mountains and Valleys, and other such corresponding *Phænomena* of the Moon, shew, that that small Planet is not nearer our Earth in place, than in quality and disposition also. If we compute the true mag-

E 4 nitude

nitude or quantity of matter in the Earth, it will
appear that she is not the 6oth part so big as *Jupiter*, nor the 3oth as *Saturn*, nor the 6[...]th as
the Sun. So that she is very inconsiderable, if
compar'd with the rest of the *Solar Vortex* only ;
but if with the intire Universe or Systems of the
Isa. xxxix.
15, 17. fixt Stars, in the elegancy of the Prophetick Expressions, *as a drop of a Bucket, as the small dust
of the Balance, yea less than nothing, and vanity.* Insomuch, that to all those remote Systems of the Heavenly Bodies, this Earth, with
all its fellow Planets, are no more visible than
those which, 'tis probable, revolve about any of
them, are to us in these our Planetary Regions.
And as we usually little think of those invisible
Globes, so any of their Inhabitants never once
imagine that there is such a Planet as ours (about
which we make such a mighty stir) in the whole
World. As to the main use of this Earth, 'tis to
afford habitation to a sinful and lapsed Race of
Creatures, of small Abilities or Capacities at present, but of great Vices and Wickedness ; and is
esteemed, as far as appears, in its present constitution so peculiarly and solely fit for them, that
when they are gone, or their Dispositions and
Faculties reform'd and improv'd, a better scene
of Nature, (*a new Heaven,* and *a new Earth,*) is
to be introduc'd, for such better and more noble
Creatures. The Old one, which now obtains,
being, it seems, only a sort of Prison or Confinement, which is to be our Lot whilst we are
sinful and miserable, but no longer.

And is this the only Darling of Nature, the
prime Object of the Creation and Providence
of God? Can such a Globe's original, nay, of
the external and visible Parts of it only, claim
four parts of six of that entire space, which the
Wisdom

Wisdom of God allotted for the Formation of all things in the whole World, while the Origin of the Sun, Moon, and numberless Systems of Stars has only a poor single part allotted to it? Must the expanding the Air between the Earth and the Clouds, be thought to equal the disposal of all those Cœlestial Bodies into their several Regions? and the producing a few Fish and Fowl, be a weightier concern, and require more time than the replenishing all the other habitable Worlds with Beings suitable to their several Constitutions? Will a wise Builder bestow twice as much time in decking and adorning of one By-closet of inferior use, and that only to some of the meanest Servants too; as of the Royal Palace, with all its stately Rooms and Apartments, intended for the King himself, and his Courtiers? Should we hear of such strange Actions, and disproportionate Procedure among Men, we should not be able to induce our selves to give credit thereto. But it seems Suppositions ten thousand times more disproportionate and unaccountable, when ascrib'd to God Almighty, are easily believ'd. So far can Ignorance, Prejudice, and a misunderstanding of the Sacred Volumes carry the Faith, nay, the Zeal of Men! and to such a mean Opinion of the most glorious and perfect of Beings are we thereby reduc'd, that as if we were not content to think him such a one as our selves, but intended to depress him below the very meanest of us, we venture with confidence and eagerness to ascribe to him that disproportionate, unequal, and unaccountable disposal of the Works of Creation, which the simplest Artificer could not bear the Imputation of

I:

It muſt here be confeſs'd, That ſuch Notions of the *Mosaick* Creation, as I now oppoſe, having begun, or at leaſt been chiefly eſtabliſh'd and propagated when the *Ariſtotelean* Philoſophy, and *Ptolemaick* Aſtronomy were believ'd; thoſe who have embrac'd them till this Age were leſs abſurd, and nearer to ſome tolerable degree of probability. For ſo long as the Earth with its adjoyning Elements was ſuppos'd the Center and Baſis of all the World; while the diſtance of the Heavenly Bodies was believ'd to be, comparatively to what we now find, very ſmall and inconſiderable; and all their Motions perform'd about us their proper and immovable Center; while the whole Series of Spheres above (tho' the ſeveral diſtinct ones mov'd the contrary way by their own peculiar Motions) was in twenty four hours conſtantly hurried from *Eaſt* to *Weſt* by the *Primum Mobile*, on purpoſe to cauſe Day and Night to us below; while Comets were eſteem'd Exhalations from the Stars, and ſent only at certain Seaſons to affright Mankind with their fiery Tails, and then to be diſſipated and vaniſh into Vapours again; while the Sun and Stars, in the Opinion of the Philoſophers themſelves, were nouriſh'd by the Steams from our Earth; and while the laſt named were either ſtuck in one Spherical Superficies as the fix'd Stars, or faſtned in their Solid Orbs, like a Nail in a Cartwheel, as the Planets, and no other uſe imagin'd but to twinkle to us in Winter Evenings, and by their Aſpects to forebode what little Changes of Weather, or other Accidents were to be expected below; while no other habitable World was dream'd of than this Globe of Earth; no other Animals once conjectur'd at, beſides thoſe on the face thereof; while Mankind was look'd on

as

as the sole Lord of the Creation, and Him for
whose sake all other Creatures in the World
were made; and while 'twas commonly granted that, as all things, the visible Heavens and
Earth, with their intire Furniture began with
him; so at the Conclusion of his Succession, or
the period of Humane Generations here, must
they for ever cease and be annihilated; While
all this, I say, was the current Philosophy, 'tis
not very surprizing that the *Mosaick* History we
are now upon was understood in the Vulgar
Sense, and seem'd not wholly disagreeable to the
presumed Frame of Nature; and 'twas not hard
to believe, that this Earth and its Inhabitants,
in the Opinion of the World, the main and
principal concern of all, and that to whose uses
every thing else intirely serv'd, had the principal care bestow'd upon it, both in its Original
Creation, and its subsequent Changes and Revolutions.

But tho' such a Scheme, and such an Apprehension were passable enough in the days of our
Forefathers; 'tis by no means so now. Those
greater degrees of Knowledge which the Providence of God has in this Age afforded us, make
such Opinions intolerable in the present, which
were not so in the past Centuries. 'Tis now evident, That every one of the Planets, as well as
that on which we live, must have a right in its
proportion to share in the care of Heaven, and
had therefore in all probability a suitable space
or number of Days allow'd to its proper Formation; much what the same Separations of Parts,
Digestions, and Collections, being no doubt to
be suppos'd in the Original Formation of any
other, as in that particular Planet, with which
Moses was concern'd. And if one or two on account

count of their fmallnefs, might be finifh'd in lefs; the reft on account of their bignefs, from a parity of Reafon, would take up much more than that fix days time which was fpent in our Earth's Formation.

And let the *Reader* judge, if it be fo impoffible to reduce the Planets alone within the fourth days Work, how much more fo it will be (in cafe we allow degrees of impoffibilities) to reduce thither that vaft noble and ufeful Body the Fountain of our Light and Heat, the Sun; and ftill in a prodigious degree more fo, to include the immenfe and numberlefs Syftems of the fixt Stars; among whom when the Sun is but one, and perhaps no bigger than the reft; (and confequently to have in reafon but an equal portion of time with them allotted for its Origination;) It muft, tho' above Sixty thoufand times as big as the Earth, while the Earth takes up four intire ones, be thruft into the Corner of a fingle Day; Corner, did I fay? rather Minute, nay, Moment of a Day; and 'tis uncertain whether even that pittance of time can fairly and feparately be allow'd to it. So that one need not fear to affert, That he who fhould affirm the Divine Power to have fpent four entire Days in the Formation of a Fly or Worm, nay, of a fingle Plant or Herb; and but one in the Formation of the Terraqueous Globe with all its Parts, Regions, and Furniture, would be lefs unreafonable than fome Expofitors now are, and more obferve Decorum, Fitnefs, Agreement, and Proportion, than they do in the Vulgar Interpretations of the *Mofaick* Creation. And I need not be afraid to call all that Aftronomy and Philofophy are Matters of, to atteft the fairnefs of fuch a Comparifon. And can any one who is fenfible of this, and entertains no other than

great

great and worthy Thoughts of his Alwife Creator, embrace fo fond and fo ftrange an Opinion?
And if the Reader will pardon a fhort Digreffion, and give me leave to fpeak a great Truth on
this occafion, I cannot but obferve,That 'tis not
the genuine Contents of the Holy Books themfelves, but fuch unwary Interpretations of them
as thefe, which have mainly contributed to their
contempt, and been but too Inftrumental to make
'em appear Abfurd and Irrational to the Free
Reafon of Mankind. For when Men found
that the Scriptures, according to the Univerfal
Senfe of Expofitors, afcribed fuch things to God,
as their plaineft reafon could not think compati-
ble to a Wife Man, much lefs to the All-wife
God ; they were under a fhrewd Temptation of
thinking very meanly of the Bible it felf, and by
degrees of rejecting it, and therewith all Divine
Revelation to the Sons of Men. How fatally
this Malady hath fpread, of late efpecially, I need
not fay ; and tho' I fully believe the main ftroke
or ftep, as to the generality, be Vicious Difpofitions and a Debauched Temper, yet how far fuch
Ill-contriv'd, Unfkilful, and Unphilofophical Interpretations,or rather Mifreprefentations of Scripture, particularly relating to the Material World of
which we are now fpeaking, may have contributed
to fo fatal and pernicious an effect, deferves the
moft ferious and fober confideration.
This Mifchief is not to be remedied, nor the
Veneration due to the Sacred Volumes retriev'd
by an obftinate maintaining fuch ftrange opinions as thofe here refer'd to, by patronizing the
fame with Divine Authority, and then making
vehement Invectives againft fuch (as many unfkilful, yet good men, are ready to do) whole only fault is this that they can no more be induc'd to
believe

believe what is plainly unworthy of, and unsuitable to the Divine Perfections, than what is evidently contradictory to Divine Revelation. Wise Men would rather set themselves carefully to compare Nature with Scripture, and make a free Enquiry into the certain *Phænomena* of the one, and the genuin Sense of the other; which if Expositors would do, 'twere not hard to demonstrate in several such cases, that the latter is so far from opposing the truths deducible from the former, or the common notions of Mankind, that 'tis in the greatest harmony therewith; and in those cases (where the thing mention'd is within the sphere of human Knowledge) no less accountable to the reason, than enforc d on the belief of Mankind. And I persuade my self if there were a careful collection made of the Ancient knots and difficulties in the several parts of the Bible, with relation to such points as we are upon, or any others of a different nature; and how very many of them, as preludes and pledges of the rest, are now intirely clear'd, or might easily be so; it would more contribute to the recovery of the Ancient Honour, and due Esteem of the Sacred Scriptures, than all the most Zealous and general Harangues from some popular Topicks, either for them, or against their Contemners, the loose *Deists* and pretended *Socinians* of this Age. For my own part I cannot but profess, that tho' I be very nice and tender in the reasonableness of my Faith, and desirous to admit nothing but what agrees to the Divine Attributes, the common notions of our Souls, and the *Phænomena* of Nature; yet upon an Impartial Enquiry into some of the most perplexing difficulties occurring there, I have obtain d so great a Measure of satisfaction about them, that my

scruples

fcruples now intirely ceafe, and I cannot doubt
either of the Truth or Divine Authority of the
Scriptures. I do not mean, that all the difficulties
are in particular vanifh'd and perfectly clear'd to
me : That is what is fcarce to be hop'd for in this
World : But I have fo frequently met with fewer
difficulties in the confideration of the Books
themfelves, than in the common Interpretations,
and thofe very Comments which ought to affoil 'em : And in fo many, and thofe moft remarkable Points of all, have met with fuch clear
and plenary, tho' unexpected fatisfaction, that I
have all imaginable reafon to believe the reft
equally capable of the fame, and to remain conftant in this affurance, That 'tis the ignorant or
foolifh Expofitions of Men, not the natural and
genuine Senfe of the Words themfelves,that makes
us imagine Scripture, Reafon, and the Nature of
Things irreconcileable or contradictory to one a-
nother. And I hope the inftances he will meet with
in the following Theory, will go a great way to
perfuade the unbyafs'd Reader of the fame Truth;
and to convince him,that greater fatisfaction is to
be look'd for from the view of God's own Books
of Nature and Scripture, than thofe of any Men
whatfoever. Whatever incompetent Judges may
fay, nothing will fo much tend to the vindication
and honour of reveal'd Religion, as free enquiries into, and a folid acquaintance with, (not ingenious and precarious Hypothefes, but) true and
demonftrable principles of Philofophy, with the
Hiftory of Nature, and with fuch ancient Traditions as in all probability were deriv'd from
Noah, and by him from the more Ancient Fathers of the World. From which *medium,* what
furprizing and unhop'd for light may be given to
fome famous portions of the Holy Scriptures, the
following

following Pages will, 'tis hop'd, afford some convincing Instances, and prove sufficient to take away mens ungrounded Fears and Apprehensions in such matters: And, by the Divine Blessing, appear a seasonable Attestation to the Certainty and Authority of those *Lively Oracles* on which our Happiness in this, and the next World does so vastly depend. But I must leave this digression, and proceed,

VI. The Vulgar Scheme of the *Mosaick* Creation, besides the disproportion as to time, represents all things from first to last so disorderly, confusedly, and unphilosophically, that 'tis intirely disagreeable to the Wisdom and Perfection of God.

And here I might justly Appeal to the Conscience of every careful Reader, even tho' his Knowledge of the true System of the World were not great, whether the vulgar account has not ever seem'd strange and surprizing to him? But if he were one Philosophically dispos'd, and allow'd himself a free consideration of it ; whether it has not ever been the most perplexing thing to his thoughts that could be imagin'd ? 'Tis well known how far this matter has been carried by Wise and Good Men; even to the taking away the literal, and the resolving the whole into a Popular Moral or Parabolick sense: And under what notion this History on the same account has appear'd to others, of no less free, but less Religious Dispositions and Thoughts, I need not say: What is indeed matter of doubt and perplexity to pious men, being unquestionably to the Loose and Profane, the Subject of Mirth and Drollery, and the sure encouragement to Atheism and Impiety. But I shall not

content

content my felf with this general reflection; but inftead of profecuting fuch a Difcourfe any farther, fhall affign fuch particular inftances of the irregular and unbecoming procedure in the vulgar Scheme of the Creation, as are plainly difagreeable to the Divine Wifdom, and unfuitable to the nature of things.

(1.) Bodies Alike in Nature have here an unlike Original.

(2.) Bodies Unlike in Nature have a like Original.

(3.) Bodies moft confiderable in themfelves, have the moft inconfiderable accounts given of them.

(4.) No Bodies but the Earth have either time for, or particulars of, the formation of the feveral parts affign'd.

(5.) The Light appears before its Caufe and Fountain the Sun was made.

(6.) The Excavation of the Channel of the Ocean, and the Elevation of the Mountains is unnatural and indecent. Of each of which I fhall fay but a word or two, and then as briefly argue from them.

(1.) Bodies Alike in nature, have an unlike Original. Our Earth is one of the Planets, and in all reafon belonging to their formation; yet is fhe the Subject of the Second, Third, Fifth, and Sixth days works, while the reft are included in the Fourth Day.

(2.) Bodies Unlike in nature have a like Original. The Sun, a glorious Body of Light, with his Fellows the fixt Stars, are join'd in the fourth day with the Opake and Dark Globes of the Planets.

F (3.) Bodies

(3.) Bodies most confiderable in themfelves, have the moft inconfiderable accounts given of them. This is very obvious in that mighty adoe about our poor Earth, while the vaftly greater and nobler Bodies of the Sun and Stars are fcarce taken any notice of. And how difproportionate fuch a procedure is, the comparifon already made of the Earth on one fide, with the reft of the World on the other, does more than fufficiently demonftrate.

(4.) No Bodies but the Earth have either time for, or particulars of, the formation of the feveral parts affign d. For when four days are wholly taken up with the particulars relating to our Earth ; the divifion of its Aerial from its Earthly Waters ; the diftinguifhing the latter from the dry Land, and draining 'em into the Channels of the Seas ; the growth of Plants ; generation of Fifh, Fowl, and Terreftrial Animals; and at laft the Creation of Man, with feveral circumftances relating to him, and the other Creatures ; not a fyllable as to the particulars of the reft of the World. Light is only commanded to fhine on the Firft Day ; and the Heavenly Bodies made on the Fourth, and there's all, as to themfelves, which occurs here.

(5.) The Light appears before the Creation of the Sun, from whence it is deriv'd : That being the Work of the Firft, This of the Fourth Day. Which how Philofophical and Accountable 'tis, let the Reader judge.

(6.) The Excavation of the Channel of the Ocean, and the Elevation of the Mountains, is unnatural and indecent. For when the Earth was at firft even, and cover'd with Waters, Expofitors imagine, that God, as it were, digg'd a vaft Channel for the Ocean, and heav'd away
the

the Earth, and plac'd it on all parts of the Globe, to make the Mountains. Which how indecent it is, I had rather leave to the judgment of the Reader, than stand here to exaggerate; especially where the naked reprefentation of the thing it felf is a fufficient expofing thereof to free Thinkers.

Thefe obvious Remarks on the vulgar Scheme of the Mofaick Creation (to omit the paffing by of the intire invifible World, whether within or without the furface of the Earth, whether corporeal or fpiritual) are, I think, fufficient demonftrations that 'tis a very diftant one from the true nature of things; and fuch as is both unworthy of the Writer and Author of the Sacred Hiftory. Whoever will take the pains carefully to confider the Syftem of Nature, and compare it with thefe Remarks, and the common Opinion of the proper Creation of all things in the fix Days Works, will not, I believe, be at a lofs for Arguments to over-turn the old, and to prove that a new Theory is to be enquir'd after, and a narrower World to be expected in the Firft Chapter of *Genefis*, than has generally been.

But Before I conclude this Head, I muft here obferve, that the confideration of thefe matters has had fo great influence on our late moft Excellent Commentator on *Genefis*, that tho' he keep more ſtrictly to the letter of *Mofes* than others, yet he finds occafion and room for thefe four great Conceffions, no lefs contrary to the vulgar, than approaching to the prefent Account of the Hiftory of the Creation.

Bishop of Ely.

(1.) He is willing to allow that *Mofes* meddles not with the intire Univerfe, but with the Planetary Syftem only.   P 2   (2.) He

(2.) He allows the Creation of the World to have been over before the six Days Work begins.

(3.) He grants the fame six Days Works to be the regular and orderly reduction of a confufed Chaos into a habitable World, without any ftrange Miracles in every part.

(4.) He fuppofes, that for a confiderable time before the fix Days Work began, there were fuch preparatory agitations, fermentations and feparations or conjunctions of parts, as difpofed the whole to fall ino the fucceeding method, and introduce the fix Days Productions following.

Which Conceffions of fo great a Man and excellent a Commentator, as they argue his fenfe of the neceffity of receding from the vulgar Hypothefis, fo they, I confefs, leffen and diminifh the difficulties in this Hiftory. *Leffen*, I fay, and *diminifh*; not take them away. For befides the want of any foundation in Scripture, as far as I fee, for the diftinction between the fixt Stars and Planets; the Arguments I have all along urged, reach, and are fram'd with regard to this limited Hypothefis alfo; and, with thof et to come, are I think more than fufficient to my purpofe ftill, and will demonftrate the unaccountablenefs of the Hiftory of the Creation even on this, tho' much more on the common Interpretation.

VII. The *Mofaick* Creation does not extend beyond this Earth, becaufe the alone final caufe of all therein contained, is the advantage of Mankind the Inhabitant thereof.

Now

Now that the final caufe of all the particulars mention'd in the Hiftory before us, is here rightly affign'd , is not only vifible in almoft every verfe of it , and in the places of Scripture afterwards referring to the fame thing ; but commonly acknowledg'd , nay contended for , by the Patrons of the vulgar account: So that I fhall here take it for granted. But then as to the confequence , that therefore the Creation is no farther to be extended , or at leaft not fo far as here it muft otherwife be, to the Sun and Planets ; nay with the moft , to the innumerable Syftems of the fix'd Stars ; 'tis to me fo natural and neceffary , that methinks 'tis perfectly needlefs to go about the proof of it. That fo vaft and noble a Syftem , confifting of fo many , fo remote , fo different , and fo glorious Bodies , fhould be made only for the ufe of Man , is fo wild a Fancy , that it deferves any other treatment fooner than a ferious confutation : And one may better think filently with ones felf , than with due deference and decency fpeak , what naturally arifes in ones Mind on this occafion.

If 'tis an inftance of, or confiftent with the Divine Wifdom, to make thoufands of glorious Bodies for the fole ufe of a few fallen and rebellious Creatures, which were to live for a little while upon one of the moft inconfiderable of them ! To create an innumerable multitude of Suns and Planets , and place them at prodigious diftances from us and from one another, (the greateft part of which were never feen till the late invention of the Telefcope ; and of fuch as are vifible, the Sun excepted, the fingle Moon, as defpicable a Body as it is in comparifon to the

F 3

most

moſt of the others, is much more beneficial to us
than they all put together) for the meer convenience of one little Earth! If 'tis Wiſe and
Rational to make the Sun more than Sixty thouſand times as big as that Globe it was to ſerve,
only that it might be plac'd above Fifty millions
of Miles off: (for in a nearer poſition it would
have ſcorch'd and burnt, inſtead of warm'd
and invigorated the Earth) when a ſmall Fiery
Ball plac'd near us would have done as well!
To make a vaſt number of Planets, (every
way as capable of Creatures of their own)
only for the ſake of us on Earth; that we might
in the night time view and calculate their po-
ſitions and motions! To place five ſecondary
Planets about *Saturn*, and four about *Jupiter*,
that after for more than Five thouſand years
no one had dream'd of their Exiſtence, a few
Aſtronomers might, with their Glaſſes, peep
at them, and obſerve their periods! To appoint the orbit of one of the primary Planets
(*Mercury*) ſo near the Sun, that not one in a
hundred ever gets a diſtinct view of him all
his Life! To move the Comets in orbits ſo extremely large and elliptical or oblong, that by
their diſtance from the Planetary Regions moſt
part of each revolution, they ſhould be ſo
little obſervable, that the World were juſt end-
ing before they could be known to be other
than Maſſes of Vapours ſoon conjoin'd, and
as ſoon diſſipated again, and now not viſible
the hundredth or perhaps thouſandth part of
their periods! To make all this immenſe frame
of the Heavenly Syſtems; ſo Glorious, Auguſt, and Magnificent, and ſo deſerving of
our Contemplation; and yet withal to frame
                                                    our

our Eyes and Senfations in that manner, as
to be uncapable to difcern or imagine any thing
thereof in comparifon! fo that had not Aftronomical obfervation rectify'd our miftakes, we
muft have thought the whole World not near
fo big as one of its leaft bodies really is; and
all this without any farther profpect, or nobler
defign than the fingle Ufe and Advantage of
Mankind! If, I fay, all this be the effect of In-
effable Wifdom and Contrivance, and worthy
to be believed of the All-wife God; 'tis fcarce
poffible to fuppofe, in the Material World at
leaft, what will not be equally fo. And fuch
ftrange and aftonifhing incongruities, which
among poor Mortals would unqueftionably argue
the moft extravagant degree of folly, in the
Deity, *Bleffed for evermore*, muft be Arguments of unbounded Perfection, and Effluxes
of Infinite Reafon, Wifdom, and Prudence.
Certainly one ought to be very well afcer-
tain'd of the fenfe of Scripture, before from
thence one venture to affert fuch unreafonable
opinions.

Nay even tho' the Senfe of Scripture feem'd
exceeding favourable to any Scheme of this Nature, yet in that cafe, a confidering Perfon
would chufe rather honeftly to own his Ignorance, and confefs he did not underftand the
matter, than be pofitive in that which is fo
plainly repugnant to the Divine Perfections.

And this (to digrefs a little) is methinks the
only fafe and rational way of procedure in thofe
cafes, where we cannot reconcile the Divine
Attributes, the *Phænomena* of the World, or
the Reafon of our own Minds, to the Revealed
Word of God, *viz.* In the firft place carefully

to

to confider the Texts concern'd , and whether
they are not mifapply'd ; if on fuch a confideration we cannot find them to be fo , and that
without a forc'd , unnatural and violent fenfe
be put upon plain words , the difficulties ftill appear infuperable ; 'tis then our Duty and our
Wifdom to imitate the *Jews* in that admirable
and pious Proverb in thefe cafes , *Cvm Elias ve-*
nerit , folvet Nedos. To fit down and reft fatisfied with this expectation , That when the
Divine Wifdom fees it a fit time , all will be
affoil'd ; and every one of the Knots of Scripture and of Providence unty'd. To ftay with
patience for thofe *idia καιροῖ* peculiar · feafons ,
which with regard both to the · improvement of
Knowledge , and unvailing of Myfteries , no
lefs than the fulfilling Decrees , *the Father has*
put in his own power. And as the Old *Jews*
fhould in vain have attempted the intire underftanding of their own Ceremonial Law till the
ídi⊙ καιροῖς , the coming of Chrift ; fo I believe we muft not expect the clearing of every
Text of Scripture , and of every fecret of Providence , till the *ídi⊙ καιροῖς* , *the time appointed*
of the Father. Till then we ought not , where
infuperable difficulties occur, by a bold determination to run counter to God , either in his
Word , whether engraven on our Minds , or
written in the Bible , or his Works vifible in
the World.

'Tis hard to fay whether thofe difhonour God
moft who embrace Doctrines, fuppos'd deducible from Scripture , tho' plainly abfurd and
unreafonable in themfelves; or thofe who venture to deny or at leaft wreft and prevaricate
with the obvious meaning of fuch Texts whence
those

thofe Doctrines us'd to be infer'd. Both thefe
methods of procedure are bold and dangerous;
Effects of our own Pride, and too high an opinion
of our proper apprehenfions and abilities, and
of fad confequence to our felves, to others,
and to Divine Revelation. There is a third or
middle way, which, tho' an inftance of real
felf-denial, we both may and ought to take.
Let God be true, but every man a liar. Our Un- Rom. iii. 4.
derftandings are finite, our Capacities fmall,
our Sphere of Knowledge not great. We depend on God Almighty as to what we *know*,
as well as what we *have*, or what we *are*. 'Tis
poffible it may not yet be the proper feafon for
unravelling the Myftery, and fo the requifite
helps not yet afforded; our own unskilfulnefs
or prejudices; fome falfe notions or precarious
Hypothefes we have embrac'd; our mifunderftanding the nature of the Scripture Stile; a
miftake of a Copy; the ignorance of the various ftages and periods of the World to which
the particulars belong; with many other fuch
circumftances, may juftly be fuppofed the occafions of our difficulties, without calling in
queftion either the truth of our humane faculties, the Attributes of God, the *Phænomena* of
Nature, or the genuine fenfe of the Holy
Scriptures. And truly were I asked in fuch a
cafe how I could fatisfie my felf, or refolve the
point; I could not more properly anfwer than
by alluding to the *Jewifh* Proverb before-mention'd; and alledging that, *Cùm Meffias vene-
rit, Solvet Nodum*; till which time I might defire leave to defer my farther anfwer.

And here from a general View of what has
been faid on thefe three laft Arguments, we cannot

not but obferve, into what Erroneous Extreme: Good Men have been betray'd, with relation to feveral main difficulties occurring in the Sacred Writings : While, from a profound refpect to the revealed Word of God, the moft were willing to lay afide the ufe of their own Reafon ; and others from a no lefs veneration for the Divine Attributes, and regard to thofe common notions which God had implanted in their Souls, were willing to indulge too great a liberty in the Interpretation of Scripture. The former, being generally Pious and Devout Souls, but little vers'd in contemplation, or the improvements of natural knowledge, were difpos'd to receive all that a Vulgar and Religious, tho' lefs Wary and Prudent Expofition, fhould recommend to their Affent. The latter having added to their Piety and Vertue, a careful enquiry into Nature, and a freer exercife of their Humane Faculties, and obferving how heavy imputations fome common Interpretations laid on the Divine Majefty, how difagreeable they were to External Nature, as well as the Reafon of Mankind ; were carried too far on the other hand ; and when the latter were fecur'd, were not proportionably folicitous about the former : I mean, fo that nothing but what Reafon, the Attributes of God, and the Syftem of the World allow'd, were admitted; thefe did not take a proportionable care that the natural fenfe of Scripture were equally provided for.

What I would here further obferve, is, the equal Condition and Deferts, but the unequal Reputation and Fate thefe two forts of Men have generally met with in the Chriftian World. Their

Their Characters to me feem fo correfpondent,
and their contrary Miftakes fo equally wide from
Truth, equally derogatory to the Honour of
God, and yet equally proceeding from a Religious Principle, a defire to fecure the Intereft of
Divine Revelation; that to me they feem to deferve the fame Refpect and Commendation for
their fincere Endeavours, and pious Intentions;
the fame Pity and Pardon for their Errors and
Miftakes. But it has happen'd much otherwife;
for by reafon of the little Leifure and Abilities
of the generality of Teachers to cultivate their
own Reafon, or make any fuccefsful enquiries
into the Natural World; the former fort being
in themfelves moft numerous, and as muft
needs happen, having the moft part of Chriftian People on their fide, did with Zeal and Ear-
neftnefs decry the latter; and tho' themfelves on
one fide did as highly Difhonour the Sacred Oracles, as the other on the oppofite, yet they vehe-
mently laid *that* Imputation on the latter, and
decry'd them as fecret Underminers of that
Word of God they pretended more rationally to
explain. 'Twere eafy to give Examples in this
cafe, but I fhall content my felf with one concerning thofe very Hiftories of the Creation and
Deluge, which I am to explain in the following
Theory.

'Tis well known what great, and hitherto infuperable Difficulties thefe Hiftories have involv'd
in them, to the general view of Mankind; and
how much ftill greater, and ftill more infuperable thofe Difficulties appear'd to Philofophick En-
quirer's, who came more nicely to confider them,
and compare what was afferted in the Holy
Scriptures, with the true Frame and Syftem of
External

External Nature. The confideration of thefe things fo affected a great and good Man, that he refolv'd on a noble Attempt, and undertook to clear thofe Points, and fhew that the temporary Origin of the World from a *Chaos*, and a Univerfal Deluge, were rational and accountable Theorems, and thereby take away that Blot and Obftacle, which the feeming impoffibility of thefe things laid in the way of ill-difpofed Perfons. In which matters, he employ'd his utmoft skill in the beft Syftem of Philofophy then known in the World; his moft diligent refearches into the facred and prophane Accounts relating to thofe anciently more known *Phænomena* of Nature, together with fuch other helps as his own excellent Abilities could afford him; and that as to feveral main and principal ftrokes, to very great Satisfaction, and to the very remarkable Illuftration of the Holy Scriptures. But in the Profecution of this Scheme, being fo vaft, fo noble, fo uniform, fo coherent, and withal fo new and furprizing, it at laft appear'd that fuch his Theory would not in feveral Particulars accord with the letter of Scripture. This unhappy diffonancy the Theorift was foon fenfible of, and no doubt not a little concern'd about. In which ftreight, feeing no poffible way of fecuring the main Points without fo unpleafing a Conceffion; inftead of refolving to reft fatisfied in the natural Senfe of Scripture, and acquiefcing in the Divine Revelation, till farther means of clearing the whole fhould offer themfelves, which I think is a good Man's Duty in fuch cafes, he ventur'd to fuppofe that the Sacred Books were not always to be fo literally and naturally underftood, as was generally

nerally believ'd hitherto. He alledg'd, That
confidering the mean Capacities of the *Jews*,
which were not capable of fuch Points of Philofophick Truths, confidering the moft ancient
way of conveying (or rather of concealing)
fublime Theorems, by Parables, Fables, and
Hieroglyphicks; confidering the Scripture Stile
in fome other cafes, very much different from
the prefent plain and explicit way of Difcourfe,
and nearer a-kin to that moft ancient Method;
confidering the main end of the Holy Writings,
the benefit of the Moral World, feem'd not to
require a ftrict adherence to truth in every
circumftance relating to the Natural; nay, rather enforc'd a receeding from it in fome cafes;
confidering, laftly, That all Ages had in vain
endeavoured to clear thefe Points according to
the ftrictnefs of the moft obvious Senfe, and
that the greater Improvements in Philofophy
feem'd but to render them ftill more unaccountable; confidering, I fay, all thefe things, He
fuppos'd that the Holy Writers only fecur'd the
Fundamental and General Verities, involving the
reft under, and explaining the whole by a way
of fpeaking, which was Myftical and Mythological; rather popular than true, and fitted
more to the needs of Men, than to the reality
of Things. This is, I think, a fair and full Account of the Opinion, and a genuine Explication of the occafion of this unhappy Slip of our
late Excellent Theorift; and fuch an one I
acknowledge 'tis, as in it felf, has no folid or
neceffary Foundation, is of ill confequence to
the Authority of the Holy Scriptures, and difhonourable both to their Penmen, and chiefly

to their Principal Inditer, the Blessed Spirit of God.

In which Censure, if the Learned Author think me too free, or too severe, he will, I hope, see reason to excuse, and not to be displeas'd with me, when I have own'd, as I must ingenuously do, That *in accusing him, I condemn my self, for I my self, in great measure, have thought the same things.* For I cannot but with the Theorist confess, That the Difficulties in the Vulgar Expositions were so great; such absurd Incongruities ascrib'd to God by them; the true System of the World did so disagree, and increase the Scruples; the main Histories themselves appear'd so impossible to be any other way secur'd; Several of the Accounts given by the Theorist were in the main so ingenious, so probable, and so agreeable to Ancient Tradition, upon a cursory Consideration; and the Arguments before-mention'd seem'd to me so considerable, that 'twas not easy for me to deny all Assent to that very Conclusion, which yet on farther Enquiries and Discoveries, I think not unworthy of the foregoing Censure. And I should esteem it a very signal happiness, if, as *that* Theory was so instrumental in drawing me into the foremention'd Mistake; so *this* might be fortunate enough to perswade the Author of that, of the opposite Verity, in which the Discoveries it contains have fully settled my own Mind, and are, I think, sufficient in themselves to settle the minds of others.

But to wave these too ambitious Expectations, I cannot but say so much in behalf of that Learned Theorist, That as he justly deserves the highest

highest Commendations for so generous and
worthy an Attempt; for the great Illustration
he has given those Histories from the most Ancient Traditionary Learning; and the Light afforded to the Holy Scriptures in several, and
those very considerable Points: So he has, I
think, reason to expect an easy Pardon where
he was not able to do the same; especially,
when not only Pardon, but the freest Praises
are bestowed on those, who as I before observ'd, equally have expos'd the Honour of God,
and equally derogated from the Reputation of
the Sacred Writings by their unwary and unskilful Interpretations. A good Man, who to
the highest Veneration for the Perfections of the
Divine Nature, has joyn'd a careful Enquiry into the Frame of the World, and a free, but
modest use of those Faculties God has given
him; and has withal exactly consider'd the undoubted evidence for the Divine Authority of
the Scripture; ought to be, and will be as tender of believing a Sense which is contrary to
his innate Notions, to the Perfections of God,
and the certain Observations of Nature, as of
that which puts a force upon the Words themselves, and renders them meerly Popular and
Mythological. And by consequence either those
who so frequently and zealously do the former,
are to be condemn'd, which yet the Christian
World has been far from doing; or those who
have been forc'd upon the latter, ought to escape
any greater Severity. For my own part, as in
such difficult Cases, I easily pass over the Mi-
stakes, and value the Truths discover'd by any
well-dispos'd Persons; which is but a due Debt
owing from one fallible Creature to another:

ther : So I humbly blefs God, the Author and Giver of all good things, for that Light he has afforded me (and which, by the Divine Blefsing, I hope the following Pages will afford the *Reader*) in thefe matters; by which I am convinc'd of the no-neceffity of oppofing the *literal* to the *true*; the Obvious and Natural, to the Rational and Philofophick Interpretations of the Holy Scriptures; and fhall chearfully wait for that happy time, when all Doubts being remov'd, and all Objections prevented by the Improvement of our Knowledge, and the Conduct of the Divine Providence, Reafon and Revelation, fhall reciprocally bear Witnefs to, and embrace each other; when no one fhall be able to pretend to the one, but he who is equally acquainted and fatisfied with the other; and the whole reafonable Creation fhall unite their Hearts and Tongues in Hymns to God. *All thy*

Pfal. cxix. *Commandments are faithful. Thy Statutes are right*
86. *rejoicing the heart. Thy Judgments, O Lord, are*
Pfal. xix. *true and righteous altogether. Righteous art thou, O*
8, 9. *Lord, and juft are thy judgments. Great and mar-*
Apoc. xv. *vellous are thy works, O Lord God Almighty! Juft*
3. *and true are thy ways, O King of Saints!* But to return from this Digreffion, and to proceed.

VIII. I prove the *Mofaick* Creation extends no farther than our Earth, and is of no other Nature than is affign'd here; becaufe neither the Intentions of the Author require, nor the Capacities of the People could bear either a ftrictly Philofophical, or a truly Univerfal Account of the Origin of things.

The

The defigns of *Mofes*, the infpired Penman, or rather of that Bleffed Spirit which infpir'd him, in this Hiftory of the Creation, were not the gratifying the Curiofity, or fatisfying the Philofophick Enquiries of a few elevated Minds, but of a more general and ufeful Nature; namely, To inform the *Jews*, and the reft of the World, that all the vifible Frame of Heaven and Earth was neither exiftent from all Eternity, nor the refult of blind Chance, fatal Neceffity, nor unaccountable Accidents, but the Workmanfhip of God Almighty. To make them fenfible that every Being they had any knowledge of, was deriv'd from, and fubject to that *Jehovah* whom they worfhipp'd, and that in him *themfelves* with all their fellow Creatures in the open Air, on the wide Earth, or in the deep Seas, *liv'd, mov'd, and had their Being*; who therefore muft needs be the Governor and Ruler of them all. To affect their Minds, by this means, with the awfulleft Veneration for the God of *Ifrael*, and infpire them with a juft Gratitude to him for all their Enjoyments, who had not only created this Earth for Mankind, and furnifh'd it with various Creatures for their ufe, but befide thefe Terreftrial, had made the very Celeftial Bodies fubfervient to their Neceffities. To demonftrate the Original Goodnefs and Perfection of things, and that therefore whatever was Evil muft have been the confequent of Man's Fall, and not of God's primary Introduction; and thereby to teach men Humility, and raife their abhorrence of Sin, the caufe of all their Miferies. To fhew them the unreafonablenefs of all forts of Idolatry, or of the Worfhip of any vifible Beings, tho' never fo ufeful or glorious, by affuring them they were all in common the Creatures of God,

Acts xvii. 28.

G   and

and all their Influences, of what kind foever, intirely deriv'd from him, and under his difpofal. In fhort, the main defign was to fecure Obedience to thofe Laws he was about to deliver from God to them, by giving them the greateft and jufteft Idea's of their Legiflator, the *Almighty Maker of Heaven and Earth.*

Thefe were, I fuppofe, the principal Reafons of thus recording the Creation of the World, and thefe Reafons made a particular Account of the vifible Parts of this Earth, with all its Furniture, that was obfervable and expos'd to their daily view, neceffary and expedient; nay, they enforc'd fome kind of mention of the Heavenly Bodies, fo far as they were concern'd with us below, and fo far as to fhew, that God originally created them, as well as the more ordinary Bodies on the Face of the Earth. All this was but proper and neceffary in order to the foremention'd purpofes. But why a Natural and Philofophical Account of the primary Formation of fuch remote and different Syftems of Bodies, whofe real Bignefs, Diftances, Natures, and Ufes, abftractedly confider'd, never came into Mens thoughts, nor were once imagin'd by them, I cannot fo eafily tell.

Efpecially, if it be confider'd, That the Capacities of the *Jews,* to whom *Mofes* peculiarly wrote, were very low and mean, and their Improvements very fmall, or rather none at all in Philofophick Matters. 'Tis not to be imagin'd that an intire Account of the Origine of the whole Frame of Nature (the nobleft and moft fublime Theory the higheft Philofopher could exercife his thoughts upon) fhould be within the reach of the *Jewifh* Apprehenfions. We do not find in our Learned and Inquifitive Age,

fuch

such a ready Comprehension and Reception of
Truths in Philosophy among the generality of
Men ; and 'tis so lately, that an easy Proposition
of the Earth's Motions, diurnal and annual, rais'd a
mighty Dust, and was very difficultly embrac'd by
even those who call'd themselves Philosophers,
that from such an instance we may easily imagine
how any natural Notions relating to the Constitution and Original of all the Bodies in the Universe must have been entertain'd among the rude
and illiterate *Jews*, newly come from the *Egyptian* Bondage, and destitute of the very first
Elements of Natural Knowledge. Every one in
the History of the Bible may with ease observe,
That the Abilities and Studies of the *Israelites*
(as indeed 'tis true of most of them to this day)
were of another Nature and Size, than must
here be suppos'd, if we bring in all the World
into the *Mosaick* Creation. If an indifferent
Stander by, who had never read the first of *Genesis*, were to judge what a sort of a κοσμοποιΐα
were to be given to so Ignorant and Unskilful
a Nation; he could not with common Prudence suppose either that it ought to be perfectly
Philosophical, or include any more than the
Senses and Capacities of the *Jews* could arrive
at, the Earth with its Appurtenances, and the
Heavens so far as they were plainly therewith
concern'd. Indeed, not only the *Jews*, but the
generality of Mankind's Apprehensions always
were, and still are much too narrow for any
noble Discoveries relating to Universal Nature;
and a Chapter about *Algebra* might almost
as suitably to Reason be recommended to them,
as an Account of the true Origination of all the
World. Nay, *de facto*, it appears, That *Moses*
was so far from deeming his People capable of

G 2   under-

understanding the intire System of Bodies remote and distant; that 'tis clear, he esteem'd it improper to say a word about the internal Constitution and Parts of our own Earth, contenting himself with what the Surface afforded, and what unavoidably came under the notice of their Senses, as is too plain to be deni'd in the History before us.

And shall we after all this believe or imagine that 'twas fit and proper, nay, or barely possible, for *Moses* to give a full Account of the beginning of all the World? And impress a just, true, and adequate *Idea* thereof on the Minds of the People! I believe 'twas so far from it, that still after all the Accommodation to the Senses and Capacities of Men, which he and the other Holy Writers use on such occasions; yet ,the meer Observation of the Truth of things forc'd them sometimes to speak what the others were not able rightly to comprehend; and they seem rather, in Natural Truths, to have gone too high, than descended too low, considering the gross Ignorance of their *Readers,* in those Matters.

Those Expressions of Scripture concerning the roundness of the World; the Earth's being founded on the Seas, and established on the Floods; a Compass or Orb being set on the Face of the Deep; the stretching out the Earth above the Waters, and its consisting out of the Water and in the Water; of most of which we shall take notice hereafter. Those Expressions, I say, are exactly accommodate to the real Constitution of the Earth, as will appear in due place; but were, 'tis plain, very much mistaken afterward. Men generally took the Earth to be round, not as a Sphere, but a Circle; and suppos'd the

Vid. Phæn. 13. infrà.

Abyss

Abyſs, on which 'twas founded to be the Ocean, or Great Sea; on whoſe Surface, in their Opinion, it ſwam, and which on every ſide encompaſs'd it as far as the very Firmament gave leave, and the ends of the Heaven would permit. That Continent we inhabit, was taken for the whole World, and its Middle or Center, imagin'd by moſt to be near the place where himſelf dwelt. The Horizon or Sea, and the Firmament, were believ'd to bound and terminate each other. The Sun, Moon, and Stars, were ſuppos'd at their deſcending below the Horizon, to be immers'd in the Sea; and at their aſcending above it, to emerge out of it again. How ridiculous theſe Conceits are, every one will eaſily judge, who has but a ſmall inſight into the Syſtem of the World; and how little they are countenanc'd by the Texts before referr'd to, 'twere eaſy to ſhew; but 'tis plain, They were ſo apply'd, and the particulars pretty handſomely adjuſted to Mens own Fancies, on theſe *Hypotheſes.*

When therefore we obſerve the Expreſſions of Scripture about the Conſtitution of our own Earth, to have been ſo miſerably miſunderſtood and miſapply'd, we may eaſily collect what fate any Notions of a ſublimer Nature, concerning the Heavens, and the whole Syſtem of Beings, muſt have undergone amongſt them. If the Apoſtles in a more Learned Age had began their Preaching with the requiring Mens belief to the Motion of the Earth, the being of Antipodes, or any other ſuch *Paradox* in Philoſophy, nay, or given them a true and rational Scheme of the Origin of the Univerſe in all its Parts, we may ſoon gueſs at the Reception they would have met with, and at the Succeſs of their Miniſtry. This procedure

G 3 could

could contribute nothing to their defign, neither
could the People be made to underftand and
believe fuch ftrange Notions. And as in this
cafe, every one will allow the Abfurdity of fuch
a method, and never imagine it probable that
the Apoftles could make ufe of it ; fo ought
we, by only changing the Scene, to conclude,
à priori, that 'tis highly unlikely that *Mofes*
would take fuch a courfe ; and that, unlefs the
words of the Hiftory were too exprefs and plain
to be deny'd, 'tis extremely improbable fo great
a Lawgiver (to go no farther) would extend his
Cofmogony beyond the ends of his Writing it,
and the Abilities of thofe who fhould read it;
or in other words, 'tis extreamily improbable that
the *Mofaick* Creation is of any other Nature or
Extent than the Propofition we are upon does
affert.

IX. Laftly, I prove the *Mofaick* Creation extends no farther than this Earth and it's Appendages, becaufe the Deluge and Conflagration,
whofe Boundaries are the fame with that of the
Mofaick Creation extend no farther.

I fhall here take it for granted, That the limits
here affign'd to the Deluge and Conflagration
are juft; it being certain as to the former, and
I think more than probable as to the latter; and
only quote a place, or two to prove the fix Days
work to be of the very fame, and no larger extent than thofe are, and leave the whole to the
Judgment of the *Reader*. *There fhall come in the*
2 Pet. iii.
4, &c.
laft days fcoffers walking after their own lufts, and
faying, Where is the promife of his coming? for fince
the fathers fell afleep, all things continue as they were
from the beginning of the creation. For this they wil-
lingly are ignorant of, that by the word of God the
heavens

heavens were of old, and the earth standing out of the water and in the water, whereby the world that then was being overflowed with water, perished: But the heavens and the earth which are now, by the same word are kept in store, reserved unto fire against the day of judgment, and perdition of ungodly men. The day of the Lord will come as a thief in the night, in the which the heavens shall pass away with a great noise, and the elements shall melt with fervent heat; the earth also, and the works that are therein, shall be burnt up. In the day of God the heavens being on fire shall be dissolved, and the elements shall melt with fervent heat. Nevertheless we, according to his promise, look for a new heaven, and a new earth, wherein dwelleth righteousness.

Verse 10.

Verse 12, 13.

Thou, Lord, in the beginning hast laid the foundation of the earth, and the heavens are the works of thine hands: They shall perish, but thou remainest; and they all shall wax old as doth a garment; and as a vesture shalt thou fold them up, and they shall be changed.

Heb. 1. 10, 12, 13.

I have now finish'd all those Arguments which to me are fully satisfactory, and I think prove beyond rational contradiction, That not the vast Universe, but the Earth alone, with its dependencies, are the proper subject of the Six Days Creation: And that the *Mosaick* History is not à Nice, Exact and Philosophick account of the several steps and operations of the whole; but such an Historical Relation of each Mutation of the Chaos, each successive day, as the Journal of a Person on the Face of the Earth all that while would naturally have contained. The sum of all is this:

(1.) The very Words and Coherence of *Moses* himself require such a Construction.

G 4 (2.) The

(2.) The Words of Creating , Making or Framing things here us'd, are commonly of no larger importance than this Proposition allows.

(3.) The *World* , or *Heaven and Earth* , the objects of this Creation , are alike frequently reftrain'd to the fublunary World , the Air and Earth.

(4.) The Chaos , that known fund and feminary of the. Six Days Creation , extended no farther.

(5.) On the contrary fuppofition, the time of the Creation of each Body is extremely difproportionate to the work it felf.

(6.) On the fame fuppofition there is an intolerable a   ler, difproportion , and confufion in the works themfelves.

(7.) The final caufe of the fix days Creation is the advantage of Mankind , the Inhabitant of the Earth.

(8.) Neither the intention of the Author, nor the capacity of the Readers require or could bear any other account of the origin of things.

(9.) Laftly , Neither the Deluge nor Conflagration , whofe extent appears commenfurate to that of this Creation , are of any larger compafs than is here affign'd.

Upon this view of the whole matter give me leave to fay, That to make the Univerfal Frame of Nature concern'd in the particular Fates and Revolutions of our Earth , is at this time of day, to demonftrate either very mean thoughts of the Ends of the Divine Workmanfhip , and of the Effects thereof in the World ; or elfe very proud and extravagant conceits of our own
worth

worth and dignity ; and at beſt argues a narrow, ignoble, and unphilofophical Soul. 'Tis much ſuch another Wiſe and Rational Notion , as it would be to ſuppoſe that the whole Terraqueous Globe , with all its parts and dependencies , all its furniture and productions , was alike concern'd in the *Fates* and *Revolutions* (pardon the expreſſions) of one ſingle Fly or Worm belonging to it. And we may e'en as fairly allow the intire dependence of this ſublunary World on the fortune of ſuch a ſingle *animalculum* ; That on its peeping into the World , the whole Earth muſt ariſe out of nothing to afford it a reſting place ; while it was growing, and continued in its prime , all things below muſt ſpring and flouriſh , rejoyce and look gay ; on its decay, all things muſt put on a mournful countenance ; and on its deſtruction , Univerſal Nature here beneath muſt expire together , and return to its primitive nothing. This repreſentation will , I imagine , ſeem bold and extravagant. But 'twill be hard to prove it ſo. And I may appeal to Aſtronomy whether the Earth can be ſhewn to bear as conſiderable a proportion to the Univerſe, as ſuch a poor *animalculum* does certainly bear to it.

I would not by this , or any thing elſe I have heretofore ſaid in this Diſcourſe, be ſo far miſtaken , as to be believ'd prone to depretiate and and debaſe Mankind ; or to put a ſlight on all thoſe Works of Nature and Providence which are ſubſervient to it. Neither do I deny that in ſome ſenſe all the Viſible World , Heaven and Earth , are ordain'd for our uſe and advantage; I fully believe that we are the Creatures of God , of whom he has a tender regard , and over whom

whom he exercifes a conftant, a fpecial Care
and Providence. As I look upon the Souls of
Men, in their proper and primitive perfection,
when they came out of their Maker's Hands,
to be Noble, to be Glorious, to be Exalted
Beings, and perhaps in capacities or faculties,
in dignity or happinefs, not inferior to fome of
the Angelick Orders; fo I alfo moft undoubtedly believe what our Saviour affirms of good mens
ftate hereafter, that they fhall be Ἰσάγγελοι,
equal to the Angels; and Ὑιοι τ̃ Θεε̃ *Children*
of God himfelf. While I am perfwaded that
the Creation of Man was not effected without
the concurrence and joint confultation of the
Blefled Trinity; Nor his Redemption without
the Acceptance of the Father, the Sacrifice
and Death of the Son in his Humane Nature;
and the Sanctification and Operation of the Holy Spirit. While I am perfwaded that the Divine Λόγος Θεάνθρωπος has ever fince the Fall of
Adam been follicitous about our Reconciliation to
God, and made it his conftant bufinefs, even
before as well as fince his Incarnation, to mediate for us, and take care of our eternal happinefs. While I believe that by the new Covenant Good Men, even in this Imperfect ftate,
are efteem'd Heirs of God, joint-Heirs with
Chrift, and denominated the Brethren and
Friends of their Glorious Redeemer. While I
do not doubt but our Humane Nature is now,
in the Perfon of our Blefled Saviour, in Heaven,
and there on account of the Hypoftatical Union
with the Eternal Λόγος; and as a reward of
that Obedience and Suffering, it underwent for
us on Earth, advanc'd above the moft exalted
Intellectual Orders, at the Right Hand of the
Majefty

Luke xx.
36.

Majefty on High. While I expect the fame Perfon in the Glory of the Father, coming to Judge the World in Righteoufnefs; and Mankind, after that final doom, to be partaker of everlafting Joy or Mifery according to their behaviour here on Earth. While, I fay, I believe all this, as I moft fincerely do, I can be under no temptation of looking with contempt upon, or of entertaining a mean opinion of Mankind, or of thofe Syftems of Nature and Providence relating to it. Yet all this notwithftanding, I think that Opinion I am now expofing, deferves no other Character than I have before given of it.

Tho' I look upon Mankind as one Species of very Noble and Glorious Creatures, yet I fuppofe it but *One,* and that there may be Millions of others at the leaft not inferior to him. Tho' I believe Humane Nature, when Innocent and Perfect, at that height of Purity and Felicity which it once had, and by the Chriftian Difpenfation may be again advanc'd to, as fo confiderable and exalted a Species of Beings; yet withal I look upon it at prefent as under a very different Character. We are all now in a deprav'd, a finful, and fo in a low, a miferable ftate. We have by our own wilful Rebellion and Difobedience, made it neceffary for God to place us in a fhort, a vicious, in an uneafie and vexatious World; where at prefent we are under a fort of confinement in a place of Trial and Probation; and through a doleful Wildernefs muft make our way to the Land of *Canaan. Quifque fuos patimur manes.* We here feel the fad effects and punifhments of former Sins. We are left to ftruggle with great difficulties, abide many affaults, assaults , and undergo severe Agonies, e're we must expect to recover our native dignity, to retrieve our ancient felicity again, *Exinde per amplum Mittimur Elysium, & reduces læta arva tenemus.* As *flesh and blood cannot inherit the kingdom of God*, so *that Kingdom is not of this World.* I see no reason to esteem the present condition of Mortality as at all considerable *in it self*, (tho' in its *consequences* it extremely be so) in comparison of the past and future periods of our Beings; and therefore without believing the Earth one of the greatest or noblest Globes in the World , I can suppose it a very proper and suitable habitation for us at present: Most wisely contriv'd, (as it certainly is) and its Funiture peculiarly and wonderfully adapted to our needs , capacities and operations. I acknowledge that Providence has so constituted our Earth that we receive some advantages from all, and very great ones from some other parts of the external and visible World. All which were in the Original Creation of things both foreseen and foredesign'd by God, and so may not improperly be so far said to have been made for our use, and appointed to serve our necessities. I do not think that those Systems of the Universe we here speak of, are ever a whit the less useful to us, or the benefits we reap from them ever the less in themselves , or less worthy of our notice and observation, our admiration and gratitude to God, because they also are subservient to other noble purposes, and are by Divine Providence made use of in several great designs over and above those advantages we are able to take notice of, or can our selves enjoy from them. I cannot imagine that God is peculiarly

1 Cor. xv. 50.
Joh. xviii. 36.

culiarly fond of any particular parts of the Material Creation , or any more a *Respecter of* some *inanimate Bodies,* than of *Persons.* He no doubt equally makes use of them all , according to their several kinds and capacities , in the service of the various species of Intelligent Creatures , and in the bringing about the great Periods of Nature , and the Decrees of Heaven ; which as they are in great measure unknown to us , so may they regard Rational Beings very different and remote from us and our concerns.

If we duly reflect on the Infinite Nature , and unlimited Perfections of the Divine Being , the Creator and Original of all things , as well as on the number, vaſtneſs, and glory of those his works which are within our view , we shall see reason to confeſs , there may be millions of Nobler Intellectual Beings interpoſed between Man and God : And the whole World might be more reaſonably ſuppos'd made at the Creation , and for the ſole uſe of any one ſpecies of thoſe, than of Mankind. If therefore we be unwilling to be our ſelves excluded from a ſhare in the intentions and deſigns of Heaven , let us not exclude any other rational Creatures from the ſame ; but be willing to ſuppoſe as this Earth was form'd in ſix days for the ſake of Man ; ſo were the reſt of the Heavenly Bodies, form'd at other proper times, for the ſake of other of God's Creatures; for whom Providence ought to be allow'd to have taken a proportionable Care , and made a ſuitable proviſion , as we our ſelves find has been done with regard to us and our affairs. Let us learn humble and modeſt ſentiments of our ſelves, from the contempla-

tion

tion of the immensity of the Works of God in
the World.   Which useful Lesson the Holy Psal-
mist would by his own example teach us.   With
whose Natural and Pious Reflection in this very
Psal. viii. case I shall conclude this whole discourse.   *When*
3, 4. *I consider thy Heavens , the work of thy fingers , the*
Moon and the Stars which thou hast ordained; Lord!
what is Man that thou art mindful of him! And
ver. ult. *the Son of Man that thou visitest him ! O Lord our*
Lord! How excellent is thy name in all the Earth !

P O S T U L A T A.

POSTULATA.

I. **T**HE Obvious or Literal Sense of Scripture is the True and Real one, where no evident Reason can be given to the contrary.

II. That which is clearly accountable in a natural way, is not without reason to be ascrib'd to a Miraculous Power.

III. What Ancient Tradition asserts of the constitution of Nature, or of the Origin and Primitive States of the World, is to be allow'd for True, where 'tis fully agreeable to Scripture, Reason, and Philosophy.

A

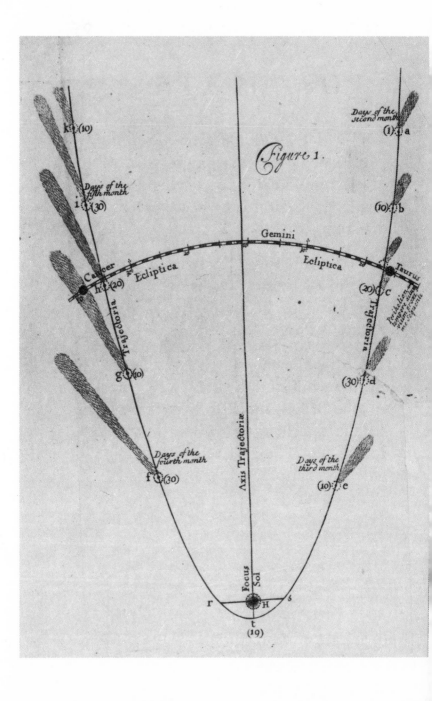

Figure 1.

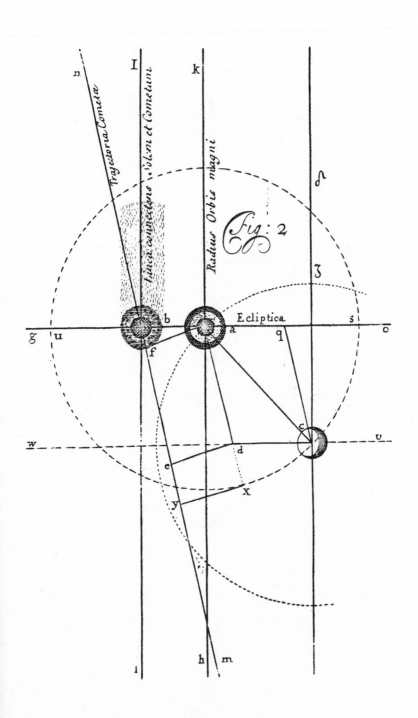

Fig: 2

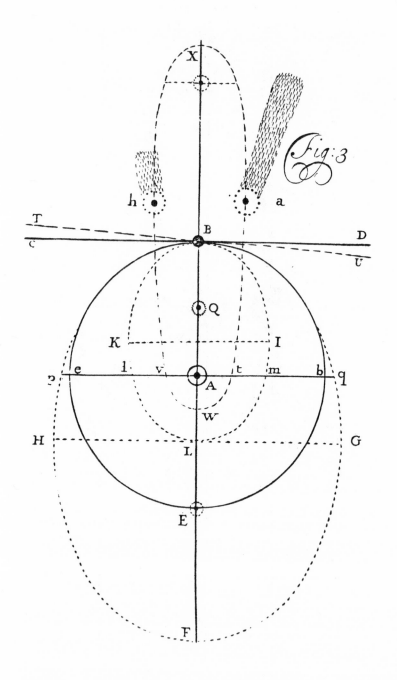

Fig: 3

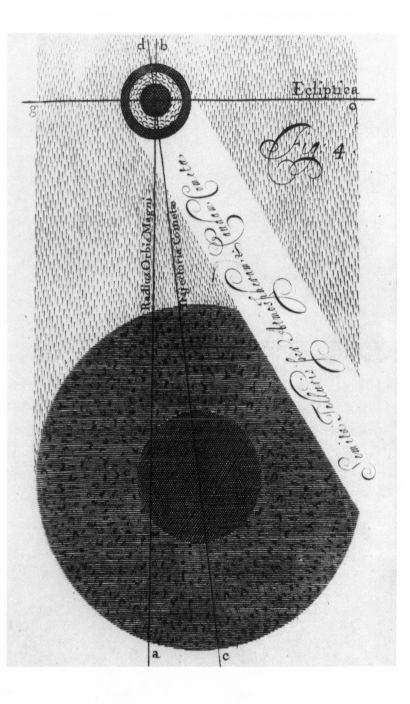

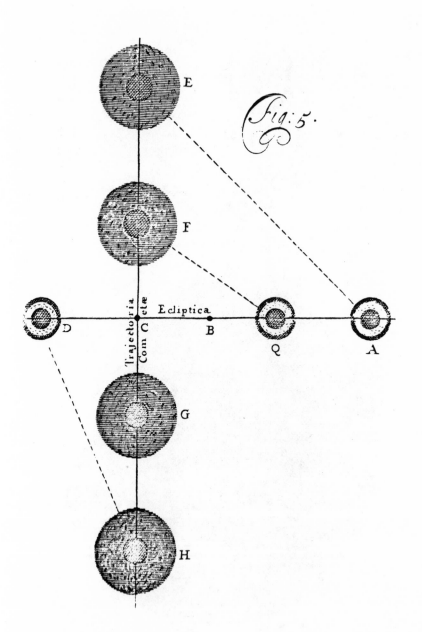

Fig: 5.

E

F

Ecliptica

Trajectoria Cometæ

D   C   B   Q   A

G

H

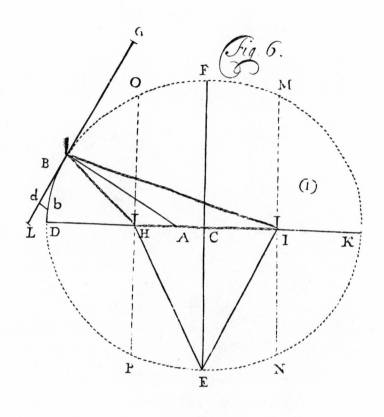

Fig. 6.

(1)

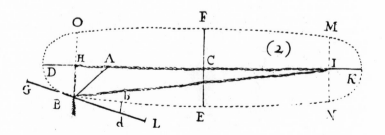

(2)

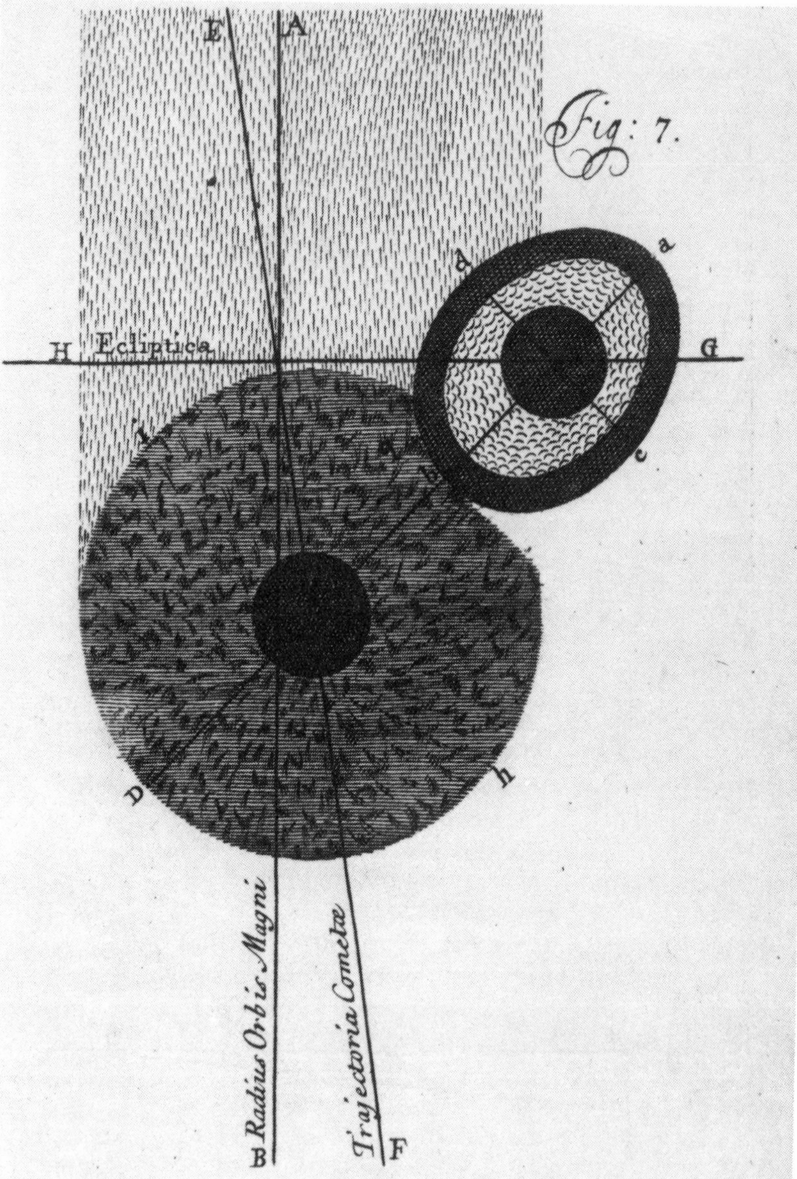

Fig: 7.

E A
H Ecliptica G
Radius Orbis Magni
Trajectoria Cometæ
B F

A
NEW THEORY
OF THE
EARTH.

BOOK I.

LEMMATA.

I. ALL Bodies will perfevere for ever in that ftate, whether of Reft or Motion, in which they once are, if no other force or impediment act upon them, or fuffer by them.

II. All Motion is of it felf rectilinear, and with the fame conftant uniform Celerity, if no other external Caufe difturb it.

Corollary 1. *'Tis evident from thefe two Propofitions, that Matter is intirely a paffive Subftance.*

Coroll. 2. *No Spontaneous Motion or Action can be the effect of meer Matter.*

Coroll. 3. *The Soul of Man, whofe leaft Power feems to be that of Spontaneous Motion, is incorporeal: which is alfo a neceffary confequence of the firft Co-*

H   *rollary*

rollary ; for if Matter be perfectly a passive Thing, the Soul, which is so active a Being, cannot be material.

Coroll. 4. The Brut Creatures giving all possible Demonstrations of Spontaneous Motion, and of a principle of Action, cannot reasonably be suppos'd meerly Corporeal Machines.

III. All those single Corpuscles of which Bodies are compos'd, do attract all other single Corpuscles of which other Bodies are compos'd, and are alike mutually attracted by them. If this Affection of the Parts of Bodies be consider'd with respect to those towards which the Motion is, 'tis call'd *Attraction*, and they are said to *draw* all others. But if it be consider'd with respect to those which are mov'd, 'tis call'd *Gravitation*, or a *Tendency* in them towards others. Thus in Magnetism we imagine a Power of Attraction belonging to the Loadstone; and in the Iron a Tendency, or (as I may call it, tho' somewhat improperly) Gravitation towards it. Tho' indeed, by the way, the Force or Affection being found to be mutual and equal on both sides, the Terms might justly be so too; and a Loadstone might as properly be said to tend or gravitate towards the Iron, or Iron to attract the Loadstone, as the contrary; just as 'tis in the Point before us. This however will serve for an Illustration, and explain our meaning in the present case, where all the Parts of Bodies are endew'd with such a mutual Gravitation and Attraction with respect to all others.

SCHOLIUM.

That no prejudice nor misunderstanding may arise, 'tis to be observ'd, That when we use the

terms

terms of Attraction or Gravitation, we do not
thereby determine the Phyfical Caufe or Seat
of any effects, as if fome innate Power or *occult
Quality* were to be fuppos'd in Bodies (as will
appear prefently); but only ufe fuch familiar
Terms whereby our meaning may be eafily underftood, and the Effects of Nature explain'd,
even where the laft and proper efficient Caufe
is not mechanically affignable. Thus we do and
may fay, as before, That the Loadftone attracts
the Iron, or the Iron tends or gravitates to the
Loadftone, not afcribing thereby any proper and
pofitive Quality or Power to thefe Bodies, but
for eafe of Expreffion, and for fupplying what
we cannot otherwife readily explain relating to
them. Thus alfo we commonly fay, That Stones
are heavy, or tend towards the Center of the
Earth; and the Expreffions, rightly underftood,
are true and natural: Tho' perhaps in both cafes
the real caufe of thofe Effects which we afcribe
to fuch an Attraction, Tendency, or Gravitation, is External, and fome continual Impulfe
from without, not any inherent Power really
Exiftent within, is the Original of all. But in
fuch cafes, where the true Agent is invifible or
unknown, we muft have leave to ufe thofe terms
which the Matter will bear, or Cuftom has rendred familiar; without which, uneafy and troublefome Circumlocutions will be unavoidable;
efpecially, feeing that no Error can hereby creep
into our Reafonings, becaufe 'tis evident, that
all the Effects of Nature are exactly the very
fame in the World, and not otherwife, which
they certainly would and muft be if Bodies did
really and properly, by their own inherent Vir-
tue or Quality, attract, and were attracted by all
others.

IV. This Affection of mutual Attraction or Gravitation is univerfal in *extent* ; all Bodies in the whole World, as far as we have any means of knowing wherefoever they are plac'd , being in common fubject thereto, and concern'd therein.

V. This Affection is alfo univerfal as to the *kinds* of its Objects; it belonging equally to all the Parts of Matter, of what Sort or Form, in what Figure or Condition foever they are: the difference of Bodies as to Texture and Compofition, Fluidity and Firmnefs, Motion and Reft, Bignefs and Subtilty, or any other fuch mutable Qualities, not in the leaft diminifhing the Influence thereof.

VI. This Affection is alfo univerfal and equable as to *Time*, without all manner of intermiffion; without any increafe or diminution in different Ages.

VII. The Quantity of the force of Attraction at equal diftances is exactly proportionable to the Quantity of Matter in the attracting Body, being in reality nothing but the Refult or Summe of the united Forces of all thofe fingle Particles of which 'tis compos'd. Thus if A be double to, *i. e.* has twice as much matter as B; A will have a double force of Attraction alfo, at equal diftances from their Centers refpectively. If A reprefent the Earth, B the Moon ; if B contain but the twenty fixth part of the matter in A, (as it really does contain no more) and a Globe or Ball were plac'd at the fame diftance from the Center of B, at which another equal to it were from that of A, it would be but the twenty fixth part fo heavy towards B, as the other were towards A.

Lem. 33. *infra.*

VIII. This

VIII. This mutual tendency of Bodies is greater or lefs, according as the Bodies themfelves are nearer to, or farther from each other.   The fame Body more forcibly attracting thofe which are near, than thofe which are farther off.   So that Stone or Pillar which is with us very heavy, would be comparatively very light, if it were as far diftant from us as the Moon.

IX. The proportion of the Increafe and Decreafe of this Gravity of Bodies in their approach to, or recefs from each other, is neither that of Similar Lines nor Solids, but of Superficies or Plains: The force of Attraction in feveral diftances being reciprocally in a Duplicate Proportion thereof.   Thus when the fame Body, without the Surface of the Earth, is twice as near its Center, as it was before, 'tis four times as heavy; when thrice as near, 'tis nine times as heavy; when four times as near, 'tis fixteen times as heavy as before.   In like manner, the fame ftrength which were able to fuftain a Body of one hundred weight here, would at twice our diftance from the Earth's Center, be equally able to fuftain four hundred weight; at three times our diftance, nine hundred weight; at four times our diftance, fixteen hundred weight, and fo, *in infinitum*, at all other diftances.   For as the Squares of the diftances increafe, fo does the Power of Attraction decreafe; and as the Squares of the diftances decreafe, fo does the Power of Attraction at the fame time increafe proportionably; as will be prov'd prefently from the known *Phænomena* of Aftronomy.

Corollary 1. *From the Comparifon of the two firft Propofitions with the feven laft, 'tis evident, That this univerfal force of mutual Attraction or Gravitation of Bodies is not a refult from the Nature of Mat-*

Vid Bentley. Serm. 7. p. 25, &c.

Matter; *which being circumscrib'd within its own bounds, being incapable of acting at a distance, and besides being intirely passive in its very Essence, cannot possibly draw others, or tend towards them of it self.*

Coroll. 2. *This universal force of Gravitation being so plainly above, besides, and contrary to the Nature of Matter; on the formention'd Accounts must be the Effect of a Divine Power and Efficacy which governs the whole World, and which is absolutely necessary to its Preservation.*

Coroll. 3. *When the Divine Power is inseparable from the Essence of God, 'tis evident, the latter is Omnipresent as well as the former, and every where equally diffus'd through the Universe; and that therefore in God we properly* live, move, *and have our* being.

Coroll. 4. *The Divine Nature is Incorporeal and Spiritual, as being equally present, and equally powerful in the midst of the material World, as in those immense Spaces which every where distinguish the Parts, and surround the Limits of it.*

Coroll. 5. *The Providence of God in the Natural World is not meerly a Conservation of its being, or a Non-annihilation thereof; but a constant, uniform, active Influence or Energy in all the Operations done in it; the very same which was exerted in the Original Impression of those Laws of Motion on which it depends. The two first Propositions, 'tis true, seem to require only a Continuation of Existence, without any new or continual Action; but the seven last plainly require more; and no less than I am here pleading for. So that if we should suppose God Almighty to withdraw or suspend this his actual Efficacy and Influence on all the Bodies in the World, tho' he preserv'd their being; the whole would immediately be dissolv'd, and each of the Heavenly Bodies be crum-*
bled

bled into Duſt; the ſingle *Atoms* commencing their ſeveral *Motions* in ſuch ſeveral ſtraight *Lines*, according
to which the *Projectile Motion* chanc'd to be at the inſtant when the *Divine* Influence (the cauſe of *Gravitation*, and all ſuch other *Affections* of *Matter*) was
ſuſpended or withdrawn.

Coroll. 6. *Mechanical Philoſophy*, which relies
chiefly on the *Power of Gravity*, is, if rightly underſtood, ſo far from leading to *Atheiſm*, that it ſolely
depends on, ſuppoſes, and demonſtrates the *Being and
Providence of God*; and its Study by conſequence is the
moſt ſerviceable to *Religion* of all other.

Coroll. 7. The Epicureans, who endeavour'd to
caſt the belief of a *Providence* at leaſt, if not of a
Deity out of the *World* by their *Atomical* or *Mechanical Philoſophy*, very fooliſhly miſunderſtood and abus'd
their own *Principles*; which in reality, when rightly comprehended, do with the greateſt *Evidence* and
Conviction eſtabliſh them both, beyond all other what-
ſoever.

Coroll. 8. There is no ſuch *Ethereal Subſtance*, or
Subtile Matter, pervading the *Pores of Bodies*, which
being it ſelf free from the *Law of Gravity*, or endu'd
with a leſs *Proportion* thereof, might be imagin'd to be
the cauſe of it in other *Bodies*, or the means of any other
Effects in the *World*.

Coroll. 9. *A* Vacuum, or *Space* diſtinct from
Matter, is neceſſary to be admitted. For were the
World equally full every where, when all *Matter* is
equally heavy in proportion to its *Quantity*, there could
not poſſibly be any difference in the *Specifick Gravity* of
Bodies; it being on the Hypotheſis of a *Plenum* impoſſible that a *Cube of Gold* ſhould be heavier than an
equal *Cube of Air*, and its contained ſubtile *Matter*
together; and by conſequence equally impoſſible that the
former ſhould over-ballance or deſcend in the latter,
which yet all experience ſhews it really does. So that

H 4   *a* Plenum

a Plenum *is so far from accounting for the* Phænomenon *of Gravity, as some would have it , that
it utterly subverts the possibility of it ; and while the
last is evident , the first must needs be indefensible.*

X. From the Uniform Projectile Motion of
Bodies in straight lines, and the Universal Power
of Attraction or Gravitation, the curvilinear
motion of all the Heavenly Bodies does arise.
If a Body, as B, be moving uniformly along
the line D C , from D to C ; and another Body
A be present, this latter Body A must draw the
former B from its straight line D C, and by doing so continually, while at the same time the
Body B retains its Projectile force along a straight
line in every point of its Course, must make the
line of its real motion a bent one, and change
its rectilinear into a curvilinear trajectory.

Fig. 3.

Coroll. Hence we may learn what is that conatus recedendi à centro motûs *in revolving Bodies,
and in what sense 'tis to be understood. For when,
as we have already seen, all Bodies have a* vis centripeta, *or propension towards one another ; 'tis impossible they should of themselves, in as proper a manner, have a contrary propension, or* vis centrifuga ;
*an endeavour of avoiding one another, (if these im-
proper terms will be allow'd me.) The true meaning
therefore of this attempt or endeavour to get farther
off the Center of Motion is only this, That all Bodies
being purely Passive , and so incapable of altering
their uniform motion along those straight lines, or tangents to their curves, in which they are every moment,
still tend onwards in the same lines, and retain their
propension or effort towards that rectilinear motion all
the time they are obliged to move in curves ; and consequently at every point of their course, endeavour to*
fly

fly off by their Tangents. Now the parts of the Tangent to which this endeavour is, being farther from the Center than those of the Curves to which the bodies are actually forc'd, an attempt to go on in the Tangent may be, and is stil'd an attempt to go farther off or recede from that Center ; tho' from no other affection than that of inactivity, or of persevering in a rectilinear motion. So that tho' the vis centripeta, *or power of gravitation-be an active and positive force, continually renew'd and impress'd on Bodies;* the vis centrifuga, *or* conatus recedendi à centro motûs *is not so, but the mere consequent and result from their inactivity. This is evident in Bodies revolving in* Ellipses *about one of the* Foci, *in their descent towards it ; where the Tangent being oblique to the Radius, or Line, from the Point of Contact to the* Focus, *this very* conatus recedendi à çentro motûs, *by urging it along the Tangent, will for some time make it approach nearer to the* Focus; *(tho' not so much nearer as by its revolving in the Ellipsis it self) as may be seen in the Scheme, if a Body at* B. *were moving towards* L. *about the Focus* H. *And this explication is confirm'd by all experience. For let a Stone be let loose from the Sling, or any revolving body be disengag'd from the force which retain'd it in its Curve, and it will not go from the Center, but only pass along the Tangent in which it was moving as if there were no such Center near it at all.*

Schem. 1.
Fig. 6.

XI. A Rectilinear or Projectile motion of the Planets along the Tangents to their Orbits, (which when once begun, always uniformly continues) join'd or compounded with their gravitation to the Sun, in the common Center or rather *Focus* of our System, is the Original of all the Planetary Revolutions about him.
　　　　　　　　　　　　　　Thus

Fig. 3.

Thus if *Jupiter*, for inſtance, repreſented by B, were moving uniformly along the Line DC, from D towards C ; if the Sun A were abſent, the Planet would paſs on ſtraight from B to C, with the ſame velocity with which it had come from D to B. But if upon its arrival at the point B, the Sun in the Center or *Focus* A begin to affect it, the Planet, by the Sun's Attraction, muſt be drawn from a rectilinear to a curvilinear courſe; and be oblig'd, if the Sun's Power be great enough compar'd with the Planets velocity, to revolve about him, and that, the attractive force always continuing, for ever after. The caſe is juſt the ſame as if B were a Stone in a Sling, A the Hand of the Slinger, (by the help of the ſtrings united together, and repreſented by the line A B) whirling it round continually. For as the Stone at its coming to the point B, were it let looſe and left to it ſelf, would fly off in the ſtraight Line or Tangent B C, yet by force is ſtill retain'd at an equal diſtance from the hand of the ſlinger, and compell'd to revolve in a kind of circle ; ſo 'tis here. The Attraction of the Sun in the common Center or *Focus* compels all the Planets, which of themſelves would paſs along their ſeveral Tangents, to revolve about it ſelf, and deſcribe their ſeveral curvilinear Orbits. And the caſe is the ſame in the ſecondary Planets with reſpect to their primary ones, about which they revolve in the ſame manner as they all both Primary and Secondary revolve about the Sun, in the common Center or *Focus* of the intire Syſtem.

    Coroll. 1. *Hence 'tis manifeſt, that the Law of univerſal Attraction once eſtabliſhed, unleſs the Divine Power had put the Planets into a ſuitable motion in right lines, they muſt ſoon have been drawn downwards,*

wards, and fall'n into the Sun: And still, if their motions should be intirely stop'd and cease, the same must happen, and they must not only be uncapable of those noble uses to which they are now subservient, but utterly perish in the violence of the Sun's scorching heat. The preventing of which therefore ought justly to be attributed to the Wisdom and Power of God in the constitution of the World.

Coroll. 2. *If the World be limited and finite in its extent, 'tis so in its time also ; and so* vice versâ *if eternal in its time, 'tis infinite also in its extent. For when all Matter (as far as we have any means of knowing, and so in reason all Matter whatsoever) is endu'd alike with a power of attraction ; and must all thereby, without proper motions along straight lines, at last meet in the common Center of Gravity of the whole ; and when withal the other Systems of fixt Stars, suppos'd here finite, retain their site and distance from each other, and thence appear not to have any projectile motion along straight lines to prevent the same ; had the frame of the World been eternal, the effect abovemention'd must have innumerable ages ago, really come to pass ; and all the matter of the intire Universe compos'd one single dull and unmoveable heap or mass in the common Center of Gravity of the whole : Which not having happen'd, demonstrates the impossibility of the Eternity of the World, and the necessity of admitting its production in time by the Power of God. When therefore 'tis unreasonable to suppose the material World truly unlimited in extent, 'tis necessary to suppose it no more unlimited in duration also. And this reasoning is unavoidable, unless we allow the most invariable and constant property of Matter in our System to be peculiar to it, and so to be a voluntary Constitution of God Almighty ; or at least that a miraculous Providence does hinder the forementien'd Effect continually.*

Serm.7.
P. 37, 38.

*tinually. So that upon the whole, as the very Learn-
ed Mr.* Bentley *has observ'd, either the Divine
Power in Creating, or peculiar Providence in Govern-
ing the frame of Nature, is on these undoubted Principles for ever establish'd.*

XII. When the Projectile Motion of the Planets is in its Direction, Perpendicular to a Line
from the Sun, and in its degree of velocity, so
nicely adapted and contemper'd to the quantity
of the Sun's Attraction there, that neither can
overcome the other, (the force of gravitation towards the Sun, and the celerity of the Planets
proper motions being perfectly *in æquilibrio*) the
Orbits of such revolving Planets will be compleat
Circles, themselves neither approaching to, nor
receding from the Sun the Center of their motions. And the Case is the same in the Secondary Planets about their Primary ones. Thus
'tis supposable, that the Velocity of all the Planets about the Sun, was exactly accommodate
Originally to his Power of Attraction, and that
their Primitive Orbits were perfect Circles; from
which at this day they do not mightily differ.
Thus however *Jupiter's* four Satellits or little
Moons have their Motions so exactly proportion'd to their gravitation to him, that their Orbits, as far as the most nice Observations can
judge, are perfect Circles, they keeping at an
equal distance from his Center in all the points
of their courses about him.

XIII. When the Projectile Motion is not adapted to, but is either too swift or too slow for
the Attraction towards the Central Body, the
Orbits describ'd will be *Ellipses*; and in the former case, when the Projectile Motion is too
swift, the Orbit will be bigger than the Circle
before-

before-mentioned ; and the nearer *Focus* of the *Ellipsis* will be coincident with the Central Body; And in the latter cafe the Orbit will be lefs than the Circle, and the farther *Focus* of the *Ellipsis* will be coincident with that Central Body. Thus if the celerity of B, be exactly correfpondent to the attractive force of the Central Body A, neither will prevail, and the Body, preferving an equal diftance from the Center, will defcribe the Circle B e E b. If the Celerity be greater, it will overcome the Attraction, and caft it felf farther off the Center for fome time, and fo revolve about it in the larger *Ellipfis* B H F G ; the Central Body, poffeffing that *Focus* A, which is neareft the point B, where the Attraction began.   But if the Celerity be fmaller, the Attraction of the Central Body A, will be too hard for it, will force it for fome time to come nearer, and to defcribe the leffer *Ellipfis* B K L I; the Central Body poffeffing that *Focus* A which is fartheft from the point B, where the Attraction began : As will be very plain from the confideration of the Figure relating hereto.

Fig. 3.

S C H O L I U M.

'Tis indeed poffible that the Celerity of Bodies may be fo great, compar'd with the force of Attraction to the Central Body, as to caft them off with fuch violence, that the Attraction will never be able to bring them round, or make them revolve about it: In which cafe the Orbits defcrib'd will be one of the other Conick Sections, either *Parabola*'s or *Hyperbola*'s ; according to the lefs or greater violence with which the Bodies are thrown; and the Central Body will poffefs the *Focus* of fuch a Figure.   But no *Phænomena* of Nature perfuading us that *de facto* any of the
Heavenly

Heavenly Bodies do defcribe either of thofe Lines, (tho' Comets *Ellipfes* come near to *Parabola*'s; of which hereafter) I fhall not farther infift upon them here. For if what has been faid of *Ellipfes* has been well underftood, the reft can have no great difficulty in it.

XIV. Several Bodies moving about the fame Central one, tho' their Primitive Velocity were equal, and direction alike, yet if they be at different diftances from it, they will defcribe figures of different Species about it. For when that determinate degree of Velocity, which at one diftance were juft commenfurate to the Central Bodies Attraction, and fo would produce a circular Orbit, muft at a farther diftance be too hard for it, by reafon of the diminution of the Attraction there; an *Elliptical* Orbit muft be defcrib'd; whofe nearer *Focus* would be coincident with the Central Body. In like manner, when the fame determinate degree of Velocity were at a nearer diftance, where the Central Attraction is augmented, it would be too little for the fame; and an *Elliptical* Orbit muft be defcrib'd, whofe farther *Focus* would be coincident with the Central Body. This cannot be difficult if what has been hitherto faid have been rightly apprehended. For when the *fpecies* of the Planetary Orbits depend folely on the proportion between the Attraction towards the Central Body, and the Velocity of the Projectile Motion; as that proportion remaining at any diftance whatfoever, the bignefs of the Orbits will be various, but the *Species* the fame; fo when that proportion is chang'd, the *Species* of the Figures muft be chang'd alfo: Which being done, the Velocity given, by the various force of Attraction in feveral

veral diſtances from the Center, as well as by the various Velocity, at a given diſtance, of which before; 'tis evident the *Species* of the Orbits will be different in this, as well as in the former Caſe.

Coroll. *The greater diſproportion there is between the quantity of Attraction, and the Velocity of the revolving Bodies, in the circumſtances mention'd in the two laſt Propoſitions, the farther from a Circular, and the more Oblong and Eccentrical will the Orbits deſcrib'd be. And the greater approach to correſpondence there is, the nearer to circular, and the leſs Oblong and Eccentrical will the ſame Orbits be.*

XV. The circular Orbits of Planets depend not only on the exact adjuſtment of the Projectile Velocity to the attractive Power of the Sun, but upon the direction of the ſame Projectile Motion, at the original Commencing of the Attraction. Thus where the Planet is in its own Tangent neither Aſcending nor Deſcending, and the Angle preceding C B A is a right one, which we have hitherto ſuppos'd; from the correſpondence of the Velocity to the Attraction, the Orbits will be perfect Circles. Otherwiſe, when the direction of the motion is oblique, in any meaſure aſcending from, or deſcending to the Central Body, and the preceding Angle C B A obtuſe or acute, the Planet, tho' its Velocity were exactly adapted to the Attraction of the Central Body, would revolve in an *Ellipſis*; and the point B, where the Attraction began, would be the end of the leſſer *Axis* thereof. All which will become eaſier by what we ſhall preſently come to explain of that figure.

Fig. 3.

Coroll. From theſe four laſt Propoſitions, compar'd with the preſent Syſtem of the Planetary World, 'tis

obvious

*obvious to take notice of the Wise and Careful Provi-
dence of God, and his most accurate contrivance in
the disposal and regulation of the whole: Whereby the
primary Velocity of the Planets, their several distances from the Central Bodies, and the original direction
of their motions, have been each so nicely adjusted
and adapted to the force of Attraction every where,
that all the Orbits of the Planets became thereby either
truly circular, or not very much different from the
same. Which remark will appear the more just, and
considerable, if we reflect on the infinitely different degrees of Velocity, and oblique direction ; with the immensly various distances from the Central Bodies,
equally possible with those which were so fitly pitch'd
upon ; and observe, to what noble and valuable uses
these Bodies are now subservient, which, without the
foremention'd exactness of contrivance in each particular, could not have been provided for. All which
demonstrate the great necessity of interesting the Divine Providence ; and the worthiness of its so careful
interposition in such cases.*

S C H O L I U M.

In order to the easier apprehension of the Motions of the Celestial Bodies, and of those things
already said, or to be said hereafter, relating to
them, 'twill not be improper in this place to give
some account of the Generation, Nature, and
Easie Properties of *Ellipses*; in which, (including
the Circle, as is commonly done) all the Heavenly Bodies (as far as we have hitherto reason
to believe) revolve perpetually ; so far at least
as will be directly subservient to our present purpose, and give any Light to the following Theory.
Take therefore, from the great *Des Cartes*, this
natural and obvious description or delineation of
an

an *Oval* or *Ellipsis*; which tho' familiar to the Gardener and Joyner, is a very good one, and gives as juft and compleat an *Idea* of it as any other whatfoever.

Take a fmall Cord or Packthread, which is very pliable, and yet not eafily ftretch'd beyond its natural length ; Tye the two ends together, by which means it will be a fort of round or circular circumference mutable into all Figures. Let two Pins or Nails, H and I, be driven into a plain Board or Table ; put the Cord or Packthread round the two Pins or Nails H and I, and with a Pencil or any fuch thing, (which, as it is drawn along, will make a fmall ftroke) in your hand, turn it round about the two Pins or Nails, as about a double Center, till you return to the Point from whence you began. Thus if B be the Point where you begin the delineation, continue it either way, by O F M K N E P D, or D P E N K M F O, till you return to B again. By which means the Point of your Pencil will defcribe fuch a Curve as is here reprefented, and is call'd an *Ellipfis*. The nature and properties whereof, as far as at prefent we fhall confider the fame, are as follow.

Fig. 6.

Fig. 6.
Schem. 1.

(·1·) The Species of the *Ellipfis* depends on the proportion there is between the length of the Cord, and the diftance of the two Centers H and I : And confequently, wherever that determinate proportion is given, the Species is given alfo, tho' the bignefs and capacity be chang'd : But where that proportion is not given ; as, the length of the Cord remaining, where the diftance of the Centers is chang'd; or, that diftance remaining, the length of the Cord is chang'd ; or both are chang'd, but not in the fame proportion ; in all thefe cafes the Species of the *Ellipfis* is different.

I   Thus

Thus in particular where the distance of the Centers, or the Line H I, is greater in proportion to the length of the Cord, there the *Ellipsis* is farther from, and where 'tis less the *Ellipsis* is nearer to a Circle. All which is so obvious on a very little consideration of the Delineation, and Figure, as 'tis represented in the two different Schemes, that no more words need be us'd about it.

(2.) If in a considerably large Figure the two Points H and I be very near together, it will be scarce distinguishable from a Circle; and in any Figure if they be suppos'd to unite, and be coincident, the Eccentrical Curve will become Concentrical; and the *Ellipsis* degenerate into a Circle; as perfect a one, as any drawn with a pair of Compasses. Whence we see why a Circle is reckon'd among the *Ellipses*; and how it may be generated by a way very like that made use of in their delineation.

(3.) As when the Points H and I are coincident, the *Ellipsis* loses its Eccentricity, and denomination, and commences a Circle; so, on the other hand, if the distance H I be indefinitely lengthened, while the difference between that distance and the length of the Cord, (equal to D H and I K or double to one D H; as the Pencil at D is easily perceiv'd) remains the same, the *Ellipsis* will go through all Species, and at last become indefinitely Oblong and Eccentrical, and one half of it, as F D E, will degenerate into the very same Figure we call a *Parabola*. For as all degrees of Eccentricity make *Ellipses* of all Species; so no degree of Eccentricity makes a Circle; and an indefinite or infinite degree of it makes a *Parabola*: Which, tho' we have no necessity to consider it so distinctly in this place (none of the Heavenly Bodies, as far as we yet know, describing

ing truly fuch a Line,as has been already obferv'd;)
yet on account of the Comets Orbits, which Fig. 1.
are nearly *Parabolical*, at leaft deferv'd our notice;
and the firft Figure will fhew an example of it.

(4.) An *Ellipfis* being defcrib'd about two Points,
as a Circle about one, or thofe two united; hence
may appear in fome meafure the nature of thefe
Points. They are indeed called the *Foci* or *Umbilici*
of the Figure, but might not unfitly be nam'd the
Centers thereof. And how naturally each of them
bears much the fame refpect to the *Elliptick* Periphery, that the *Center* does to the circular one,
is partly obvious from the foregoing delineation;
and of which thofe who are acquainted with the
Conick Sections cannot be ignorant. To whom
the matter will be ftill plainer, if they confider
the generation of an *Ellipfis* from the Section of
a *Conick* fuperficies, by a plain interfecting the
oppofite fides of the *Cone*, and yet not parallel to
the *Bafis*; as the Geometricians ufually do. For
there the *Axis* of the *Cone*, or Line which paffes
from its *Vertex* through the Center of the Circle
its *Bafis*, does not pafs through the middle or
Center of the *Ellipfis*; but one of thofe Points we
are fpeaking of. And accordingly, if the name
Center had not by cuftom in the *Ellipfis* been bor-
rowed from the Circle on account of its pofition,
rather than fome other properties of it, and thence
appli'd to the middle point in the *Ellipfis*; it
might very fitly, as has been before faid, have
been given to the two Points H and I, now ftil'd
the *Foci* or *Umbilici* thereof. And by the fame
reafon the correfponding fingle Points, going under the fame names in the *Parabola* and *Hyperbola*, would deferve and challenge the fame denomination. And this is fo agreeable to the true
Syftem of the Planetary World, that in the new

I 2   Aftronomy

Aftronomy (and thence in thefe Papers) the
ftile is fometimes continued; and 'tis not unufual,
I may add, nor very improper, to fay, That the
Sun, the common *Focus* or *Umbilicus* of all the Ce-
leftial *Elliptick* Orbits, is in the *Center* of our
Syftem, or poffeffes the *Center* of the Planetary
World.

(5.) Tho' all the Lines paffing through the
Center in a Circle, being equal, are equally confiderable; yet 'tis otherwife in the *Conick Sections*;
where that Line through the *Focus* alone which
cuts the principal *Axis* at right Angles, is remarkable above all the reft; and in very many cafes
peculiarly confiderable. This Line is ftil'd the
Latus Rectum, and in the *Ellipfis* is, after the longer and fhorter *Axis*, the third proportional.
Thus in the Figure before us, as D K is to E F,
fo is the fame E F to O P or M N, the *Latus
Rectum* thereof, fo famous with the Writers on
the *Conick Sections*.

(6). The fubtenfe of the Angle of Contact
b d, parallel to the diftance from the *Focus* B H,
at an equal diftance from the Point of contact B,
if that diftance be fuppos d infinitely fmall, is in
all parts of the fame *Ellipfis*, or other *Conick Section* equal to it felf. The Truth and Ufe of which
property is not yet fufficiently known.

(7.) If from any Point in the circumference
of an *Ellipfis* as B, Lines be drawn to each *Focus*,
B H, B I; thefe two Lines taken together are always equal to themfelves, and to the longer
Axis K D: As the delineation of the Figure does
plainly manifeft.

(8.) If the Angle made by the Lines to the
Foci from any certain Point, H B I be divided in
the midft by the Line E A; the faid Line B A
will be perpendicular to the Tangent, or Curve
at

at the Point of contact ; and fo the Angles A B L
A B G will be right ones, and equal to each other,
as confequently will equal parts of them L B H :
I B G.

(9.) A Line drawn from either *Focus* to the
end of the leffer *Axis*, H E or I E, is equal to
half the longer Axis C D or C K : as is evident
by the laft particular but one. And the fame
Line is Arithmetically the middle proportional
between the greateft and leaft diftance from
the faid *Focus*. Thus H E, for inftance, is juft
fo much longer than H D, as 'tis fhorter than
H K ; the difference in both cafes being the Eccentricity H C or C I.

(10.) The Tangent of an *Ellipfis* L G is never
perpendicular to a Line drawn from the *Focus*,
excepting the two points which terminate the
longer *Axis* D and K. And if you imagine the
point of contact B, with the Radius B H, and
the Tangent L G, to move round the *Ellipfis* together, from B towards D ; the preceding Angle,
H B L, will, in the defcent from K by F to D,
be an acute one ; (its acutenefs increafing from
K to F, and as much decreafing from F to D)
and in the afcent from D by E to K an obtufe
one ; (its obtufenefs increafing from D to E ; and
as much decreafing from E to K :) in both femi-
revolutions arriving at rightnefs at the Points D
and K, the ends of the longer *Axis* alone ; as was
here to be obferv'd.

(11.) The *Area* of an *Ellipfis* is to that of a
circumfcrib'd Circle, (whofe Diameter is equal to
the others longer *Axis*) as the fhorter *Axis* of the
Ellipfis is to the fame longer *Axis* or Diameter.

(12.) If the Circumferences of a Circle, and
of an *Ellipfis*, be equal ; the *Area* of the Circle
is the greater. It being known, that of all Fi-

Fig. 6.
Scheme 1.

gures,

gures, whofe *Perimeters* are equal, the Circle is the moft capacious.

(13.) If an *Ellipfis*, by becoming infinitely Eccentrical, degenerate into a *Parabola*; the *Latus Rectum* will be four times as long as the neareft diftance to the *Focus* thereof. Thus r s is four times as long as H t.

Fig. 1.

XVI. All Bodies which, together with a Projectile or Uniform Motion along right Lines, are continually attracted or impell'd towards one certain Point or Center, let the attraction or impulfe be of what nature or quantity foever, will always (no other Force interpofing) by a Line drawn from that Center to themfelves, defcribe equal *Area's* in equal times, and fo proportionable *Area's* in proportionable times, through all parts of their courfes. Thus if the *Area* defcrib'd the firft minute were equal to a thoufand fquare Feet; whether the Bodies came nearer or went farther off, it would always in a minute be equal to the fame thoufand fquare feet; in two minutes double, or two thoufand; in three minutes treble, or three thoufand; in four minutes Quadruple, or four thoufand; and fo for ever proportionably. The demonftration of this noble and exceeding ufeful *Theorem* is both eafie and pleafant: But that not being my prefent bufinefs, I fhall, as in the reft, refer the Reader to the Great Author himfelf for fatiffaction.

XVII. All Bodies, *vice verfà*, which revolve in Curves; and by a Line drawn from themfelves to a certain Point or Center, defcribe *Area's* proportionable to the times of defcription; are attracted or impell'd continually towards that Point or Center.

Corollary.

Corollary. *When therefore Lines drawn from every one of the Planets to the Sun, describe perpetually* Area's *proportionable to the times of description ; as is own'd by all Astronomers ;* 'tis certain that, besides *their several Projectile Motions, they are every one continually attracted or impell'd towards the Sun ; and from such compounded forces revolve about him. And the case being the same in the* Moon *about the* Earth ; *the* Circumjovials *about* Jupiter ; *and the* Circumsaturnals *about* Saturn ; *this Corollary equally belongs to them also.*

XVIII. If Bodies from a Projectile Motion, and an attraction or impulse to a Point or Center move about the same in a *Spiral* Line, which interfects every Radius in the same Angle; the force of the attraction or impulse, at different distances from that Center is reciprocally as the Cubes of such distances : And *vice versâ,* if the force of attraction or impulse to any Center be as the Cubes of the distances reciprocally ; Bodies revolving about the same must describe *Spiral* Lines, interfecting the Radij in the same Angle.

XIX. If Bodies from a Projectile Motion and an attraction or impulse to a Point, move about it, being the *Center* of an *Ellipsis,* in the Periphery of the same *Ellipsis* ; the force of attraction is *directly* as the distance from such a Center: And *vice versâ,* if the force of attraction or impulse to any Point be as the distance from the same *directly,* Bodies revolving about it must describe an *Elliptick* Figure ; with whose Center the fore-mention'd Point will be coincident.

XX. If Bodies from a Projectile Motion, and an attraction or impulse to a Point, describe an *Ellipsis* about that Point, coincident with one of its *Foci*; the force of Attraction towards that *Focus* is *reciprocally* as the squares of the distances from the same. And *vice versâ*, if the force or attraction to any Point be in a duplicate proportion of the distances from the same *reciprocally* ; Bodies revolving about the same must describe *Ellipses* about it, coincident with one of the *Foci* thereof.

Corollary 1. *Where Bodies revolve about any Point or Central Body, from the Figure describ'd, and the Situation of the Point or Central Body, the Law of attraction or impulse tending towards the same is discovered.* And vice versâ, *where the Law of attraction or impulse is known, the Figure to be describ'd by revolving Bodies, and the Situation of the Point or Central Body, towards which the attraction or impulse is, with respect to such Figures, is* à priori *discover'd also.*

Coroll. 2. *None of the Heavenly Bodies describing either* Spiral Lines, *or* Ellipses *about their* Centers, *'tis certain no Law of Gravitation in a triplicate* reciprocal, *or* direct *simple proportion of the distance from the* Central Body, *obtains in the Planetary* World.

*Coroll. Lem. 17. prius.

Coroll. 3. * *All the Planets revolutions arising from the composition of their Projectile Motion and Gravitation towards the Sun; and they all describing* Ellipses *about him, in the* Common Focus *of all their Orbits, as is evident from Astronomy; 'tis hence certain that the force of their attraction or impulse towards the Sun is in a duplicate proportion of their distances reciprocally.*

Coroll. 4. *The case being the same as to the* Moon *about the* Earth, *and the* Circumsaturnals *about* Saturn; *this last Corollary belongs equally to them also. But* Jupiters Satellits *revolving in compleat Circles are incapable of affording evidence in his case.*

XXI. If

XXI. If feveral Bodies revolve about the fame central attractive Body at feveral diftances; and the periodical Times in which they revolve be to each other, as the Squares of their diftances from the fame; the force of Attraction or Impulfe to that central Body is in a triplicate Proportion of fuch diftances *reciprocally*; and *vice versâ*, if the force of Attraction or Impulfe be as the Cubes of their diftances *reciprocally*, the periodical Times of Revolution will be to each other, as the Squares of their diftances from the fame central Body.

XXII. If feveral Bodies revolve about the fame central attractive Body, at feveral diftances in *Circular* or *Elliptick* Orbits, and the periodical Times of revolving be all equal; the force of Attraction or Impulfe towards the central Body is *directly*, as the diftances from the fame.

XXIII. If feveral Bodies revolve about the fame central Body, in *Circular* or *Elliptick* Orbits, at feveral diftances; and the Squares of the periodical Times of revolving are to each other as the Cubes of the middle diftances from the fame central Body; the force of Attraction or Impulfe towards the fame is in a duplicate Proportion of the diftances from the fame *reciprocally*.

Corollary 1. *Where feveral Bodies, from a projectile Motion, compounded with a Gravitation towards a central Body, revolve about the fame at feveral diftances; from the Proportion there is between the periodical Times of revolving, compar'd with the diftances from the central Body, the Law of Gravitation tending towards the fame is difcovered;* and vice versâ, *where the Law of Gravitation is known, the Proportion between the periodical Times compar'd with the diftances from the central Body is,* à priori, *difcover'd alfo.*

Coroll. 2.

Coroll. 2. *None of the Heavenly Bodies periodical Times of revolving being to each other as the Squares of their distances from the central Body, nor equal to one another; 'tis certain, as before, that no Law of Gravitation in a triplicate* reciprocal, *or* direct *simple Proportion of the distances from the central Body, obtains in the Planetary World.*

Coroll.
Lem. 17.
prius.

Coroll. 3. " *All the Planets Revolutions arising from the Composition of their projectile Motion and Gravitation towards the* Sun, *and the Squares of their periodical Times of revolving being to each other as the Cubes of their middle distances from him;* 'tis hence certain, *That, as before,* 'the force of their Attraction *or Impulse towards the* Sun, *is in a duplicate Proportion of their distances* reciprocally.

Coroll. 4. *The* Case *being the same as to the* Circumjovials *about* Jupiter, *and the* Circumsaturnals *about* Saturn; *this last* Corollary *belongs equally to them also. But the* Moon *being a single Planet revolving about the* Earth, *is incapable of giving evidence in her Case.*

Coroll. 5. *As before, the Law of Gravitation being demonstrated from the Planets revolving in Ellipses about the central Bodies in one of the* Foci; *the Proportion between the periodical Times, compar'd with the distances from the central Bodies, was deducible* à priori; *so vice versâ, the periodical Times compar'd with the distances demonstrating the Law of Gravitation, thence the necessity of the Planets Revolution in* Ellipses, *about the central Bodies in one of the* Foci, *is* à priori *demonstrated also.*

Coroll. 6. *'Tis certain, That the Annual Motion belongs to the* Earth *about the Sun, not to the Sun about the Earth. For when from the Moon's Orbit, and the Planet's Orbits and periodical Times, 'tis certain, That the* Law *of Gravitation towards the* Earth, *and towards the Sun is the same; and by consequence,*
all

all the periodical Times of Bodies revolving about each of them in the same Proportion to one another, compar'd with their several Distances from each of them: On *Which* Hypothesis, *this Proportion suits the* Phœnomena *of Nature, the same must be the true one, and to be fully acquiesc'd in. Now 'tis known, That on the* Hypothesis *of the Earth's Annual Motion, her periodical Time exactly suits, and is so between that of* Venus *and* Mars, *as the Proportion observ'd through the whole System, and demonstrable* à priori, *withal, exactly requires; but on the other* Hypothesis *'tis enormously different. For when the Moon undoubtedly, and on this* Hypothesis *the Sun also, revolves about our Earth; and when the distance of the Sun is to that of the Moon as about* 10000 *to* 46; *and the Moon's periodical Time less than* 28 *days; the periodical Time of the Sun is by the* Rule of Three *discoverable thus: As the Cube of the Moon's distance,* 46 *equal to* 97336; *to the Cube of the Sun's* 10000 *equal to* 1000000000000. (*or almost as* 1 *to* 10000000) *so must the Square of the Moon's periodical Time* 28 *Days equal to* 784. *be to the Square of the Sun's periodical Time,* 7840000000; *whose square Root,* 88204, *are Days also, equal to* 242 *Years. So that on the* Hypothesis *of the Sun's Revolution about the Earth, its periodical Time must undoubtedly be* 242 *Years, which all Experience attests to be but a single one. So that at length the Controversy between the* Ptolemaick *and* Pythagorean Systems *of the World is to a Demonstration determin'd, and the Earth's Annual Motion for ever unquestionably establish'd.*

Coroll. 7. *'Tis certain those Opake Masses which sometimes appear at the Sun, are not Planets revolving at any the least distance from him, but Spots or* Maculæ *adhering to him: for whereas they revolve but once in about twenty six Days; on Calculation it will appear, that a Planet near the Sun's Surface as these*

must

*muſt be, cannot have three hours allow'd for its
periodical Revolution, which being ſo different from
the foremention'd ſpace of twenty ſix days, quite decides
that Controverſy, and demonſtrates thoſe Maſſes to be
real* Maculæ *adhering to the Body of the Sun, as is
here aſſerted.*

XXIV. If a Planet deſcribe an *Ellipſis* about
its central Body in the *Focus* thereof, it will move
faſteſt when tis neareſt to, and ſloweſt when
'tis fartheſt from the ſaid central Body or *Focus*;
and agreeably in the intermediate places. For
ſeeing whereſoever the revolving Body is, the
Area is ſtill proportionable to the time, as was
before ſhew'd; and ſo in equal times always
equal; 'tis evident by how much the Diſtance is
leſs, and the Line from the *Focus* is ſhorter; by ſo
much muſt the Bodies motion be the ſwifter to
compenſate the ſame: and *vice versâ*, by how
much the former is longer, by ſo much muſt the
latter be ſlower to allow for it.

Fig. 6.   XXV. If the Planet B deſcribe an *Ellipſis* about
the central Body in the *Focus* H; as the *Area* deſcrib'd by the Line B H, will be exactly uniform
and proportional to the time of Deſcription; ſo
the *Angular Motion*, or Velocity of the Line from
the other *Focus* B I, will be proportional to the
time, and uniform alſo; tho' not ſo Exactly and
Geometrically.

        XXVI. The Law of Gravitation already ex-
plain'd being ſuppos'd; if one Planet deſcribe
an *Ellipſis* about the central Body in the *Focus* H,
Fig. 6.   and another deſcribe a Circle about the ſame in
its Center: If the Semidiameter of the Circle be
equal to H E, the middle diſtance in the *Ellipſis* from the ſame Center or *Focus*, their periodical Times of revolving will be the ſame;
                                                and

and when the Diftances are equal, their Velocity will be fo too.

Corollary, *Tho therefore the Planets revolve in Ellipfes of feveral Species, yet their periodical Times may be as well compar'd with one another, and with their diftances from the central Bodies, as if they all revolv'd in compleat Circles; as was above done.*

XXVII. If a Body revolve about a central Body, as about A in a Circle, as B e E b; and another revolve about the fame in the *Focus* of its *Ellipfis* B H F G, fo that the Semediameter of the Circle were equal to the neareft diftance in the *Ellipfis*, A B; the Velocity of the Body at the neareft Point of the *Ellipfis* will be greater than the Velocity of the Body in the Circle ; and will be to it in half the Proportion of the *Latus rectum* of the *Ellipfis* p q, to the Diameter of the Circle e b; or as that Line p q, to a middle proportional between it felf and e b.

XXVIII. If one Body revolve round a central Body in a Circle, and another about the fame in its *Focus* defcribe fo very Eccentrical an *Ellipfis* that it may pafs for a *Parabola*; the Velocity of the Body moving along the *Ellipfis*, will be to that of the Body moving in the Circle (the Point in the *Ellipfis* being as far from the central Body as the Circumference of the Circle) very nearly as ten to fe .n.

XXIX. If a central Body have many Bodies revolving about it ; 'tis perfectly indifferent in it felf, and with regard to the central Body, in what Plains foever, or which way in thofe Plains foever, they all or any of them move.

Corollary. *Hence arifes a convincing Argument of the Interpofition of Council and Providence in the Conftitution of our Syftem; in which all the Planets revolve*
the

Fig. 3.

the same way, from West *to* East; *and that in Plains almost coincident with one another, and with that of the* Ecliptick, *as Mr.* Bentley *hath also observ'd.*

Serm. 8.
p. 13.

XXX. The Order of the Heavenly Bodies in the Solar Syſtem is as follows: *Firſt* of all, The vaſt and glorious Body of the Sun is plac'd in the middle, very near the Center of Gravity of the intire Syſtem, in the common *Focus* of every one of the Planetary Orbits. Next to him *Mercury* deſcribes his *Ellipſis*, and that ſo near, that we on Earth rarely obtain a diſtinct view of him. Next to *Mercury* is the *Elliptick* Orbit of *Venus*, our glorious Morning and Evening Star. Next to *Venus* our Earth, with its attendant the *Moon*, perform a joint Courſe, and Meaſure out the Annual Period. Next to the *Earth* the fiery Star *Mars* alone, without any viſible Guard accompanying him, revolves about the ſame Center. Next to *Mars*, tho' at a mighty diſtance from him, the largeſt of the Planets, *Jupiter*, with his four remarkable Satellits; and laſtly *Saturn* with his five little *Moons* about him, deſcribe the fartheſt and moſt remote Orbits, and compleat the intire Planetary *Chorus*, as the Frontiſpiece of the Book repreſents them to the Contemplation of the *Reader.*

SCHOLIUM.

Beſides the Planets, whoſe Orbits are not very different from Circles, there are another Species of Bodies revolving about the *Sun* in ſuch *Ellipſes*, as may paſs for *Parabola's*, they are ſo exceeding Eccentrical; but as regularly retaining their ſeveral Periods and Orbits, as the Planets

now

now mention'd. But becaufe thefe Bodies will be more diftinctly confider'd hereafter, I fhall wave their farther Confideration at prefent, and proceed.

XXXI. The periodical Times of each Planet's Revolution about the *Sun*, are as follow.

		Y.	D.	H.
Mercury		00	088	00
Venus	revolves a-	00	224	18
The Earth	bout the	00	365	06
Mars	*Sun* in the	01	315	00
Jupiter	fpace of	12	000	00
Saturn		30	000	00

XXXII. The middle diftances of the Planets from the *Sun*, are as follow.

Mercury			020952000	Statute
Venus	is diftant		039096000	Miles,
The Earth	from the		054000000	each
Mars	*Sun*		082242000	5000
Jupiter			280582000	*Paris*
Saturn			513540000	Feet.

S C H O L I U M.

The Proportions of thefe Numbers are un-queftionable: But the Numbers themfelves only within about a fourth part under or over. The Reafon of fuch uncertainty is, That the Sun's *Parallax* or Angle which the Diameter of the Earth would fubtend to an eye at the Sun, on which the whole depends, is not yet accurately determined by Aftronomers; fo that between 24 and 40 Seconds, no number can be certainly

pitch'd

pitch'd upoñ, till farther Obſervations put an end to our Doubts. On which Account I have endeavour'd to come as near to Probability as poſſible, and have ſuppos'd the Sun's *Parallax* 32 " in a middle between the two foremen-tion'd Extreams; and from this *Hypotheſis* made theſe and the following Calculations; which therefore cannot well be above a fourth part un-der or over the truth, but very probably are much nearer it.

XXXIII. The quantity of Matter in ſuch of the Heavenly Bodies as afford us means of deter-mining the ſame, is in the Proportions follow-ing.

The *Sun's* ——— ——— ———66690.
Jupiter's ——— ——— ——— 00060½.
Saturn's ——— ——— ——— 00028¼.
The *Earth's* ——— ——— ——— 00001.
The *Moon's* ——— ——— ——— 00000$\frac{1}{26}$.

S C H O L I U M.

Becauſe the Solidity or Quantity of Matter in Bodies is in a triplicate Proportion of their Dia-meters; that ſmall uncertainty in the Sun's *Pa-rallax* beforemention'd, imports a great deal in the preſent Calculation. I ſhall therefore give the *Reader* the Proportions of the Quantity of Matter in the Heavenly Bodies on the two ex-tream *Hypotheſes*, as well as I have done on the middle one; only informing him, that the *Hypo-theſis* of 24" ſeems nearer the truth than the op-poſite extream of 40", as being neareſt the ac-curate Obſervations of our great Aſtronomer Mr. *Flamſteed.* The quantities of Matter there-fore, are as follow,

The

The Sun's—28700	⎫ If the	*The Sun's*—136560	⎫ If the
Jupiter's —00026$\frac{1}{11}$	⎬ *Sun's*	*Jupiter's* —000124$\frac{1}{7}$	⎬ *Sun's*
Saturn's —00012$\frac{1}{8}$	⎬ *Paral-*	*Saturn's*——00057$\frac{9}{10}$	⎬ *Paral-*
The Earth's-00001	⎭ *lax* be	*The Earth's*-000001	⎭ *lax* be
The Moon's-00000$\frac{1}{28}$	40″.	*The Moon's*-000000$\frac{1}{28}$	24″.

Corollary. *The weight of Bodies at equal distances from the Sun and Planets, being in the same Proportion with the Quantity of their Matter, as has been* Lem. 7 *already said; the same Numbers assign'd in the last prius.* Lemma, *which explain the latter, serve equally to explain the former also.*

XXXIV. The Diameters of the *Sun* and *Planets,* are as follows.

The Sun's ——— 494100	⎫	
Saturn's——————043925	⎪	
Jupiter's———— 052522	⎪	
Mar's-————— 002816	⎬ Statute Miles, each
The Earth's ——— 008202	⎪ 5000 *Paris* Feet.
The Moon's——— 002223	⎪	
Venus's ——— —— 004941	⎪	
Mercury's —•——002717	⎭	

XXXV. The weight of Bodies on the Surface of the *Sun*, and those *Planets* mention'd in the 33^d *Lemma* before, is as follows. On the Surface of

The Sun ——— ——— ——— -10000.
The Earth ——— ——— ——-01258$\frac{1}{2}$.
Jupiter ——— ——— ——-00804$\frac{1}{2}$.
The Moon ——— —— ——— -00630.
Saturn ——— —•——— ——-00536.

K   XXXVI. The

XXXVI. The Denfities of the fame, (whatever be the *Sun's Parallax*) is as follows.

The Moon's ————— ————— ———— 700.
The Earth's ————— ———— ———— 387.
The Sun's ——— ——— ———— ———— 100.
Jupiter's ———— ———— ———— 076.
Saturn's ——— ———— ———— ———-060.

XXXVII. As the weight of Bodies without the Superficies of the Heavenly Bodies increafes in a duplicate Proportion of their nearnefs to their Centers; fo within the fame Superficies, does it decreafe in a fimple Proportion thereof; and is confequently greateft upon the Superficies themfelves. Thus a Body at 10000 Miles diftance from the Earth's Center, is four times fo heavy as it would be at 20000. But within the Earth, if a Body were twice as near its Center as 'tis on the Surface, it would be but half fo heavy as 'tis here; if thrice as near, it would be but a third part fo heavy; if four times as near, it would be but a quarter fo heavy; and fo for ever proportionably. Gravity therefore is moft confiderable on the Surface, decreafing both ways, upward in a duplicate Proportion of the *reciprocal* Diftance; and downward in a fimple *direct* Proportion thereof.

XXXVIII. If the central Regions of a Globe contain a fphærical Cavity within the fame; Bodies plac'd therein, from the equality of Attraction on every fide, will not tend any way, or gravitate at all, but be as perfectly at liberty, as if they were not affected by any fuch Law of Attraction or Gravitation.

XXXIX. The *Moon* revolves about the Earth from *Weft* to *Eaft* in 27 Days, 7 Hours, 43 Minutes;

nutes ; and in the very fame fpace of Time, by a ftrange Correfpondence and Harmony of the two Motions, revolves the fame way about its own *Axis* ; whereby (one Motion as much converting it to, as the other turns it from the Earth) the fame fide is always expos'd to our fight.

XL. The Librations of the *Moon*'s Body, which caufe not exactly the fame Hemifphere thereof to be perpetually expos'd to our fight, arife from the Eccentricity of the *Moon*'s Orbit, from the Perturbations by the *Sun*'s Attraction, and from the Obliquity of the *Axis* of the Diurnal Rotation to the *Moon*'s own Orbit, without the knowledge of which Circumftances her *Phænomena* were inexplicable, but by the confideration of them are very demonftrable.

XLI. In the 2365th year of the *Julian* Period, the Autumnal Equinox was on the 11th day of *October*. 'Tis evident from the Aftronomical Tables of the Anticipation of the Equinox, that in 4044 years (the time fince the beforemention'd Year) the Equinoxes have anticipated 30 Days 9 Hours. 'Tis alfo evident, That this Year 1696. the Vernal Equinox is on the 9th of *March*, and the Autumnal on the 12th of *September*; 'tis farther evident, That whereas now the Space from the Vernal to the Autumnal Equinox is eight or nine Days longer than from the Autumnal to the Vernal, by reafon of the Pofition of the *Perihelion* of the Earth's Orbit near the *Winter* Solftice; at the time beforemention'd it was not above five or fix Days fo. By the Anticipation therefore of the Equinoxes alone, if the Pofition of the *Perihelion* had been always the fame, the Equinoxes at the time affigned had been on the 9th of *April* in the Morn-

ing,

ing, and on the 12ᵗʰ of *October* in the Evening; and the equaller Division of the Year allow'd for, the Vernal Equinox was on the 10ᵗʰ of *April*, and the Autumnal on the 11ᵗʰ of *October*, as was to be prov'd.

XLII. Comets are a Species of Planets, or Bodies revolving about the *Sun* in *Elliptical* Orbits, whose periodical Times and Motions are as constant, certain, and regular as those of the Planets, tho' till very lately wholly unknown to the World.

XLIII. These *Elliptical* Orbits of Comets are so very Oblong and Eccentrical, that while they come within our Observation, they are but little different from *Parabola's*, and may accordingly be consider'd as such.

XLIV. The Plains in which various Comets move, are themselves exceeding various, and at all imaginable Angles of Inclination with one another, and with that of the Ecliptick.

XLV. The course of Comets in their Orbits is not determin'd one way, (as is that of the Planets from *West* to *East*) but indifferently some of them move one way, and some another.

Corollary 1. *From these two last* Lemmata, *'tis evident , that Comets move sometimes from* East *to* West, *other times from* West *to* East ; *sometimes from* North *to* South, *other times from* South *to* North; *or obliquely between any of these ways, according as the Situation of the Plains of their Orbits, and the Directions of their Courses together determine them.*

Coroll. 2. *Hence 'tis certain, That the heavenly Motions are not perform'd in corporeal* Vortices; *when the Comets exactly observe the same Laws and Velocity of Motion, whether they revolve with or against, or cross to the Planets, and the suppos'd fluid Matter of the* Vortices.

XLVI. Comets

XLVI. Comets in their defcent to, and afcent from the *Sun*, pafs quite through the Planetary Syftem; as may be feen in the Frontifpiece.

Corollary. *Hence we may obferve a new poffible Caufe of vaft Changes in the Planetary World, by the accefs and approach of thefe vaft and hitherto little known Bodies to any of the Planets.*

XLVII. If a Comet in its defcent to, or afcent from the *Sun*, approach near to a Planet as it paffes by, and its Plain be different from that in which the Planets move; by its attractive Power it will, agreeably to the univerfal Law of Gravitation of Bodies, draw it from the Plain in which it before mov'd, and fo caufe it afterward to move in a new one, inclin'd to the former, but paffing through the *Sun*, as the former did.

Corollary. *Hence 'tis fuppofable, That tho' the Planets originally revolv'd in the fame common Plain, yet by the fubfequent Attraction of Comets, their Plains may now be inclin'd to one another, and different; as 'tis certain* de facto *they now are.*

S C H O L I U M.

When the Law of Gravitation is univerfal and mutual, 'tis evident, The Planet would draw the Comet from its Plain, as well as the Comet would draw the Planet; and fo generally, what effects foever the Comets could have on the Planets, the latter would have correfpondent ones on the former. But as this Indication once given for all, there is no neceffity of taking notice of the changes in the Comets; fo accordingly, in what follows, I fhall wholly omit the fame; and confine my felf to fuch things as will be immediately ufeful in the following Theory.

XLVIII.

XLVIII. If a Comet revolving in the fame
Plain with a Planet, whofe Orbit is a perfect
Circle, as it paffes by, approach near it, by accelerating or retarding the Velocity of the Planet,
it would render its Orbit *Elliptical.* Thus if B
were a Planet revolving about the *Sun* at the
Center A, in the circular Orbit B e E b; and a
Comet either in its defcent towards, or afcent
from the *Sun* fhould pafs near it, it would agreeably to the univerfal Law of Gravitation of Bodies, accelerate it, if concurring with, or retard
ing it, if contradicting the Planet's own annual
Motion along the Periphery of its Circle. Whereupon the concentrical Orbit would become ex-
centrical, and the Planet would afterward revolve in an *Ellipfis,* which on an Acceleration
would be bigger, and on a Retardation lefs
than the Circle which it had till then defcrib'd ;
the former reprefented by B H F G, the latter
by B K L I. For when the original Velocity of
B was exactly adjufted to the *Sun's* Power of
Attraction, and its Orbit thereupon a perfect
Circle, this new Acceleration or Retardation
muft render it afterward incommenfurate, and
too great, or too little for the fame ; and accordingly the Orbit to be afterward agreeably to
what has been formerly explain'd, defcrib'd by
the Planet, muft be an *Ellipfis*; and bigger or
lefs than the former Circle, as the force was
directed for, or againft, the Planet's own Motion.

Corollary 1. *In this Cafe the* Sun *would no longer
be in the Center of the Figure, but in one of the* Foci,
viz. *in the nearer* Focus *of the larger, and the farther
of the fmaller* Ellipfis.

Coroll. 2. *If* B *were the Earth moving circularly
about the* Sun *from* Weft *to* Eaft, i. e. *from* B *by* e,
E b

Fig. 3.

Lem. 11, 12, 13. *prius.*

E b *to* B *again; and a Comet* h *in its descent towards the Sun should pass by before it, or on the East side; the annual Motion of the Earth would be accelerated, and its circular Orbit degenerate into the larger* Ellipsis B H F G, *about the Sun in its nearer Focus* A.

XLIX. If a Comet in paffing by as before, accelerate the Planets Motion, and fo enlarge the Orbit, the Planets periodical Time of revolving will be enlarg'd, and become longer thereby. In like manner, if the Comet retard the Planets Motion, and fo diminifh the Orbit, the periodical Time of revolving will be leffen'd, and become fhorter. And ftill the more confiderable the Acceleration or Retardation is, compar'd with the original Velocity of the Planet, the greater will be the eccentricity, and the greater difference between the former and latter Orbits, and the former and latter periodical Times of revolving alfo.

Corollary 1. *If in the foregoing Cafe the Semidiameter of the ancient Circle, with the middle Diftance in the Ellipfis afterward defcrib'd be given, as alfo the periodical Time of revolving in the latter, the periodical Time of revolving in the former is at the fame time determin'd. For as the Cube of the middle Diftance in the Ellipfis, to the Cube of the Semidiameter of the Circle, fo is the Square of the periodical Time in the Ellipfis, to the Square of the periodical Time in the Circle. So that three of thofe terms being known, which is here fuppos'd; the fourth, by the* Golden Rule, *is known alfo, whofe fquare Root anfwers the demand of this* Corollary.

Coroll. 2. *When therefore the three* Poftulata's *now mention'd are given in the cafe of the Earth, (fuppofing that it anciently revolv'd in a circular Orbit) as*

K 4 *will*

will hereafter appear; the time of its annual Revolution in that original and circular Orbit may easily be at this day discover'd.

L. If a Planet moving in a circular Orbit were accelerated by an Attraction directly along its Tangent or Periphery; the preceding Angle made by the Tangent and Radius C B A would still remain a right one, and the point B, where the Acceleration happen'd, would afterward be the nearest to the *Focus*, or the *Perihelion* in the *Ellipsis* afterward to be describ'd. So if it were alike directly retarded along its Tangent or Periphery, the Angle would still be a right one; and the Point B where the Retardation happen'd, would be the farthest from the *Focus*, or the *Aphelion* in the *Ellipsis* to be afterward describ'd.

LI. If therefore such Acceleration or Retardation were caus'd by a Body moving uniformly along its Trajectory on each side of the Planets circular Periphery, the oblique Acceleration above, would take off the nearly equal oblique Retardation below, or the contrary; and thereby the effect afterward remaining would be all one, as if the prevailing force, whether of Acceleration or Retardation were only along the Tangent or Periphery; all one, as if the whole Attraction were caus'd while the attracting Body was at or near that Tangent or Periphery it self; and by consequence the Point B would be, as above, the *Perihelion* or *Aphelion* of the *Ellipsis* afterward describ'd.

LII. But by reason that Bodies revolving about the *Sun*, move still swifter when nearer, and flower when farther off; the Motion of a Comet is swifter within than without the Periphery of the

Fig. 3.

the fore-mention'd Circle. If therefore (to omit here and hereafter cafes not to our purpofe) a Comet in its defcent towards its *Perihelion* pafs juft before the Body of a Planet, and Accelerate it; becaufe the time of Acceleration without the Periphery of the Circle is longer than the time of the retardation within it, the effects of the outward oblique Attraction muft be fomewhat more than of the inward; and the preceding Angle become fomewhat obtufe. Thus if a Comet in its defcent from X by h to W Accelerate the Planet B; by reafon of the prevalence of the outward oblique Attraction, the Planet will be not only Accelerated, but drawn outward in fome meafure alfo, and the preceding Angle, which before was conftantly a right one, and reprefented by C B A will be a little obtufe, and be reprefented by T B A; and by confequence the Point B will be a few degrees paft the fucceeding Perihelion, juft fo many as in the faid *Ellipfis* are neceffary to render the Angle made by the Radius, or Line from the *Focus*, and the Tangent, obtufe in the fame proportion with that above-mention'd. So that on fuch an Acceleration the *Perihelion* will be fome degrees more backward than the Point B, at which the Acceleration happen'd.

Fig. 3.

  Coroll. *If therefore in a given year, a Comet, in its defcent towards the Sun, Accelerated the Earth's Annual Motion, and chang'd its Orbit from a Circle to an* Ellipfis; *the degree of the Ecliptick, and day of the year, when the fame Attraction happen'd, may be pretty nearly determined by the place of the Perihelion at the fame time, from the Aftronomical Tables of its Place and Motion.*

LIII. If

LIII. If the neareſt diſtance of a Comet to a
Planet be given, the time of Attraction to be
conſider'd is from thence determinable. Thus
if a Comet in its Deſcent towards the Sun, as
Fig. 5. from E to H, paſs'd by a Planet moving in the
Circumference of its circular Orbit from A to D,
and ſo accelerated the ſame : Let C G be the Line
deſcrib'd by the Comet while the Planet paſſes
along from B to C, at which laſt Point C the
Comet is ſuppos'd to have been at its neareſt
diſtance, when the Planet is at B ; and let C F
be equal to C G. In this caſe the Acceleration
by the Comet between E and F, being nearly
taken off by the retardation between G and H ;
(and the like is to be ſuppos'd of the Acceleration
beyond E, and the retardation beyond H, not
to be contain'd in the Figure) 'tis evident that
all the Attraction which is to be conſider'd, is
that Accelerating the Planet while the Comet
paſſes from F to G, and the Planet from Q to
C : As the ſole view and conſideration of the
Figure it ſelf will give ſufficient evidence. Which
from the Velocity of the motion of Comets and
Planets eaſily calculated, might be ſoon determined ; if the neareſt diſtance C B were once
aſcertain'd.

Coroll. 1. *If therefore the neareſt diſtance* C B
*were known, and the bigneſs or quantity of Matter
in the Comet it ſelf ; ſeeing the time of Acceleration
is withal known ; the quantity of Acceleration, the
increaſ'd Velocity of the Planet ; and by conſequence
the Magnitude of the* Elliptick Orbit *to be afterwards
diſcrib'd ; and the periodical time of revolving anſwe-
rably thereto, might all be* à priori *determined.*

Coroll. 2. Vice verſà, *If the neareſt diſtance*
B C, *with the Eccentricity of the ſubſequent* Elliptick Orbit, *or its periodical time be given ; the bigneſs*

neſs of the Comet may, on the ſame grounds, be de-termin'd alſo.

LIV. If a Comet deſcending towards the Sun paſs'd near a Planet which had a ſecondary one revolving about it; unleſs their ſituation were ſo accurately and nicely adjuſted that it approach'd equally near to them both, theſe two Planets would no longer revolve together, but being for ever ſeparated muſt deſcribe different Orbits about the Sun. This is eaſily demonſtrable; ſince any diverſity of Attraction muſt change each of their annual Orbits and Periodical times in proportionably different degrees: The leaſt of which were more than ſufficient to ſuch a purpoſe as we here are ſpeaking of.

Coroll. *If therefore the Planetary Orbits were all or any of them Originally Circles; and by the Attraction of Comets paſſing by, were chang'd into Ellipſes; The Poſition of their ſeveral Satellits, which they ſtill retain, muſt have been moſt wiſely and wonderfully adjuſted, by the Divine Providence, with their fellows; with their Primary Planets; and with the Orbits and Periods of the Comets; without which correſpondence the preſent ſyſtem of the World muſt have been vaſtly alter'd; and the Primary Planets have loſt their Attendants for ever.*

LV. When therefore the Earth ſtill retains its Secondary Planet the Moon, which at its Original Formation belong'd to it; if its preſent *Elliptick* Orbit be the effect of the paſſing by of a Comet, the time of ſuch paſſing by muſt have been about three days after the New or Full Fig. 2. Moon. Let o g repreſent a Section of the Eccliptick Periphery; in which the Earth a is performing its annual courſe, from Weſt to Eaſt,

or

or from o towards g: Let c be the Moon, performing in like manner, (besides her menstrual revolution the same way, from t by c towards s, about the Earth,) her annual course, with the same Velocity as the Earth, from u towards w, along her Periphery u w, equidistant from the Eccliptick o g: Let n m represent the trajectory of the Comet, interfecting the Line passing through the Sun I i, in the Angle m b i of 12, 14, or 16 degrees more or less: Let b be the Comet descending from n towards m in its approach towards it *Perihelion*: From the Earth's Center, from d and x, (the Line a x being drawn parallel to the Comets Trajectory n m,) let fall perpendiculars to the Trajectory a f, d e, x y. Now if while the Comet were passing from f to y, the Moon stood still, and did not proceed in her annual course along her Periphery u w, she must have been at that Point x, or not above one day past the new at t; and so the nearest distances a f x y being equal, the Attractions of the Earth by the Comet at f, and of the Moon by the Comet at y, would have been equal also; and by consequence this position would have secur'd the future agreement and company of these two Planets, and the time of the passing by of the Comet fix'd to a single day after the New Moon. But by reason of the Moons progressive annual motion along her Periphery u w, while the Comet descends from t towards y; she must have been in that Point of her Menstrual Orbit c, where c d is to c q or d a, as her Velocity to the Comets, or as 7 to 10; that so the Comet descending from its nearest distance to the Earth at f, to its nearest distance to the Moon at e; and the Moon arriving at the same time, by her annual motion, at the Point d, the nearest distances

ftances a f; d e may ftill be equal; and the acceleration of the Earth and the Moon may ftill be
the fame.   Now this being the cafe ; the place of
the Moon c muft be about 41, 43, or 45 degrees
more or lefs paft the Point t, in its Menftrual
Orbit, or the Conjunction with the Sun or three
days paft the New Moon.   And the like will be
demonftrated of three days paft the Full Moon,
by the fame figure and reafoning ; if we do but
fhift the Scene, and let c reprefent the Earth, and
u w the Ecliptick Periphery ; a the Moon, and
o g its Periphery.   For all the reft remaining as
above ; the Angle ☾ c a which the Moon a muft
have pafs'd after the full at ☾, being equal to the
alternate c a t, would require equal time to be
defcrib'd ; and fo the time proper for the fituation of the Earth and Moon, (which is equally
neceffary in this as in the former cafe) as the
Figure reprefents it , will be three days after the
Full ; as this Corollary afferts.

Coroll. *If therefore in a given year a Comet in its
defcent towards the Sun Accelerated the Earth and
Moon's annual motions, and thereby chang'd their Orbit from a Circle to an* Elliplis ; *when the* day *of the
year, from the place of the* Perihelion, *were* pretty
nearly *determined ; by this laft* Lemma, *the* very
day *is determined alfo from the Aftronomical Tables of
the Conjunctions of the Sun and Moon.*

LVI. If our Earth once revolv'd about the
Sun in a circular Orbit, whofe Semidiameter
were equal to the Earth's original diftance from
the Sun fix degrees paft its Perihelion, the annual period was exactly equal to 12 Synodical or
13 Periodical Months. 'Tis evident that 12 *Synodical* or 13 *Periodical* Months, (equal to each
other in the prefent cafe,) are 355 days 4 hours

19 minutes. 'Tis also evident that the Eccentricity of the Earth's Orbit, or the distance between the *Focus* and Center of its *Ellipsis*, was, according to the ancient Astronomers, *Hipparchus* and *Ptolomy*, $\frac{1}{100}$ of the intire middle distance. By the Moderns 'tis found somewhat less, (and those who know Mr. *Newton*'s Philosophy will easily allow of some diversity in different ages;) by *Tycho* twas determin'd to be near $\frac{18}{1000}$; by *Cassini* since $\frac{17}{1000}$; and last of all by our most accurate Observer Mr. *Flamsteed*, (as he was pleas'd by Letter with great freedom to assure me,) $\frac{1692}{100000}$, or near $\frac{17}{1000}$, as *Cassini* had before determin'd. All which consider'd, we may very justly take the middle between the Ancient and the Modern Eccentricity $\frac{19}{1000}$ for the true original one; and about $\frac{185}{10000}$ or more nicely $\frac{1846}{100000}$ for the difference between the ancient Semidiameter of the circular Orbit, and the middle distance in the present *Elliptick* one ; (the point of acceleration being about 6 degrees past the *Perihelion*, not just at it, as is before prov'd.) Then by the Golden Rule, as the Cube of 100000, (the middle distance in the *Ellipsis*,) to the Cube of 98154, (the Semidiameter of the Ancient Circle) so is the square of 525949, (the number of minutes in our present Solar year,) to the square of the number of Minutes in the ancient Solar year, whose Root being 511459 minutes, or 355 days 4 hours 19 minutes, appears to be exactly and surprizingly equal to the Lunar year before mention'd.

Coroll. *Upon this* Hypothesis *the Ancient Solar and Lunar year were exactly commensurate and equal; and* 10 *days,* 1 *hour,* 30 *minutes, shorter than the present Solar year. Which last number tho' it be not equal to the Lunar* Epact *at present; is yet rightly assign'd ; each Synodical Month being (by the quicker*
                                                                    angular

*angular revolution of the Earth then) fo much longer,
as upon the whole adjufted, the periods as is above fta-
ted : which on calculation will eafily appear.*

LVII. As Comets agree with Planets in a regular Motion about the Sun, the common Center or *Focus* of our Syftem, fo do they as to their
bulk and magnitude; being, generally fpeaking,
about the bignefs of Planets, as the obfervations
of Aftronomers demonftrate.

LVIII. Befides the Bodies of the Comets themfelves, which are folid, compact, and durable ;
there is round about the fame a vaftly large, thin,
pellucid Fluid; containing withal great quantities of Opake or Earthy Particles; conftituting
together a confufed, irregular, unequally difpos'd, and uncertainly agitated Mafs of Bodies;
whofe Diameter is 10 if not 15 times as long as
that of the Body it felf, and this Mafs is call'd
the *Atmofphere* thereof.

LIX. By reafon of the mutual accefs, and recefs of the Comets to, and from the Sun, their
Atmofpheres are uncapable of attaining, or at
leaft of long retaining any regular and orderly
fituation and difpofition of parts according to the Law of Specifick Gravity. In fhort,
while they are mov'd in fo exceeding Eccentrical Orbits, they can neither acquire, or at leaft
not long preferve, fuch a permanent conftitution
as the Planets have, and as the confervation of
Plants and Animals do neceffarily require, and
are therefore to be look'd upon in their prefent
ftate as uninhabitable.

LX. But in cafe the Orbit of a Comet were
chang'd into that of a Planet, *i. e.* if its Eccentrical *Ellipfis* were turn'd into a Concentrical
Circle, or an *Ellipfis* not much differing therefrom

from; at a fuitable and convenient diftance from the Sun; there is no reafon to doubt but the parts of that confufed Atmofphere which now encompafs it to fuch a prodigious diftance, would fubfide and fettle downwards according to their feveral Specifick Gravities; and both obtain and preferve as fetled, fixt, and orderly a conftitution as a Planet has: Which Conftitution, if the Atmofphere of a Comet were as well predifpos'd for the fame as the original Chaos of a Planet, would produce a Planet as fit for the growth of Vegetables and the habitation of Animals as that on which we live, or any other in the Solar Syftem.

LXI. Befides the Central Solid, or Body of the Comet, and its vaft Atmofphere encompaffing it, there is alfo a long lucid Train, which in the approach to the Sun is by it acquir'd; and appears to be nothing elfe but the Lighteft and Rareft parts of its Atmofphere rarified by the Sun's heat; which becoming thereby lighter than the Sun's own Atmofphere, rife in a mift or fteam of vapours towards the parts oppofite to the Sun; and are call'd the *Tail* of it.

LXII. This immenfe Cylindrical Column of rarifi'd Vapour, tho' its Craffitude or Diameter be ufually more than 400000 miles, is fo very much expanded, and in fo exceeding rare a condition, that the fix'd Stars may be difcern'd quite through the fame.

LXIII. This fo rare, fine, expanded Vapour moves regularly with, and accompanies the Comet it felf in its intire courfe, any way whatfoever; even through the Syftem of the Planets, and that without any difturbance.

Coroll. *The vaft fpaces between, and beyond the Planets are not full of fubtile or ethereal matter;*
but

but either perfectly, or at least sensibly a real vacuum
or void.

LXIV. The *Phænomena* of Comets Motions
suppose and depend on the annual motion of the
Earth , without which they are insoluble. Thus
they sometimes seem to move with greater ,
sometimes with lesser Velocity, than the 'rules
of their own, or indeed any other regular motion require or permit: Nay sometimes they appear to us Stationary and Retrograde: All which,
as in the Planets, will naturally arise from the
motion of the Earth, and of the Spectators Eye
therewith, and is thence exactly deducible ; but
without that *Hypothesis,* cannot be accounted for.
Thus also towards the end of their appearances
they seem to deflect from that great Circle in
which they before were seen to move ; the motion
of the Earth then being more considerable compar'd with that of the Comets ; and so causing a
more sensible *Parallax* or diversity of appearance
than before, while their own motion was so
much swifter: And the same is observable in
their other *Phænomena.*

Corollary. *Hence.arises a convincing argument for
the annual motion of the Earth:Which,as 'twas known
to be necessary to account for the* Phænomena *of Planets before ; so now appears no less so in relation to those
of the Comets. All the Heavenly Motions at last attest-
ing the truth, and establishing the certainty of the same.*

LXV. Some Comets approach in their *Perihelia* so very near to the Sun, that they must be
prodigiously heated and scorch'd thereby ; and
this to such a degree that they may not be intirely cool'd in very many thousands of years.
Thus the last famous Comet 1680, 1681. at its
L   *Perihelion*

Perihelion on the 8th of *December* 1680, suftain'd a degree of heat 28000 times as great as that we feel with us in Summer ; or about 2000 times as intenfe as is that of a red hot Iron. So that, by Mr. *Newton*'s Calculation, if that Comet were as big as our Earth ; as Denfe and Solid as Iron ; and were throughout equally heated to the fore-mention'd degree, 'twould fcarce in our Air be fully cool'd in 50000 years. And by confequence in the vaftly rarer Atmofphere of the Sun, in which the Heavenly Bodies revolve, not under a vaftly longer time.

Corollary 1. *Comets do not wholly confift of va-pours, exhalations, or fuch other diffipable matter, as was formerly fuppos'd : Otherwife they muft have been utterly uncapable of fuftaining any part of fo vio-lent a heat, (which yet we fee they fometimes do) without an intire Diffipation and Diffolution.*

Coroll. 2. *When the Atmofphere of a Comet is chiefly a Fluid, and yet but a fmall part thereof by the utmoft heat capable of rarefaction (which appears from the but fmall diminution of the Atmofphere when the Tail is largeft, and the Heat moft intenfe) 'tis evident that its Fluid is a very different one from thofe we are here acquainted withal. For when the main bulk thereof retains its conftitution and fituation quite through the action of the moft violent heat imaginable; which would diffipate and rarifie all the Watery, and perhaps Earthy parts vifible with us ; it muft, by its mighty denfity, gravity, compactnefs, or fome other property not belonging to Fluids here on Earth, be un-capable of greater expanfion than it has of it felf; and be a Compact, Denfe, or Heavy Fluid, or Mafs of Fluids, of which we have no obvious example ; and for which we have no proper Epithet or Name amongft us.*

Coroll. 3. *Tho' Vapour, or the fmall parts of Wa-ter, be the fooneft fubject to rarefaction ; and the*

Tail

Tail of a Comet, before its approach to the Sun, be therefore perhaps nothing but a mist or steam of such Vapours ; yet may the same Tail after the Perihelion *be in part composed of more gross heavy and opake corpuscles. For when the intenseness of the heat in the* Perihelion *is sufficient to dissolve and rarifie not vapour alone, but Sulphur, Niter, Coal or other Gross and Earthy Steams and Exhalations ; whatsoever of such a Nature the Atmosphere of the Comet contains, will sure be in some sort affected, and elevated with the Vapour into the Tail, upon such an approach of the Comet to the Sun as we are speaking of. Tho' therefore the Tail should be suppos'd in its descent towards the Sun to be pure unmixed Vapour, or Watery Particles, (as withal the outmost regions of the Atmosphere it self in probability are) yet the same Tail after the* Perihelion, *ought to be esteem'd a more Heterogeneous and impure mixture ; especially in the lowest spaces of it, and those parts which are nearest to that Atmosphere it self, from whence the whole does proceed.*

LXVI. The Diurnal Motion of Planets is in it self perfectly diftinct from, and wholly independent on the Annual. This I hope will be universally granted without any necessity of a demonstration.

LXVII. If a *Chaos, i. e.* a confused fluid mass or congeries of heterogeneous Bodies, (suppose it were a Comets Atmosphere, or any other such like irregular *compositum* of mingled corpuscles) in its formation were subject only to an Annual motion about the Sun, without any Diurnal Rotation about an *Axis* of its own ; the Figure thereof would be that of a perfect *Sphere*; as from the uniform force of Gravity, and consequent equilibration of parts on all sides, is easily demonstrable. But if during its Formation it

had

had a Diurnal Rotation about an Axis of its own, the Figure thereof, (by reason of the great velocity and consequent *conatus recedendi à centro motus*, diminishing the force of Gravity at the Equatorial parts) would be that of an *oblate Sphæroid*, such as an *Ellipsis* revolving about its lesser *Axis* would generate.

LXVIII. If a Planet consisted in great measure of an Abyss or Dense Internal Fluid, and a Crust or Shell of Earth plac'd on its Surface; tho' the Diurnal Rotation were not begun at the Formation thereof from a *Chaos*, and so its original figure were *Sphærical*; yet upon the commencing of the said Diurnal Rotation, it would degenerate immediately into that of an *oblate Sphæroid*, and retain it afterward, as well as if it had put on the same at its primary formation.

Corollary. *When therefore the greater quickness of the vibrations of the same* Pendulum, *and the greater gravitation of Bodies near the Poles than the Equator, consequent thereupon, demonstrate the former Regions of the Earth to be nearer its Center than the latter; and that consequently the Figure is that of an* Oblate Sphæroid ; *'tis evident, that either the Diurnal Motion commenc'd before the Original of its present constitution ; or that its internal parts are in some degree Fluid, and so were pliable and alterable on the after commencing of such Diurnal Rotation. And this Corollary extends equally, if not more to* Jupiter ; *whose Diurnal Rotation is quicker than our Earth's, and by consequence its Figure farther from Sphærical. Thus by Mr.* Newton's *Calculation the Diameter of the Equator of the Earth is to the* Axis *thereof only as* 692 *to* 689. *But in* Jupiter, *according to the same Mr.* Newton's *Calculation Corrected, as about* 8 *to* 7. *Which is very considerable and sensible ; and accordingly attested to by the concurrent observations of* Cassini, *and Mr.* Flamsteed. LXIX.

LXIX. If fuch an Upper Cruft or Shell of Earth on the face of the Abyfs, were Fix'd and Confolidated before the Diurnal Rotation thereof commenc'd, it would remain intire, continued, and united all the time of its Sphærical Figure, or all the time it had no other than an Annual revolution. But by the beginning of the Diurnal Rotation ; which would make the furface of the Abyfs and its fuftained Orb of Earth put on the Figure of the *Oblate Sphæroid* before-mention'd ; that Upper Orb muft be ftretch'd, chap'd, and crack'd ; and its parts divided by perpendicular Fiffures. For the Periphery of an *Ellipfis* being larger than that of a Circle where the *Area* is equal ; and the Superficies of a *Sphæroid* generated by its circumvolution, confequently, larger than that of a Sphere generated by the like circumvolution of the Circle, which is the prefent cafe ; that Orb of Earth, 'tis plain, which exactly fitted, and every way enclos'd the Abyfs while it was a Sphere, would be too little and ftraight for it, when it after became a *Sphæroid* ; and muft therefore fuffer fuch Breaches and Fiffures as are here exprefs'd.

LXX. The ftate of Nature in a Planet, conftituted as above, while it had only an Annual revolution, would be as follows.

(1.) By reafon of the fame face of the Planet's refpecting continually the fame *Plaga* of the Heavens, or the fame fixt Stars ; and its continual parallellifm to it felf; all the apparent revolution of the Sun muft depend on the Annual Motion ; and a Day and a Year be all one. This is evident, becaufe, as a Year is truly that fpace in which the Sun feemingly, and the Earth really performs a fingle revolution round the Ecliptick ; fo a Day is truly that fpace in which

L 3 the

the Sun paſſes or appears to paſs from any certain Semi-Meridian to the ſame again once:
Which ſpaces of time are here the very ſame,
and ſo the appellations themſelves Year and Day,
may indifferently and promiſcuouſly be appli'd
thereto.

(2.) The courſe of the Sun and Planets, (for
the fixt Stars were then *Fixt* indeed; having
neither a Real nor Seeming motion) muſt be
contrary to what it has appear'd ſince: Their
Riſing being then in the *Weſt*, and their Setting
in the *Eaſt*: Which, from the way of the preſent Diurnal Rotation, has ſince, as all know,
been quite different.

(3.) There muſt be a perpetual Equinox, or
equality of Day and Night, through the whole
Planet; by reaſon of the Sun's deſcribing each
revolution a great Circle about the ſame, on
which alone ſuch an equality depends.

(4.) The Ecliptick muſt ſupply the place of
an Equator alſo; and the Torrid, Temperate,
and Frigid Zones be almoſt alike diſpos'd with
regard to that Circle, as with us they are with
regard to the real Equator.

(5.) To ſuch as liv'd under or near the ſaid
Ecliptick, the Poles of the World or Ecliptick,
the only ones then in Being, would be at the Horizon; and ſo not elevated or depreſs'd to the
Inhabitants there. But upon the commencing
of a quicker Diurnal Rotation the ſame way
with the Annual. The caſe would be in all
theſe particulars quite different. For,

(1.) By reaſon of the quickneſs of the new
Diurnal, in compariſon of the Ancient and Continued Annual Revolution, Days and Years
would be intirely diſtinct ſpaces of time: The
Sun returning to the ſame Semi-Meridian very
                                              often,

often, while (from one Tropick to another, and fo to the fame again) he appear'd to have compleated his longer Annual period.

(2.) By the Diurnal Rotation of the Planet from *Weft* to *Eaft*, the revolution of the Sun, of the other Planets, and of all the Heavenly Bodies, would be from *Eaft* to *Weft* ; and they would all Rife at the former, and Set at the latter part of the Horizon.

(3.) The perpetual *Equinox* would be confin'd to the Equatorial parts of the Planet; and all other Countries would have longer Days in Summer, and fhorter in Winter, as now obtains in the World: When only *March* 10 and *September* 12 have Day and Night equal to each other through the whole Earth.

(4.) The Ecliptick and Equator would be intirely different ; the latter a Real Circle, or Line, on the Planet ; equally diftant from its own proper Poles : The former, confin'd to the Heavens , and not with refpect to the Planet, eafily to be taken notice of. The Torrid, Temperate, and Frigid Zones would regard the new Equator, and be from it diftinguifh'd and difpos'd almoft in the fame manner as before they were from the Ecliptick, and that with greater nicenefs, and more exact boundaries.

(5.) The Poles of the World which before were to the Inhabitants at or near the ancient Ecliptick, neither elevated nor deprefs'd, but fituate at the Horizon, would feem intirely chang'd, and particularly at the Interfection of fuch ancient Ecliptick, and the fucceeding Northern Tropick, the Northern Pole would appear to be elevated above, the Southern deprefs'd below the Horizon; and the Sun and Planets, whofe Motions were before over the *Vertex*, and at right Angles with the Horizon, would appear inclin'd or bent towards the Southern parts; and that way become oblique, and at unequal Angles with the Horizon for ever after.

Corollary 1. *To the Inhabitants of that place laft mention'd, the beginning of the Night, and of the Autumn; or Sun-fet, and the Autumnal Equinox, would in fuch a Primitive State of a Planet, be exactly Coincident: And* vice verfa, *the place to which they were fo coincident, was that Interfection juft now affign'd, or at leaft under the fame Meridian therewith.*

Coroll. 2. *Such a Planet would be more equally habitable in the Second than in the Firft State. For from the Sphærical Figure of the Planet at firft, the*

Vid.Arg.7: Hypoth. 1. infra.

Central Hot Body, (of which hereafter) would equally reach all the Regions; and the Sun chiefly affect the Torrid Zone; and ftill lefs the Temperate, but leaft of all the Frigid ones; as he does at prefent. So that if any one of thefe Climates, by reafon of the due proportion of heat afforded it from the Sun, were habitable, neither of the other could with any fort of equality be fo too. But when the Figure of the Planet became an oblate Sphæroid, (*as on the commencing of the Diurnal Rotation we have fhew'd it would*) *the proportion of heat would be upon the whole more equable through the feveral Climates of the Planet; the greater vicinity of the Central Hot Body to the Frigid Zones, in fome meafure compenfating the greater directnefs of the Sun's Pofition to the Torrid one; and rendring the compleat furface of the Planet pretty univerfally habitable on account thereof.*

Coroll. 3. *Where the States of External Nature are fo very different (as on the fame Planet before and after its Diurnal Rotation begin, they appear to be) 'tis reafonable to fuppofe, that the Natures, Conftitutions, and Circumftances of Creatures, which were the Inhabitants in fuch different States, muft be suitably*

*suitably and proportionably different from one ano-
ther.*

Coroll. 4. *'Tis therefore, without due allowance
for every thing, very unfafe arguing from one State or
its Circumftances to another ; and very unjuft to conclude things unaccountable or abfurd in one, only becaufe
they are ftrange and unknown to the other State. The
like is to be faid of Phrafes, Defcriptions, or Relations
concerning one, which may eafily be mifunderftood in
the other, without an exact Confideration and Allowance for the Diverfity of things belonging thereto.*

LXXI. If the Atmofphere of a Comet, or
any other fuch a fluid confufed *Chaos*, were by
a regular and orderly Digeftion and Subfidence
brought into a confiftent and durable ftate, the
univerfal Law of fpecifick Gravity muft prevail,
and each Mafs take its place, generally fpeaking, according to it (whether 'twere fluid or
folid) from the Center to the Circumference of
the whole.

LXXII. Fluids are capable of all degrees of
Denfity and fpecifick Gravity, as well as Solids.
Thus the Proportion of the heavieft and lighteft
Fluids, Quickfilver, and Oyl, are nearly as fifteen and one; when yet the Proportion of the
heavieft folid, Gold, and the lighteft Earth or
Mold which we find here, is not quite as ten to
one. On which account 'tis highly reafonable
to allow that poffibly there may be as much Variety and Diverfity in the Fluids belonging to a
Planet, as we fee there is in the Solids thereof.

Corollary. *From thefe two laft* Lemmata, *it appears as reafonable to fuppofe a great part of the internal Conftitution of a Planet to be a Fluid, or Syftem
of Fluids, as to be a Solid or Syftem of firm and
earthly* Strata, *which yet is ufually fuppos'd ; and which*

of

of these Hypotheses *best suits the Constitution of the*
Original Chaos, *and the* Phænomena *of Nature af-*
terward, is in reason to be embrac'd.

LXXIII. In the Formation of a Planet from
a *Chaos*, it muft be much more rare and unufual
to lodge very heavy Fluids near the fuperficiary
Regions, among Bodies of a lighter and rarer
Texture, than Solids equally fo. For the Corpufcles of very denfe and heavy Solids, when
they are once entangled among, and mixed with
others, tho' of very different denfity and fpecifick
Gravity, muft afterward, let the place proper for
Bodies of their weight be never fo much nearer
the Center, lye according to their firft cafual Situation. Thus if you take duft of Gold, Silver,
or Brafs, with Sand, Gravel or Saw-duft, and mix
them, or let them fubfide indifferently together,
as they place themfelves at firft, fo, notwithftanding their different weight, will they be fituate ever after. But in Fluids the cafe is quite
otherwife, for they will obtain their due place,
not only when mixed with Fluids, but with any
folid Corpufcles whatfoever. Nay, befides that,
they will penetrate the Interftices of heavier Bodies than themfelves; and unlefs where they are
firmly confolidated or conjoin'd together, will
fettle into, and fill up the fame, without any
regard to the Situation according to fpecifick Gravity. Fluids are compos'd of moveable, fepara-
ble parts, diffufing, fubfiding, and flowing every where, and thereby will be fo far from refting at Regions too high and remote from the
Center, confidering their fpecifick Gravity, that
how light foever they are, unlefs the earthy
Parts under them be either fixt and confolidated,
or their Interftices already intirely fill'd and fa-
                                                    tur'd

tur'd, they will infinuate themfelves, and by degrees approach as near as poffible to the Center of that Planet to which they belong.

Corollary 1. *Tho' our Earth fhould contain vaft quantities of denfe and heavy Fluids within, as well as like denfe and heavy Solids; yet 'tis more ftrange that we have near the Surface one* Specimen *of the former,* (viz. Quickfilver) *than that we have fo many forts, and fo much larger Quantities of the latter* (the Mineral and Metallick Bodies) *much denfer and heavier than that common Earth among which they are found.*

Coroll. 2. *No Argument can be drawn from the variety of denfe and heavy Solids, and the fingle inftance of a denfe and heavy Fluid, to prove the improbability of a vaft fubterraneous denfe and heavy Fluid, or Syftem of Fluids, on whofe Surface our Orb of Earth may be fuppos'd to rely; if the other* Phœnomena *of Nature require fuch an* Hypothefis.

LXXIV. If a *Chaos* were chiefly compos'd of a denfe Fluid, of greater fpecifick Gravity than its folid dry or earthy Parts, the place of fuch a denfe Fluid upon a regular Formation, would be neareft the Center, and the folid or earthy Mafs would encompafs it round, enclofe it within it felf, and reft upon its Surface; and *vice versâ,* if an Orb of Earth be fituate on the Surface of a Fluid, that Fluid is denfer and heavier than the intire Columns of fuch an Orb of Earth confider'd together.

LXXV. If a Solid be either contain'd in, or fall upon a Fluid of greater fpecifick Gravity than it felf, it will neither fink to the bottom, fubfide intirely within, nor emerge quite out of the fame; but part of it remaining immers'd, the other part will be extant above the Surface of the Fluid;

and

and that in a different degree proportionably to
the different specifick Gravity of the Solid, compar'd with that of the Fluid.

LXXVI. Such a Solid will continue to that
certain depth immers'd in the Fluid before-mention'd, that if the space taken up thereby were
fill'd with the Fluid, that Portion of the Fluid
were exactly equal in weight to the whole Solid.
Thus, if a Cube of Wood or Brass were immers'd in a Fluid of twice its specifick Gravity,
it would one half subside within, and the other
half be extant above the Surface of the Fluid. If
it were immers'd in a Fluid of thrice its specifick Gravity, two thirds of it would be extant,
and but a third part inclos'd within the said Surface, and suitably hereto in all other Proportions
whatsoever. These two Propositions are demonstrated by *Archimedes*, and are the known Foundations of *Hydrostaticks*.

LXXVII. If therefore solid Bodies, equal in
visible Bulk, or taking up equal Spaces, but of
unequal density and specifick Gravity, rest upon
the Surface of a Fluid denser and heavier than
themselves, they must remain immers'd in the
same in different degrees; the heaviest sinking
deepest, and the lightest being the most extant
above the Fluid. Thus, if six several Cubes of
equal apparent Magnitude, made of Gold, Lead,
Silver, Brass, Iron, and Stone, were laid upon the
same Fluid, denser and heavier than any of them,
every one severally would sink so much deeper
as it was heavier, and thereby the upper Surface
arising from them all, become very unequal.

LXXVIII. If upon the first general Digestion
and Separation of Parts in a *Chaos*, the upper
Regions are for the most part compos'd of liquid
or fluid Bodies, with only a few dry, solid, or earthy

Parts

Parts intermixt; the outward Surface, after the
Formation is intirely over, will be smooth and
even, as the Surface of Liqours constantly of
it self is. But if, on the contrary, the quantity
of dry, solid, or earthy Parts be vastly greater
than of the liquid or fluid ones, the Surface will
be rugged and uneven, by the different degree
of the Immersion of the different Columns thereof, in that dense Fluid or Abyss upon which the
Orb is plac'd.

    Corollary 1. *In the former case all the Corpuscles*
will obtain their proper place, (the Fluidity freely per-
mitting their passage) according to their respective spe-
cifick Gravity. But in the latter they must take their
places rather according as they chanc'd to be before si-
tuate, than according as their specifick Gravity would
of it self determine them. The case of that part of the
Lemma, *and of this* Corollary, *being almost the*
same with that before mention'd; where the Dust of
Gold, Silver, or Brass, with Sand, Gravel, or
Saw-dust, are suppos'd to be let fall uncertainly upon a
Fluid heavier than the whole mixed Mass taken toge-
ther; For those Columns where the Gold, and other
Metallick Dust were predominant sinking farthest, and
those where Sand or the other lighter Particles were
so, not so far into the Fluid; the upper Surface must
be uneven, and withal the several Species of Corpus-
cles retain that place where they chanc'd to be at first
dispos'd, without any possibility of recovering any other
which by the Law of specifick Gravity were due to
them.

    Coroll. 2. *If therefore the upper Regions of a*
Chaos, *whose quantity of Liquid is very small in*
comparison of its solid Corpuscles, do subside into a Fluid
of greater specifick Gravity than its own Columns ta-
ken together are; an Orb of earth will be compos'd
on the Surface of the Fluid, and its different Columns
being

*being made up of Bodies of very different Natures and
specifick Gravities, (as must happen in such a confused heterogeneous Mass, as we call a* Chaos, *particularly the Atmosphere of a Comet) that Orb will
sink into the Fluid in different degrees, and thereby
render its Surface unequal, or distinguished into Mountains, Plains, and Vallies. So that by how much any
Column was compos'd of rarer, more porous, and
lighter Bodies, by so much would it produce a higher
Mountain; and in like manner, by how much a
Column was compos'd of more close, fix'd, dense and
solid Bodies, by so much would it produce a lower
Valley; and so* vice versâ, *the higher any Mountain,
the more rare, porous, and light its Column; and the
lower any Valley, the more fix'd, close, dense, and solid
its Column must needs be suppos'd.*

Coroll. 3. *If therefore any Planet be immediately
on its first Formation of an unequal Surface, compos'd
of Mountains, Plains, and Valleys; and the order of its
internal* Strata *be disagreeable to the Law of specifick
Gravity; it has exactly proper Indications to prove,
that the quantity of Fluids in the upper Regions was
originally small in comparison of its earthy Parts,
and that such an uneven Orb is situate on a Fluid
denser and heavier than it self.* [Which case how exactly it corresponds to the known Circumstances of our Earth, is left to the consideration of the
Reader.]

LXXIX. If any of the Heavenly Bodies be
plac'd near a Planet, by the inequality of its
Attraction of the Parts at unequal distances from
it, a double Tide, or Elevation of the Fluids
thereto belonging, whether they be inclos'd
within an Orb of Earth, or whether they be on
its Surface above, must certainly arise, and the
Diurnal Rotation of such a Planet being suppos'd,

pos'd, muſt cauſe ſuch a ſucceſſive Flux and Reflux of the ſaid Fluids, as our Ocean is now
agitated by. Thus, if a d b c be the Earth, and Fig. 7.
b i D h be a Comet, or any one of the Heavenly Bodies plac'd near the ſame, and the upper
Orb of Earth be ſituate above a vaſtly large fluid
Abyſs, the Comet or Heavenly Body will conſiderably more attract the nearer parts about b,
than it does thoſe about the Line d c, or the
middle parts of the Earth; by which Attraction
whereever the Particles attracted are not ſolid,
fixed, and unmoveable, they will be elevated or
raiſed into a Protuberance d b c. In like manner,
the Comet or Heavenly Body will conſiderably
more attract the middle parts near the Line d c,
than thoſe more remote about a, and thereby
occaſion their ſlower Motion towards it ſelf, than
that of the foreſaid middle parts; and conſequently permit them to remain farther off the
Center; or which is all one, to elevate themſelves into the oppoſite Protuberance d a c. And
this Effect not depending on the Situation of the
Fluid under the Orb of Earth, is equally evident
with reſpect to the Atmoſphere and Ocean upon, as any Abyſs beneath the ſame, and ſo
muſt cauſe a double Tide or Elevation of the
Fluids of the Globe. And this double Tide, by
the Diurnal Rotation of the Earth from *Weſt* to
Eaſt, will ſhift continually from *Eaſt* to *Weſt*,
and cauſe that Elevation and Depreſſion of the
Ocean twice each Revolution, which we ſo
wonder at, and take ſo much notice of
amongſt us.

Corollary 1. *When therefore the Vicinity of the*
Moon, and the Vaſtneſs of the Sun's Body, make
their force conſiderable with regard to the Fluids of our
Earth, their ſeveral Attractions muſt produce two ſe-
veral

veral double Protuberances, Tides, or Elevations of the Ocean and Atmosphere thereof; whence must arise very remarkable Phænomena *relating thereto; of which in the following* Corollaries.

Coroll. 2. *The sensible Elevation or Tide would be only double, as if it arose from one of the Luminaries, but such as from the Composition of their attractive Power were to be expected.*

Coroll. 3. *When therefore the* Sun *and* Moon's *Forces unite, or when they are situate in or near the same Line through the Center of the Earth, which happens only at the* New *and* Full Moon, *the Tides must be the greatest; and when their Forces contradict each other, or when they are situate in the middle between the* Now *and* Full, *at the Quadratures, the Tides must be the least. In the former case, the visible Flux and Reflux arises from the Summe; and in the latter, from the* Difference *of their Attractions; and so the Spring-Tides, after the* New *and* Full, *are the result of the Elevation and Depression of both the* Sun *and* Moon *conjoyntly; but the Nepe-Tides, after the Quadratures, the result only of the prevailing Elevation and Depression of the* Moon *above those of the* Sun; *and by consequence, exactly agreeable to experience, much less than the other.*

Coroll. 4. *As if the Luminaries were situate in the* Axis *of the Earth, the Diurnal Revolution would not more expose any places to their force one time than another, and no Reciprocation of Flux and Reflux would arise; so the nearer they are to such a Position, the less must such a Reciprocation be, and the farther from such a Position, the greater. On which account, The Elevation or Tide must be greater after the* Equinoxial New *and* Full Moon, *than after the* Solstitial; *and the highest Spring-Tides be those about* March 10. *and* September 12. *as all Experience attests them to be; and the Situation of the Luminaries*

near

near the Equator of the Earth, and farthest from the Poles, does require.

Coroll. 5. *When by the Vicinity of the* Moon, *the visible Tides follow her Influence; and when withal our Earth in about* 24¾ *Hours, recovers the same Situation with regard to her; 'tis evident, That in the said space, each Part of the Ocean must have twice been elevated, and twice depress'd, or had a double Flux, and double Reflux of its Waters, as all Observation assures us it really has.*

LXXX. The Elevations or Tides caused by two different Bodies at the same distance, are always proportionable to the Quantity of Matter in the same attractive Bodies; as from the force of Gravitation in general, proportionable to the attracting Body, will easily be understood. Thus if a Comet or Planet, whose Quantity of Matter were ten or twelve times as much as the *Moon's*, were at an equal distance with her from the Center of the Earth, the Tides, whether of the internal Abyss, if such there be, or external Air and Water, would be ten or twelve times as high as those she is the cause of with us.

Vid. *Lem.* 7. *prius.*

LXXXI. The Elevations or Tides caused by the same, or an equal Body at various distances, are *reciprocally* in a triplicate Proportion of such distances. Thus if the *Moon* should approach as near again to the Earth's Center, as now she is, the Tides would be eight times as high; if thrice as near, twenty seven times as high; if four times as near, sixty four times as high as those she at her present distance produces.

Corollary 1. *Hence appears (which Mr.* Bentley *has in part also observ'd) a signal Influence of the Divine Providence respecting the Constitution of the World, in placing the Heavenly Bodies at so vast a*

Serm. 8. p. 14.

M

distance

diſtance from each other, and thegreateſt at the greateſt diſtance, that when we conſider it, we cannot but be amazed at it. For had they been ſituate any whit near to one another, they would have cauſ'd prodigious Diſorders; and in particular, ſuch deſtructive Tides, whenever there was vaſt quantities of Fluids, or a great Ocean, that neither Plant nor Animal could have avoided its force, or ſuſtain'd its fury, which by the wiſe placing the Heavenly Bodies at ſo vaſt a diſtance is intirely prevented.

Coroll. 2. The ſame careful Providence is alike, and on the like accounts, conſpicuous in the ſmallneſs of the ſecondary Planets; whoſe nearneſs otherwiſe being ſo great, muſt have been attended by the foremention'd Inconveniences, but is now perfectly ſecure from them. Thus for inſtance, our ſecondary Planet, the Moon, which is ſo near to us, is withal ſo ſmall; (but the

Lem 33. prius.

26th part ſo big as the Earth, not the 700th part ſo big as Saturn, nor the 1400th as Jupiter, nor near the millioneth as the Sun) that the Tides ſo cauſed are but of ſome few Feet in height, very moderate, not at all incommodious, nay in truth very advantagious to us, which in the other ſecondary Planets is alſo no leſs true, and no leſs remarkable.

Fig. 7.

LXXXII. Of the two Protuberances produc'd by the preſence of a Comet, or other Cœleſtial Body, that which is directly towards that Body, as d b c, is larger and higher than the oppoſite one, d a c. This is *à priori* demonſtrable, and found agreeable to experience alſo.

LXXXIII. If ſuch a double Tide were very great, and ſhould on a ſudden be produc'd in a ſubterraneous Abyſs, on whoſe Surface an Orb of Earth, fix'd and conſolidated together, were ſituate, it would raiſe or depreſs the Regions of that Orb, as it ſelf was raiſ'd or depreſs'd; and by by putting on the Figure of an *Oblong Sphæroid*, (such as an *Ellipsis* revolving about its longer *Axis* would generate) and thereby increasing its Surface so much, that the Orb of Earth could not fit and enclose it Uniformly as before, would strain and stretch the said Orb of Earth, would crack and chap it, and cause Fissures and Breaches quite through the same. All which is easily understood from what has been already said of a Case very agreeable to this we are now upon, and so can stand in need of no farther Explication here.

BOOK

BOOK II.

HYPOTHESES.

I. THE Ancient *Chaos*, the Origin of our Earth, was the Atmofphere of a Comet.

This Propofition, however new and furprizing, will, I hope, appear not improbable, when I fhall have fhewn, That the Atmofphere of a Comet has thofe feveral Properties which are recorded of the Ancient *Chaos*: That it has fuch peculiar Properties befides, as lay a rational Foundation for fome of thofe *Phænomena* of our Earth, which can fcarce otherwife be Philofophically explain'd; and that no other Body, or Mafs of Bodies now known, or ever heard of in the World, can ftand in Competition, or fo much as pretend to the fame Character, which it fo agreeably correfponds to: Which will be the defign of, and fhall be compriz'd under the following Arguments.

See the Teftimonies *about the* Chaos *cited at the* first Phæ-nomena *afterward.*

(1.) The Names of thefe two Bodies, or Syftems of Bodies, are exactly the fame, and equally agreeable to the Nature of each of them. The Original *Chaos*, by the Ancient Tradition of the *Phænicians*, was ftil'd, Ἀὴρ ζοφώδης καὶ πνευματώδης, & Πνοὴ Ἀέρος ζοφώδης; in *Englifh*, A dark and ftormy *Atmofphere*. Which Appellation,

tion, (the conftant Character of that Mafs encompaffing the Body of a Comet, and at the
fame time of the old *Chaos*) if we fuppofe it to
have been as fitly by Antiquity appli'd to the
latter, as certainly, Obfervation being judge, it
is to the former; is as proper a one for our prefent purpofe, as could poffibly be defir'd.

(2.) The main bulk of the ancient *Chaos*, and
of the Atmofphere of a Comet, is a Fluid, or Syftem of Fluids. As to the former, 'tis both neceffary to be prefuppos'd in order to the fucceeding Separation, and regular Difpofition of the
Parts; and is confirm'd by all the Accounts of it.
But *Mofes* himfelf being exprefs, I fhall content
my felf with his fingle Teftimony; who not only calls it an *Abyfs*, but gives it the ftile of *Waters*. *Darknefs was upon the face of the deep, and*

Gen. i. 2. *the Spirit of God moved upon the face of the waters.*
Now, that the main part of a Comet's Atmo-
fphere is alfo a Fluid, appears both by its Pellu-
cidnefs, (a thing unufual in Bodies, but fuch as
are, or once were in a fluid Condition) and by
thofe perpetual Changes and Agitation of Parts
within the Regions of it, which in any other
than a Fluid are plainly impoffible; and which
indeed, withal, have hitherto feem'd fo vifible
and remarkable, that thence men were ready to
imagine the whole Mafs to be nothing elfe but a
Congeries of Vapours or Clouds, uncertainly
jumbled together, and as uncertainly diffipated
again.

(3.) The *Chaos* is defcrib'd to have been very
ftormy and tempeftuous; of which fome of the
Ancient Writers take particular notice. To
which thofe frequent and violent Agitations and
Changes, thofe ftrange, uncertain Hurries of
Opake Maffes hither and thither, which the
Phænomena

Phænomena of Comets Atmofpheres prefent us with, moft exactly agree.

(4.) The *Chaos* was a mixed Compound of all forts of Corpufcles, in a moft uncertain confus'd and diforderly State; heavy and light, denfe and rare, fluid and folid Particles were in a great meafure, as it were at a venture, mingled and jumbled together. The Atoms, or fmall confti-tuent Parts of Air, Water, and Earth, (to which, together with Fire, the name of *Element* has been peculiarly appli'd) every one were in eve-ry place, and all in a wild and difturbed Corfu-fion. This is the very Effence, and enters the Definition of a *Chaos*; in which therefore all both do, and muft agree. And if any one care-fully confider the perpetually various Vifage of a Comet's Atmofphere, its vaft Extent, the no manner of Order or Method of its feveral Ap-pearances, and remember that in fome Comets it has in its near approach to the *Sun*, been fcorch'd and burn d by a degree of heat many hundred times as Intenfe as the *Sun*'s is with us in the midft of *Summer*, he will not wonder that I affert the Parts of this Atmofphere to be in a perfectly confus'd and *Chaotick* Condition. One might indeed as well, and as reafonably, expect Order and Method in the ruinous Re-liques of a City burnt to Afhes, or in the Smoke proceeding from the fame, as in feve-ral, at leaft, of thofe Atmofpheres we are fpeak-ing of.

(5.) The ancient *Chaos*, juft before the be-ginning of the fix days Creation, was very dark and caliginous. *Darknefs was upon the face of the deep*, fays the Sacred, and the very fame fay the prophane Writers. Now, when we every Year fee how far that fmall Company of col-lected

Gen. i. 2.

lected Vapours, of which a Cloud confifts, can
go towards caufing darknefs on the Face of the
Earth; we may eafily guefs how thick the Darknefs of the Comet's Atmofphere muft needs be,
when all thofe earthy and watery Corpufcles,
which flying up and down in the vaft Regions
thereof do now fo often, and fo much obfcure
the Comet's central Body, and are here fo very
fenfible; when all thefe, I fay, fhall rife up,
and make a confus'd cloudy Orb on the more
confin'd Surface of the Atmofphere of fome
fcores, if not hundreds of Miles thick, as muft
happen in the beginning of its Formation.
If this be not fufficient to account for this thick
Darknefs on the Face of the Abyfs, 'twill, I imagine,
be difficult to folve it better.

(6.) Our upper Earth, the Product of the ancient *Chaos*, being in all probability founded on
a denfe Fluid or Abyfs, as will appear in the
Sequel, the main part of the Fluid of that ancient *Chaos* by confequence muft have been fuch
a denfe and heavy one as is here mention'd
And indeed, 'tis in it felf but very reafonable,
if not neceffary, to allow the inferior Parts of
a fluid *Chaos*, to have been compos'd of much
denfer and heavier Maffes than the fuperior, or
than Water, the main vifible Fluid of our Globe.
For, if we confider the matter in any fort according to the Law of fpecifick Gravity; all
heavy Fluids muft, at leaft, as certainly be near
the Center, as like heavy Solids; and 'tis but
mechanical to allow that in a confufed Fluid *in
fome meafure*, as well as *exactly* in a digefted
one, the Fluids contain'd in the inner Regions
muft be much heavier than thofe at or near the
outer Surface thereof. But befides, 'twill be
hard to account for the confus'd moving ftate
of

of the earthy Parts, or, which is much the fame, the fluidity of the intire *Chaos*, without allowing a much greater quantity of Fluids in it, than what we now fee with us, the Waters of our prefent Earth; and thofe of a Denfity and Gravity fit to retain their Pofts, as well nearer the Central, as the fuperficiary Parts. And that on this account, (of the Comet's Atmofphere's fixed and denfe Fluid) 'tis peculiarly adapted to the forefaid Defcription of the *Chaos*, is evident by what has been already obferv'd of the fame; to which I refer the *Reader* for fatisfaction.

(7.) Whereas very many, and very confiderable *Phænomena* of Nature, (which Dr. *Woodward* has excellently obferv'd) as well as ancient Tradition, require and fuppofe a Central Fire, or internal Heat diffufing warm and vigorous Steams every way from the Center to the Circumference of the Earth; and whereas 'tis very difficult on the common *Hypothefis*, or indeed on any hitherto taken notice of, to give a Mechanical and Philofophical Solution of the fame: If we will but allow the Propofition we are now upon, and that the Earth, in its *Chaotick State*, was a Comet, a moft eafy and Mechanical Account thereof is hereby given, and the *Phænomena* of Nature rendred plain and intelligible. For a Comet, befides its thinner fluid Atmofphere, confifting of a large, denfe, folid, central Body; and fometimes approaching fo near the *Sun* that the immenfe Heat acquir'd then, tho' fooner failing in the thinner and expos'd Atmofphere, will not do fo in the central Solid, under very many thoufands of Years; nothing can better fuit the cafe of our prefent Earth, than to allow a Comet's Atmofphere to have been her *Chaos*; and the Central Body of the Comet, the Source and

Coroll. 2.
Lem. 65.
prius.
Effay, Part
3. Sect. 1.

Vid. L. m.
65. prius.

and Origin of that Central heat, which our Earth appears still to inclose within it.

(8.) The bigness of Comets and their Atmospheres agrees exactly with the supposition we are now upon. For tho' the Atmospheres are 10 or perhaps 15 times in Diameter as big as the Central Bodies, (which yet have been formerly observ'd to be near the Magnitude of the Planets) and thereby of a much larger capacity than this Argument supposes ; yet if, from that thin, rare, expanded state in which they now are, they were suppos'd to subside or settle close together, and immediately rest upon the Central Body ; as on a Formation they must do ; the intire mass would make much such Bodies in Magnitude, as the Planets are : As Astronomers, from the observations made about them, must freely confess. So that when to all the other inducements to believe these Atmospheres to be the same Masses of Bodies we call *Chao*'s, (from one of which all Antiquity Sacred and Prophane derive the Origin of our Earth) it appears that the Magnitude is also exactly correspondent ; I know not what can be alledg'd to take off or weaken the force of them. Which general conclusion might be confirm'd by some other similitudes between them and the Planets, observable in the succeeding Theory, or probably deduc'd from their *Phænomena*; which I shall not at present insist particularly upon. So that on the whole matter, upon the credit of the foregoing Arguments united together and conspiring to the same Conclusion ; I may, I think, venture to affirm, That as far as hitherto present Nature and Ancient Traditions are known, 'tis very reasonable to believe, that a *Planet* is a *Comet* form'd into a regular and lasting constitution, and

Lem. 57, 58. *prius.*

Vid. Newt. p. 508. & *Corell.* 1. *Solut.* 71. *infra.*

and plac'd at a proper diftance from the Sun in
a Circular Orbit, or one very little Eccentrical ;
and a *Comet* is a *Chaos*, *i. e.* a *Planet* unform'd,
or in its primæval ftate, plac'd in a very Eccentrical one : And I think I may fairly appeal to all
that the moft Ancient Hiftory, or Solid Philofophy can produce hereto relating, in atteftation
to fuch an Affertion. Efpecially confidering
withal,

(9.) Laftly, That there is no other pretender,
no other Mafs of Bodies now known, or ever
related to have been known in the whole Syftem
of Nature, which can ftand in competition, or fo
much as feem to agree to the defcription of the
Ancient *Chaos*, but that which is here affign'd
and pleaded for. Now this I am fecure of, and
all will and muft grant : They cannot but be
forc'd to confefs, that, (the Atmofphere of a
Comet fet afide) they have no other *Idea* of the
Nature and Properties of that Mafs of Bodies
call'd a *Chaos*, but what profane Tradition, with
the concurrence of the Holy Books, afford them ;
without any vifible inftance or pattern in Nature.
Which acknowledgement, join'd to the remarkable correfpondence of the particulars before-
mention'd ; and the no objection of any moment, as far as I fee, to be produc'd to the contrary ; is, I think, a mighty advantage in the prefent cafe. All that can reafonably be requir'd
farther is, that the *Phænomena* of the Earth, to be
fuperftructed on this foundation, and deriv'd fucceffively through the feveral Periods, to the confummation of all things, prove coincidents to
this *Hypothefis*, and confirm the fame : Which
being the attempt of the following Theory, muft
be by no means here pretended to before-hand ;
but left to the Impartial Judgment of the Reader,
when

when he is arriv'd at the end of his Journey, and digested the whole Scheme. From the intire and conjoint View whereof, and not from any particulars by the way occasionally reflected on, a prudent and well-grounded Sentence is to be pass'd upon it, and upon several of the *prior* Conclusions themselves also. However, when here is a known and visible foundation to depend on; and the Reader is refer'd to no other *Chaos* than what himself has seen, or, 'tis probable, may in a few years have opportunity of seeing; it must be at the least allow'd a fair and natural procedure, and of the consequences whereof every thinking and inquisitive Person will be a proper Judge. The reasonings proceeding, without begging any precarious *Hypothesis* at first, of the nature of that old fund and promptuary whence all was to be deriv'd, or sending the Reader to the utmost Antiquity for his Notion thereof; to which yet, in the most Authentick accounts of the Primitive *Chaos* now extant, I fear not to appeal, and submit my self.

II. The Mountainous Columns of the Earth are not so dense or heavy as the other Columns.

This Proposition will also I imagine, be new and unexpected to very many; but I hope the following Arguments, which I shall very briefly propose, will demonstrate it to be no unreasonable or precarious one.

(1.) Mountains are usually Stony and Rocky, and by consequence lighter than the main Body of the Earth. For tho' Stone be somewhat heavier than
the

the uppermoft *Stratum* or *Garden Mold*, as fome ftile it; yet 'tis confiderably lighter than that beneath the fame. For if we compare its weight with that in the bottom of our Mines, which is alone confiderable to our purpofe, (our upper *ftrata*, as will hereafter appear, being generally factitious, or acquir'd at the Univerfal Deluge) we fhall be forc'd to own the neceffity of the confequence of the prefent Argument. The Specifick Gravity of Stone, is to that of Water, as 14 to $5\frac{1}{3}$, but the Specifick Gravity of the Earth at the bottom of our Mines, is to that of Water, as 3 to 1, fometimes as 4 to 1, nay fometimes almoft as 5 to 1, and therefore to be fure confiderably Denfer and Heavier than Stone. So that were the Mountainous Columns of the Earth intirely made up of Stone, they would, (without the confideration of thofe empty Caverns they inclofe) be plainly the lighteft parts of the whole Earth.

Newt. p. 417.

(2.) Thofe very Denfe and Heavy Corpufcles of Gold, Lead, Silver, and other fuch like Metals and Minerals, are moftly, if not only, found in the Bowels of Mountains. Now, when the Gravity of thefe Bodies is fo great, that in a regular formation they ought to have feated themfelves, one would think, much nearer the Center, than they now are; to account for fuch their pofition, it muft be fuppos'd, that the Columns under them, and the Earth among them, were lighter and rarer than the Neighbouring Columns did afford; that upon the whole, the intire *Compofitum* or Mafs taken together, may be allow'd to be, if not lighter, yet, at leaft, not heavier than others at the fame diftance from the Center. So that by a juft, tho' a little furprizing way of reafoning, from the greater weight of fome parts of the Mountainous Columns, the lefs weight of the whole is infer'd. (3.)

(3.) Mountains are the principal Source and Origin of Springs and Fountains. Now Dr. *Woodward*, from his own obfervations, afferts, That thefe are neither deriv'd from Vapours condens'd in the Air at the Tops of Mountains, nor from meer Rains, or fall of Moifture, as feveral have differently afferted ; but from the Waters in the Bowels of the Earth ; and that 'tis a Steam or Vapour rais'd by the Subterraneous Heat which affords the main part of their Waters to them. On which Hypothefis, which I take to be the trueft, and moft rational of all others, the Vapours appear to have a more free and open vent or current up the Mountainous Columns, than the neighbouring ones; and confequently, They are more rare, laxe and porous, or lefs denfe and weighty than the others.

(4.) All *Volcano*'s, or fubterraneous Fires, are in the Bowels of fome Mountain, to which a Plain or a Valley was never known to be liable. Which obfervation affords a double Argument for fuch a levity and rarenefs as we are now contending for: The One, from the temper of an inflammable Earth, Sulphureous and Bituminous; which being in part made up of Oily Particles, the lighteft Fluid we have, muft in likelihood be the lighteft of all *Strata* whatfoever. The other, from the free admiffion of Air into the Bowels of thefe Mountains; without which no Fire or Flame can be preferv'd: Which alfo infers fuch a porofity and laxenefs as we are now concern'd to prove.

(5.) Mountainous Countries are chiefly fubject to Earthquakes, and confequently are as well Sulphureous and Inflammable, as Hollow and Cavernous, Loofe and Spungy in their inward parts ; without which properties the *Phænomena*
of

of Earthquakes were difficultly accountable : Especially according to Dr. *Woodward's Hypothesis* of them; who deriving them from steams of Subterraneous heat ascending from the Central parts, and collected in great quantities together, must by consequence own that the Bowels of Mountains, so commonly subject to Earthquakes, are most Pervious, Porous, and Cavernous of all other. All which Arguments, especially taken together with some other coincidences hereafter observable, will, I hope, be esteem'd no inconsiderable evidence of the Truth of the Proposition we are now upon.

Essay. p. 134,&c.

III. Tho' the *Annual Motion* of the Earth commenc'd at the beginning of the *Mosaick* Creation ; yet its *Diurnal Rotation* did not till after the Fall of Man.

Tho' I cannot but expect that this will appear the greatest *Paradox,* and most extravagant Assertion of all other, to not a few Readers ; yet I hope to give so great evidence for the same from Sacred as well as Prophane Authority , that competent and impartial Judges shall see reason to say, that if it be not sufficient to force their assent, yet 'tis such as they did not expect in so surprizing, remote, and difficult a case ; the Records relating to which (the Sacred Ones excepted) are so few, so dubious, and so ancient; and the constant opinion of the World, within the Memory of History, so fixt and setled on the contrary side. Let it only be, by way of Preparation, remark'd, That the Annual and Diurnal Motions are in themselves wholly

Lem. 66. prius.

wholly independent on each other, as was before
taken notice; and consequently, that 'tis as rational to suppose the former without the latter, if
there be evidence for the same, in the Original
State of Nature, as 'tis to believe them capable
of being conjoin'd, from the known *Phænomena*
of the World, in the present state. Let it also
be observ'd, that there is yet no evidence
that either the Central Bodies of any of the
Comets, or that even several of the Planets,
who undoubtedly have an Annual Motion about
the Sun, have yet any Diurnal Rotation about
Axes of their own: And let it, lastly, be consider'd,
that when the Diurnal Rotation must have an
Original, a time when it began; that time may
as rationally and naturally be suppos'd after the
Fall, as before the Creation, or Six days Work;
and which was the true and real one, must be
determin'd by the Testimonies of Antiquity, or
other Collateral Arguments to be from thence,
or from the *Phænomena* of Nature Ancient or
Modern, deriv'd and infer'd. Which things beings suppos'd, I thus attempt to prove the present
Assertion; If the Primitive State of Nature before the Fall, had those peculiar *Phænomena* or
Characters which certainly belong to a Planet before its Diurnal Rotation began; and are as certainly impossible in the present state of the Earth
revolving about its own *Axis*; 'tis plain the Assertion before us is true and real: But that
those peculiar *Phænomena* or Characters did belong to that Primitive State, the Testimonies of
Sacred and Profane Antiquity, to be presently
produc'd, do make appear; and by consequence
the Assertion before us is true and real. The
Phænomena or Peculiar distinguishing Characters
here intended have been already mention'd, and
are

are thefe five. (1.) A Day and a Year are all one. (2.) The Sun and Planets Rofe in the *Weſt* and Set in the *Eaſt.* (3.) There was through the whole Earth a perpetual *Equinox.* (4.) The Ecliptick and Equator were all one ; or rather the latter was not in Being, but all the Heavenly Motions were perform'd about the fame invariable *Axis,* that of the former. (5.) To fuch as liv'd under the Ecliptick, the Poles of the fame (or of the World , they being then not different,) were neither elevated nor depreſt, but at the Horizon. Thefe are the certain and undeniable Characters of fuch a ſtate : And that they belong'd to the Primitive State of our Earth, before the Fall, I am now to prove.

(1.) In the Primitive ſtate of the World Days and Years were all one. Which Aſſertion I endeavour to Evince by the following Arguments. (1.) On this *Hypotheſis* the Letter of *Moſes* is as exactly followed as in the contrary one. 'Tis agreed that *Moſes* calls the ſeveral Revolutions of the Sun, in which the Creation was Perfected, *Days,* every where in that Hiſtory. Now as a *Year* is properly the fucceſſion of the four ſeveral Seaſons, Spring, Summer, Autumn and Winter, ariſing from *one ſingle* Revolution of the Earth about the Sun ; fo a *Day* is the fucceſſion of Light and Darkneſs *once* ; or the ſpace of *one ſingle* apparent Revolution of the Sun from any certain Semimeridian, above or below the Horizon, till its return thither again. Now in the cafe before us, both thefe Periods are exactly coincident ; and both are perform'd in the fame ſpace of time : Which ſpace therefore in equal propriety of ſpeech belongs to either or both thofe names indifferently ; and by confequence, may with the exacteſt Truth and Propriety be ſtil'd a

Day

Day or a Year. Which thing duly confider'd, if I had no pofitive evidence for the Propofition before us, yet, fetting afide prepoffeffion, I had an equal right and pretence to Truth with the Common Expofitors; i keeping equally clofe to the Letter of the Sacred Hiftory. (2.) This *Hypothefis* gives a rational account of the Scripture ftile, wherein a *Day*, even in after Ages, very frequently denotes a *Year*; as is commonly taken notice of by Expofitors. Thus by *Mofes* himfelf the Word *Day* is not only, in the very recapitulation of the Creation, us'd for the intire *Six*; (*Thefe are the Generations of the Heavens and of the Earth when they were Created, in the Day that the Lord God made the Earth and the Heavens, and every Plant of the Field before it was in the Earth, and every Herb of the Field before it grew.*) But, in other places, as it feems, for the juft fpace of a *Year. And at the end of Days, or after fome Years, it came to pafs, that Cain brought of the fruit of the ground an offering unto the Lord. The days of Adam after he had begotten Seth were eight hundred years. And all the days that Adam lived were nine hundred and thirty years, and he died.* And fo of the reft of the Genealogies in that Chapter. Thus in others of the Holy Writers, *I will give thee ten fhekels of Silver by the days,* i. e. *per annos,* by the *years,* or every *year.* Thus what in one place is, *Jofhuah waxed Old, and came into Days;* is in another, *Jofhuah was old, and ftricken in years.* The like phrafes we have of *David; the number of Days that David was King in Hebron, over the houfe of Judah, was feven Years and fix months. The Days that David reigned over Ifrael were forty years.* So, what was in the Law, *Bring your Tyths after three Years;* is in the Prophet, *Bring your Tyths after three Days.* Which ways of fpeaking, with others that follow,
may

Gen ii,
4, 5.

Cap. iv. 3.

Cap. v. 4, 5.

Jud. xvii.
10.
Jofh. xiii.
1.
Cap. xxiii.
1.
2 Sam. ii.
11.
1 King. ii.
11.
Deut. xiv.
28.
Amos iv.
4.

may feem alluded to, and explain'd by thefe two, tho' themfelves fomewhat of a different nature. *Your children,* fays God to the Ifraelites, *fhall wander in the Wildernefs forty Years; after the number of the Days in which ye fearched the land, even forty Days, each Day for a Year, fhall you bear your iniquities, even forty Years.* Lye thou, fays God to the Prophet *Ezekiel, on thy left fide, and lay the iniquity of the houfe of Ifrael upon it; according to the number of the Days that thou fhalt lye upon it, thou fhalt bear their iniquity: For I have laid upon thee the Years of their iniquity, according to the Number of the Days, three hundred and ninety Days; fo fhalt thou bear the iniquity of the houfe of Ifrael. And when thou haft accomplifh'd 'em, lye again on thy right fide; and thou fhalt bear the iniquity of the houfe of Judah forty Days; I have appointed thee a Day for a Year.* But what I mainly and principally intend here is, that known, frequent and folemn way in the Prophetick Writings of determining *Years* by *Days;* the inftances of which are very obvious, fome whereof I fhall here barely quote for the Reader's fatisfaction; (and more in a cafe fo notorious and remarkable need not be done.) *How long fhall be the vifion concerning the daily facrifice, and the tranfgreffion of defolation, to give both the Sanctuary, and the Hoft to be trodden under foot? And he faid unto me, Unto two thoufand three hundred Days; then fhall the Sanctuary be cleanfed. From the time that the daily facrifice fhall be taken away, and the abomination that maketh defolate be fet up, there fhall be one thoufand two hundred and ninety Days. Bleffed is he that waiteth, and cometh to the one thoufand three hundred five and thirty days. But go thou thy way till the end be; for thou fhalt reft, and ftand in thy Lot at the end of the days. I will give power unto my two witneffes, and they*

Marginal references:
Num. xiv. 33, 34.

Ezek. iv. 4, 5, 6.

Dan. viii. 13, 14.

Cap. xii. 11, 12, 13.

Apoc. xi. 3.

Cap. xii.6. *they shall prophecy one thousand two hundred and sixty days, cloathed in sack-cloth. The Woman fled into the Wilderness, where she hath a place prepared her of God, that they should feed her there, one thousand two hundred and sixty days.* Agreeably whereto a *Week* consisting of *seven days*, denotes *seven years*; and a *Month*, consisting of *thirty days*, denotes *thirty years*, in the same Prophetick Writings. Thus in that most famous of all Prophecies, concerning the death of the *Messias*. Dan. ix. 24.25,26. *Seventy Weeks are determin'd upon thy people, and upon thy holy city; to finish the transgression, and to make an end of sins, and to make reconciliation for iniquity, and to bring in everlasting righteousness, and to seal up the vision and prophecy, and to anoint the most Holy. Know therefore and understand, that from the going forth of the commandment to restore and to build Jerusalem, unto the Messiah the Prince, shall be seven weeks, and sixty and two weeks; the street shall be built again, and the wall, even in a straight of times. And after the sixty and two weeks shall Messiah be cut off: but not for himself. The Holy City shall they tread underfoot* Apoc. xi. 2. Cap. xiii. 5. *forty and two months. Power was given to the Beast to continue forty and two months.* All which expressions, with others of the same nature, are not accountable; I mean there is no satisfactory reason can be given why a *Day* should so frequently denote a *Year* in the Sacred Writings, on any other *Hypothesis*. We usually indeed content our selves in these cases with the bare knowing the meaning of Scripture expressions, as if they were chosen at a venture; and so, for instance, finding a *Day* to represent a *Year* in the same Books, we rest satisfi'd, without enquiring why a *Day* rather than an *Hour*, a *Week*, or *Month*, (the two latter of which terms are yet us'd by these Authors) were pitch'd upon to signifie the before-mention'd space to us;

or

or why if the word *Day* muft be made ufe of,
it muft mean a determinate juft *Year*, rather than
a *Week*, a *Month* or a *Thoufand Years*, (for which
laft it yet feems fometimes to be taken) fo frequently in the Sacred, efpecially the Prophetick Pf. xc. 4.
Writings. But 'tis very fuppofable, that 'tis our 2 Pet.iii.8.
Ignorance or Unskilfulnefs in the Stile of Scrip- Gen· ii.17.
ture, and thofe things therein deliver'd (not the
Inaccuracy of the Writers themfelves) which
occafions our fo laxe and general Interpretations.
It will fure at leaft be allow'd me, that wherever
not only the Meaning of Phrafes, but the Original and Foundation of fuch their Meaning is
naturally and eafily affignable, an account thereof is readily to be embrac'd. And certainly the
Primitive *Years* of the World being once fuppos'd
to have been *Days* alfo ; and call'd by that name
in the Hiftory of the Creation ; this matter will
be very eafie ; the fucceeding Stile of Scripture will appear only a continuation of the Primitive, and fitted to hint to us a time wherein a
Day and a *Year* were really the fame: And this
without any diminution of the true defigns of
the Prophetick numbers ; I mean the involving
their Predictions in fo much, and no more obfcurity, as might conceal their meaning till their
completion, or till fuch time at leaft as the Divine Wifdom thought moft proper for their manifeftation in fucceeding Ages. So that this Argument demonftrates the prefent Expofition to
afford a natural foundation of accounting for
fuch ways of fpeaking in the Holy Scriptures,
which otherwife are, as to their Occafion and
Original, unaccountable; and confequently,
proves it to be as truly agreeable to the *Stile*, as
the former did to the Letter thereof. (3.) The
fix *Days* of Creation, and the feventh of Reft,

were, by Divine Command, to be in after Ages commemorated by *Years* as well as by *Days*; and so in reason answered alike to both those denominations. 'Tis evident, that the Works of

Gen. ii. 1, 2, 3.

the Creation were compleated in six *Evenings* and *Mornings*, or six Revolutions of the Sun, call'd *Days*; and that the seventh was immediately set apart and sanctified as a *Day* of Rest, and Memorial of the Creation just before compleated ; and 'tis evident that this Sanctification of the seventh, as well as the operations of the six foregoing, belong'd to the Primitive state of the World, before the Fall. Now that we may know what sort of *Days* these were, 'twill be proper to enquire into the ensuing times ; and observe, after the distinction of *Days* and *Years* undoubtedly obtain'd, what constant Revolutions of six for Work, and a seventh for Rest there appear ; or in what manner, and by what spaces these Original ones were commemorated; which will go a great way to clear the Point we are upon. And here, 'tis evident, that when God gave Laws to the *Israelites*, he allow'd them six ordinary Days of Work, and ordain'd the seventh for a *Day* of Rest or Sabbath, in Imitation and Memory of His Working the first six, and Resting or keeping a Sabbath on the Seventh *Day*, at the Creation of the World. This the Fourth Commandment so expresly asserts, that 'tis past possibility of question. 'Tis moreover, evident that God, upon the Children of *Israel's* coming into the Land of *Canaan*, ordained (with reference, as 'tis reasonable to suppose, to the same

Lev. xxv. 3, 4.

Primitive State of the World, the six Days of Creation and the Sabbath) That six *Years* they should Sow their Fields, and six *Years* they should Prune their Vineyard, and gather in the Fruits thereof; But

But in the feventh *Year* fhould be a Sabbath of Reft unto the Land, a Sabbath for the Lord: They were neither to Sow their Field, nor Prune their Vineyard: Then was the I and to keep a Sabbath unto the Lord. So that if we can juftly prefume that the primary fpaces of the World, here refer'd to, were proper *Evenings* and *Mornings*, or Natural *Days*, becaufe they were reprefented and commemorated by fix Proper and Natural *Days* of Work, and the feventh of Reft: I think 'tis not unreafonable to conclude they were Proper and Natural *Years* alfo; confidering they appear to have been among the fame People, by the fame Divine Appointment, reprefented and commemorated by thefe fix Proper and Natural *Years* of Work, and the feventh of Reft alfo. Nay, if there be any advantage on the fide of Natural *Days*, from the exprefnefs of the reference they had to the Primitive ones (which the Fourth Commandment forces us to acknowledge) there will appear in what follows fomewhat that may juftly be efteem'd favourable on the fide of *Years*. Befides the fix *Days* for Work, and the feventh for Reft, the *Jews* were commanded (on the fame account, as we may juftly fuppofe) to number from the Paffover feven times feven *Days*, or feven Weeks of *Days*, and at the conclufion of them to obferve a folemn Feaft, call'd the Feaft of Weeks or of Sabbaths, once every year. In like manner befides the *Yearly* Sabbath as I may call it, or the feventh *Year* of Reft and Releafe after the fix *Years* of Work, the *Jews* were commanded (on the fame account, as we may juftly fuppofe) to number feven Sabbaths of *Years*, feven times feven *Years*; and at the conclufion thereof to celebrate the great Sabbatical *Year*, the *Year* of *Jubilee*: They

ver. 1.
Vid. Deut.
xv.

Lev. xxiii.
15--21.

Cap. xxv.
3--16.

N 4   were

were neither to Sow, nor Reap, nor Gather
in the Grapes, but esteem it Holy, and suffer
every one to return to his Possession again.
Where that which is remarkable is this, that
when the Sabbatical *Days,* and Sabbatical *Years*
equally return'd by perpetual revolutions
immediately succeeding one another; yet the
case was not the same as to the Feast of
Weeks at the end of seven times seven *Days*;
that following the Passover, and not returning
till the next Passover again, and so was but
once a Year: Whereas its corresponding Solem-
nities, the *Jubilees,* or great Sabbatical *Years,* at
the end of seven times seven *Years,* did, as the
former, return by perpetual revolutions immediately succeeding one another for all future Generations. All which duely consider'd, I think
upon the whole, 'tis but reasonable to conclude,
That seeing the Primitive spaces, or periods of
Work and Rest, appear, by Divine Appointment, to have been commemorated among the
Jews by *Years* as well as by *Days*; the same Primitive spaces or periods were equally *Days* and
Years also. (*4.*) The Works of the Creation, by
the Sacred History, concurring with Ancient
Tradition, appear to have been leisurely, regular, and gradual, without any precipitancy or
acceleration by a Miraculous hand on every occasion : Which is impossible to be suppos'd in
those *Days* of twenty four short hours only; but
if they were as long as the present *Hypothesis* supposes, they were truly agreeable and proportionable to the same productions. Which consequence will be so easily allow'd me, that I
may venture to say, That as certain as is the regular and gentle, the natural and leisurely procedure of the Works of the Creation (of which I
know

know no good Reafon from any Warrant facred
or prophane to make any queftion) fo certain is
the Propofition we are now upon, or fo certainly the Primitive *Days* and *Years* were all one.
(5.) Two fuch Works are by *Mofes* afcrib'd to
the third *Day*, which (if that were not longer
than one of ours now) are inconceiveable and
incompatible.   On the former part of this *Day*   Gen. i.
the Waters of the Globe were to be drain'd off   9—13.
all the dry Lands into the Seas; and on the fame
Day afterward, all the Plants and Vegetables were
to fpring out of the Earth. Now the Velocity of
running Waters is not fo great, as in a part of
one of our fhort *Days*, to defcend from the middle
Regions of the dry Land into the Seas adjoyning to them; nor if it were, could the Land be
dry enough in an inftant for the Production of
all thofe Plants and Vegetables, which yet we
are affur'd appear'd the fame *Day* upon the face
of it; which Difficulties vanifh, if we allow the
primitive *Days* to have been *Years* alfo, as will
more fully be made appear in due place. (6.)
Whatever might poffibly be faid of the other
Days works, by recurring to the Divine miraculous Power; (which yet is here not only unnecef-
farily, and without warrant from the Sacred Hiftory it felf, but fometimes very *indecently* done)
yet the numerous Works afcrib'd to the fixth *Day*
plainly fhew, That a fpace much longer than we
now call a *Day*, muft have been referr'd to in
the Sacred Hiftory.   The bufinefs of the fixth
Day includes evidently thefe following particulars.
(1.) The Production of all the bruit dry-land
Animals. (2.) The Confultation about, and the   Gen. i. &
actual Creation of the Body, and Infufion of the   ii.
Soul of *Adam*.   (3.) The Charter or Donation of
Dominion over all Creatures beftow'd on *Adam*.
(4.) The

(4.) The Exercise of Part of that Dominion, or the giving Names to all the dry-land Animals; which sure suppos'd some acquir'd knowledge in *Adam*, some Confideration of the Nature of each Species, some skill in Language, and the ufe of Words; and withal, fome proportionable Time for the gathering fo great a number of Creatures together, and for the diftinct naming of every one. (5.) When on this review it appear'd, that among all thefe Creatures there was not a Meet-help, or fuitable Companion for him; God then caft him into a deep Sleep, (which 'tis probable lafted more than a few minutes to deferve that Appellation) took out one of his Ribs, clofed up the Flefh inftead thereof, and cut of that Rib made the Woman. (6.) After this God brings this Woman to *Adam*, he owns her Original, gives her an agreeable Name, takes her to Wife, and they together receive that Penediction, Increafe and Multiply. (7.) God appoints them and their Fellow-Animals, the Vegetables for Food and Suftenance.

Vid *Bifhop* Patrick on *Gen.* in Initio. *Gen.* ii. 4, &c.

All which (to omit the *Jews* Tradition of the Fail of Man this fixth *Day*, and fuch things prefuppos'd thereto which muft belong to it, even by the *Mofaick* Hiftory it felf) put together, is vaftly more than is conceivable in the fhort fpace of one fingle Day in the vulgar Senfe of it. 'Tis true, God Almighty can do all things in what portions of Time he pleafes. But 'tis alfo true,

On *Gen.* 3. init.

(as Bifhop *Patrick* well obferves in a like cafe) that Man cannot. He muft have time allotted him, in proportion to the bufinefs to be done, or elfe 'tis not to be expected of him. And 'tis plain, That *Adam* and *Eve* were mainly concern'd in the latter Actions of this *Day*: fo that by a juft and neceffary confequence, That *Day*

in

in which *they* went through fo many and different Scenes, and perform'd fo many Actions, requiring at leaft no fmall part of a *Year*; and that
after themfelves and all the dry-land Animals had
been on the fame *Day* produc'd, was certainly fuch
a *Day* as might be proportionate to fuch Operations, and not fhorter than a *Year*, which the prefent *Hypothefis* allows in the cafe. (7.) If the
Hiftory of the Fall of Man be either included
in the fixth *Day*, according to the Ancient Tradition of the *Jews*, which I confefs to be very
improbable; or belong to the feventh, as might,
by coming as near as poffible to fuch old Tradition, more probably be allow'd: On either of
thefe Suppofitions, there is the greateft neceffity
imaginable of fuppofing fuch a *Day* much longer than is commonly done. Which I think
is of it felf fo plain, that I need not aggravate
the matter, but leave it to the free Confideration of the *Reader*. All which Arguments to
me appear very fatisfactory, and evince, that
the firft diftinguifhing and peculiar Character
of fuch a primitive State of Nature as was before-mention'd did really belong to our Earth
before the Fall, and that then a *Day* and a
Year were exactly one and the fame fpace of
Time.

(2.) In the primitive State of the World the
Sun and *Planets* rofe in the *Weft*, and fet in the
Eaft, contrary to what they have done ever
fince. This may feem to have been the foundation of that Story in *Herodotus*, who tells us, Lib. 2.
That the *Sun*, in the fpace of 10340 Years, four cap. 142.
times inverted his Courfe, and rofe in the *Weft*.
But what I mainly depend on, is that Difcourfe
in *Plato*, who relating fome very ancient Tradi- *Archæol.* p.
tions about the primitive State of things, and 250, 251,
what 252.

what a mighty and remarkable Change was effected by a certain mighty and remarkable Alteration in the Heavenly Motions, (which Alteration in general deserves also to be taken notice of, as agreeing so well with the present *Hypothesis*) the most surprizing, and of the greatest consequence of all others, and the cause of suitably surprizing and considerable Effects in the present State of Nature, makes it to be this change of the Way or Course of the Heavenly Bodies, which is the consequence of the present Assertion. For this grand thing of which he had spoken so highly, is this, Ἐστι ⳤ ἔν δὴ τῦτ αὐτὸ, Ίἠν τῦ παντὸς φορὴν, ποτὲ μὰ, ἐϕ᾽ ἃ ϝῦ κινεῖϑ᾽, φέρεῖς, ποτὲ δ᾽ ἐπὶ τ᾽ἀναντία. *The Motion of the Universe sometimes revolves the same way that it does now, and sometimes the contrary way.* Which Testimony is very plain, and full to our present purpose.

(3.) In the primitive State of Nature there was a perpetual *Equinox*, or Equality of Day and Night through the World. This *Phænomenon*, or such Effects as in part suppose it, is usually by the Christian Fathers applied to the Paradisiacal State; and by the Ancient Heathens to the Golden Age, or the Reign of *Saturn*: (coincident, 'tis probable, at least in part, thereto) For they all with one consent deny that the *Sun*'s Course was oblique from one Tropick to another, or that the difference and inequality of Seasons, which must have followed therefrom, did belong to that first and most happy State of the World, as may at large be seen the places quoted in the Margin, too long here to Transcribe; to which therefore I refer the *Reader*, and proceed.

Dicor. lib. 2. cap. 1. & 10. *Archæol.* lib. 2. cap. 5. & 6.

(4.) In

(4.) In the primitive State of the World, there was no Equator diſtinct from the Ecliptick; all Motions were perform'd about one invariable *Axis*, that of the latter ; (for the Plains of the Planet's Orbits, I conſider as nearly coincident with that of the Ecliptick) without the Obliquity of one Circle or Motion to another. Tho' this be ſomewhat related to the former particular, yet I ſhall diſtinctly quote a Teſtimony or two directly belonging hereto, and not ſo properly reducible to the other. The firſt is that of *Anaxagoras*, who ſays, Τὰ δ' ἄϛϱα ϗατ' ἀϱχὰς μὲν ϑολοειδῶς ἐνεχϑῆναι, ὥϛε ϗτ κορυϕὴν τ̃ γῆς τ̃ ἀεὶ ϕαινόμενον ῖ) πύλον. That *the Stars in their primitive State revolv'd in a Tholiform manner, inſomuch, that the Pole appear'd perpetually at the* Vertex *of the Earth.* Whoſe meaning, tho' ſomewhat obſcure, ſeems to be, That the Motion of the Heavens was originally about one Center or *Axis*, that of the Ecliptick, whoſe Pole was continually over againſt the ſame Point of the Earth; which on the *Hypotheſis* before us is true, but in the preſent Frame of Nature impoſſible. The next Author, whom I ſhall produce, is *Plato*, who in the foremention'd Diſcourſe about the Ancient and Modern States of the World, ſays, That in the former of them the Motion of the Heavens was uniform, which thing was the cauſe and original of the Golden Age, and of all that happineſs which therein Mankind enjoy'd, or external Nature partook of; which, how well it ſuits the preſent *Hypotheſis*, I need not ſay. All that exceeding happy State of Nature, which innocent Man enjoy'd, beyond what he does ſince the Fall, being therein owing to ſuch a Conſtitution of the World as this Author intimates, and I am now proving. Which in the laſt place, ſhall be

Theor. lib. 2. cap. 10. p. 293.

Archæol. p. 251.

Ibid. p.
273.

be confirm'd from *Baptista Mantuanus,* who says,
(relating the Opinion of the old Aftonomers)
All the Cœleftial Spheres were in the beginning
of the World concentrical and uniform in their
Motion; and the *Zodiack* of the *Primum Mobile,*
and that of the Planets (the Equator and Ecliptick) were united and coincident, by which
means all fublunary Bodies were more vivid and
vigorous at that time than in the prefent Ages of
the World; as the *Theorift* fums up the force of his
Teftimony, very agreeably to the *Hypothefis* before
us, of the Aftronomy in the primitive State of the
Heavens.

(5.) To the firft Inhabitants of the Earth,
(dwelling at the Interfection of the ancient
Ecliptick with the prefent *Northern* Tropick; of
which hereafter) the Poles of the World were
Hypoth. 4.
infra.
neither elevated nor deprefs'd, but at the Horizon. But fometime after the Formation of things,
they fuddenly chang'd their Situation; the *Northern* Pole appear'd to be elevated above, and
the *Southern* deprefs'd below the Horizon; and
the Courfe of the Heavens feem'd bent or inclin'd to the *Southern* Parts of the World; or in
plain words, there was a new Diurnal Rotation
began about the prefent *Axis* of the Earth;
which I take to be the true and eafy Expofition of the fame *Phænomena.* This Matter is
much infifted on by the Ancients, and being fo,
will fully confirm our Affertion, and give light
and ftrength to fome of the former Teftimonies.
Theor. lib.
2. cap. 10.
Plutarch has a Chapter entituled, Περὶ Ἐγκλίσεως
Γῆς, Of the Inclination of the Earth; in which
he thus recites the Opinion of *Leucippus,* Παρεκ-
πεσεῖν ᾗ γῆν εἰς τὰ μεσημβεινὰ μέρη, διὰ τῶν ἐν τοῖς
μεσημβεινοῖς ἀραιότητα, ὅτε δὴ πεπηγότων ἐπὶ βορείαν
διὰ τὸ καταψύχθαι τοῖς ἠυμοῖς, ἐπὶ δ' ἀντιθέτων πε-
πυρωμένων.

ϱωμχ́ων. *That the Earth fell, or was enclin'd towards the* Southern *Regions, by reason of the rareness of those Parts; The* Northern *Regions being grown rigid and compact, while the* Southern *were scorch'd or on fire.* Whose Opinion is also recited by *Lærtius* in almost the same words, Ἐκλείπειν ἢ ἥλιον χ̀ σελήνω τῷ κεκλίθ τ̀ὼ γλὼ πρὸς μεσημβείαν. τὰ ὃ πρὸς ἄρκτον ἀείτε νίφεσ̃. χ̀ κατὰψύχεα ἢ), χ̀ πήγνυσ̃. *By reason of the failure in the* Sun *and* Moon, *the Earth was bent or inclin'd towards the* South. *But the* Northern *Regions grew rigid and inflexible by the snowy and cold Weather which a〈ct〉ed thereon.* To the same purpose is the Opinion of *Democritus,* Διὰ τὸ ἀσϑενέϛεϱν εἶ) τὸ μεσημβεινὸν ῶ̃ ϖεϱιϵχον̃Θ, αὐξομίνω τὼ γλὼ χ̀ ῶῶ̃ ἐγκλιϑ̃ιαι: τὰ ῶὴ βόϱεια ἄκϱατα, τὰ ὃ μεσημβεινὰ κέκϱα̃), ὅϑεν χ̀ ῶῶ̃ βεϐάϱη̃) ὅτϛ ϖεϱισὶ ὅϖι τοῖς καϱποῖς χ̀ τὰ αὐξίσαι. That *by reason of the* Southern 〈elements〉 〈air's〉 imbecillity, *or smaller* Fro〈sts〉, *the Earth in those Parts increas'd in bulk, and so sunk and bent that way.* For the Northern Regions were ill temper'd, but the Southern very well; whereby the latter becoming fruitful, waxed greater, and by an over-weight preponderated and inclin'd the whole that way. *As exprest to the full is the Testimony of* Em〈pedocles〉, Τὸ ἀέϱ〈Θ〉 εἴξαν〈Θ〉 τῷ τὶ ἡλίε ὁϱμ̃, ἐϛ̃ϱίϑωσαι τὰς ἄϱκΤες, χ̀ τὰ μὲν βόϱεια ὑ̇ψωϑῆναι, τὰ ὃ νότια τατειν̃ωϑῆναι, χ̀̃ ὁ χ̀ ῶ ὅλον κόσμον. *The* North, *by reason of the* Air's *yielding to the* Sun's *force, was bent from its former Position; whereupon the* Northern *Regions were elevated, and the* Southern *depress'd; as together with them, was the whole* World. *To which agrees* Anaxagoras *in these words, which immediately follow those just before quoted,* Πϱϵῖν ὃ ετεϱ τὼ Ἐ〈ϖ〉οιϛϛν λαβεῖν. *But afterward the Pole received a turn or inclination.* These so many, and so pregnant Testimonies of Antiquity, as to the matters

of

of fact foregoing, (for as to the several Reasons
assign'd by them, they being, I suppose, but
the single Conjectures of the Authors, must be
uncertain, and need not be farther consider'd
or insisted on in the present case) seem to me
so weighty, that I cannot but build and rely
very much upon them. How should such
strange and surprizing *Paradoxes* run so universally through the eldest Antiquity, if there were
not some ground or foundation in earnest for
them? 'Twould be hard wholly to reject what
were so unanimously vouched by the old Sages of
Learning and Philosophy, even tho' there were
no other evidence or reason for our belief. But
when all these Authors, *the only competent Wit-
nesses in the Case*, do but confirm what on other
Accounts, as we have seen, and shall farther
see, there is so good reason to believe; and
when so great light is thereby afforded to the
primitive Constitution of Nature, and the Sacred
History of the State of Innocency; their Atte-
stations are the more credible, and the more
valuable, and in the highest degree worthy of
our serious Consideration. What I can foresee
of Objection, deserving our notice, against
what has been advanc'd from the Testimonies
of the old Philosophers, is this, That they seem
to favour the perpetual *Equinox* before the Flood,
by the right Position of the present *Axis* of the
Earth, parallel to that of the Ecliptick, (as the
Theorist imagines) and its Inclination or oblique
Position acquir'd at the Deluge, (as the same
Author supposes) rather than the original Absence, and subsequent commencing of the Diurnal Rotation after the Fall of Man, as I here
apply them. I answer, (1.) The Parallelism of
the *Axis* of a Diurnal, to that of an Annual Revolution,

volution, is as far as I find, a perfect ſtranger to
the Syſtem of the World; there being, I think,
not one of the Heavenly Bodies, *Sun* or *Planet,*
but has its own *Axis* oblique to the Orbit in
which it moves. (2.) It will be farther evinc'd
hereafter, That, *de facto,* before the Flood, the
Axis of the Earth was Oblique to its Annual
Orbit, the Plain of the Ecliptick; and the Year
diſtinguiſh'd into the preſent Seaſons, *Spring,*
Summer, Autumn, and *Winter.* (3.) That equable and healthful Temper of the Air, which the
Theoriſt chiefly relied upon, as neceſſary to the
Longevity of the Antediluvians, and fully prov'd
by Antiquity, ſhall be accounted for without
ſuch an *Hypotheſis.* (4.) The Teſtimonies before
alledg'd do not, if rightly conſider'd, ſuit this
Hypotheſis; nay, in truth, they fully confute it.
Of the five Characters before-mention'd, under
which we have reduc'd the main Teſtimonies,
there are two which are common to this, and
to the *Theoriſt's Hypotheſis, viz.* (1.) The perpetual and univerſal Equinox. (2.) The coincidence of the Equator and Ecliptick (tho' in ſomewhat a different manner). So that the Teſtimonies for theſe two can neither eſtabliſh the one,
nor the other, as equally ſuiting them both. The
other three are peculiar to that *Hypotheſis* we have
been proving, and by conſequence at the ſame
time eſtabliſh that, and confute the *Theoriſt's Hypotheſis.* And theſe three are, (1.) The Equality
of a *Day* and a *Year.* (2.) The *Sun* and *Planet's*
riſing in the *Weſt,* and ſetting in the *Eaſt.* (3.)
The Poſition of the Poles at the Horizon, with
the after Elevation of the *Northern,* the Depreſſion of the *Southern* Pole, and the inclination or
bending of the Heavenly Bodies Courſes towards
the *South.* 'Tis evident at firſt view, That the

O two

two former of these three last mention'd *Phæno-mena*, are inconsistent with the *Theorist's Hypo-thesis*, and on a little Consideration 'twill be so of the last also. For while the Poles of the Earth or World remain in being the same, as depending on the same proper *Axis* of the Earth's own Diurnal Revolution; 'tis plain, the Latitude of Places on the Earth, or the Eleva-tion of the Pole equal thereto, remains invaria-ble; and so that Pole which to the Inhabitants of Paradise was elevated at the least $23\frac{1}{2}$ degrees, could not be at the Horizon, whatever right Po-sition the *Axis* of the Earth might have with re-spect to the Ecliptick. On the same account there could, even in the *Theorist's* own *Hypothesis,* be no new Elevation of the one, or Depression of the other Pole at the Deluge, nor inclination of the Courses of the *Sun* and *Planets* towards the *South.* All that could on the *Theorist's* Prin-ciples be effected, (besides the Earth's Equator and Poles pointing to different fix'd Stars, and its Consequences) was only this; that whereas before the *Sun* was always in the Equator, or middle distance from any Climate, it afterwards by turns came nearer to them (as we commonly, tho' carelesly express it) in *Summer,* and went farther from them in *Winter,* than before; which upon the whole, was no more a bent or inclina-tion to one part of the Heavens than to the other; and so of the Planets also. And the case is the same as to the Poles of the Ecliptick; the *Nor-thern* one being as much elevated above that of the World at one hour of the Day, as depress'd beneath it at another. All which is, I think, sufficient to shew, That the Testimonies of An-tiquity alledg'd by the *Theorist* for the perpetual *Equinox,* or the right Position of the Earth's *Axis*

till

till the Deluge, and the oblique Pofition, and different Seafons then acquir'd, are fufficient of themfelves alone to confute *his*, and eftablifh the *prefent Hypothefis.* (5.) All things confider'd, fuch a Pofition as the *Theorift* contends for, was more likely to incommode, than be ufeful to Mankind. Taking the Matter wholly as the *Theorift* puts it, it would prevent the Peopling of the *Southern* Hemifphere, by the fcorching heat juft under the Equator, without the leaft Intermiffion at any time of the Year. It would render the Earth utterly unferviceable, both under the Equator and Poles, and in the Climates adjoyning, and fo ftreighten the Capacity of the Earth in maintaining its numerous Inhabitants; which, were the whole inhabitable, will appear but juft fufficient to contain them. It would by the Perpetuation of one and the fame Seafon continually, hinder the variety of Fruits and Vegetables of every Country; and many other ways fpoil the fetled Courfe of Nature, and be pernicious to Mankind. (6.) No mechanical and rational Caufe of the Mutation of the Earth's *Axis* either has been, or, I believe, can be affign'd on the *Theorift's Hypothefis*, or any others which fhould embrace the fame Conclufion. (7.) Laftly, to name no more Arguments, The Teftimonies of *Diogenes* and *Anaxagoras*, are as exprefs almoft to the Time, as to this Change it felf. The words being exceeding remarkable, are thefe, as *Plutarch* himfelf relates them, Διογένης κỳ Αναξαγόεας μεʃὰ τὸ συsῆσαι τ̕ κόσμον, κỳ τὰ ζῶα ἐκ τ̕ γῆς ἐξαγαγᾶν, ἐκκλιθῆναί πῶς τ̕ κόσμον ἐκ τ̕ αὐ-ʃομάτȣ εἰς τὸ μεσημβεινὸν αὐτᾶ μέεΘ ἴσως ἀπὸ πρϑ-ʃοίας, ἵνα ἅ μὲν τινα ἀοίκητα γένη), ἃ ỳ οἰκητὰ μέεη τᾶ κόσμȣ, χτ̕ ʬύξιν, κỳ ἐκπύρωσιν. κỳ ἐυκρασίαν. 'Twas the Doctrine both of Diogenes *and* Anaxagoras,

Vid. Phæ-nom. 33. *infrà.*

Vid. Bentley, Serm. 8. p. 22, &c. And Dr. *Woodward's Effay,* p.267. &c.

Theor. lib. 2. cap. 10.

That after the Creation or primary Constitution of the World, and the Production of Animals out of the Earth, the World, as it were of its own accord, was bent or inclin'd towards the South. And truly 'tis probable this Inclination was the Effect of Providence, on purpose that some Parts of the World might become habitable, and others uninhabitable, by reason of the difference of the frigid, torrid, and temperate Climates thereof. Which obfervable and most valuable Fragment of Antiquity ought to have been before mention'd, but was on purpofe referv'd for this place; where it not only fully attefts the matter of fact, the Inclination of the Heavens towards the *South*; not only affigns the final Caufe truly enough, (confidering the uninhabitablenefs of the Torrid, as well as of the Frigid Zones, in the Opinion of thofe Ages) the Diftribution of the Earth into certain and fix'd Zones, Torrid, Temperate, and Frigid; but fo accurately and nicely fpecifies the time alfo, That fucceeding the Creation, agreeably to the prefent *Hypothefis*; that were I to wifh or chufe for a Teftimony fully to my mind, I could fcarcely have defir'd or pitch'd upon a better. To thefe five foregoing Arguments, for the proof of my main Conclufion, I fhall, by way of fupernumerary ones, or Appendages, add one or two more, and fo leave the whole to the Confideration of the Impartial *Reader.*

(6.) The State of Mankind without queftion, and perhaps that of other Animals, was before the Fall vaftly different from the prefent; and confequently requir'd a proportionably different State of external Nature; of which, without the *Hypothefis* before us, no Account can be given, or at leaft has not yet by any been attempted. The World, as to other things, feems to have
been

been at firft, in great meafure, put into the fame
Condition which we ftill enjoy; and yet Reafon, as well as Scripture, affures us, That fo
different a condition of things in the Animal,
Rational and Moral, muft be fuited with an
agreeably different one in the Natural and Corporeal World. Which being confider'd, and that
at the fame time no remarkable difference has
been, or perhaps can be affign'd, but what the
Hypothefis before us, and its confequences afford
us; and that withal a fatisfactory account of the
feveral Particulars is deducible from the fame,
as I hope to make appear hereafter; upon the
whole, I think this a very confiderable Atteftation to what has been before infifted on. 'Tis
indeed poffible, that what I look on as an advantage to, others may imagine to be a prejudice againft the prefent *Hypothefis*; as inferring,
among other things, a half year of Night, as
well as a half year of Day, which may be fuppos'd too difproportionate to the State and Condition of Mankind; and efpecially, too inconvenient for fo happy and eafy a Life, as that of
Mankind in Paradife undoubtedly was, without
any confideration of the other Creatures. But it
ought to be confider'd, as has been already remark'd, that our judging of one Scheme or Syftem of Nature by another, is very fallacious,
and very unreafonable. Almighty God adapts
each particular State to fuch rational and animal
Beings as are on purpofe defign'd for the fame;
but by no means thereby confines his Power and
Providence, which can with the fame eafe adapt
other Beings, or the fame in other Circumftances, to a very different and clean contrary
Condition. The Days in *Jupiter* are not ten
hours long; thofe in the *Moon* near Seventy two

Coroll. 3. &
4. *Lem.* 70.
præs.

O 3   times

times as long as they, or a Month; yet any one
who fhould thence conclude, that either *Jupiter*
or the *Moon*, if not both, were uncapable of Inhabitants, he would, I think, be very rafh, not
to fay prefumptuous, in fo doing. 'Tis true, he
might juftly conclude, That fuch Creatures as
dwell on this *Earth* in their prefent Circumftances
could not, or at leaft could not with conveni-
ency, inhabit either of them. But the neceffary
confequence of that is only this, That as the State
of external Nature appears to be in *Jupiter* and
the *Moon*, very different from ours on *Earth*
now; fo moft probably are the State and Circumftances, the Capatitities and Operations of
their feveral Inhabitants equally different from
thofe of Mankind at prefent upon it; which is
what I fully allow, and plead for, in the Cafe
before us; and which, when rightly confider d,
may fave me the labour of returning any other
Anfwer to the particular difficulty here mention'd, and of enlarging upon feveral other things
which might be faid to great fatisfaction on the
prefent occafion; which in profpect thereof,
fhall therefore be no further profecuted in this
place.

(7.) Laftly, The prefent *Hypothefis* gives an eafy Account of the vaft change in the Natural, on
the change in the Moral World; and of the fad
Effects of the Divine Malediction upon the Earth
after the Fall of Man; which till now has not,
that I know of, been fo much as attempted by
any. Several have been endeavouring to account
for that change which the Deluge made in the
World: But they are filent as to the natural caufes
or occafions of a Change, which (Antiquity, Sacred or Prophane, being judge) was in all refpects vaftly more remarkable: The State of Innocency,

nocency, and that of Sin, being fure on all accounts more different from, and contradictory to
each other, than the Antediluvian and Poftdilu-
vian, either in reafon can be fuppos'd, or in fact
be prov'd to be. Now as to the particulars of this
Change, and the caufes of them; and how well,
on the *Hypothefis* we are upon, they correfpond to
one another, I muft leave that to the Judgment
of the Reader, when I come to treat of 'em in
their own place hereafter. In the mean time this
may fairly be faid, that *This* being the *firft* attempt
at an *Intire Theory*, or fuch an one as takes in *All*
the great Mutations of the Earth; As it will on
that account claim the Candor of the Reader, and
his unbiafs'd Refolution of embracing the Truth
(however new or unufual the Affertions may feem)
when fufficiently evidenc'd to him; So the coincidence of things from firft to laft, through fo
many ftages and periods of Nature, and the folution of all the main *Phænomena* of every fuch
different ftage and period from the Creation to
the confummation of all things; if they be found
juft, mechanical, and natural, will it felf deferve
to be efteemed one of the moft convincing and
fatisfactory Arguments for any fingle particular of
this Theory that were to be defir'd; and fhew, that
not any great Labour or Study of the Author, but
the happy Advantage of falling into true and real
Caufes and Principles is, under the Divine Providence, to be own'd the occafion of the Difco-
veries therein contain'd. In all which, may
thefe my poor Endeavours prove as fatisfactory
to the minds of others, as they have been to my
own, and give them the fame affurance of the
Verity and Divine Authority of thofe Holy
Books, where the feveral Periods are recorded,
and the *Phænomena* chiefly preferv'd, which the

difcovery

difcovery of thefe things has afforded my felf,
and I am fure that my Labours will not be in
vain.

IV. The ancient Paradife or Garden
of *Eden*, the Seat of our firft Parents in the State of Innocence,
was at the joynt Courfe of the Rivers *Tigris* and *Euphrates* ; either before they fall into the *Perfian Gulf*,
where they now unite together,
and feparate again ; or rather where
they anciently divided themfelves
below the Ifland *Ormus*, where the
Perfian Gulf, under the Tropick of
Cancer, falls into the *Perfian-Sea.*

That fomewhere hereabouts, on the *Southern*
Regions of *Mefopotamia*, between *Arabia* and *Perfia*, was the place of the ancient Paradife, 'tis
paft reafonable doubt from two of its Rivers,
Tigris and *Euphrates*, occuring in the Defcription

Gen. ii. of its Situation by *Mofes*. And when the follow-
14. ing Theory is underftood, perhaps there will appear reafon to alter the place, where more nicely
it may be fuppos'd to have been, to that other
here conjectur'd. I fay, *When the following Theory
is underftood*; for tho' the particular place affign'd
be now under Water, and a Branch or Bay of
the great Ocean ; yet in probability it might not
be fo then, as will hereafter appear. My reafons
for this Situation of Paradife, are thefe,

(1.) The

(1.) The Ancient Tradition of the *Jews* and *Archæol.* p. *Arabians* was, that Paradise was seated under the 269. Primitive Equinoctial ; which is impossible, unless it were as far South as the Tropick of *Cancer* : Under which therefore it ought to be, and accordingly is by this *Hypothesis* plac'd and determin'd.

(2.) 'Twill be easie on this *Hypothesis* for every one to suppose that the other two Rivers, or Branches of these, *Pison* and *Gihon*, which have been in vain hitherto sought for, must be now lost in the *Persian* Sea ; and therefore not to be discover'd, nor their discovery to be expected, since the Deluge.

(3.) The Countries encompass'd by, and bordering on, these four Streams or Rivers, being alike, in part, under Water; the difficulties arising from the common mistaken Suppositions relating thereto will cease , and Light be afforded to the *Mosaick* Description on the particular consideration thereof.

(4.) The most literal and obvious sense of the Words of the Sacred Historian concerning the situation of *Eden*, and its *Garden* or *Paradise*, will be accountable , and exactly suitable to the state of these Countries, according to the present Geography. The words of *Moses* are, *And the Lord* Ger. ii. 8, *God planted a Garden eastward in Eden ; and* 10. *there he put the man whom he had formed. And a River went out of Eden to water the garden; and from thence it was parted and became into four heads.* To which the present *Hypothesis* is correspondent to the greatest niceness, if we suppose that *Tigris* and *Euphrates* being united, as they are now, in *Babylonia*, ran in one Stream quite through that Valley, which is now cover'd with Water, and call'd

call'd the Gulf of *Perfia* (I fuppofe the Country
of *Eden* then) upon the Exit of which, beyond
Ormus, the faid United Streams divided themfelves (as *Nile* into feven) into four feparate
branches; and by them, as by four Mouths,
difcharged it felf into the *Perfian* Sea : Two of
which Streams retain'd the Names of the Original ones, *Tigris* and *Euphrates* ; and the other two
acquir'd new ones, and were call'd *Pifon* and
Gihon ; juft before or about which Divifion, that
Country ftil'd *Paradife*, or the *Garden of Eden* was,
I imagine, accordingly fituate. This I take to
be the moft probable account of this Point ; and
fuch an one as takes away the perplexities of this
matter ; agrees to the Letter of *Mofes*, and the
Geography of the Country ; and is fuitable
withal both to what the *Jewifh* and *Arabian* Tradition before-mention'd affert, and what the
next *Hypothefis* requires.

V. The Primitive Ecliptick, or its correfpondent Circle on the Earth, interfected the Prefent Tropick of *Cancer* at Paradife ; or at leaft at its Meridian.

When from the laft *Hypothefis* but one, it appears that the Primitive Ecliptick was a fixed
Circle on the Earth, as well as in the Heavens ;
and muft both equally divide the prefent Equator, and touch the prefent Tropicks; 'tis proper to fix, if poffible, the Point of Interfection
with the Northern Tropick ; whereby the intire
Circle may be ftill defcrib'd, and its Original Situation determin'd. Which is the attempt of
this

this *Hypothesis* we are now upon ; and which I thus prove.

(1.) Without this *Hypothesis* the before-mention'd *Jewish* and *Arabian* Tradition, of the situation of Paradise under the Primitive Equinoctial, is unaccountable and impossible to be true. For Paradise being, at the most southern Position suppofable, but just under the Tropick of *Cancer* , it could no where be under the ancient Equinoctial or Ecliptick, but at their mutual Interfection ; which muft therefore have been as this Propofition afferts.

(2.) The Production of Animals out of the Earth and Waters, at or near Paradife, feems to have requir'd all the heat poffible in any part of the Earth; which being to be found only under the Equinoctial , confirms the laft mention'd Argument, and pleads for that fituation of Paradife which is here affigned to it.

(3.) And Principally, This fituation is determin'd by the coincidence of the Autumnal Equinox, and the beginning of the Night or Sun-fet, at the Meridian of Paradife. 'Tis known that at Paradife, or the place of the Creation of Man, the Νυχϑήμερον, or Natural Day, commenc'd Gen. i. 5, with the Sun-fetting, Six a Clock, or coming on 8, 13, 19, of the Night. 'Tis granted alfo, that the begin- 23, 31. ning of the moft Ancient Year, (which fhall prefently be prov'd to have been at the Autumnal Equinox) was coincident with the beginning of the World, or of the *Mofaick* Creation. Which things compar'd together, do determine the queftion we are upon. It being impoffible, on the grounds here fuppos'd, that Sun-fet and the Autumnal Equinox fhould be coincident to any but thofe in the Northern Hemifphere, at the Point

of

of Interſection of the Ancient Ecliptick, and the preſent Tropick of *Cancer* ; or ſuch as were under the ſame Meridian with them ; as any ordinary Aſtronomer will ſoon confeſs: Which Argument is Decretory, and fixes the place of Paradiſe to the greateſt exactneſs and ſatisfaction.

    Corollary 1. *Hence a plain reaſon is given, of the Days of Creation commencing at Evening ; which otherwiſe is a little ſtrange : It being but a neceſſary reſult of the time of the Year, and Region of the Earth, when, and where the Creation began.*

    Coroll. 2. *As alſo why the Jewiſh Days, eſpecially their Sabbath-Days, began at the ſame time ever ſince : The Memory of the Days of Creation being thereby exactly preſerv'd.*

Lev. xxiii. 32.

    Coroll. 3. *As alſo why their Civil Years, but eſpecially their Sabbatical Years, and Years of Jubilee, (even after their Months were reckon'd from the Vernal,) began at the Autumnal Equinox : The memory of the Years of the Creation being thereby alike exactly preſerv'd.*

VI. The Patriarchal, or moſt ancient Year mention'd in the Scripture, began at the Autumnal Equinox.

Vid Calviſ. Prolegom. de tempore Mundi Conditi Cap. 34.

    The Reaſons of this Aſſertion are theſe enſuing.

    (1.) The principal Head or Beginning of the Jewiſh Year in all Ages was the firſt Day of their Autumnal Month *Tiſri* ; and was accordingly honour'd with an extraordinary Feſtival, the Feaſt of Trumpets: When the Head or Beginning of
their

Lev. xxiii.
ſa. 25.
Numb.
xxix.1---6.

their Sacred Year, the firft of *Nifan*, had no fuch folemnity annex'd to it : As is known and confefs'd by all.

(2.) When God commanded the *Jews* on their coming out of *Egypt*, to efteem the Month *Nifan*, the Firft in their Year; it feems plainly to imply, that till then it had not been fo efteemed by them. The words are thefe. *The Lord fpake unto Mofes and Aaron in the Land of Egypt, faying, This Month* (fhall be) *unto you the beginning of Months; it* (fhall be) *the firft Month of the Year to you.* And this is ftrengthened by confidering, that tho' we here find an Original of the Sacred Year in the Spring ; yet we no where do of the Civil in Autumn : Which therefore, 'tis very probable, was the immemorial beginning of the Ancient Year long before the times of *Mofes.* Exod. xii. 1, 2. with xiii. 4.

(3.) Whatever beginning of the *Jewifh* Year there might be on other accounts; 'Tis confefs'd by all, That the beginning of the Sabbatical Years, and Years of Jubilee, (by which in all probability the Primary Years of the World were commemorated and preferv'd) was at the Autumnal Equinox: Which is a very good Argument that thofe Ancient Years, fo commemorated and preferv'd, began at the fame time alfo.

(4.) The Feaft of Ingathering, or of Tabernacles, which was foon after the Autumnal Equinox, is faid to be *in the End*, or *after the Revolution of the Year* : Which is a peculiar confirmation of the Affertion we are now upon. Exo. xxiii. 16. & xxxiv. 22.

(5.) Unlefs that Year at the Deluge commenc'd at the Autumnal Equinox, we muft (fays the Learned *Lightfoot* in his Scheme thereof) fuppofe one Miracle more than either Scripture or Reafon give us ground to think of ; and that is,

that

that the Waters fhould increafe, and lie at their height all the Heat of Summer, and abate and decreafe all the cold of Winter. Which, without Reafon, he fuppofes is not to be allow'd.

(6.) What was alledg'd under the laft Propofition is here to be confider'd, That on this *Hypothefis* a clear Reafon is given of the Nights preceding the Day in the Hiftory of the Creation, and ever fince among the *Jews*; which otherwife is not fo eafily to be accounted for.

(7.) The teftimony of the *Chaldee* Paraphraft, (to which *Jofephus* does fully agree) is as exprefs as poffible, upon 1 *Kings* 8. 2. where the words are, *In the Month Ethanim, which is the feventh Month*; (*viz.* as all confefs, from the Vernal Equinox) upon which the Paraphrafe is, *They call'd it of Old the Firft Month*; *but now it is the Seventh Month:* Which may well counterpoife all that from fome later Authors can be produc'd to the contrary. So that upon the whole I may fairly conclude, notwithftanding fome fmall Objections, (which either lofe their force on fuch Principles as are here laid down, or will on other occafions be taken off) That the moft Ancient or Patriarchal Year began at the Autumnal Equinox.

VII. The Original Orbits of the Planets, and particularly of the Earth, before the Deluge, were perfect Circles.

This is in it felf fo eafie and natural an *Hypothefis*, that I might very juftly take it for granted, and make it a *Poftulatum*: And in cafe I could

prove

prove every thing to agree to, and receive Light from the fame, and withal account for the prefent Eccentricity, no man could fairly charge it with being a precarious or unreafonable one. But although the main reafons for fuch a Propofition are, I confefs, to be taken from the confequences thence to be deriv'd; and the admirable correfpondence of them all to Ancient Tradition, to the *Phænomena* of the Deluge, and to the Scripture Accounts thereto relating, as will be vifible hereafter; yet there being fome Arguments of a different nature which may render it probable, and prepare the Reader for admitting the fame, before the confequences thereof come to be fully underftood, I chufe to place this Affertion here, among my *Hypothefes*; tho' I do not pretend that the Arguments *here* to be made ufe of, ought to put the fame fo near to certainty, as its fellows have, I think, reafon to expect with unprejudic'd Readers. But to come to the matter it felf : The Reafons I would offer are thefe following.

(1.) The Defigns and Ufes of Planets feem moft properly to require circular Orbits Now in order to give a rational guefs at the fame Defigns and Ufes of Planets, I know no other way than that from comparifon with the Earth. And here, when we find one of the Planets, and that plac d in the middle among the reft, to agree with the others in every thing of which we have any means of enquiry; 'tis but reafonable to fuppofe, that it does fo alfo in thofe, which 'tis impoffible for us, by any other certain way, to be affured of. If we obferve a certain Engin in one Country, and fee to what ufe 'tis put, and to what end it ferves; and if afterward we fee another,

tho'

tho in a different Country, agreeing to the former in all things, as far as we are able to difcover : Tho' we are not informed of its defign and ufe, we yet very naturally, and very probably, believe that it ferves to the fame purpofe, and was intended for the fame end with the former. Thus it ought fure to be in the cafe before us; and by the fame way of reafoning we may fairly conclude to what ufes all the Planets ferve, and on what general defigns Providence makes ufe of them, *viz.* To be the feat or habitation of Animals, and the Seminary of fuch Plants and Vegetables as are neceffary or convenient for their fupport and fuftenance. Which being therefore probably fuppos d of the reft, and certainly known of the Earth, I argue, That a circular Orbit being the moft fit and proper for fuch purpofes, may juftly be prefum d the original fituation of the Planets, and the primary work of Providence in ordering their courfes. Such Creatures, Rational, Senfitive, or Vegetative, as are fit and difpos'd for a certain degree of the Sun's heat, are very much incommoded by one much greater, or much lefs ; and by confequence are peculiarly accommodate to a Circular, but by no means to an Eccentrical Orbit. And tho' the inequality of the Earth's diftance from the Sun, in the different Points of its Orbit, be fo inconfiderable, that we obferve little effect of it; yet in fome of the other Orbits, which are much *Vid. Arg.2.* more Eccentrical, it muft be very fenfible, and *Hypoth.* 1c. have a mighty influence on the productions of *infra.* Nature, and the conftitution of Animals in Planets revolving therein. And what reafon can we imagine why the Southern Hemifphere, for inftance, of a Planet, by the fituation of the *Perihelion* near its Summers Solftice, fhould be fo

different

different from the Northern, in the primary contrivance of the Divine Providence? This seems not so agreeable to the original regularity and uniformity of Nature ; nor does it look like the immediate effect of the Divine Power and Wisdom in the first frame of the World, when all things just coming out of the Creator's hands, must be allow'd to have been perfect in their kind, and exceeding good ; when the rational Creatures being Pure and Innocent, the natural state of things was to be suited to them ; and dispos'd agreeably to reason, proportion, and the convenience of the same unspotted and sinless Creatures.

(2.) The opposite position and use of the opposite Species of Bodies the Comets, seem, by the rule of contraries, to suppose what we have been contending for. If indeed we had found a mixture of Planets and Comets in the same Regions of the Solar System, and a confusion of the Orbits and Order of both : If we had discover'd all species of *Ellipses*, with all degrees of Eccentricity from the Circle to the *Parabola* ; the Proposition I am upon would be more than precarious, and but too disagreeable to the frame of Nature. But when we find no such thing, but the clean contrary; namely, That all the Comets revolve in Orbits so extremely Eccentrical, that such segments of them as come within our observation are almost *Parabolical,* or of an infinite degree of Eccentricity; 'Tis not unreasonable to conclude, That likely enough the contradistinct Species of Bodies the Planets originally revolv'd in Orbits of no degree of Eccentricity, that is, in perfect Circles : The Eccentrical or *Elliptick* Orbits of the one, among other things, probably distin-

P guishing

guiſhing them from the other ; which originally moved in Concentrical or Circular ones.

(3.) This *Hypotheſis* is favour'd by the Ancient Aſtronomy ; which ſo pertinaciouſly adher'd to the Circular *Hypotheſis*, notwithſtanding all its Eccentricks , Epicycles , and ſtrange Wheelwork ; that it may ſeem the effect of Ancient Tradition , that once the Heavenly Motions were really Circular. And This is the more remarkable, becauſe, not only the true Syſtem of the World, but the *Conick Sections*, and among them the *Elliptick* Figure was very anciently known and conſider'd. By the introduction of which, all the fanciful and uncouth figments they were forc'd upon, might have been wholly ſpar'd, and an eaſie and natural *Idea* of the Planetary Motions obtain'd. Which if ever it had been ſtarted, by its exact agreement to the *Phænomena*, could ſcarce ever have been loſt ; and which yet, as far as I know, never came into the Minds of Aſtronomers till the Great *Kepler*'s time ; who firſt prov'd the Orbits to be *Elliptick* too plainly to be denied, or almoſt doubted any longer.

(4.) The Quantity of the ſeveral Orbits *Eccentricity*, and the Poſition of their *Aphelia*, are ſo various, different, and without any viſible deſign, order or method, as far as is hitherto diſcover'd, that the Whole looks more like the reſult of Second Cauſes, in ſucceeding times, than the Primary Contrivance and Workmanſhip of the Creator himſelf. 'Tis indeed poſſible that there *may* be Deſign and Contrivance in theſe things, tho' we cannot diſcern them ; yet ſeeing we have, on the common grounds, no Reaſon to affirm ſuch a thing ; ſeeing the equidiſtant ſituation from the Sun would more clearly ſhew ſuch Deſign and Contrivance ; ſeeing alſo, the original circular

Motion

Motion of the Earth granted, the Pofition of
the Earth's *Aphelion*, and the quantity of its Orbit's *Eccentricity*, do fo remarkably infer the Divine Wifdom and Artifice therein, and are wonderfully fubfervient to the higheft purpofes; (By
the one, the Day of the Year when the Flood
began; by the other, the length of the Antediluvian Year, being nearly determinable; of
which hereafter) 'tis I think, but fair reafoning
to conclude, That that *Hypothefis* which does fo
certainly argue Art and Contrivance, Order and
Providence, is to be prefer'd to another, which
feems to infer the clean contrary, or at beft only
leaves room for a poffibility thereof; as 'tis in
the prefent cafe. I do by no means queftion but
thefe uncertain *Eccentricities* and various Pofition
of the *Aphelia* of the Planets, with all other fuch
feemingly Anomalous *Phænomena* of Nature, happen'd by a particular Providence, and were all one
way or other fitted to the ftate of each Species of
Creatures Inhabiting the feveral Planets, according as their refpective Behaviours or Circumftances, in their feveral Generations requir'd:
(of which the fucceeding Theory will be a pregnant inftance) But my meaning is this; That
before any good or bad actions of Creatures,
when every thing was juft as the Wifdom of
God was pleas'd to appoint; when each Creature was compleat and perfect in its kind, and fo
fuited to the moft compleat and perfect ftate of
external Nature; 'tis highly probable that the outward World, or every fuch ftate of external Nature was even, uniform, and regular, as was the
temper and difpofition of each Creature that was
to be plac'd therein: And as properly fuited to
all their neceffities, and conveniences, as was
poffible and reafonable to be expected. Such a
P 2 ftate,

state, 'tis natural to believe, obtain'd through the Universe till succeeding changes in the Living and Rational, requir'd proportionable ones in the Inanimate and Corporeal World. 'Tis most Philosophical, as well as most Pious, to ascribe only what appears wise, regular, uniform, and harmonious, to the First Cause ; (as the main *Phænomena* of the Heavenly Bodies, their Places, and Motions, do, to the degree of wonder and surprize) but as to such things as may seem of another nature, to attribute them intirely to subsequent changes, which the mutual actions of Bodies one upon another, fore-ordain'd and adjusted by the Divine Providence, in various Periods, agreeably to the various exigencies of Creatures, might bring to pass.

(5.) It being evident, that multitudes of Comets have pass'd through the Planetary System; that in such their passage they were sometimes capable of causing, nay, in very long periods must certainly, without a Miracle, have caused great alterations in the same ; and that the nature and quantities of the present *Eccentricities* or Anomalies are no other than what must be expected from such Causes; 'tis very reasonable to allow these effects to have really happen'd, and that consequently all might be, as I here contend it was originally, orderly, uniform, and regular ; and particularly the Planetary Orbits uniform, concentrical, and circular, as I am here concern'd to prove. If any one of us should observe that a curious Clock, made and kept in order by an excellent Artist, was very notably different from the true time of the day, and took notice withal of a certain rub or stoppage, which was very capable of causing that Error in its Motion ; he would easily and undoubtedly

conclude

conclude that such an Error was truly occasion'd by that visible Impediment; and never design'd at first, or procur'd by the Artist. The application of which resemblance, is too obvious to need a Comment, and naturally enforces what I am now contending for.

(6.) 'Tis evident that all the little Planets about *Jupiter* move in Orbits truly Circular, without the least sensible degree of Eccentricity: On which account the present *Hypothesis* appears to be far from contrary to the frame of Nature; nay to be no other with regard to the *Primary*, than is *de facto*, true in this *Secondary* System: And from that so remarkable a parallel, may the more easily be believ'd to have once been the case of this also.

(7.) 'Tis evident, that in case the Comets Attractions were the cause of the Eccentricity of the Planets, they would usually draw them also from the Plains of their former Orbits, and make them inclin'd or oblique to one another: So that where the Orbits are Eccentrical, 'tis probable, according to the present *Hypothesis*, the Plains must be different, and oblique to each other; and where the Orbits are Circular, the Plains of the several Orbits must be as they were at first, or, in probability, coincident. Now this is really observable in the two Systems last mention'd: The Plains of the Circular Orbits about *Jupiter* being nearly, if not exactly coincident, and those of the Eccentrical ones about the Sun being oblique to each other. Which Observation is no inconsiderable Argument, that originally the Planetary Orbits were exactly Circular; as well as that at the same time they were every one in the same common Plain, or in Plains coincident to one another. Which

last

laſt mention'd *Hypotheſis*, (to ſpeak a word or two of that by the way) tho' I look upon it as not unlikely, and ſuch an one as ſeveral of the foregoing Arguments might be apply'd to, and do plead for; yet I ſhall not inſiſt farther upon it here: Both becauſe the following Theory does not directly depend upon it in any part; and becauſe the moving in different Plains does not cauſe any ill effects, or notable inconveniences, in the Syſtem of Nature, as we have ſhewn the Eccentricity does; and ſo cannot with the ſame clearneſs and force be urg'd againſt its being the Original Workmanſhip of God, as I have above diſcours'd in the other caſe. Only this I may ſay, That ſeeing the Planetary Orbits are ſtill almoſt in the ſame Plain; ſeeing the Comets Paſſages are capable of cauſing ſuch little obliquity; nay were they originally in the ſame Plain, in length of time, by the fore-mention'd Attraction, they muſt without a Miracle, have been drawn from their common Plains, and been obliged to revolve in thoſe different from each other, as they now do; and ſeeing withal that *Eccentricity* and *Obliquity*, *as uniformity of diſtance from the Center, and coincidence of the Plains*, go together in the World, as has been juſt before noted; this *Hypotheſis* of the Original coincidence of the Planetary Plains, is an opinion neither improbable, nor unphiloſophical; and only a *little leſs* evident than what this Propoſition was to prove, *viz.* That the Primary Orbits of the Planets were perfect Circles; but otherwiſe very much a-kin, and exceeding correſpondent thereto; they at once receiving light from, and affording light to one another mutually.

VIII. The

VIII. The Ark did not reft, as is commonly fuppos'd, in *Armenia*; but on the Mountain *Caucafus*, or *Paropamifus*, on the Confines of *Tartary*, *Perfia*, and *India*.

This Propofition is proved by thefe following Arguments.

(1.) This Mountain agrees to the place where the Firft Fathers after the Deluge Inhabited; which any part of *Armenia* does not. 'Tis evident from Scripture, that the firft removal of the Fathers after the Flood there mention'd, was from the parts on the *Eaft* of *Babylon*: It came to pafs *as they journeyed from the Eaft, that they found a plain in the land of Shinar, and they dwelt there*; and accordingly there they built the Tower of *Babel*, as you find in the following Hiftory. Now *Armenia*, on one of whofe Mountains the Ark is commonly fuppos'd to have refted, is fo far from the Eaftern Point from *Babylon*, that 'tis fomewhat towards the Weft, as any Map of thofe Countries will eafily fhew. But the Mountain here pitch'd upon, *Caucafus*, or *Paropamifus*, being fituate near to the Eaft Point from *Babylon*, is on that account peculiarly agreeable to the Hiftory of *Mofes*, of the Habitation of the firft Fathers after the Flood, and fo to the Seat of the Ark thence to be determin'd.

(2.) Notwithftanding we meet with few or no Colonies fent Eaftward, after the confufion of Tongues, as we do into other quarters; yet the Eaftern Nations appear, in the moft Ancient

Gen. xi. 2.

P 4 Prophane

Prophane Hiftories of the World, to have been
then the moft numerous of all others. On which
account thofe Countries muft have been firft
Peopled before the Defcent of the Sons of Men
to *Babylon,* which the remotenefs of *Armenia*
is uncapable of; but the Neighbourhood of *Caucafus* permits, and naturally fuppofes. It being
probable that if the Sons of *Noah,* for the firft
Century after the Flood, dwelt upon or near that
Mountain, they would firft fend Colonies, or
leave a Company thereabouts, which fhould
ftock thofe Eaftern Countries adjoining, before
they fpred themfelves into the remoter parts of
Afia, Europe, and *Africa;* and *vice verfa,* feeing
they appear to have firft Peopled thofe Regions,
'tis equally probable that they originally were
fituate at or near the fame Regions, *i. e.* at or
near the Mountain here determin'd.

(3.) The Teftimony of *Porcius Cato* is exprefs
in the Point, who affirms, That two hundred
and fifty years before *Ninus,* the Earth was over-
flown with Waters; and that *In Scythia Sagà re-
natum mortale Genus*: Mankind was renew'd or re-
ftor'd in that part of Scythia which is call'd Saga,
which Country, fays Sir *Walter Raleigh,* is
undoubtedly under the Mountain *Paropamifus.*

(4.) The fame Affertion is confirm'd by the
Tradition of the Inhabitants, who, fays Dr. *Heylin,* aver, That a large Vineyard in *Margiana,*
near the Foot of Mount *Caucafus,* was of *Noah's*
Plantation, which may juftly be fet againft any
pretended Reliques or Tradition for *Armenia;*
and agreeing with the place determin'd by the
other Arguments, deferves juftly to be preferr'd
before them. Thefe are the Arguments, which
from

from *Goropius Becanus*, Sir *Walter Raleigh*, and Dr. *Heylin* make ufe of in the Cafe, and which I think are very fatisfactory. But I fhall add one more, which they take no notice of, but which I efteem fo clear, that it might almoft alter the Denomination of the Propofition, and give it a claim to a place among the foregoing *Lemmata*, which I propofe as certain; not thefe Propofitions, which whatever degree of evidence they or any of them may have, I yet chufe to propofe under a fofter Name, and call them *Hypothefes.* And the Argument is this;

(5.) The Ark refted upon the higheft Hill in all *Afia*, nay, at that time the higheft Hill in the World; but *Paropamifus* (the true and moft famous *Caucafus*, in the old Authors) is the higheft Hill in all *Afia*, nay, was then of the whole World; and is by confequence, the very fame on which the Ark refted. Now, in this Argument, I fuppofe it will be allow'd me, That *Caucafus* is the higheft Mountain in *Afia* (Sir *Walter Raleigh* fays 'tis *undoubtedly* fo); that it was the higheft in the World alfo at that time, will from the fame Affertion be hereafter prov'd, whatever pretence the *Pike of Teneriff*, or any other may at prefent make: All that therefore I am here to make out, is, That the Ark muft have refted on the higheft Mountain in the World, which is eafily done: For the Waters covering the Tops of all the higheft Hills on the Face of the Earth, fifteen Cubits; and yet the Ark refting the very firft day of the abatement of the Waters, above two Months before the Tops of other Mountains were feen (as will be proved hereafter:) 'Tis evident, That not only the lower Hills of *Armenia*, but all other in the World, befides *Caucafus*, were uncapable of receiving the Ark

at

Sir *Walter Raleigh's* Hift. lib. 1. cap. 7. fect. 10. And *Heylin's* Cofmog. p. 7, 8.

Lib. 1. cap. 7. fect. 10. fubj. 12. Solut. 59. infrà.

Phæn. 59. *infrà.*

at the time affigned for its refting in the Sacred
Hiftory; and by confequence, That and That
only was the Mountain on which it refted. If
it be here objected, That *Ararat*, where the Ark
refted, is in Scripture taken for *Armenia*; and by
confequence it muft be an *Armenian* Mountain
which we are enquiring for. In Anfwer, I grant
that *Ararat* is in Scripture taken for *Armenia*;
but I deny, that all the Mountains of *Ararat* are
included in that Country. 'Tis poffible the *Alps*
or *Pyrenees*, might give or receive their Names
to, or from fome fmall Country at which they
rofe, or through which they paffed; but it
would not from thence follow, that all the
Alps or *Pyrenees* belong'd to, and were contain'd
in fuch a Country. 'Tis ufual for vaft and
long Ridges of Mountains to be call'd by one
Name, tho' they pafs through, and thereby belong to many and diftant Regions, which I take
to be the prefent Cafe; and that the intire Ridge
of Mountains running *Weft* and *Eaft* from *Ar-*
menia to the Fountains of the Rivers *Oxus* and
Indus, call'd fince by the general Name of
Mount *Taurus*, were anciently ftil'd *Ararat*, or
the Mountains of *Ararat*. To which the *Mo-*
faick Hiftory does well agree, by ufing the plu-
ral number, *The Ark refted on the Mountains of*
Ararat, *i. e.* on one of thofe Mountains, or of
that ridge or aggregate of Mountains going by
the general Name it has at its *Weftern* rife, and
ftil'd *Ararat*. This is, I think, a fair and fatisfactory Interpretation of the Mountains of *Ara-*
rat; and fuch an one as Bifhop *Patrick* embraces,
tho' he be by no means partial to that Opinion
I here defend thereby. But if any be not yet
fatisfied of the truth of the Propofition we are
upon, they may confult the Authors abovemention'd,

Gen. viii.
4.

2 Kings
xix. 37.
Ifa. xxxvii.
38.

In Loc.

tion'd, who have more at large infifted on it, and alledg'd other Arguments on the fame account, to which I fhall therefore refer the *Reader.*

IX. The Deluge began on the 17th Day of the fecond Month from the Autumnal Equinox, (or on the 27th Day of *November* in the *Julian* Stile extended backward) in the 2365th year of the *Julian* Period, and in the 2349th year before the Chriftian *Æra.*

In this account of the number of Years from the Deluge, I follow the moft Reverend and Learned Archbifhop *Ufher's* Chronology, deriv'd from the *Hebrew Verity*, without taking notice of what Years the *Samaritan* and *Septuagint* have added thereto; they being, as will hereafter appear, added without reafon, and not at all to be confider'd. Now, that the number of Years affign'd by Archbifhop *Ufher* is rightly deduc'd from the *Hebrew*, is, I think, notwithftanding the wide and manifold Miftakes of the former, pretty well agreed upon among the lateft Chronologers; and capable of a much more fatisfactory Proof, than from fo great Differences before thereto relating one would be ready to imagine, as upon a little enquiry I eafily found. Indeed, the Archbifhop has made the matter fo plain, that one cannot but wonder how former Chronologers came fo ftrangely to be miftaken; and 'tis perhaps one of the moft difficult things to give

Coroll. 6.
Hypoth. 10.
infra.

give a good account of, that is readily to be pitch'd upon. I once intended to have here not only given the *Canon* of the feveral Periods, but confirm'd the fame from the Scripture, and anfwer'd the principal Objections made againft any parts thereof; as well from the faid Archbifhop's incomparable, tho' imperfect *Chronologia Sacra,* as from fuch other Obfervations as having been fince made, (efpecially by the very Learned Sir *John Marfham,* who has intirely and evidently clear'd what the Archbifhop principally labour'd at without fuccefs, the Chronology in the Book of *Judges)* give farther light and ftrength to the fame Accounts. But this would perhaps be too much like a Digreffion, and fomewhat foreign to my main Defign, fo I forbear, and only fet down the *Chronological Canon,* according to which I reckon from the Creation to the prefent time, as follows.

I. From

I. From the beginning of the
Mofaick Creation, till the Crea-
tion of *Adam*, 29½ (Days to a
Month, till the Deluge.) ——— } Y.   M. D.
0005—06—11

II. From the Creation of *Adam*,
till the day when the Earth began to be clear of the Waters,
or the Autumnal Equinox, in
the Year of the Deluge. ——— } 1656—05—14

III. From the Autumnal Equinox
in the Year of the Deluge, till
the departure of *Abraham* out
of *Haran.* (30½ Days to a Month
fince the Deluge.) ——— } 0426—06—15

IV. From *Abraham's* departure
out of *Haran*, till the *Exodus* of
the Children of *Ifrael* out of
Egypt. ——— } 0430—00—00

V. From the *Exodus* of the Children of *Ifrael* out of *Egypt*, till
the Foundation of *Solomon's*
Temple. ——— } 0479—00—17

VI. From the Foundation of *Solomon's* Temple, till its Conflagration. ——— } 0424—03—08

VII. From the Conflagration of
Solomon's Temple, till the Ka-
lends of *January*, which began
the Chriftian *Æra.* ——— } 0587—04—25

VIII. From the beginning of the
Chriftian *Æra*, till this Autumnal Equinox, *Anno Do-
mini*, 1696. ——— } 1695—08—26

Sum of all. ——— 5705—00—00

From the firft day of the Deluge,
till the 28th of *October* in this
fame Year, 1696. ——— } 4044—00—00

This

This *Canon* agrees with the Archbifhop's in
every thing, but that, for exactnefs, I make ufe
of *Tropical*, or natural Solar Years, inftead of *Julian* ones ; to which accordingly I proportion the
Months and Days; I add thofe five Months fourteen Days which his *Hypothefis* forc'd him, without ground, to omit between the Creation and
the Deluge; and I give the primitive Years of
the Creation their place, which having been taken for fhort Days of twenty four Hours long,
were not hitherto fuppos'd to deferve the fame.
All which being obferv'd, I refer the *Reader*,
who defires farther fatisfaction, to the Archbifhop
himfelf, where he may find the particulars of the
feveral Periods clear'd to him.

X. A Comet, defcending, in the Plain of the Ecliptick, towards its *Perihelion*; on the firft Day of the Deluge paft juft before the Body of our Earth.

That fuch a Pofition of a Comet's Orbit, and
fuch a paffing by as is here fuppos'd, are in
themfelves poffible, and agreeable to the *Phænomena* of Nature, All competent Judges, who are
acquainted with the new and wonderful Difco-
veries in Aftronomy, according to the *Lemmata*
hereto relating, muft freely grant. But that it
really did fo at the time here fpecified, is what I
am now to prove. 'Tis true, when upon a meer
Suppofition of fuch a paffing by of a Comet, I
had in my own mind obferv'd the *Phænomena* relating to the Deluge to anfwer to admiration, I
was not a little furpriz'd, and pleas'd at fuch a
Difcovery.

Lem. 42,
&c. *priùs.*

Difcovery. It gave me no fmall Satisfaction to fee, that upon a poffible and eafy *Hypothefis*, I could give fo clear an Account of thofe things, which had hitherto prov'd fo hard, not to fay inexplicable, and could fhew the exact coincidence of the particulars with the Sacred Hiftory, and the *Phænomena* of Nature. I thought to be able to proceed fo far, was not only more than had been yet done, more than was generally expected ever would be done; but abundantly fufficient to the beft of purpofes, to clear the Holy Scriptures from the Imputations of ill-difpofed Men, and demonftrate the Account of the Deluge to be in every part neither impoffible nor unphilofophical. But proceeding in fome farther Thoughts and Calculations on the faid *Hypothefis*, I, to my exceeding great Content and Admiration, found all things to correfpond fo ftrangely, and the time of the Year by feveral concurring ways fo exactly fix'd, agreeably to the Sacred Hiftory thereby; that, as I faw abundant Reafon my felf to reft fatisfi'd of the reality, as well as probability of what I before barely fuppos'd; fo I thought the producing the Particulars I had difcover'd might afford evidence to the minds of others, and go a great way to the intire eftablifhing the certainty of that, of whofe great probability the Correfpondence of the feveral *Phænomena* of the Deluge had before afforded fufficient fatisfaction. But before I come to the Arguments to be here made ufe of themfelves, give me leave by way of Preparation, to fhew what fort of evidence fuch Affertions as this before us, when good and valid, are capable of; and how great or fatisfactory it may be in any other, and fo may be expected to be in the prefent Cafe. 'Tis evident, That all Truths are

not

not capable of the fame degree of evidence, or manner of Probation. Firſt Notions are known by Intuition, or ſo quick and clear a Perception, that we ſcarce obſerve any Deduction or Ratiocination at all in our Aſſent to them. Some principal Metaphyſical Truths have ſo near a Connexion with theſe, that the manner of reaſoning or inferring is ſcarce to be trac'd or deſcrib d; a few obvious and quick Reflections enforcing our hearty acquieſcence : Among which, the belt of Metaphyſicians Mr. *Lock,* in his *Eſſay of Humane Underſtanding,* very rightly placesthe Being of God. Purely Mathematical Propoſitions are demonſtrated by a chain of deductions, each of which is certain and unqueſtionable. So that on a clear view of the truth and connexion of each Link, or Member of the intire Argumentation, the Evidence may ſtill be look'd on as infallible. Propoſitions in mixt Mathematicks, as in Opticks, Geography, and Aſtronomy, depending partly on abſtract Mathematick Demonſtrations, and partly on the Obſervations of the *Phænomena* of Nature ; tho' not arriving to the ſtrict infallibility of the evidence with the former ſort, are yet juſtly in moſt caſes allow d to be truly certain and indubitable. Hiſtory is all that we commonly can have for matters of fact paſt and gone ; and where 'tis agreed upon by all, and uncontroulable, 'tis eſteemed fully ſatisfactory, tho' not abſolutely certain in common Caſes. And Laſtly, To come cloſer to the Point, the knowledge of Cauſes is deduc'd from their Effects. Thus all Natural Philoſophy, *i. e.* the knowledge of the Cauſes of the ſeveral viſible *Phænomena* of the World, is ſolely deriv'd from thoſe Effects, or *Phænomena* themſelves, their accurate Correſpondence

Lib. 4.
cap. 10.

to

to, and neceffary dependance on certain fuppofed Caufes, and their infolubility on any other
Hypothefes, with the coincidence of the particular
Calculations of the Quantities of Motion, Velocity, Periods, and Species of Figures to be every
where accounted for. On the Univerfal Con-
fpiration and Correfpondence of which, with
the impoffibility of producing an inftance to the
contrary, depends what may be truly ftil'd a
Phyfical Demonftration. I mean, Then, and only
Then is a Phyfical Caufe to be efteem'd *Demonftrated*, when all the *Phænomena* of the World
may be certainly fhewn to be juft fo, and no
otherwife, as they neceffarily would, and muft
be on fuppofition thereof. This laft method is
that which our beft of Philofophers has taken in
his Demonftration of the Univerfal Affection or
Property of Bodies, which he calls *Mutual Attraction* or *Gravitation*, and which accordingly he has
eftablifh'd beyond poffibility of Contradiction;
and this is the fole way of bringing natural
Knowledge to perfection, and extricating it from
the little *Hypothefes*, which in defect of true Science, the World has till lately been forc'd to be
contented with. In the Point before us, there
are only three poffible ways of proving the truth
of the Affertion here laid down. The firft, that
of Propofitions in mixt Mathematicks, by Calculation of the Motion of fome Comet, as we
do of Planets from the Aftronomical Tables,
and thence demonftrating the certainty thereof.
But befides the improbability of this Comet's having ever return'd fince the Deluge; 'tis plain,
the defect of old Obfervations, and the fo late
difcovery of the Laws and Orbits of their Motions, do render fuch a way of Probation, at
leaft at prefent, impoffible. The fecond way

Q   of

of Probation, is that of Hiftorical Relation, that
at the Deluge a Comet did fo pafs by; of which
there is directly none in the prefent Cafe. Nor
feeing the poffibility of the fame was not
known, nor the thing vifible to the Inhabitants
Coroll. 4. that out-liv'd the Flood. as will hereafter ap-
Solut. 50. pear; is this kind of Evidence to be at all ex-
infra. pected? But the third and laft way, poffible, is
the Being of fuch plain and fenfible Effects, as
muft be undoubted confequents of fuch an Affertion, and without the fuppofal thereof were
perfectly unaccountable; which is the very method of Probation I fhall here ufe, and do wholly depend upon. There are feveral degrees of
evidence, and kinds of proofs, very different
from thofe made ufe of in the Mathematicks,
which yet are little lefs fatisfactory to the minds
of wife Men, and leave little more room for
doubting than they. Several forts of Propofitions muft be evinc'd by feveral forts of Arguments; and whatever poffible and eafy Affertion
has all the proofs which its nature requires, or
could juftly be expected upon fuppofal of its
real Exiftence, ought to be admitted for true
and evident. Thus in that fort of things we are
now upon; if a certain Caufe be affign'd, which
being fuppos'd would neceffarily infer feveral
plain and vifible Effects, and occafion feveral
fenfible *Phænomena*; 'tis plain, if thofe Effects
and *Phænomena* be upon Examination found to
be correfpondent, and as they muft and would be
on the real being of fuch a Caufe, the exiftence
of that Caufe is prov d. And as where the Effects
are few, ordinary, otherwife accountable and
incapable of Reduction to Calculation, or accuracy of correfpondence in the juft Quantity and
Proportion neceffary; the proof is weak and only

ly probable; and as where several of the consequents of that Cause agree well enough, yet some others disagree, the disagreement of one or two, is a stronger Objection against, than the coincidence of the rest an evidence for the same, and the proof none at all: So on the other side, where a Cause is assigned, whose certain consequent Effects must be very many, very surprizing, otherwise unaccountable, correspondent on the greatest niceness of Calculation in the particular Quantity and Proportion of every Effect, and where withal no disagreeing *Phænomenon* can be urg'd to the contrary; the evidence hence deriv'd of the reality of the assigned Cause, tho' of a different nature, and, if you will, degree too, from Demonstration, is yet little less satisfactory to the minds of wise and considering Men, than what is esteem'd more strictly so. Thus, for instance, Astronomers at this day find little more Inclination or Reason to doubt of the Annual and Diurnal Motions of the Earth, than of any strictly demonstrated Proposition; and as much, in a manner, take it for granted in all their Reasonings, as they do the Propositions in *Euclid*, tho' the evidence for the same be in its kind different from, and inferior to the other. And thus, as I have before observ'd, Mr. *Newton* has given sufficient evidence of the Universal Law of *Mutual Attraction* and *Gravitation* of Bodies, which accordingly there is no more occasion to doubt of, than of those common matters of Fact or History, of which no wise Man ever made any question. And thus it is, that I hope to evince the truth and reality of that Cause assigned in this Proposition, *viz.* by proving that those visible Effects or *Phænomena* relating to the Universal Deluge, which are very many, very sur-

Q 2
prizing

prizing, hitherto unaccountable, feveral of which
are capable of Calculation as to the particular
Time, Quantity, and Proportion of the refpective particulars, are every one fo, and no otherwife, as on fuppofal of the affigned Caufe they
either certainly muft, or at leaft probably would
have been. And as upon a Demonftration of the
difagreement of any one *Phænomenon*, which
were a neceffary confequence of the fame, I
muft own the falfenefs of the Propofition before
us; fo I hope, if the univerfality of Correfpondence, even to the exactnefs of Calculation in
proper cafes be eftablifh'd, and no contradictory
inftance can be produc'd; it will be allow'd,
that I have fufficiently evinc'd the reality, and,
in a proper Senfe, certainty of the fame Affertion. This then being premis'd, 'tis plain, that
every one of the particular *Phænomena* of the Deluge afterward accounted for, is a proper Argument of this Propofition, and might juftly
claim a place here on that account. But becaufe fuch an Enumeration of them before-hand
would prevent their own more peculiar place
hereafter, and difturb the propos'd method of
the enfuing Theory, I fhall leave them to their
proper places, tho' with this Premonition, That
feveral of them do fingly fo exactly fit the
otherwife unaccountable *Phænomena* of Nature,
and of the Deluge, and determine the time and
circumftances of the latter fo nicely, that their
feparate evidence is confiderable; but when
taken conjointly with the reft, as fatisfactory as
I think the Nature of the thing is capable of.
But befides thefe particular correfpondent *Phænomena* of the Deluge, and after the difcovery of
the moft of them, I found proofs of fomewhat
another nature; which not only confirmed all
that

that I had before obferv'd, but enabled me to determine the time when the Flood began, to the greateft exactnefs poffible; which therefore I fhall alone produce here, referving thofe other for their own places hereafter. Now on the *Hypothefis*, that a Comet pafs'd by the Earth, till then revolving circularly about the *Sun* at the time, and in the manner affign'd by the Propofition, the neceffary Effects or Confequents of it are thefe Five. (1.) The circular Orbit of the Earth would be chang'd into that of an *Ellipfis*; and the *Sun*, which was before in the Center of the Circle, would be afterward in that *Focus* of the *Ellipfis*, which were neareft the place at which the Attraction of the Comet happen'd. (2.) The Year, after fuch a paffing by of the Comet, would be increafed ten Days, one Hour, thirty Minutes. (3.) The time of the paffing by of the Comet, or the beginning of the Deluge to be determin'd by the place of the *Perihelion*, muft be coincident with that affigned in the *Mofaick* Hiftory. (4.) The very day of the Comet's paffing by, or of the beginning of the Deluge, to be determin'd from the Aftronomical Tables of the Conjunctions of the *Sun* and *Moon*, muft be coincident with the time determin'd by the faid place of the *Perihelion*, and with the very day affign'd in the *Mofaick* Hiftory. (5.) The quantity of Acceleration, to be determin'd *à Priori*, from the force of the Comet's Attraction, muft correfpond with that which the prefent *Elliptick* Orbit does require. All which that they are, *de facto*, true and real, I fhall now prove.

Hypoth. 7.
prius.

Lem. 48.
cum Coroll.
prius.

Lem. 56.
cum Coroll.
prius.
Lem. 52.
cum Coroll.
prius.

Lem. 55.
cum Coroll.
prius.

Lem. 53.
cum Coroll.
prius.

(1.) The Orbit of the Earth is now *Elliptical*, and the Sun is in that *Focus* thereof, which was

neareft

neareſt the place of the Earth, when the Deluge
began. This Propoſition is ſufficiently known
to Aſtronomers, as to the former part of it:
And if it be conſider'd, That the Earth when the
Deluge began, was but juſt paſt that degree of
the *Ecliptick*, where the *Perihelion* was afterward, as will preſently appear; the latter
part will be equally evident with the former.

Arg. 3.
Hypoth hu-
jus, infrà.

(2.) The Year before the Flood was ten
days; or more nicely, ten days one hour
and thirty minutes, ſhorter than the preſent.
In order to the proof of which I ſhall ſhew
firſt in general, that the Antediluvian Year was
different from, nay ſhorter than the preſent
Year; and afterwards determine the particular length thereof more exactly; and ſhall com-
priſe wh reaſons I have for theſe Aſſertions in
the following Arguments.

Vid. Phæ-
nom. 22.
infra.

(The true length of the Solar Year was
ſo g unknown after the Deluge, that there
m have happen'd ſome mighty change and
length ni g thereof at the Deluge, or elſe no
rational account can be aſſign'd of ſuch groſs
and laſting an ignorance. 'Tis not to be
queſtion d but the Antediluvian Patriarchs were
perfectly acquainted with the Antediluvian
Year; every one of thoſe mention'd in Scripture
having ſeen ſo many Summers and Winters, or
natural ſolar Years, that himſelf were able to
aſcertain their length, and correct any miſtake
about them. Tis alſo not to be doubted but
the Poſtdiluvians would have retain d the ſame
Year, and determin d it by the ſame number of Days, as their Fore-fathers, had they
found it to agree with the Courſe of the Sun
then,

then, as it did formerly. But 'tis evident from the Ancienteſt Authors, that 'twas many hundreds of Years after the Deluge e're the moſt Learned Nations rectifi'd their Year to the Sun's Courſe, or arriv'd at more than three hundred and ſixty Days in their Accounts. Which number accordingly was the Standard of a Year for many Ages, (The full proof of which, and the clearing thereby of ſeveral Prophetick Periods, that famous one of *Daniel*'s Seventy Weeks eſpecially, is what we impatiently expect from a moſt Learned Prelate of our Church) till Aſtronomical Obſervations forc'd Men to correct the ſame. Now all this on the preſent *Hypotheſis* is eaſie and natural; That when the Antediluvian Year was but a few hours above three hundred and fifty five Days; and at the Deluge was inſenſibly become ſome odd hours above three hundred and ſixty five Days, without the leaſt knowledge or ſuſpicion of any change therein; 'Tis, I ſay, very eaſie and natural in this caſe to ſuppoſe, that upon their obſerving the ſeaſons to be protracted, and return ſtill later every Year than other; (as on the retaining the Antediluvian Year muſt needs happen,) and conſequently their Ancient Standard of three hundred and fifty five days, to be too ſhort for the Sun's Revolution; that they ſhould lengthen their accounts to thirty Days in every Month, and the even number three hundred and ſixty Days in the whole Year. Which convenient and remarkable number three hundred and ſixty, being probably fixt at the time when Aſtronomy began to be improv'd, or at leaſt reviv'd after the Deluge, and ſo become the diviſion of the Ecliptick, and of every Circle of the Sphere; was not quickly chang'd, but meaſur'd the Ancient Year among not a few Nations,

and

and that not a few Ages together : As being alfo
lefs obfervably different from the Sun s Courfe,
and correfpondent both to the degrees of a
Circle, and twelve even Months of thirty Days
a-piece. And indeed this adjuftment of the Year
and Months, with the degrees of a Circle, and
of each Sign in the Ecliptick, was found fo eafie,
ready, and ufeful on all accounts, that even when
the odd five days were added afterward, they
were not inferted into the Months, nor perhaps
efteem'd part of the Year, but look'd upon as
'Ημέραι 'Επαγόμεναι, *adventitious* or *odd days*, of a
quite different denomination and character from
all the reft. However 'tis ftill agreeable to the
prefent *Hypothefis*, that on the farther obfervation
of the protraction of the Seafons, and on the improvement of Aftronomy ftill higher, as the
Year had been increas'd before from three hundred and fifty five to three hundred and fixty, fo
afterward it fhould be increas'd from three hundred and fixty to three hundred and fixty five
days; and at laft, (the Obfervations of the more
Learned Aftronomers enforcing it,) from three
hundred fixty five to 365¼ or the *Julian* Year,
which with us is retain d to this very day. All
this is I think eafie and natural in the prefent
cafe, upon that *Hypothefis* which is here defend-
ed ; but without it 'tis very ftrange and unaccountable. 'Tis, I fay, very *ftrange* and *unaccountable* either how the Antediluvian Patriarchs
fhould not know the length of their own Year;
or that none of their Pofterity, who were deftitute of Divine Revelation, fhould retain the
fame afterwards, but be forc'd to make ufe of
one that was fo far from correfponding to thofe
Seafons, and that Revolution of the Sun which
a Year was on purpofe defign d to be commen-
　　　　　　　　　　　　　　　　　　　　　　　　furate

furate to. Which concluſion is farther confirm'd,

(2.) By the Eſſential difference of the Ancient
Years among ſeveral Nations ſince the Deluge :
Some of which made uſe of *Solar*, and others of
Lunar ones, or endeavour'd to adjuſt their periods to thoſe of each of theſe Luminaries. This
difference of Years, is known in Antiquity, has
been the occaſion of great diſputes; and is not
yet a ſtranger to the World. Nay, as far as I
find, ſome of thoſe Nations who agreed with the
moſt general Standard of three hundred and ſixty
days, ſuppos'd that number agreeable in ſome
meaſure to the *Lunar*, as well as to the *Solar*
courſe, as conſiſting nearly of twelve Synodical
or Monthly Revolutions of the former, as well
as of a ſingle Annual one of the latter; and embrac'd it as much, if not more on the account
of its imagin'd correſpondence with the *Moon*,
as of a like imagin'd correſpondence with the
Sun. Now this Eſſential difference of *Solar* and
Lunar Years in the eldeſt Antiquity after the
Flood, is on no other grounds ſo accountable
as that the Antediluvian Year having been
delivered down from their Fore-fathers to have
agreed with the courſes both of the *Sun* and *Moon*,
(as on the preſent *Hypotheſis* it really did) ſome
Nations followed *one* Branch, and others *another*
of the ſame Tradition : And when they no longer were commenſurate, accommodated their accounts to the one or the other, according as the
one or the other was moſt prevalent, and univerſal among them. This is an eaſie and rational account of this Eſſential difference of *Solar*
and *Lunar* Years, ſo variouſly followed by ſo many Nations ſince the Deluge : Which otherwiſe,
if the Year was of the ſame length with the preſent,

fent, and fixt before the Flood, 'tis hard to affign
the Original of. But That it were, as in this *Hypothefis*, both a *Solar* and *Lunar* Year, all is very
eafie, and what muft naturally happen upon an
imperceptible change at the Deluge. Which
will be ftill farther confirm'd if we confider,

(3.) That the Moon's other Motions, *Diurnal*
and *Menftrual*, are ftill fo accurately adjufted and
commenfurate to each other, that 'tis very probable the *Annual* was alike adjufted and commenfurate to thofe in the primitive Conftitution of Nature. 'Tis certain the Moon accompanies our Earth, and has her *Annual* Revolution exactly equal to the others. 'Tis alfo certain, as has been before obferv'd, that her *Men-*
ftrual Periodical Revolution about the Earth, is
exactly equal to her *Diurnal* about her own *Axis*:
Which wonderful and remarkable coincidence or
correfpondence of two fuch intirely diftinct motions, renders it highly probable that the third
or *Annual* Revolution was not by Providence
Originally defign'd to be fo incommenfurate to
thofe others, as fince the Deluge it moft evidently has been; and that to the greateft trouble and
perplexity of many Ages, and the intire difturbance of the Ancient Chronology. Where we
cannot but in one cafe acknowledge, the moft exact interpofition of Providence in the Equality
of the *Menftrual* and *Diurnal* Revolutions; and
the notable effect thereof, the expofition of the
fame Hemifphere of the Moon to the Earth continually: We cannot fure be unwilling to own
a like Interpofition in the other, in the commen-
furability and correfpondency of the fame *Men-*
ftrual and *Diurnal* Revolutions to the *Annual* one
of it felf, and of its Companion the Earth: Efpecially where the reafon and advantage of fuch
an

Lem. 39.
prius.

an adjuftment, (the eafie and regular accounts of Time through the World thence arifing) is much more plain and evident than in that other cafe, of which yet there can be no poffibility of doubt or hefitation : Which therefore confiderably enforces the fore-mention'd *Hypothefis*, according to which the Wife and Careful Interpofition of Providence in the Original Conftitution of the World, appears to have been as accurately follicitous, and engag'd in the adjuftment of the *Annual* Motion to the *Menftrual*, as 'tis unqueftionably true in the like correfpondence of the *Menftrual* to the *Diurnal*, fo worthy the prefent confideration and admiration of Aftronomers: Which will be moft of all confirm'd by the exact agreement of the feveral Periods, to be taken notice of in the next place.

(4.) The *Eccentricity* of the Sun is fo exactly coincident with the *Epact* of the Moon ; or the Annual Motion in the Circular Orbit before the Deluge, fo nicely equal to thirteen Periodical, and twelve Synodical Revolutions of the Moon; that 'tis very improbable it fhould be wholly by chance, or without any relation of one to another. The Eccentricities of Planets are various, uncertain, and boundlefs ; and 'twill be next to impoffible in fuch cafes to obferve accurate coincidences where nothing but Chance is concern'd, and there is no Analogy or Connexion in Nature for 'em. If there were a certain Watchword out of 500 pitch'd upon among certain Confpirators, and a Perfon was taken on fufpicion, and prov'd to have nam'd that very word to his fuppofed Partner ; it were in reafon, and the opinion of the World 499. to one he before knew of it, and did not by chance only hit upon it. If any Ancient Hiftorian fhould affert,
that

that a certain remarkable accident happen'd on such a Day, and such an Hour, of a given Year, and a way was afterward difcover'd of determining the time on which, if it really did happen, it muft have done fo ; tho' the Authority of the Author were not confiderable otherwife, no doubt would be any more made of his veracity in that point, if the coincidence was fo exact as to determine the fame hour mention d by the Hiftorian. Thus if on other intimations it be conjectur'd, that the Earth mov'd circularly before the Deluge, and the Year was both a Solar and Lunar one ; and if afterward the *Eccentricity* of the Earth's Orbit, and the Lunar *Epact,* or difference between the Solar and Lunar Year, be reduc'd to Calculation, and found accurately coincident, when the *Eccentricity* of no other of the Planetary Orbits , is at all Correfpondent ; There is, I think, very great probability to believe that coincidence founded in Nature, and that the alteration of the Year juft fo much as thofe agreeing-quantities require, was the true occafion thereof. The *Eccentricity* requifite to correfpond to the Lunar *Epact,* muft be $\frac{12}{1000}$ of the intire middle diftance : That of *Saturn* is $\frac{57}{1000}$ that of *Jupiter* $\frac{48}{1000}$ that of *Mars* $\frac{21}{1000}$ that of *Venus* $\frac{10}{1000}$ that of *Mercury* $\frac{210}{1000}$ that of the *Moon* $\frac{43}{1000}$ which all widely differ from the quantity here neceffary. But when we confider the Eccentricity of the *Magnus Orbis,* or Orbit of the Earth's and Moon's Annual Courfe, it exactly accords , and is $\frac{12}{1000}$ of the intire middle diftance; as we have before particularly obferv'd, and as the Moon's Epact moft nicely requires. 'Tis, I confefs, not *impoffible* that Calculations and Numbers, in which there is all imaginable room for diverfity under or over, *may* be coincident, without any natural Dependance or Analogy

logy

logy one to another. Tis *poſſible*, that I may
ſeveral times by gueſs, or at a venture, hit upon
any number which another Perſon has in his
mind. 'Tis *poſſible*, a Gameſter may, without
any foul dealing, throw all Sizes or Aces, be the
Dice never ſo many, a hundred times together.
Theſe things it muſt be own'd are *poſſible*, and
ſo no Compact or Colluſion can be *demonſtrated*
by ſuch Coincidences; neither, conſequently,
do I pretend that this, or any of the like Coincidences in the preſent Theory do abſolutely *demonſtrate* that Aſſertion they are brought to prove.
But as in the former caſes, the Obſervation of
the mention'd Coincidences would afford evidence fully *ſatisfactory* of ſome Myſtery, Cunning, or Artifice us'd therein; ſo I think it ought
to be in the preſent caſe; I mean where all
things elſe are rightly correſpondent, and no
contradictory inſtances to be alledg'd, the nice
and accurate Coincidences of Calculations in
this, and the other proper caſes through this
Theory, ought to ſatisfy the minds of conſidering Men of the real truth and evidence of the
Propoſition on which they all depend, and from
which they are deriv'd; and particularly, that
the Lunar *Epact* and *Sun's Eccentricity* which are ſo
nicely equal to each other, muſt have a natural
Relation, and a common Occaſion; the alteration of the Year at the Deluge: Which being ſo
far eſtabliſh'd by theſe Chronological and Aſtronomical Arguments, ſhall be now confirm'd from
the Holy Scripture.

(5.) This *Hypotheſis* of the ten days addition to
the year, is very agreeable to the Hiſtory of the
Deluge in the *Hebrew* it ſelf; and abſolutely neceſſary to reconcile the Text as we have it from the
ſame *Hebrew* verity, with that Tranſlation which
the

the *Septuagint*, and from them *Josephus*, give us thereof. 'Tis commonly, and probably suppos'd, That the space in which *Noah* was in the Ark was a just Solar year: 'Tis expresly so in the *Septuagint* and *Josephus*; the entrance and exit being

on the same day of the same month; when yet 'tis in the *Hebrew*, and our Bibles, a year and ten days; the entrance on the 17th, and the exit on the 27th of the second month, as is evident in the Texts quoted in the Margin. Which seeming repugnances have not hitherto met with any satisfactory conciliation, and are generally allow'd to be inconsistent with one another. Some great Men are willing to suppose the year referr'd to at the Deluge, to have been a Lunar one, such as was in after-ages made use of; which in the common years having eleven days less than the Solar, will nearly account for this matter, and pretty well accommodate the whole. But this, I think, will not satisfy, because the *Jewish* Lunar year began at the Vernal, but this at the Autumnal Equinox: because five, at least, of these months had thirty days a-piece, whereas the Lunar had generally thirty, and twenty nine, by turns throughout the year: Because withal this brings the matter only *nearer*, but does not reconcile it, there still wanting a day to that purpose: For when the Moon's Epact is eleven days, the *Hebrew* affords only ten; so that *Noah* must both prevent the Solar year one day, and the *Septuagint* be still irreconcilable with the *Hebrew*, though this conjecture were admitted. All which rightly consider'd, 'tis, I think, evident that this *Hypothesis* of the Lunar year is not only wholly precarious, but indeed indefensible; and were it otherwise, would not be at all advantagious in the case before us; to which therefore

some-

Marginalia (left column):

Gen. vii. 11, 13. & viii. 14, 15, 16, 17.

Vid. Bishop *Patrick in Loc.*

Gen. vii. 24. & viii. 3. with viii. 4.

somewhat elfe muft be anfwer'd, and fomewhat
farther advanced, or the Knot muft remain
ftill unfolved at leaft, if not infoluble. I affirm
then, That the allowance of thofe days, which
we have before endeavoured to fhew were wanting in the year before the Flood, will take off
the difficulty, and reconcile the *Hebrew* with the
Septuagint to the greateft exactnefs : And 'tis not
a little obfervable, That the number of days
requifite to this reconciliation, are the very fame
that we have already, from the Eccentricity of
the Sun, and the Lunar Epact confpiring together, determined to have been the difference between the Antediluvian and the Poft-diluvian
year. Let us but therefore fuppofe the *Hebrew*
to make ufe of that year which was in ufe at
that time to which the Hiftory belongs, and
which *Noah* in a journal of the Deluge muft be
allowed to reckon by; and the Tranflators,
after obfervation had forc'd men to increafe the
year ten days, to allow for the fame, and exprefs
the duration of the Deluge, or the fpace of
Noah's remaining in the Ark, according to that
juft year then only current among them, and
there is no difficulty left. Now this procedure
of receding from the very words or numbers of
an Author, in order the more eafily and juftly
to exprefs his meaning and give a truer *Idea* to
the prefent age, of what was reprefented at firft
in a way fuitable to that of any Hiftory or occurrence, but afterwards forgotten, is a very rational one ; and if applied to other Authors and
Cafes, is neither unufual nor inconvenient.
Thus if in an Hiftory of the ancient ftate of
Egypt, the *Egyptian* years were made ufe of; a
Tranflator who fhould, upon the introduction
and fole ufe of the *Julian* year afterwards, reduce

duce them all to that, and reckon all the months and days according to that only, he would do at once the greatest justice to the Author, and deserve the thanks of the Reader, for so much easier and more familiar an *Idea* of each period, than a rigid and scrupulous keeping to the Author's own words and numbers could ever have given him. The case is the same as to Weights and Measures us'd by former Ages, or Foreign Nations; which when reduc'd to others equivalent to them in Terms familiar and known, are much more useful than when word answers to word, and number to number in every thing. And if we allow but this to have been the case between *Moses* himself who wrote the *Hebrew* Text, and the *Septuagint* who many Ages after Translated it, we shall find, according to our foregoing calculations, that the year us'd by *Noah* was but Three hundred fifty five days; and that by the *Septuagint*, Three hundred sixty five; and so that space, which with the first Author is certainly a year and ten days, from the 17th to the 27th of the second Month; and is alike evidently a just year from the 27th to the 27th of the same second month with the Translators, are coincident, or the same entire Solar year. Whereby our *Hypothesis* is at once confirmed, and the difficulty arising from the *Hebrew* Text it self, but chiefly as compared with the *Septuagint*'s Translation, does entirely vanish and disappear: Which Argument join'd to the foregoing, will, I hope, be thought not inconsiderable.

(3.) The time of the passing by of the Comet, or of the beginning of the Flood, determin'd by the place of the *Perihelion*, is exactly agreeable to that mention'd in the *Mosaick* History. 'Tis certain, That the place of the *Perihelion* of the Earth's

Earth's Orbit is now in the beginning of the eighth degree of *Cancer* : And by Mr. *Flamsteed's* Astronomical Table of its Motion, it goes forward in 4044 Years full 56 Degrees : So that by going back to the time following the Deluge, the *Perihelion* must then have been at the beginning of the 12th Degree of *Taurus.* It has also been before proved, that the place of the Comets passing by must have been a few Degrees, as five, six or seven, past the *Perihelion,* that is, on or near the 18th Degree of *Taurus* : Which in the Ancient Year, beginning at the Autumnal Equinox, will fall upon or near the 17th Day of the Second Month : On which very Day, by the express Testimony of the Sacred Historian (agreeing within a Day or two with the Corrected Testimonies of *Abidenus* and *Berosus*) the Deluge began. Which exactness of coincidence I look upon as so remarkable and surprizing, that nothing can be more so; and I need not fear to appeal to the Confidering Reader, if this be not the most peculiar and convincing Attestation to our *Hypothesis,* which could easily be defir'd, or in the least wish'd for: That from it not only the several *Phænomena* of the Deluge, but the time of its commencing is so precisely determin'd also; and that in the greatest Correspondence and Harmony with the Sacred History of the same thing imaginable.

(4.) The very day of the Comets passing by, or of the beginning of the Deluge determin'd from the Astronomical Tables of the Conjunctions of the *Sun* and *Moon,* is exactly coincident with that before *nearly* determin'd by the place of the *Perihelion,* and *exactly* by the *Mosaick* History. It has been before prov'd, that seeing the *Moon* still accompanies the Earth, it must

Gen. vii. 11. Vid. Verba ipsa apud Langium de annis Christi. p. 255.

Lem. 5; prius.

R   needs

needs have been three Days paſt the New or Full, at the paſſing by of the Comet. It has alſo been before prov'd, that the Flood began in the Year of the *Julian* Period 2365, or the 2349ᵗʰ before the Chriſtian *Æra.* Now it appears by the Aſtronomical Tables of the Conjunctions of the *Sun* and *Moon,* that the mean New Moon happen'd at the Meridian of *Babylon* juſt before Eleven a Clock in the Forenoon, on the 24ᵗʰ day of *November,* (in the *Julian* Year) and ſo at Eleven a Clock on the 27ᵗʰ of *November,* 'twas three days after the New. Which being the 1−ᵗʰ day of the Second Month, from the Autumnal Equinox, is the very ſame pitched

Gen. vii. 11.

upon from the place of the *Perihelion,* and expreſly mention'd in the Sacred Hiſtory : And by ſo wonderfully correſponding therewith, gives the higheſt Atteſtation to our *Hypotheſis* that could, for the completion and conſummation of the foregoing Evidence, be reaſonably defir'd.

(5.) The Quantity of Acceleration determin'd *à priori* from the force of the Comets Attraction, does very well correſpond with that which the preſent *Elliptick* Orbit does require. Upon Calculation according to the *Lemma* quoted in the

Lem. 27. prius.

Margin, the Velocity acquir'd by the Earth on its firſt change, from a Circular to an *Elliptick* Orbit appears to have been about $\frac{1248}{131250}$ of the intire Velocity ; or ſuch as would carry it in three hours and a half's time 1248 Miles. 'Tis alſo upon calculation evident, from what has been

Lem. 53. cum coroll. prius.

already obſerv'd, that in caſe the Comets neareſt diſtance were a quarter of the Moons, or ſixty thouſand Miles, and it ſelf of much the ſame bigneſs with the Earth ; (two very probable and eaſie *Hypotheſes;*) the time of the Comets Attraction to be ſolely conſider'd is three hours and
a half,

a half, and the quantity of Velocity therein produc'd is the requisite quantity $\frac{1248}{131253}$ of the intire Velocity, or so much as carries a body 1248 Miles in the fore-mention'd space of three hours and a half. And in case the Comets nearest distance were less, if the Comet withal be supposed in the same proportion less also; the effect will be the same, and the fore-mention'd Velocity equal to what the former Calculation assign'd, and the *Elliptick* Orbit of the Earth does exactly require. Which accuracy of correspondence, in the due quantity of Velocity, added to the former Arguments, cannot but be esteem d a mighty Evidence for the reality of our *Hypotheses*: All whose consequents are so surprizingly true, and so fully bear Witness to one another.

Corollary I. *From what has been said under this Proposition, we may pretty nearly determine the Constitution of the* Antediluvian *Year. For when it consisted of three hundred and fifty five Days, four Hours, and nineteen Minutes, and had for at least five Months together, from the second to the sixth, thirty Days to a Month, or one hundred and fifty to five Months, as we have seen, it must in all probability have consisted of twelve Months; The first seven whereof had thirty, and the last five only twenty nine days apiece, Or rather the first eleven Months had thirty, and the twelfth only twenty five Days. That as in the famous* Egyptian *Year, or that of* Nabonassar *after the Deluge, every Month had thirty Days a piece, and the supernumerary five were added by themselves, and stil'd* 'Ημέραι 'Επαγόμεναι; *so before the Deluge all the Months, as near as possible, had thirty days apiece also; and the five deficient ones were taken from the last, and might be denominated* 'Ημέραι 'Απαγόμεναι. *And possibly might give occasion to that*

method

method of the before-mention'd Year in the following Ages. How often the odd Hours and Minutes were intercalated, and came to just even Days before the Deluge, 'tis not, for a certain reason not here to be mention'd, easie, very exactly to determine; nor perhaps of consequence that it should be so determined. Only in general every sixth year at least, one with another, must be Leap-Year, and have three hundred and fifty fix days; as every fourth is Leap-Year, and has three hundred and sixty fix days now among us.

Coroll. 2. Every Antediluvian *Year* and *Season*, *Spring*, *Summer*, *Autumn*, and *Winter*, began at Sunset following the Solar ingress into a Cardinal Point, and the Full Moon. It appears, as has been before prov'd, that the Autumnal Equinox preceding the Deluge, happen'd on the 11th day of October. It also appears, by the Astronomical Tables of the Conjunctions of the Sun and Moon, that 'twas Full Moon the same Day: The Night succeeding which Day, began the First Day of Autumn, and the First Day of the Year also. Which being suppos'd, and that, as we have prov'd, the Solar Year was exactly coincident with twelve Synodical Months, or the Lunar Year, it must necessarily have been ever so. And not only the other particular Seasons, but the Year it self began at the most remarkable time possible. The Astronomers had a double coincidence to observe, at the conclusion of one, and the commencing another year, viz. The Autumnal Equinox, and the Full Moon: Which must for ever fix and establish the constancy of their Annual space. And even the Countryman had somewhat easily observable to fix his Account, and Characterize his Year, the Full Moon Rising when the Sun set, as the same common period of the Old, and introducer of the New Year. So that in so regular and truly natural Solar and Lunar Years

as

Lem. 4'. prius.

as then obtain'd, no *Obfervations of Aftronomers were* neceffary to adjuft or calculate their meafures of Time; Nature, or rather Divine Providence, having fo fitted the Heavenly Revolutions, that nothing more than the eafie obfervation of a Full Moon was neceffary to determine their Seafons, and their Years, and to retain them at a conftant fetting out, with the Equinoctial and Solftitial Points in the Heavens. Than which Difpofition, nothing of fuch a nature could more clearly demonftrate the Wife Provifion of the great Creator; or more ufefully be fubfervient to Mankind.

Coroll. 3. Hence we eafily underftand the primary occafion of the confufions in Aftronomy and Chronology after the Flood, notwithftanding they might have been well underftood before it. While the Solar and Lunar Years were equal, and every one of them began both at the Equinox, and at the Full Moon; (this latter, obfervable by all, fixing the former, obfervable but by a few,) 'Twere next to impoffible to fuppofe any difference in Years, or in the Accounts of Time depending thereon. But upon an imperceptible change of the Year at the Deluge, and the confequent incommenfurate duration of the Solar and Lunar Periods, 'Tis natural to fuppofe great diverfity of Years, and perplexity of Accounts. Some might long retain their Ancient Year, and fuffer its Head to wander through all Seafons: Others might retain their Ancient Year, as far as it agreed with the twelve Lunations or Months afterward, and make ufe of a Lunar-year: Whofe Head they might either, as the former, fuffer to wander through all Seafons, or fix as well as they could by the intercalation of a Month, as oft as they found fo much deficiency from the Solar Year. And as the former fort, having a regular Cycle, or conftant method for the finding the Head of their Months and Years, needed no other Obfervations, fo

the

the latter muſt always remark the ʒiʒʒus of the Moon, *and begin their Months, or Years, or both at ſome obſervable Point of an entire Lunation, as at the* Full *or* New Moon, *or ſo ſoon as any decreaſe or increaſe of its Light became ſenſible. Some might ſtrive to find out the number of Days neceſſary to be added to their old Year, and ſo to reduce the ſame to the true Solar Revolution; and accordingly might firſt make every Month thirty Days, and the Year three hundred and ſixty, till that appearing too little, five more Days, and at laſt the odd ſix Hours were by degrees added, and the Civil became almoſt equal to the Natural Year. While others were intent upon the Adjuſtment of the Solar and Lunar Periods, and inventing* Cycles *for the correſpondence of thoſe ſeveral Accounts, which were reſpectively followed by ſeveral Nations. All which variety of reckoning, with its natural conſequences, muſt cauſe ſtrange Confuſion in the accounts of Time, and create mighty Difficulties in the Ancient Chronology; very agreeably to what every one knows to have been really the caſe, who ſearches into ſuch Matters, to what our* Hypotheſis *lays a rational Occaſion and Foundation for, and to what, without ſuch a ſuppoſed change at the Deluge, is by no means accountable.*

     Coroll. 4. *When the number* Three hundred and ſixty *is not only a middle proportional between the Days in an Antediluvian and Poſtdiluvian Year, and nearly between the preſent Solar and Lunar Year, is not only the number of Degrees in the Ecliptick, and in every Circle or Orbit; but was the juſt number of Days in a Year among ſo many Nations, for ſo many Ages. The reaſon of that Prophetick Stile, in which a Day, or Year thereby meant, does plainly ſignify Three hundred and ſixty Days, and no more, is clear and evident. What Difficulties the want of this Obſervation, that* Daniel's *Pro-*
phetick

*phetick Year confifted of Three hundred and fixty Days,
has left unfolv'd, and what light may be afforded to
fome places of the higheft importance thereby, I had
rather the Reader fhould be left to his own Obfervations, and that Work fo impatiently expected, of
which I made mention before, than prepoffefs him
with any more particular inftances thereof in this
place.*

Coroll. 5. *When the very day of the beginning of
the Deluge, nearly determin'd by the place of the*
Perihelion, *and* exactly *by the Aftronomical Tables
of the Conjunctions of the* Sun *and* Moon, *is the very fame individual Day with that mention'd by the
Sacred Writer; hence arifes a very furprizing and unexpected Confirmation of the Verity of the Scripture
Hiftory. Here is a great and fignal inftance of the
wonderful Providence of God indeed, and of his care
for the Credit and Eftablifhment of the Holy Books;
that he has left us means fufficient, after above Four
thoufand Years, of examining and afcertaining the Veracity of the moft Ancient of its Writers, and in one
of the moft fcrupled and exceptionable Points of his
Narration, that of the Univerfal Deluge; and that
from unexceptionable Principles, the Aftronomical Tables of the Cæleftial Motions. To how great a degree
this thing will deferve the moft ferious Confideration of
every one, efpecially in this our Sceptical Age, I need
not determine. The importance of the concern, and the
greatnefs of the Evidence hence afforded, fufficiently
enforcing this Point, without any farther Application.*

Coroll. 6. *The years added in the* Samaritan Pentateuch *and* Septuagint *to the accounts of Time,
from the* Hebrew Verity, *fince the Deluge, are
added without reafon, and are contrary to the Truth,
and to the Sacred Writings together. For whereas,
by the* Hebrew Verity, *and the Aftronomical Tables*

R 4 *of*

of the place of the Perihelion, *and of the Conjunctions
of the* Sun *and* Moon; (*not to mention the Testimonies of* Abidenus *and* Berosus *here*) *the Deluge's
beginning is fix'd to the Seventeenth day of the Second
Month from the Autumnal Equinox, or to the* 27th *of*
November *in the Year of the* Julian Period 2365,
and the 2349th *before the Christian Æra;* (*by reason of
the just number of* 4044 *Years since past and elapsed;*) *In
case those Eight hundred or Nine hundred Years which
the* Samaritan *and* Septuagint *have added, are to
be allowed for, all is put thereby into Confusion. The
Situation of the* Moon *necessary to this matter is lost,
and no reasonable Account to be given of her still accompanying the Earth. The place of the* Perihelion,
*and Day of the beginning of the Deluge thence nearly
determin'd, must have been about twelve Degrees, and
as many Days sooner; and the Day which* Noah *entred into the Ark must have been not the Twenty seventh
of the Second Month, as even the* Septuagint *by their
way of reckoning were oblig'd to express it; nor the
Seventeenth day of the same Month, as the* Hebrew
Verity *and* Samaritan *Pentateuch do rightly determine it; but rather the Fifth of the same Month,
contrary to the Faith and Agreement of all Copies and
Translations in the World. So that upon the whole,
the intire force of this Reasoning, and the conjoint
Influence of the several ways by which this* Hypothesis *fixes the day of the* Deluge *so nicely, conspires
to confirm and give undoubted Attestation to the*
Hebrew Verity; *and consequently to destroy the Authority of the* Samaritan *and* Septuagint, *so far as
they contradict the same, in the matters herein concern'd.*

Coroll. 7. Hence the Chronology *of the* Bible *is
establish'd, and all the pretended immense numbers of
Years, which the Annals of some Nations recount, are
confuted. For as the Year of the* Deluge, *from the*
Hebrew

Hebrew *Chronology given*, *the Day of the beginning of the Deluge therein assign'd is fully attested to, and determin'd on our* Hypothesis, *from Astronomy*; *so, vice versâ, the Day of the beginning of the Deluge from the same Sacred History given, (and within a Day or two confirm'd from* Abydenus *and* Berosus *corrected) the number of Years thereby assign'd, is at the same time establish'd also. The Methods before-mention'd of fixing that Day, not permitting the Addition or Subtraction of a few* hundreds, *much less* many thousands *of Years, to or from those Four thousand and forty four, which the Holy Scriptures require us to account since that time: Which therefore ought to be fully acquiesced in; and all other wild and extravagant Numbers be utterly rejected.*

Coroll. 8. *Hence, upon supposition that the Comet was of any given Magnitude, the height of the Tide, or elevation of the Abyss, with its incumbent Orb, may be reduc'd to Calculation, and its Quantity consider'd and compar'd with the Phænomena depending on it. Thus for instance, if the Comet were half as big as the* Earth, *which will hereafter appear not far from truth, and consequently approach'd eight times as near as the* Moon, *or Thirty thousand Miles of us; at its nearest distance, the elevation of the Abyss, or the height of the Tide above its former Position must have been near eight Miles. For the* Moon *elevates the Ocean about six Feet above its moderate State; a Comet at the same distance, (half as big as the* Earth, *which is) Thirteen times as big as the* Moon, *would elevate the same Thirteen times as high, or Seventy eight Feet; and at an eighth part of its distance Five hundred and twelve times as high as the last, or Thirty nine thousand nine hundred and thirty six Feet, which is very near the before-mentioned height of eight Miles. Which Elevation of the Abyss seems very agreeable*

Vid. Solut.
58. infrà.

Lem. 80,
81. prius.

able

able to the Phænomena *afterwards to be obſerv'd, and ſo within a due Latitude eſtabliſhes the foregoing* Hypotheſes *of the nearneſs of the Comets approach, and the conſequent bigneſs of the Comet it ſelf before-mention'd.*

S C H O L I U M.

Having thus eſtabliſh'd this main Propoſition, twill here be proper to deſcribe as near as the *Phænomena* of Comets, and of the Deluge, afford us any guidance, the particular *Trajectory* of the Comet, or that part of it which could be concern'd with us, and our lower Planetary Regions, which accordingly, in a mean between ſuch as approach exceeding near to, and ſuch as remain at ſomewhat remoter diſtances from the *Sun* in their *Perihelia,* and agreeably to that Hiſtorical *Trajectory* of the laſt famous Comet delineated by Mr. *Newton,* I ſhall here attempt. For tho' 'twere folly to think of delineating the very ſame in which the Comet revolv'd, yet we may eaſily come pretty near it; we may give the *Reader* a clear and diſtinct *Idea* of the whole matter, and enable him to judge of any particular conſequences occaſionally to be drawn therefrom. Now verbal Deſcriptions in ſuch caſes being of ſmall advantage, compar'd to Schemes and Graphical Delineations, I ſhall wave more *Fig. 1.* words about it, and exhibit an intire Figure of the whole to the view and conſideration of the *Reader.* From the careful Obſervation whereof the following inferences may be eaſily drawn.

Corollary 1. *The Earth would twice paſs quite through the Tail of the Comet ; the firſt time at the beginning of the Deluge, and the ſecond about Fifty three*

*three or fifty four Days after : Their several Motions,
then bringing them to the Situation describ'd in the
Figure.*

Coroll. 2. *At the second passing by of the Comet,
before its cutting the Ecliptick in its Ascent from the
Sun, about Sixty two Days after the former passage,
the Moon, which at the first was three Days past
the New, at this last time must have been within a
day or two of its Quadrature, past the like Conjunction.*

Coroll. 3. *If at the first passing by of the Comet, the
Moon was a small matter nearer the Comet than the
Earth had been just before ; she would be accelerated
somewhat more than the Earth, and by her Position
at the second passage she would be a little more retarded
than the Earth; and upon the whole might afterward retain an equal Velocity with it, as 'tis certain
she still does.*

Coroll. 4. *That former superabundant Velocity
would in the intermediate space cast the Moon farther off the Sun, and thereby make it approach nearer
the Earth at the Conjunction or New ; and recede
farther from it at the Opposition or Full than it did
before. Which things being so, it may deserve consideration, whether the present* Eccentricity *of the*
Moon's *Orbit about the Earth, might not, without
any change in its periodical Revolution, be hence derived? And so, Whether the* Menstrual Course *were
not as truly* circular *before the* Deluge, *as we have
already shew'd the* Annual *to have been?* Especially,
when the Situation of the Moon's Apogæon *was,
from the present Astronomical Tables, somewhat near
that place which according to such an* Hypothesis ,
and such a Trajectory *of the Comet, it ought to have
been, I mean the latter degrees of* Cancer, *or the former of* Leo.

Coroll.

Coroll. 5. '*Twas almoſt the New* Moon *when the Comet's Tail involv'd the Earth and the* Moon *the ſecond time* ; *as the Poſition of the Earth in the Figure, with the conſideration of the place of the* Moon *then, will eaſily ſhew.*

BOOK

BOOK III.

PHÆNOMENA.

CHAP. I.

Phænomena *relating to the* Mosaick *Creation, and the Original Constitution of the Earth.*

I. ALL those particular small Bodies of which our habitable Earth is now compos'd, were originally in a mixed, confused, fluid, and uncertain Condition; without any order or regularity. It was an *Earth without form, and void*; had *darkness* spread over *the face of its Abyss*; and in reality was, what it has been ever stil'd, a perfect *Chaos*.

Gen. i. 2. Grot. Ver. Rel. Chrift. l. 1. Sect. 16. Burn. Theor. l. 1. c 4. and l. 2. c. 7. 8. Arch. l. 2. c. 1.

The Testimonies for this are so numerous, and the Consent of all Authors, Sacred and Prophane, so unanimous, that I need only refer the *Reader* to them for the undoubted Attestation of it.

II. The Formation of this Earth, or the Change of that *Chaos* into an habitable Word, was not a meer result from any

necessary

neceffary Laws of *Mechanifm* independently on the Divine Power; but was the proper effect of the Influence and Interpofition,
and all along under the peculiar Care and
Providence of God.

The Teftimonies for this are fo numerous, and
fo exprefs, both in the *Mofaich* Hiftory it felf,
in the other parts of Scripture relating thereto,
and in all Antiquity, that I may refer the *Reader* to almoft every place where this matter is
fpoken of, without quoting here any particulars.
He who is at all acquainted with the Primitive
Hiftories of this rifing World, whether Sacred or
Prophane, can have no reafon to make any doubt
of it.

III. The Days of the Creation, and that
of Reft, had their beginning in the Evening.

Gen. 1. 5, *The Evening and the Morning were the firft Day.*
8, 13, 19, And fo of the reft afterward.
23, 31.

IV. At the time immediately preceding
the fix days Creation, the face of the *Abyfs,*
or fuperior Regions of the *Chaos,* were involv'd in a thick Darknefs.

Gen. i. 2. *Darknefs was upon the face of the Deep.* To which
Teftimony the Prophane Traditions do fully
agree; as may be feen in the Authors before refer'd to.

V. The vifible part of the firft days Work,
was the Production of Light, or its fucceffive appearance to all the Parts of the Earth;
with the confequent diftinction of Darknefs
and Light, Night and Day upon the face
of it.

God

God said, Let there be Light ; and there was Gen. i. 3,
Light : And God saw the Light that it was good, 4, 5.
and God divided the light from the darkness : And
God called the light, Day, and the darkness he called
Night : And the Evening and the Morning was the
first day.

VI. The visible part of the Second Days
Work was the elevation of the Air, with
all its contained Vapours ; the spreading
it for an *Expansum* above the Earth ; and
the distinction thence arising of Superior
and Inferior Waters: The former consisting of those Vapours, rais'd and sustain'd
by the Air ; the latter of such as either
were enclosed in the Pores, Interstices and
Bowels of the Earth, or lay upon the Surface thereof.

God said, Let there be a firmament, or Expan- ver. 6,7,8.
sum, in the midst of the waters, and let it divide
the waters from the waters. And God made the fir-
mament, and divided the waters which were under
the firmament, from the waters which were above
the firmament: And it was so ; and God called the
firmament Heaven. And the Evening and the Morn-
ing were the second day.

VII. The visible parts of the Third
Day's Works were two, the former the
Collection of the inferior Waters, or such
as were now under the Heaven into the
Seas, with the consequent appearance of
the dry Land ; the latter the production
of Vegetables out of that Ground so lately
become dry.

God

ver. 9, 10, 11, 12, 13. God *faid, Let the waters under the heavens be ga-thered together unto one place, and let the dry land ap-pear; and it was fo. And God called the dry land Earth; and the gathering together of the waters called he Seas: And God faw that it was good. And God faid, Let the Earth bring forth grafs, the herb yield-ing feed, and the fruit-tree yielding fruit after his kind, whofe feed is in it felf upon the earth; and it was fo. And the earth brought forth grafs, and herb yielding feed after his kind, and the tree yielding fruit, whofe feed was in it felf after his kind; and God faw that it was good. And the Evening and the Morning were the third day.*

VIII. The Fourth Day's Work was the Placing the Heavenly Bodies, Sun, Moon and Stars, in the *Expanfum* or Firmament, *i. e.* The rendring them Vifible and Con-fpicuous on the Face of the Earth: Toge-ther with their feveral Affignations to their refpective Offices there.

ver. 14, 15, 16, 17, 18, 19. God *faid, Let there be lights in the Expanfum, or, firmament of heaven, to divide the day from the night; and let them be for figns and for feafons, and for days and years; and let them be for lights in the firmament of heaven, to give light upon the earth; and it was fo. And God made two great lights; the greater light to rule the day, and the leffer light to rule the night; he made the ftars alfo. And God fet them in the firmament of the heaven, to give light upon the earth; and to rule over the day, and over the night, and to divide the light from the darknefs; and God faw that it was good. And the Evening and the Morning were the fourth day.*

IX. The Fifth Day's Work was the Pro-duction of the Fifh and Fowl out of the Waters;

Waters; with the Benediction beftow'd on them in order to their Propagation.

God faid, Let the Waters bring forth abundantly ver.20,21, *the moving creature that hath life, and fowl that may* 22, 23. *fly above the earth in the open firmament of heaven. And God created great Whales, and every living creature that moveth, which the waters brought forth abundantly after their kind ; and every winged fowl after his kind ; and God faw that it was good. And God bleffed them, faying, Be fruitful and multiply, and fill the waters in the Seas; and let fowl multiply in the earth. And the Evening and the Morning were the fifth day.*

X. The Sixth Day's Work was the Production of all the Terreftrial or Dry-land Animals ; and that in a different manner. For the Brute Beafts were produc'd out of the Earth, as the Fifh and Fowl had been before out of the Waters: But after that the Body of *Adam* was form'd of the Duft of the Ground ; who by the Breath of Life breath'd into him in a peculiar manner, became a Living Soul. Some time after which, on the fame day, he was caft into a deep Sleep, and *Eve* was form'd of a Rib taken from his fide. Together with feveral other things, of which a more particular account has been already given on another occa- Hypoth.3. p. 89, &c. prius.
fion.

God faid, Let the Earth bring forth the living ver.24,25, 26,27. *creature after his kind, cattel and creeping thing, and beaft of the Earth after his kind; and it was fo. And God made the beaft of the earth after his kind, and cattel after their kind, and every thing that*

creepeth

creepeth upon the earth after his kind; and God saw that it was good. And God said, Let us make man in Our Image, after Our likeness, and let them have dominion over the Fish of the sea, and over the fowl of the air, and over the cattel, and over all the earth, and over every creeping thing that creepeth upon the earth. So God created Man in his own image, in the image of God created he him ; Male and Female created he them, &c. Vid. ver. 28, 29, 30, 31. and Cap. 2. 7, 15, &c.

XI. God having thus finiſh'd the Works of Creation, Reſted on the Seventh day from the ſame; and ſanctified or ſet that day apart for a Sabbath, or day of Reſt, to be then and afterward obſerv'd as a Memorial of his Creation of the World in the ſix foregoing, and his Reſting or keeping a Sabbath on this ſeventh day. Which Sabbath was reviv'd, or at leaſt its Obſervation anew enforc'd on the *Jews,* by the Fourth Commandment.

Gen. ii. 1, 2, 3. *Thus the Heavens and the Earth were finiſhed, and all the hoſt of them, and on the ſeventh day God had ended his work which he had made; and he reſted on the ſeventh day from all his work which he had made. And God bleſſed the ſeventh day, and ſanctifyed it, becauſe that in it he had reſted from all his work which God created and made.*

Exod. 20. 8,9,10,11. *Remember that thou keep holy the Sabbath day. Six days ſhalt thou labour, and do all thy work : But the ſeventh day is the Sabbath of the Lord thy God ; in it thou ſhalt do no manner of work, thou, nor thy ſon, nor thy daughter, nor thy man-ſervant, nor thy maid-ſervant, nor thy cattel, nor the ſtranger which is within thy gates : For in ſix days the Lord made Heaven and Earth, the Sea, and all that in them is,*
and

and refted the feventh day; wherefore the Lord blef-
fed the feventh day, and hallowed it.

XII. There is a conftant and vigorous heat diffufed from the Central towards the Superficiary parts of our Earth.

Tho' I might bring feveral Arguments from Ancient Tradition, the Opinion of great Philofophers, and the prefent Obfervations of Nature for this Affertion ; yet I fhall chufe here, for brevities fake, to depend wholly on the laft evidence , and refer the inquifitive Reader to what the Learned Dr. *Woodward* fays in the prefent cafe ; which I take to be very fatif-factory. Effay, Part 3. Sect. 1.

XIII. The Habitable Earth is founded or fituate on the Surface of the Waters ; or of a deep and vaft Subterraneous fluid.

This Conftitution of the Earth is a natural re-fult from fuch a *Chaos*, as we have already af-fign'd ; affords foundation for an eafie account of the Origin of Mountains; renders the Hiftories of the feveral ftates of the Earth, and of the Univerfal Deluge very intelligible ; is as Philofophical, and as agreeable to the common *Phænomena* of Nature as any other; without this fuppofition 'twill be, I believe, impoffible to explain what Antiquity, Sacred and Prophane, affures us of relating to the Earth, and its great *Cataftrophes* ; but this being allow'd, 'twill not be difficult to account for the fame to the greateft degree of fatisfaction, as will appear in the progrefs of the prefent *Theory* : And Laftly, The fame affertion is moft exactly confonant to, and confirm'd by the Holy Scriptures ; as the following Texts will fairly evince. *Vid. Theor. L. 1. Cap. 5 & 11. & , 2. Ca L. & 10. 7,*

Prov. viii.
27,28,29.

*When the Lord prepared the heavens I was there:
When he set a compass (Circle or Orb) on the face
of the deep: When he established the clouds above,
when he strengthened the fountains of the deep: When
he gave to the sea his decree, that the waters should
not pass his commandment; when he appointed the
foundations of the earth.*

Psal. xxiv. 2.

*He hath founded the earth upon the seas, and
establish'd it upon the floods.*

& cxxxvi.
6.

*To him that stretched out the earth above the wa-
ters; for his mercy endureth for ever.*

2 Pet. iii.
5, 6.

*This they willingly are ignorant of, that by the
word of God the heavens were of old, and the Earth,
standing out of the water, and in the water; whereby the world that then was, being overflowed with
waters, perished.*

Gen. vii.
11.

*The fountains of the great deep were broken
up.*

& viii. 2.

The fountains of the deep were stopped.

XIV. The interior or intire Constitution
of the Earth is correspondent to that of an
Egg.

Vid. Theor.
L. 1. C. 5.
& L. 2.
C. 10.

'Tis very well known that an *Egg* was the so-
lemn and remarkable Symbol or Representation
of the World among the most venerable Antiquity; and that nothing was more celebrated
than the Original, Ὠον Ὀρφικον, in the most early
Authors; which if extended beyond the Earth
to the System of the Heavens, is groundless and
idle; if referr'd to the Figure of the Earth, is
directly false, and so is most reasonably to be
understood of the intire and internal Constitution
thereof.

Lem. 67,
& 68. cum
Coroll.
prius.

XV. The Primitive Earth had Seas and
Dry-land distinguish'd from each other in
great measure as the present; and those situate

tuate in the fame places generally as they ftill are.

This is put paft doubt by part of the third, the intire fifth, and part of the fixth Day's Works. One half of the third being fpent in diftinguifhing the Seas from the Dry-land; the intire fifth in the Production of Fifh and Fowl out of the Waters, and in the affigning the Air to the latter fort, and the Seas to the former for their refpective Elements; and on the fixth, God beftows on Mankind the Dominion of the Inhabitants, as well of the Seas as of the Dry-land. All which can leave no doubt of the truth of the former part of this Affertion. And that their Difpofition was originally much what as it is at prefent, appears both by the Rivers, *Tigris* and *Euphrates,* running then into the fame *Perfian* Sea that now they do; And by the Obfervations of Dr. *Woodward* fully confirming the fame.

Gen. i. 9, 10. *Verfe* 20, 21, 22, 23.

Verfe 26. 28.

Effay, pag. 252, 253.

XVI. The Primitive Earth had Springs, Fountains, Streams, and Rivers, in the fame manner as the prefent, and ufually in or near the fame places alfo.

This is but a proper confequence of the Diftinction of the Earth into Seas and Dry-land; the latter being uninhabitable without them; and fuch Vapours as are any way condenfed into Water on the higher parts of the Dry-land, naturally defcending and hollowing themfelves Channels, till they fall into the Seas. However, the other direct proofs for both parts of the Affertion are fufficiently evident.

I was fet up from everlafting, from the beginning, or ever the earth was. When there were no depths, I was brought forth; when there were no fountains abounding with water.

Prov. viii. 23, 24.

S 3

A river

Gen. ii.
10, &c.
A river went out of Eden *to water the garden;
and from thence it was parted, and became into four
heads,* Pison, Gihon, Tigris, *and* Euphrates: *The
two latter of which are well-known Rivers to
this very day.* And the fame thing is confirm'd

Eff. p.
255.
by Dr. *Woodward*'s Obfervations.

XVII. The Primitive Earth was diftinguifh'd into Mountains, Plains, and Vallies,
in the fame manner, generally fpeaking,
and in the fame places as the prefent.

This is a natural confequent of the two former: The Caverns of the Seas, with the extant
Parts of the Dry-land, being in effect great Vallies and Mountains; and the Origin and Courfe
of Rivers neceffarily fuppofing the fame. (For
tho' the Earth, in the *Theorift*'s way, were Oval,
which it is not, 'tis demonftrable there could be
no fuch defcent as the courfe of Rivers requires.)
However the direct proofs are evident.

Prov. viii.
22,23,25,
26.
*The Lord poffeffed me in the beginning of his way,
before his works of old. I was fet up from everlafting, from the beginning, or ever the Earth was. Before the mountains were fetled: before the Hills was
I brought forth: While as yet he had not made the
earth, nor the fields, nor the higheft part of the duft of
the world.*

Job xv. 7.
*Art thou the firft man that was born? or waft thou
made before the hills?*

Pfalm xc.
1,2.
*Lord, thou haft been our dwelling place from one ge-
neration to another. Before the mountains were brought
forth, or ever thou hadft formed the earth and the
world, even from everlafting to everlafting, thou art
God.* And indeed thefe three laft *Phænomena*
are in their own Natures fo linked together, they
fo depend on, and infer one another mutually,
that the proofs of each of them fingly may juftly
be

be efteemed under the fame Character to both the other ; and all of them are thereby eftablifh'd paft all rational Contradiction. Of which whole matter, Dr. *Woodward*'s Obfervations are a fuffi- *Essay,* p. cient Atteftation alfo.

XVIII. The Waters of the Seas in the Primitive Earth were *Salt*, and thofe of the Rivers *Frefh*, as they are at prefent, and each, as now, were then ftor'd with great plenty of Fifh.

Essay, p. 249——— 252. and 255——— 258.

This appears from the difference of the *Species* and Natures of Fifhes, fome being produc'd and nourifh'd by Salt Water, others by Frefh ; and yet all created on the fifth Day. And this in all its parts is confirm'd by Dr. *Woodward*'s Obferva- *Essay.* p. tions.

Essay. p. 253, 254, 255.

XIX. The Seas were agitated with a like *Tide*, or *Flux* and *Reflux*, as they are at prefent.

There is in it felf no reafon to doubt of this ; and tis moreover attefted by Dr. *Woodward*'s Ob- *Essay,* p. fervations.

Essay, p. 254.

XX. The Productions of the Primitive Earth, as far as we can guefs by the remainders of them at the Deluge, differ'd little or nothing from thofe of the prefent, either in Figure, Magnitude, Texture of Parts, or any other correfpondent refpect.

This is prov'd by Dr. *Woodward*'s Obferva- *Essay,* p. tions.

Essay, p. 22, 23, 258.

XXI. The Primitive Earth had fuch *Metals* and *Minerals* in it, as the prefent has.

In the land of Havilah *there was gold ; and the gold* Gen ii. *of that land was good, there was* bdellium *and the* 11, 12. onyx-ftone. S 4 Tubal-

Gen. iv. 22. Tubal-cain, *was an instructer of every artificer in brass and iron.* Which is withal attested by Dr. Essay, Part 4. Vid. p. 258, 259. *Woodward's* Observation.

XXII. Arts and Sciences were invented and improv'd in the first Ages of the World, as well as they since have been.

Gen. iv. 2. Abel *was a keeper of sheep,* but Cain *was a tiller of the ground.*

Verse 17. Cain *builded a city, and called it after the name of his son* Enoch.

Verse 20. Jabal *was the father of such as dwell in tents, and of such as have cattel.*

Verse 21. Jubal *was the father of all such as handle the harp and organ.*

Verse 22. Tubal-cain *was an instructer of every artificer in brass and iron.* See also the Right Reverend Bishop *Patrick,* on *Gen.* iv. 20, 21, 22, 25. and v. 18.

CHAP. II.

Phænomena *relating to the* Primitive State *of the Earth.*

XXIII. THE *Primitive* State of the Earth admitted of the primary Production of Animals out of the Waters and dry Ground , which the subsequent Vid. *Grot. Verit. Rel. Christ.* l. 1. sect. 16. States, otherwise than in the ordinary method of Generation have been incapable of.

This appears from the History of the Creation, compar'd with that of Nature ever since. Theor. l. 1. c. 5. l. 2. c. 7. By the former of which, (agreeing with the oldest eft Traditions) 'tis evident, That the Fifhes and Fowls were the immediate Productions or Off-fpring of the Waters, and the Terreftrial Animals of the Dry-land in the *Primitive* State of the Earth: And by the latter 'tis equally fo, that nei-ther of thofe Elements have afforded the like ever fince.

XXIV. The Conftitution of Man in his *Primitive* State was very different from that ever fince the Fall, not only as to the Temper and Perfections of his Soul, but as to the Nature and Difpofition of his Body alfo.

This the whole Drift and Series of the Sacred Hiftory of this Primitive State fuppofes; in which thefe two Particulars may here be taken notice of: (1.) Nakednefs was no fhame, and fo no fenfe of any need to cover it does appear. Thofe Inclinations which provide for the Propa-gation of Mankind were, it feems, fo regular, and fo intirely under the command of Reafon, that not fo much as an Apron was efteem'd ne-ceffary to hide thofe Parts, which all the World have fince thought proper to do. (2.) The Temper of the Humane Body was more foft, pliable, and alterable than now it is: Some forts of Fruits and Food were capable of caufing a mighty change therein, either to fix and adapt it to its prefent Condition, or difcompofe and diforder it; *i. e.* in other words, either to render it Permanent and Immortal on the one hand; or to devolve upon it Difeafes, Corruption, and Mortality on the other. What concerns the Soul, or its moral Perfections, is without the compafs of this *Theory*, and not here to be confider'd.

Gen. ii. 25.and iii. 7, 10, 11.

Cap. ii. 9, 16, 17. and iii. 1, &c.

XXV. The

XXV. The Female was then very different from what she is now ; particularly she was in a state of greater equality with the Male, and little more subject to Sorrow in the Propagation of Posterity than he.

(1.) Her Names were as much as possible the very same with his. The Husband was call'd *Adam*, the Wife *Adamah*; the Husband *Iffch*, the Wife *Iffchah*. *God called their Name* Adam *in the day that they were created. She shall be called* Iffchah *, because she was taken out of* Iffch. (2.) We find little to infer any Inequality or Subjection till after the Fall. *Adam* said , *This is now bone of my bone, and flesh of my flesh: Therefore shall a man leave his father, and his mother, and shall cleave unto his wife, and they shall be one flesh. Unto the woman God said,* (after the Fall) *thy desire shall be (subject to) thine husband, and he shall rule over thee.* (3.) Her pains in Conception and Childbirth were inconsiderable in comparison of what they since have been. *Unto the woman God said,* (after the Fall) *I will greatly multiply thy sorrow, and thy conception; in sorrow thou shalt bring forth children.*

Gen. v. 2. and ii. 23, 24.

Chap. iii. 16.

Ibid.

XXVI. The other Terrestrial Animals were in a state of greater Capacities and Operations ; nearer approaching to reason and discourse, and partakers of higher degrees of Perfection and Happiness, than they have been ever since.

This appears, (1.) From the necessity or occasion of a particular view and distinct consideration of each *Species* of Animals before *Adam* was satisfied that none of them were a Help meet

Gen. ii. 20.

meet for him, or fuitable to his Faculties and
Condition. (2.) From the *Serpent*'s difcourfe with
the Woman: In which, tho' the *Old Serpent, the
Devil,* was alfo concern'd, yet the particular *Subtilty
of the Serpent* is taken notice of as a means of her
Deception, and a Curfe denounced and inflicted
on the fame Beaft upon account thereof. *Now
the Serpent was more fubtil than any beaft of the
field, which the Lord God had made,* &c. *I fear
left by any means, as the Serpent beguiled Eve
through his fubtilty. The Lord God faid unto the* fer-
pent, *Becaufe thou haft done this, thou art curfed
above all cattel, and above every beaft of the field;
upon thy belly fhalt thou go, and duft fhalt thou eat
all the days of thy life.* (3.) From St. *Paul*'s Difcourfe in the Eighth Chapter to the *Romans,
For the earneft expectation of the creature waiteth for
the manifeftation of the Sons of God. For the creature was made fubject to vanity, not willingly, but by
reafon of him who hath fubjected the fame in hope:
Becaufe the creature it felf alfo fhall be delivered from
the bondage of corruption, into the glorious liberty of
the children of God. For we know that the whole
creation groaneth and travelleth in pain together, until
now.*

Gen. iii. 1.
2 Cor. xi.
3.
Gen. iii.
14.

Rom. viii.
19, 20,
21, 22.

XXVII. The temper of the Air, where
our firft Parents liv'd, was warmer, and the
heat greater before the Fall than fince.

This appears, (1.) From the heat requifite to
the Production of Animals, which muft have been
greater than we are fince fenfible of. Of which
the hot Wombs in which the *Fœtus* in *viviparous*
Animals do lye, and the warm brooding of the
Oviparous, with the hatching of Eggs in Ovens, are
good evidence. (2.) From the nakednefs of our
firft Parents. (3.) From that peculiarly warm
cloathing

Gen. ii. 25.

cloathing they immediately ftood in need of afterwards, the Skins of Animals. *Unto* Adam *alſo,*

Chap. iii.
21.
(after the Fall) *and to his wife, did the Lord God
make coats of skins, and cloathed them.*

XXVIII. Thofe Regions of the Earth
where our firft Parents were plac'd, were
productive of better and more ufeful Vegetables, with lefs Labour and Tillage than
fince they have been.

Gen. ii. 15.
*The Lord God took the man, and put him into the
garden of* Eden *to dreſs it, and to keep it;* (before
the Fall).

Chap. iii.
17, 18, 19.
The Lord God faid unto Adam, (after the Fall)
*Curſed is the ground for thy ſake; in ſorrow ſhalt
thou eat of it all the days of thy life. Thorns alſo and
thiſtles ſhall it bring forth to thee, and thou ſhalt eat
the herb of the field. In the ſweat of thy face ſhalt
thou eat bread, till thou return unto the ground, for
out of it waſt thou made.*

XXIX. The *Primitive* Earth was not
equally Paradifiacal all over. The Garden of
Eden or Paradife being a peculiarly fruitful
and happy foil, and particularly furnifh'd
with the neceffaries and delights of an innocent and bleffed life, above the other Regions
of the Earth.

Gen. ii. 8,
9.
The Lord God planted a Garden Eaſtward in Eden,
*and there he put the man whom he had formed : And
out of the ground made the Lord God to grow every
tree that is pleaſant to the ſight, and good for food;
the tree of life alſo in the midſt of the garden, and the
tree of knowledge of good and evil.*

Chap. iii.
23, 24.
*The Lord God ſent the Man forth from the garden
of* Eden *to till the ground from whence he was taken :
So he drove out the man.*

XXX.

XXX. The place of Paradife was where the united Rivers *Tigris* and *Euphrates* divided themfelves into four ftreams, *Pifon*, *Gihon*, *Tigris* and *Euphrates*.

Of this fee the fourth *Hypothefis* before laid down.

XXXI. The Earth in its *Primitive* State had only an *Annual* Motion about the Sun: But fince it has a *Diurnal* Rotation upon its own *Axis* alfo: Whereby a vaft difference arifes in the feveral States of the World.

Of this with all its confequents fee the third *Hypothefis* before laid down.

XXXII. Upon the firft commencing of this *Diurnal* Rotation after the Fall, its *Axis* was oblique to the plain of the Ecliptick as it ftill is: Or in other words, the prefent viciffitudes of Seafons, *Spring*, *Summer*, *Autumn* and *Winter*, arifing from the Sun's accefs to, and recefs from the *Tropicks*, have been ever fince the Fall of Man.

God faid, on the fourth Day, *Let there be lights in the firmament of the heaven, to divide the day from the night*; which was their proper office till the Fall. *And let them be*, ever after, *for figns, and for feafons, and for days, and years*. After the Flood, *While the Earth remaineth, Seed-time and Harveft, and Cold and Heat, and Summer and Winter, and Day and Night fhall not ceafe*. Implying, that tho' the Seafons, as well as Night and Day, had been, during the Deluge, fcarcely diftinguifhable from one another; yet the former as well as the latter diftinction had been in nature before:

And

Gen. i. 14.

Cap. viii. ult.

And furely the Spring, Summer, Autumn and Winter, with their varieties of Cold and Heat, Seed-time and Harveft, were no more originally begun after the Deluge, than the fucceffion of Day and Night mention'd here together with them is by any fuppos'd to have been. But of this we have at large difcours'd under the third *Hypothefis* foregoing already ; to which the Reader is farther referr'd for fatisfaction.

CHAP. III.

Phænomena *relating to the* Antediluvian *State of the Earth.*

XXXIII. THE Inhabitants of the Earth were before the Flood vaftly more numerous than the prefent Earth either actually does , or perhaps is capable to contain and fupply.

In order to the proof of this Affertion, I obferve, (1.) That the Pofterity of every one of the *Antediluvians* , is to be fuppos'd fo much more numerous than of any fince, as their lives were longer: This is but agreeable to the Sacred Hiftory, in which we find two at fixty five, and one at feventy years of Age to have begotten Children : While the three Sons of *Noah* were not begotten till after their Father's five hundredth year: When yet at the fame time the feveral Children of the fame Father appear to have fucceeded as quickly one after another as they ufually do at this day. For as to *Cain* and *Abel*, they

Gen.v. 15, 21.
ver. 12.
ver. 32.

appear

appear to have been pretty near of an Age, the
World being at the death of the latter, not without confiderable numbers of People, tho' their
Father *Adam* was not then an hundred and
thirty years old; and fo in probability contain'd
many of the Pofterity of both of them. (Which
by the way fully eftablifhes the early begetting
of Children juft now obferv'd in the *Antediluvian* Patriarchs, and if rightly confider'd, over-
turns a main Argument for the *Septuagint's* Addition of fo many Centenaries in the Generations Before and After the Deluge.) And as to
the three Sons of *Noah*, born after the five hundredth year of their Father's Life, 'tis evident
that two of them at the leaft, *Japhet* and *Sem*,
were born within two years one after another.
All which makes it highly reafonable to fuppofe,
that in the fame proportion that the Lives of the
Antediluvians were longer, was their Pofterity
more numerous than that of the *Poftdiluvians.*
(2.) The Lives of the *Antediluvians* being pretty
evenly prolong'd, without that mighty inequality in the periods of humane Life, which we
now experience, the proportion between the
Lives of the *Antediluvians* and thofe of the *Poftdiluvians*, is to be taken as about nine hundred the
middle period of their Lives; to twenty two,
the middle period of ours: Which is full forty to
one. And accordingly in any long fpace, the *Antediluvians* muft have forty times as numerous a
Pofterity, as we ufually allow with us for the fame
fpace, on account thereof. (3.) On account of
the *Coexiftence* of fo many of fuch Generations as
are but fucceffive with us, we muft allow the
Antediluvian number of prefent Inhabitants to
have been in half an Arithmetical proportion of
fuch their longer lives after the duration of the
firft

Gen. iv.
14, 15.
with 25.

Vid. Cap.
vii. 13.
with v. 32.

Gen. v. 32.
& vii. 11.
& viii. 13.
with xi.
10.

Vid. Graunt
On Bills
of Mor-
tal. p. 84.

firſt Fathers is expir'd, and a gradual decreaſe of the Ancient ſtock going off, as well as a gradual increaſe of the New ſtock coming on, to be allow'd for : Till which time the proportion is not to be diminiſh'd. So that on this account for the firſt nine hundred years of the World the number of Inhabitants on the Face of the Earth, muſt be eſteem'd forty times as great as in ſo long time are now derivable from a ſingle Couple ; and afterwards twenty times ſo; which *Poſtulata* ſuppos'd, I ſhall propoſe a Calculation (built upon certain matter of fact) firſt how many they *might* have been by the Deluge; and afterward another or two, relying alike on Matter of fact, how many 'tis probable they *really were*, and muſt have been at the ſame time.

Exod. xii. 37. Numb. i. 45, 46. (1.) 'Tis evident from the Sacred Hiſtory, and not to be denied by thoſe who forſake the *Hebrew* Chronology themſelves, or who would leſſen the numbers of the *Antediluvians*; That in the ſpace of about two hundred ſixty ſix years, the Poſterity of *Jacob* alone, by his Sons, (without the conſideration of *Dinah* his Daughter) amounted to ſix hundred thouſand Males, above the Age of Twenty, all able to go forth to War.

Pag 85. Now by Mr. *Graunts* Obſervations on the Bills of Mortality it appears that about $\frac{34}{100}$ are between the Ages of ſixteen and fifty ſix : Which may be near the proportion of the *Males* numbred, to the intire number of them all. So that as thirty four to an hundred, by the Golden Rule, muſt ſix hundred thouſand be to the intire number of the Males of *Iſrael* at that time : Which was therefore one Million ſeven hundred ſixty four thouſand and ſeven hundred. To which add *Fe-*Pag. 64. *males*, near $\frac{1}{15}$ fewer, as ſuppoſe, to make the ſum even, one Million ſix hundred thirty five thouſand

thoufand, three hundred, the *Total* is, three
millions, and three hundred thoufand ; add forty
three thoufand for the *Levites,* (not included in
the former accounts,) the intire Sum will at laft
amount to three millions, and three hundred
forty three thoufand Souls. Now if we fuppofe
the increafe of the Children of *Ifrael* to have
been gradual, and equal through the whole two
hundred fixty fix years, it will appear that they
doubled themfelves every fourteen years at leaft ;
which proportion , if we fhould continue it
through the entire hundred and fourteen Periods, (which the fpace from the Creation to the
Deluge admits) the product or number of People
on the face of the Earth at the Deluge would be
the hundredth and fourteenth place in a Geometrick double proportion, or feries of numbers,
two, four, eight, fixteen, *&c.* where every
fucceeding one were double to that before it :
Which to how immenfe a Sum it would arife,
thofe who know any thing of the nature of
Geometrick Progreffions will eafily pronounce,
and may be foon tried by any ordinary Arithme-
tician. So that without allowing· for the *Longæ-*
vity, and that *Coexiftence,* and more numerous
Off-fpring thereon depending, without taking
as advantagious an *Hypothefis* as one might precarioufly, tho' poffibly, do in fuch a cafe ; If
the *Antediluvians* had only multiplied as faft before, as 'tis certain the *Ifraelites* did fince the
Flood for the affigned term ; the numbers of Mankind actually Alive and *Coexifting* at the Deluge,
muft have been, not only more than the Earth
now does or poffibly could maintain, but pro-
digioufly more than the whole number of Mankind can be juftly fuppos'd ever fince the Deluge,
nay indeed, with any degree of likelihood, ever

T   fince

since the Creation of the World. On which account this Calculation muſt not be at all eſteem'd a real one, or to exhibit in any meaſure the juſt number of the Poſterity of *Adam* alive at the Univerſal Deluge. But it ſerves to ſhew how vaſtly numerous, according to the regular method of humane Propagation, the Offſpring of a ſingle perſon may certainly be ; and this on a Calculation from undoubted matter of fact, not from a meer poſſible *Hypotheſis,* (according to which numbers prodigiouſly greater would ſtill ariſe.) It demonſtrates the probability, if not certainty, of Mankind's Original from a common head as well before as ſince the Deluge, and that within a few Millenaries of years. It, laſtly, is more than ſufficient to demonſtrate the Propoſition we are upon, that the whole Earth muſt have been peopled long before the Flood, and at its approach have contain'd vaſtly more in number than the preſent does or can do. So that altho' I do not pretend to give a particular gueſs at the number of the *Antediluvians* thereby, yet I thought it not improper to be here inſerted. Which firſt Computation being thus diſpatch'd I come to the (2.) which I take to be very probable, and very rational ; and perhaps, within certain limits, to be admitted in the preſent caſe : Namely, That the Primary increaſe of Mankind after the Creation, (that the World might not be deſtitute of Inhabitants for many Ages) was not, at leaſt conſidering their greater *Longævity,* leſs than that of the *Iſraelites* in *Egypt* before-mention'd : But that afterwards, (which was the caſe of the *Iſraelites* alſo) a much leſs proportion obtain'd. Upon which fair and modeſt *Poſtulata* I ſhall demonſtrate the truth of that propoſition

pofition we are now upon. In order to which
I obferve, from Mr. *Graunt*, that at this day the Pa. 59.
number of People does fo increafe, that in two 85, 86.
hundred and eighty years, the Country doubles
its People, and the City of *London* much fooner.
Let us therefore fuppofe that after the firft two
hundred and fixty fix years of the World, the
former of thofe proportions were obferved (and
that muft by all be own'd fufficiently fair;) and
compute how many the number of People muft
on fuch a Calculation arife to before the Deluge.
When therefore after the firft two hundred and
fixty fix years, there was near five periods, each
of two hundred and eighty years, (if the *Longævity* of the *Antediluvians*, and the confequent
Coexiftence and more numerous pofterity were excluded) the number of the Inhabitants by the
Deluge would amount to about thirty times the
former fum of three millions three hundred forty
three thoufand, or one hundred millions two hundred and ninety thoufand of Souls. But if we withal
allow, as we ought, that this number is on account
of *Coexiftence* to be twenty times as great; and on
account of more numerous pofterity forty times
fo (which is on both accounts eight hundred
times as great as the laft mention'd); the number of People at the Deluge will amount to
eighty thoufand two hundred and thirty two
millions; which number, fince the prefent Inhabitants of the Earth, as fome conjecture,
fcarcely exceed three hundred and fifty millions,
is above two hundred and twenty nine times
as great as the Earth now actually contains upon
it, and by confequence many more than at prefent
it could contain and fupply. And this *Hypothefis*
and Calculation are confirm'd by what I fhall
propofe in the (3.) Place, and which muft by

all

all be allow'd very fair and reasonable, namely,
That tho' Mankind, *Cæteris Paribus,* increas'd but
in the same proportion before, as they have
done since the Deluge; we shall find, upon a
due allowance for the two things before-mention'd, *Coexistence* and more numerous *Posterity,*
that the number last assign'd is rather too small
than too great, and the numbers of the Inhabitants of the Earth were more than the present
Earth does or can maintain, many years before
the approach of the Deluge. For if the number
of years before had been the same as that since
the Flood, the Inhabitants, tho' they had been no
longer livers than we now are, would have
been as numerous as the present. But because
the number of years before the Deluge wanted
about two thousand four hundred of that since;
we must allow or abate the increase, which has
arisen in the last two thousand and four hundred
years: Which, since in these latter ages it has
been double in two hundred and eighty years,
and so in two thousand and four hundred years
about three hundred times as great as before;
the *Antediluvians,* if their lives had been no
longer than ours since, must have been but the
three hundredth part so many as the Earth now
contains upon it. But when on the two fore-
mention'd accounts, the number is to be eight
hundred times as great, and on this only three
hundred times as small; the excess is on the side
of the *Antediluvians,* and their number five hundred times as great as that of the present Inhabitants of the Earth. So that on this last *Hypo-*
thesis, which I suppose none can justly except
against, tho' the present Earth be allow'd capable of maintaining five times as many People
as are now by computation upon it; yet will
it

it appear that the *Antediluvian* Earth maintain'd an hundred times as many. Which I imagin not to be wide from probability; and, being so near the calculation before, may be allow'd as reasonable in the present case.

XXXIV. The Bruit Animals whether belonging to the Water or Land, were proportionably at least, more in number before the Flood than they are since.

This is I think generally look'd upon as no other than a reasonable deduction from the last Proposition; and is very fully attested by Dr. *Woodward's* Observations, as far as the remains of those Ages afford any means of knowing the same: And so ought in reason to be universally allow'd. *Essay, pa. 257, 258*

XXXV. The *Antediluvian* Earth was much more fruitful than the present; and the multitude of its vegetable productions much greater.

This is both necessary to be allow'd by reason of the multitude of its Inhabitants, rational and irrational, maintained by them; of which before: And abundantly confirm'd also by Dr. *Woodward's* Observations. *Essay, pa. 84, &c. & 257, 258.*

XXXVI. The Temperature of the *Antediluvian* Air was more equable as to its different Climates, and its different Seasons; without such excessive, and sudden heat and cold; without the scorching of a *Torrid Zone*, and of burning Summers; or the freezing of the *Frigid Zones*, and of piercing Winters; and without such sudden and violent changes in the Climates or Seasons from one extreme to another, as the present Air, to our sorrow, is subject to.

Theor. 1.
c. 1. &
2. Archæ-
2. c. 5,
& 6.

These Characters are extremely agreeable to, and attested by, the ancient Accounts of the Golden Age. The gentleness of the *Torrid* and *Frigid Zones* is necessary to be suppos'd in order to the easie Peopling of the World, with the dispertion and maintenance of those numerous Inhabitants we before prov'd it to have contain'd: Which if they were as now they are, would be very difficultly accountable. The gentleness of Summer and Winter, with the easie and gradual coming on, and going off of the same Seasons, are but necessary in order to the very long lives of the *Antediluvians*; which else 'twere not so easie to account for. And indeed the most of those Testimonies which have been suppos'd favourable to a perpetual *Equinox* before the Deluge, are resolv'd into this Proposition; and if it can be separately establish'd, need not be extended any farther.

XXXVII. The Constitution of the Antediluvian Air was Thin, Pure, Subtile and Homogeneous, without such gross Steams, Exhalations, Nitrosulphureous, or other Heterogeneous mixtures, as occasion Coruscations, Meteors, Thunder, Lightening, Contagions, and Pestilential Infections, in our present Air; and have so very pernicious and fatal (tho' almost insensible) effects in the World since the Deluge.

This is the natural consequent, or rather original, of the before-mention'd equability and uniformity of the *Antediluvian* Air: This must be suppos'd on the account of the *Longævity* of the Inhabitants: And this is very agreeable to the last cited descriptions of the Golden Age.
The

The contrary Heterogeneous and Grofs *Atmo-fphere*, which now encompaffes the Earth, is difagreeable to a reguiar ftate, (which an original formation from the *Chaos* fuppofes) as containing fuch Denfe and Bulky Exhalations, and Maffes, which at firft muft have obtain'd a lower fituation, and were not to be fuftain'd by the Primitive Thin' and Subtile Air or Æther. Such mixtures as this Propofition takes notice of, or thofe effects of them therein mention'd, have no Footfteps in Sacred or Prophane Antiquity, relating to the firft Ages of the World; there is no appearance of them in the Serene and Pellucid Air of the Moon, or of the generality of the Heavenly Bodies, and fo there can be no manner of reafon to afcribe them to the *Antediluvian* ftate.

XXXVIII. The *Antediluvian* Air had no large, grofs Maffes of Vapours, or Clouds, hanging for long feafons in the fame. It had no great round drops of Rain, defcending in multitudes together, which we call Showers: But the Ground was watered by gentle Mifts or Vapours afcending in the Day, and defcending, in great meafure, again in the fucceeding Night.

This Affertion is but a proper confequent of fuch a Pure, Thin, Rare Æther as originally encompafs'd the Earth. 'Tis very agreeable to the defcriptions of the Golden Age, and to the prefent *Phænomena* of moft of the Planets (efpecially of the Moon, whofe face, tho' fo near us, is never obfcur'd or clouded from us.) 'Tis neceffary to be fuppos'd in an Air without a Rainbow, as the *Antediluvian* was; (of which prefently)

Theor. 1. 2. c. 1.

fently) and is indeed no other than the words of the Sacred Hiftory inform us of.

Gen. ii. 5, 6. *The Lord God had not caufed it to Rain upon the Earth, —— But there went up a Mift from the Earth, and watered the whole face of the ground.*

XXXIX. The *Antediluvian* Air was free from violent Winds, Storms, and Agitations, with all their effects on the Earth or Seas, which we cannot now but be fufficiently fenfible of.

This the foregoing *Phænomena* enforce: So Homogeneous, Pure, and Unmix'd a Fluid, as that Air has been defcrib'd to have been, by no means feeming capable of exciting in it felf, or undergoing any fuch diforderly commotions or fermentations. Where no Vapours were collected into Clouds, there muft have been no Winds to collect them; where the Climates preferv'd their own proper temperature, no Storms muft have hurried the Air from colder to hotter, or from hotter to colder Regions; where was no Rainbow, there muft have been no driving together the feparate Vapours into larger *Globules,* or round drops of Rain, the immediate requi- Vid. Phæ- nom. 55. infià. fite thereto. This is alfo highly probable by reafon of the perpetual tranquility of the Air for the firft five intire Months of the Deluge, (as will be prov'd anon) which is fcarce fuppofable if Storms and Tempefts were ufual before.

XL. The *Antediluvian* Air had no Rainbow; as the prefent fo frequently has.

Gen. ix. 12,13,14, 15, 16,17. Vid. Theo. l. 2. c. 5. *God faid,* (after the Deluge) *This is the token of the covenant which I make between me and you, and every living creature that is with you, for per- petual generations. I do fet my bow in the cloud; and it fhall be for a token of a covenant between me and*

and the earth. And it shall come to pass when I bring a cloud over the earth, that the bow shall be seen in the cloud. And I will remember my covenant, which is between me and you, and every living creature of all flesh ; and the waters shall no more become a flood to destroy all flesh. And the bow shall be in the cloud, and I will look upon it, that I may remember the everlasting covenant between God and every living creature of all flesh that is upon the earth. And God said unto Noah, this is the token of the covenant which I have establish'd between me and all flesh that is upon the earth.

XLI. The *Antediluvians* might only Eat Vegetables ; but the Use of Flesh after the Flood was freely allow'd alfo.

God *said*, (to our firft Parents in Paradife) *Behold I have given you every herb, bearing feed, which is upon the face of all the earth ; and every tree, in the which is the fruit of a tree yielding feed, to you it shall be for meat ; and to every beaft of the earth, and to every fowl of the air, and to every thing that creepeth upon the earth wherein there is life ; I have given every green herb for meat : And it was fo.*

God *blessed Noah and his fons*, (after the flood) *and faid unto them, Be fruitful and multiply, and replenish the earth. And the fear of you, and the dread of you shall be upon every beaft of the earth, and upon every fowl of the air, upon all that moveth upon the earth, and upon all the fishes of the fea ; into your hand are they delivered. Every moving thing that liveth shall be meat for you ; even as the green herb have I given you all things.* To which when the Prince of Latin Poets fo exactly agrees, let us for once hear him in the prefent cafe.

Gen. i. 29, 30.

Cap. ix. 1, 2, 3.

Ante

Vir. Georg
lib. 2. fub
calce.

*Ante etiam fceptrum Dictæi Regis, & antè
Impia quàm cæfis gens eft epulata juvencis,
Aureus in terris hanc vitam Saturnus agebat.*

XLII. The Lives of the *Antediluvians*
were more univerfally equal, and vaftly
longer than ours now are: Men before the
Flood frequently approaching near to a
thoufand, which almoft none now do to a
hundred years of Age.

Grot. ubi
fuprà.
Theor. 1.
2. c. 3.
Hor Ode
3.

This is both fully attefted by the moft ancient Remainders of prophane Antiquity, and will
be put paft doubt hereafter by a Table of the
Ages of the *Antediluvians*, out of the fifth Chapter of *Genefis*. *Semotique priùs tarda neceffitas Lett
corripuit gradum.*

XLIII. Tho' the *Antediluvian* Earth was
not deftitute of leffer Seas and Lakes, every where difper'd on the Surface thereof;
yet had it no *Ocean*, or large receptacle of
Waters, feparating one Continent from another, and covering fo large a portion of it,
as the prefent Earth has.

Vid. etiam
Coroll. 2.
Solut. 7.
infrà.

This is evident, Becaufe (1.) the number of
the *Antediluvians* before affign'd, muft have been
too numerous for the Continents alone to maintain. (2.) The Ark appears to have been the
firft Pattern and Inftance for Navigation (which
had there been an *Ocean*, muft have been very
perfect long before); and this feems probable
from the conftant filence concerning Navigation
in the Golden Age, from the common Opinion
of all Authors; and from the neceffity of the

Gen. vi.
14,15,16.

moft minute and particular Directions from God
himfelf

himfelf to the Fabrick of it in the *Mofaick* Hiftory. (3.) That famous Tradition among the
Ancients of the drowning a certain vaft Continent, call'd *Atlantis*, bigger than *Africa* and *Afia*,
feems to be a plain Relique of the Generation
of the *Ocean* at the Deluge, and confequently of
that *Antediluvian* State, where the greateft part
of what the *Ocean* now poffeffes was Dry-land,
and inhabited as well as the reft of the Globe.
(4.) The Generation of the *Ocean*, with the Situation of the prefent great Continents of the
Earth, will be fo naturally and exactly accounted for at the Deluge, that when that is underftood there will remain to thofe who are fatisfied
with the other Conclufions, fmall reafon to
doubt of the truth of this before us. (5.) The
Teftimony of *Jofephus* (if the *Theorift* hit upon
his true Senfe) is agreeable, who fays, At the
Deluge God 'Εἰς θάλασσαν τ̔ ἤπειρον μετέβαλε; *chang'd
the Continent into Sea.*

Archæol.
p. 241.
Theor. L
1. c. 6.

Theor. L
2. c. 10.
p. 280.

C H A P. IV.

Phænomena *relating to the Univerfal De-*
luge, and its Effects upon the Earth.

XLIV. **I**N the Seventeenth Century from
the Creation, there happen'd a
moft extraordinary and prodigious Deluge
of Waters upon the Earth.

This general Affertion is not only attefted by
a large and fpecial Account of it in the Sacred
Writings, but by the univerfal Confent of the
moft ancient Records of all Nations befides, as
may

188 *PHÆNOMENA.* Book III.

Grot. ubi suprà. Bish. Stillingfleet's Orig. l. 3. may be seen in the Authors quoted in the Margin; and is put moreover past doubt by Dr. *Woodward's* Natural Observations *

c. 4. *Edward's* Authority of Script. p. 118, &c. And Commentators on Gen. 6. and 7. * Essay, Pref. and Part 3. Sect. 2.

XLV. This prodigious Deluge of Waters was mainly occasion'd by a most extraordinary and violent Rain, for the space of forty Days, and as many Nights, without intermission.

Gen.vii.4. *Yet seven days, and I will cause it to rain upon the earth forty days and forty nights.*

Verse 11, 12. *The windows of heaven were opened, and the rain was upon the Earth forty days and forty nights.*

Verse 17. *And the flood was forty days upon the earth.*

XLVI. This vast quantity of Waters was not deriv'd from the Earth or Seas, as Rains constantly now are; but from some other Superior and Cœlestial Original.

This is evident, Because (1.) the *Antediluvian* Air (as was before prov'd) never retain'd great quantities of Vapours, or sustained any Clouds capable of producing such considerable, and so lasting Rains, as this most certainly was. (2.) The quantity of Waters on the *Antediluvian* Earth, where there was no Ocean, (as we saw just now) was very small in comparison of that at present, and so could contribute very little towards the Deluge. (3.) If the quantity of Waters on the Face of the Earth had then been as great as now, and had all been elevated into Vapours, and descended on the Dry-land alone, it were much too small to Vid. Th. l. 1. c. 2. cause such a Deluge as this was. (4.) But because, if the Waters were all rais'd into Vapours, and descended in Rain, they must either fall upon, or run down into the *Ocean,* the Seas, and those

Declivities

Declivities they were in before, they could only take up and poſſeſs their old places; and ſo could not contribute a jot to that ſtanding and permanent Maſs of Waters which cover'd the Earth at the Deluge. (5.) The Expreſſion us'd by the Sacred Hiſtorian, that the Windows, Flood-gates, or *Cataracts* of Heaven were open'd at the fall, and ſhut at the ceaſing of theſe Waters, very naturally agrees to this Superior and Cœleſtial Original.

Gen. vii. 11. And viii. 2.

XLVII. This vaſt fall of Waters, or forty Days rain, began on the fifth day of the Week, or *Thurſday* the twenty ſeventh day of *November*, being the ſeventeenth day of the ſecond Month from the *Autumnal Equinox;* (correſponding this Year 1696. to the twenty eighth day of *October*.)

In the ſix hundredth year of Noah's *life, in the ſecond month, the ſeventeenth day of the month, the windows of heaven were opened, and the rain was upon the earth forty days and forty nights.*

Gen. vii. 11.

Thus *Abydenus* and *Beroſus* ſay it began on the fifteenth day of *Dæſius,* the ſecond Month from the *Vernal Equinox;* which, if the miſtake, ariſing 'tis probable from the ignorance of the change in the beginning of the Year at the *Exodus* out of *Egypt,* be but corrected, is within a day or two agreeable to the Narration of *Moſes,* and ſo exceedingly confirms the ſame.

Langius de annis Chriſti, p. 255.

XLVIII. The other main cauſe of the Deluge, was the breaking up the Fountains of the great *Abyſs*, or the cauſing ſuch Chaps and Fiſſures in the upper Earth, as might permit the Waters contain'd in the Bowels of it when violently preſs'd and ſqueez'd fqueez'd upwards to afcend, and fo add to the quantity of thofe which the Rains produced.

Gen. vii. 11. Job xxxviii. 8.

All the fountains of the great deep were broken up.

The fea brake forth, as if it had iffued out of the womb.

XLIX. All thefe Fountains of the great Deep were broken up on the very firft day of the Deluge, or the very firft day when the Rains began.

Gen. vii. 11.

In the fix hundredth year of Noah's *life, in the fecond month, the feventeenth day of the month, the fame day were all the fountains of the great deep broken up, and the windows of heaven were opened:*

L. Yet the very fame day, *Noah*, his Family, and all the Animals entred into the Ark.

Gen. vii. 13, 14.

In the felf-fame day, laft mention'd, entred Noah, *and* Shem, *and* Ham, *and* Japheth, *the fons of* Noah, *and* Noah's *wife, and the three wives of his fons with them into the ark: They, and every beaft after his kind, and all the cattel after their kind, and every creeping thing that creepeth upon the earth after his kind, and every fowl after his kind, every bird of every fort.*

LI. Tho' the firft and moft violent Rains continued without intermiffion but forty days, yet after fome time the Rains began again, and ceafed not till the feventeenth day of the feventh Month, or a hundred and fifty days after the Deluge began.

This is very probably gather'd from the mighty increafe of the Waters, even after the firft forty days Rain were over; and from the exprefs fixing of the ftoppage of the Rains to the laft day here affigned.

The

The Waters prevailed, and were increafed greatly. And the waters prevailed exceedingly upon the Earth.

Gen. vii. 18. Verfe 19.

The waters prevailed (or were increafed) *upon the Earth an hundred and fifty days. And God remembred* Noah, *and every living thing, and all the Cattel that was with him in the Ark : And God made a wind to pafs over the Earth, and the waters affwaged. The fountains alfo of the deep, and the windows of heaven were ftopped; and the rain from heaven was reftrained.*

Verfe 24.

Cap. viii. 1, 2.

LII. This fecond, and lefs remarkable Rain was deriv'd from fuch a caufe as the former was.

This Propofition is (1.) Very fair and probable in it felf. (2.) Gives an account of the augmentation of the Waters by their fall, when had they been only exhaled and let fall again, as our Rains now are, they would have added nothing thereto. (3.) Is exactly agreeable to the expreffions in *Mofes*; who fays *the Windows of Heaven* which were *open'd* at the beginning of the firft, were not fhut or *ftopped* till the end of this fecond Rain; thereby plainly deriving this latter, as well as the former, from a Superiour and Celeftial original. *The fountains of the deep and the windows of heaven were ftopped, and the rain from heaven was reftrained.*

Gen. viii. 2.

LIII. Tho' the fountains of the great deep were broken up, and the forty days Rain began at the fame time, yet is there a very obfervable mention of a threefold growth, or diftinct augmentation of the Waters; as if it were on three feveral accounts, and at three feveral times.

The

Gen. vii.
17.

The flood was forty days upon the earth, and the waters increased, and bare up the ark, and it was lift up above the earth.

Verse 18.

And the waters prevailed, and were increased greatly, and the ark went upon the face of the

Verse 19.

waters.

And the waters prevailed exceedingly upon the earth, and all the high hills that were under the whole heaven were cover'd.

LIV. The Waters of the Deluge increas'd by degrees till their utmost height; and then decreas'd by degrees till they were clearly gone off the face of the earth.

This is evident from the intire series and course of the *Mosaick* History, in the seventh and eighth chapters of *Genesis*.

LV. The Waters of the Deluge were Still, Calm, free from Commotions, Storms, Winds, and Tempests of all sorts, during the whole time in which the *Ark* was afloat upon them.

Gen.vi.15.

This is evident from the impossibility of the *Ark*'s abiding a Stormy Sea, considering the vast bulk, and particular figure of it. For since it was three hundred Cubits long, fifty Cubits broad, and thirty Cubits high: Which is, according to the most accurate determination of the Cubits length, by the Right Reverend the Lord Bishop of *Peterborough*, above five hundred and forty seven English feet long, above ninety one feet broad, and near fifty five feet high: And since withal it appears to have been of the figure of a Chest, without such a peculiar bottom, and proportion of parts, as our great Ships are contrived with; 'tis evident, and will be allow'd by Persons skill'd in Navigation, that

Bishop Cumberland's Weights and Measures, p. 34.

'twas

'twas not capable of enduring a Stormy Sea. It muſt, whenever either the Ridges or Hollows of vaſt Waves were ſo ſituate, that it lay over-croſs the one or the other, have had its back broken, and it ſelf muſt have been ſhatter'd to pieces; which having not happen'd, 'tis a certain evidence of a calm Sea during the whole time it was afloat.

LVI. Yet during the Deluge there were both Winds and Storms of all ſorts in a very violent manner.

God made a wind to paſs over the earth, and the waters aſſwaged. Gen.viii.1.

Thou coveredſt the earth with the deep, as with a garment; the waters ſtood above the mountains. At thy rebuke they fled; at the voice of thy thunder they haſted away. They go up by the mountains; they go down by the vallies unto the place which thou haſt appointed for them. Pſalm civ. 6, 7, 8.

LVII. This Deluge of Waters was univerſal in its extent and effect; reaching to all the parts of the Earth, and deſtroying all the Land-animals on the intire Surface thereof; thoſe only excepted which were with *Noah* in the Ark. Vid. Philonis deſcriptionem Diluvii apud Burnetium, Archæol. p. 236.

The following Texts, eſpecially if compar'd with the thirty third foregoing *Phænomenon,* and added to Dr. *Woodward's* Obſervations atteſting the ſame thing, will put this Aſſertion beyond rational Exception. Eſſay. Pref. and Part 3. Sect. 2, Vid. Th. I. 1. c. 3.

God looked upon the earth, and behold it was corrupt; for all fleſh had corrupted his way upon the earth. And God ſaid unto Noah, *The end of all fleſh is come before me.* Gen. vi. 13.

Behold, I, even I do bring a flood of waters upon the earth, to deſtroy all fleſh, wherein is the breath of life, Verſe 17.

V

life from under heaven: and every thing that is in the
earth ſhall dye.

Chap. vii.
4.
Verſe 19,
20, 21,
22, 23

Every living ſubſtance that I have made, will I
deſtroy from off the face of the earth.

All the high hills that were under the whole heaven
were covered.———— And all fleſh died that moved
upon the earth, both of fowl, and of cattel, and of
beaſt, and of every creeping thing that creepeth upon
the earth, and every man. All in whoſe noſtrils was
the breath of life; all that was in the dry land died.
And every living ſubſtance was deſtroyed which was
upon the face of the ground, both man, and cattel,
and the creeping thing, and the fowl of the heaven,
and they were deſtroyed from the earth; and Noah
only remain'd alive, and they that were with him in
the Ark.

LVIII. The Waters at their utmoſt
height were fifteen Cubits above the higheſt
Mountains, or three Miles at the leaſt per-
Vid. Va-
ren. Geog.
p. 60.
Gen. vii.
19, 20.
pendicular above the common Surface of the
Plains and Seas.

All the high hills under the whole heaven were co-
ver'd. Fifteen cubits upwards did the waters prevail,
and the mountains were cover'd.

LIX. Whatever be the height of the
Mountain *Caucaſus*, whereon the *Ark* reſted
Now; it was *at that time* the higheſt in the
whole World.

Vid. Hy-
poth. 8.
priùs.

This is evident from what has been already
obſerv'd, That tho' the utmoſt height of the
Waters were fifteen Cubits above the higheſt
Mountains, and ſo many hundreds, nay, thouſands above the moſt of them; yet, did the
Ark reſt on the very firſt day on which the Waters
began to diminiſh, more than two Months before the emerging of the tops of the other
Mountains;

Mountains; As is evident from the Texts following.

The waters prevailed upon the earth (from the seventeenth day of the second, to the seventeenth day of the seventh month) *an hundred and fifty days. And God remembred* Noah, *and all the cattel that was with him in the Ark; and God made a wind to pass over the earth, and the waters assuaged. The fountains also of the deep, and the windows of heaven were stopped, and the rain from heaven was restrained. And the waters returned from off the earth continually, and after the end of the hundred and fifty days the waters were abated. And the* Ark *rested in the seventh month, on the seventeenth day of the month, upon the mountains of* Ararat. *And the waters decreased continually until the tenth month: in the tenth month, on the first day of the month, were the tops of the mountains seen.* Gen. vii. ult. (with verse 11.) Chap. viii. 1, 2, 3, 4, 5.

LX. As the Fountains of the great Deep were broken up at the very same time that the first Rains began, so were they stopp'd the very same time that the last Rains ended; on the seventeenth day of the seventh Month.

The fountains also of the deep, and the windows of heaven were stopped, and the rain from heaven was restrained. Gen. viii. 2.

LXI. The abatement and decrease of the Waters of the Deluge was first by a Wind which dried up some. And secondly, by their descent through those Fissures, Chaps, and Breaches, (at which part of them had before ascended) into the Bowels of the Earth, which received the rest. To which latter also the Wind, by hurrying the Wa-

ters

ters up and down, and so promoting their lighting into the beforemention'd Fissures, was very much subservient.

Gen. viii. 1. *God made a wind to pass over the earth, and the waters asswaged.*

Verse 3. *The waters returned from off the earth continually,* or *going and returning.*

Job xxxviii. 8, 10, 11. *Who shut up the sea with doors, when it brake forth as if it had issued out of the womb?——— When I brake up for it my decreed place, and set bars and doors, and said, Hitherto shalt thou come, but no further; and here shall thy proud waves be stayed.*

Psalm civ. 6, 7, 8, 9. *Thou coveredst the earth with the deep, as with a garment : the waters stood above the mountains. At thy rebuke they fled: at the voice of thy thunder they hasted away. They went up by the mountains : they went down by the vallies unto the place which thou hadst appointed for them. Thou hast set a bound that they may not pass, that they turn not again to cover the earth.*

LXII. The dry Land, or habitable Part of the Globe, is since the Deluge divided into two vast *Continents*, almost opposite to one another, and separated by a great Ocean interpos'd between them.

This every Map of the Earth is a sufficient proof of.

LXIII. One of these *Continents* is considerably larger than the other.

This is evident the same way with the former.

LXIV. The larger *Continent* lies most part on the *North-side* of the Equator, and the smaller most part on the *South*.

This

This (if we take *South-America*, the moft confiderable and intire Branch of the whole, for the
Continent here referr'd to, as 'tis reafonable to
do) is alfo evident the fame way with the former.

LXV. The Middle or Center of the
North-Continent is about fixteen or eighteen
degrees of *Northern* Latitude ; and that of
the *South* about fixteen or eighteen degrees
of *Southern* Latitude.

This may foon be found by meafuring the
Boundaries of the feveral *Continents* on a Globe
or Map, and obferving the Pofition of their
Centers.

LXVI. The diftance between the *Continents*, meafuring from the larger or *Northern South-Eaftward*, is greater than that
the contrary way, or *South-Weftward*.

This is evident by the like means with the
former : It being farther from *China*, or the
Eaft-Indies to *America* going forward *South-Eaft*,
than from *Europe* or *Africa* going thither *South-
Weft*.

LXVII. Neither of the *Continents* is terminated by a round or even circular Circumference, but mighty Creeks, Bays, and
Seas running into them ; and as mighty
Peninfula's, Promontories, and Rocks jetting out from them, render the whole very
unequal and irregular.

This none who ever faw a Globe or Map of
the World can be ignorant of.

LXVIII. The depth of that *Ocean* which
feparates thefe two *Continents* is ufually
V 3 greateft

greateſt fartheſt from, and leaſt neareſt to
either of the ſame *Continents* ; there being
a gradual deſcent from the *Continents* to the
middle of the *Ocean,* which is the deepeſt
of all.

This is a Propoſition very well-known in Navigation ; and in ſeveral Sea-*Charts* relating thereto, may eaſily be obſerv'd.

LXIX. The greateſt part of the *Iſlands*
of the Globe are ſituate at ſmall diſtances
from the Edges of the great *Continents* ;
very few appearing near the middle of the
main *Ocean.*

This the bare Inſpection into a Map or Globe
of the World will ſoon give ſatisfaction in.

LXX. The Ages of Men decreas'd a-
bout. one half preſently after the Deluge ;
and in the ſucceeding eight hundred or nine
hundred Years were gradually reduced to
that ſtandard at which they have ſtood ever
ſince.

This

This the following Tables will eafily evince.

Ages of the *Antediluvi-ans* in their Years.	Ages of the *Poftdiluvians* in the prefent Years.	
Adam ——————— 930	Noah ——————— 950	Gen. v. 11.
Seth ——————— 912	Sem——————— 600	and xxv. 7.
Enos ——————— 905	Arphaxad ———— 438	and xxxv.
Cainan—————— 910	Salah ——————— 433	28. and
Mahalaleel————— 895	Heber —————— 464	xlvii. 28.
Jared- —————— 962	Phaleg-—————— 239	and L. 26.
Enoch (tranflated)--365	Reu ——————— 239	
Methufelah———— 969	Serug ——————— 230	
Lamech —————— 777	Nahor —————— 148	
Noah ——————— 950	Terah ——————— 205	
Sem ——————— 600	Abraham——— 175	
	Ifaac ——————— 180	
	Jacob ——————— 147	
	Jofeph —————— 110	

The days of our years are threefcore years and ten; and if by reafon of ftrength they be fourfcore years, yet is their ftrength labour and forrow: for it is foon cut off, and we fly away. In the Days of *Mofes.* — Pfalm xc. 10.

LXXI. Our upper Earth, for a confiderable depth, even as far as we commonly penetrate into it, is *Factitious,* or newly acquir'd at the Deluge: The ancient one having been covered by frefh *Strata* or *Layers* of Earth at that time, and thereby fpoil'd or deftroy'd as to the ufe and advantage of Mankind.

I will deftroy them with the Earth.
Neither fhall there any more be a flood, Διαϕθειϱει, *to deftroy,* corrupt, or fpoil *the Earth.* — Gen. vi. 13. and ix. 11.

V 4   This

This is moreover evident by the vaſt numbers
of the Shells of Fiſh, Bones of Animals, Intire
or Partial Vegetables, buried at the Deluge, and
Incloſed in the Bowels of the preſent Earth,
and of its moſt ſolid and compacted Bodies, to
be commonly ſeen at this day. Whoſe truth
is atteſted not only by very many occaſional remarks of others, but more eſpecially by the
careful and numerous Obſervations of an Eye-
witneſs, the Learned Dr. *Woodward.* 'Tis true,
this excellent Author was forc'd to imagine,
and accordingly to aſſert, That the Ancient
Earth was diſſolv'd at the Deluge, and all its
parts ſeparated from one another; and ſo the
whole, thus diſſolv'd and ſeparate, taken up into the Waters which then cover'd the Earth;
till at laſt they together ſetled downward, and
with the fore-mentioned Shells, Bones, and Vegetables, incloſed among the reſt of the Maſs,
compos'd again that Earth on which we now
live. But this *Hypotheſis* is ſo ſtrange, and ſo miraculous in all its parts; 'tis ſo wholly different
from the natural *Series* of the *Moſaick* Hiſtory
of the Deluge; takes ſo little notice of the forty
days rain, the principal cauſe thereof; is ſo contrary to the Univerſal Law of mutual Attraction, and the ſpecifick gravities of Bodies; accounts for ſo few of the before-mention'd *Phænomena* of the Deluge; fixes the time of the year
for its commencing ſo different from the truth;
implies ſuch a ſort of new Formation or Creation of the Earth at the Deluge, without warrant for the ſame; is in ſome things ſo little
conſiſtent with the *Moſaick* Relation, and the
Phænomena of nature; and upon the whole is
ſo much more than his Obſervations require,
that I cannot but diſſent from this particular *Hypotheſis,*

Eſſay.
Paſſim.

pothefis, tho' I fo juſtly honour the *Author*, and
fo highly eſteem, and frequently refer to
the *Work* it felf. All that I ſhall fay farther is
this, That the *Phænomena* of the interior Earth,
by this *Author* fo exactly obferv'd, are on the
common grounds or notions of the Deluge,
(which fuppofe the Waters to have been pure,
without any other mixtures) fo unaccountable,
and yet fo remarkable and evident, that if no
other rational folution could be offer'd, 'twere
but juſt and neceſſary to admit whatever is afferted by this *Author*, rather than deny the reality
of thofe *Phænomena*, or afcribe the plaineſt remains of the Animal and Vegetable Kingdom
to the fportings of Nature, or any fuch odd and
Chimærical occaſions, as fome perſons are incli-
nable to do. But withal, I muſt be allow'd to
fay, and the *Author* himſelf will not difagree,
That his *Hypothefis* includes things fo ſtrange,
wonderful, and furprizing, that nothing but the Effay, p.
utmoſt neceſſity, and the perfect unaccountable- 82.
nefs of the *Phænomena* without it, ought to be
eſteem'd fufficient to juſtifie the belief and introduction of it. Which ſtraits that account. of
the Deluge we are now upon, not forcing me
into, as will appear hereafter; I have, I think,
but juſt reafons for my disbelief thereof, and as
juſt, or rather the fame reafon to embrace that
Affertion we are now upon, That this upper
Earth, as far as any Shells, Bones, or Vegetables
are found therein, was *adventitious*, and newly
acquir'd at the Deluge, and not only the old
one diſſolv'd, and refetled in its ancient place
again.

LXXII. This *Factitious Cruſt* is univerfal, upon the Tops of the generality of
Mountains,

Mountains, as well as in the Plains and Valleys; and that in all the known Climates and Regions of the World.

Essay, p 5, 6, 7.
This is fully attested by the Observations of the same *Author*, and those which he procur'd from all parts of the World conspiring together.

LXXIII. The Parts of the present upper *Strata* were, at the time of the Waters covering the Earth, loose, separate, divided, and floated in the Waters among one another uncertainly.

Pref. and p. 74.
This is proved by the same *Author's* Observations.

LXXIV. All this Heterogeneous Mass, thus floating in the Waters, by degrees descended downwards, and subsided to the bottom, pretty nearly, according to the Law of Specifick Gravity ; and there compos'd those several *Strata* or *Layers*, of which our present upper Earth does consist.

P. 75.
This is prov'd by the same Observations.

LXXV. Vast multitudes of Fishes, belonging both to the Seas and Rivers, perish'd at the Deluge ; and their Shells were buried among the other Bodies or Masses which subsided down, and compos'd the *Layers* of our upper Earth.

P. 75, 76, 77.
This is prov'd by the same Observations.

LXXVI. The same Law of Specifick Gravity which was observ'd in the rest of the Mass, was also observ'd in the subsidence of the Shells of Fishes; they then sinking together with, and accordingly being

ing now found enclos'd among thofe *Strata* or Bodies which are nearly of their own feveral-Specifick Gravities: The heavier Shells being confequently ftill enclos'd among the heavier *Strata*, and the lighter Shells among the lighter *Strata*, in the Bowels of our prefent Earth.

This is prov'd by the fame Obfervations.   P. 75, 76, 77.

LXXVII. The *Strata* of *Marble*, of *Stone*, and of all other folid Bodies, attained their folidity as foon as the *Sand*, or other matter whereof they confift, was arriv'd at the bottom, and well fetled there. And all thofe *Strata* which are folid at this day, have been fo ever fince that time.

This is prov'd by the fame Obfervations.   P. 79.

LXXVIII. Thefe *Strata* of *Stone*, of *Chalk*, of *Cole*, of *Earth*, or whatever matter they confifted of, lying thus each upon other, appear now as if they had at firft been parallel, continued, and not interrupted : But as if, after fome time they had been diflocated and broken on all fides of the Globe, had been elevated in fome, and deprefs'd in other places ; from whence the fiffures and breaches, the Caverns and *Grotto's*, with many other irregularities within and upon our prefent Earth, feem to be deriv'd.

This is prov'd by the fame Obfervations.   P. 79, 80, 81.

LXXIX. Great numbers of Trees, and of other Vegetables were alfo, at this fubfidence of the Mafs aforefaid, buried in the
Bowels

Bowels of the Earth: And fuch very often as will not grow in the places where they are lodg'd: Many of which are pretty intire and perfect, and to be diftinctly feen and confider'd to this very day.

P. 77, 78.   This is prov'd by the fame Obfervations.
513.

LXXX. It appears from all the tokens and circumftances which are ftill obfervable about them, That all thefe Vegetables were torn away from their ancient Seats in the Spring time, in or about the Month of *May.*

P. 274,   This is prov'd by the fame Obfervations.
275.

LXXXI. All the *Metals* and *Minerals* among the *Strata* of our upper Earth owe their prefent frame and order to the Deluge ; being repofed therein during the time of the Waters covering the Earth, or during the fubfidence of the before-mention'd Mafs.

P. 179,   This is prov'd by the fame Obfervations.
180.

LXXXII. Thefe *Metals* and *Minerals* appear differently in the Earth, according to the different manner of their firft lodgment : For fometimes they are in loofe and fmall Particles, uncertainly inclos'd among fuch Maffes as they chanc'd to fall down withal: At other times fome of their Corpufcles happening to occur and meet together, affix'd to each other ; and feveral convening, uniting, and combining into one Mafs, form'd thofe *Metallick* and *Mineral Balls* or *Nodules* which are now found in the Earth: And according as the Corpufcles chanc'd

to

to be all of a kind or otherwife, fo the
Maffes were more or lefs fimple, pure, and
homogeneous. And according as other Bodies, Bones, Teeth, Shells of Fifh, or the
like happen'd to come in their way, thefe
Metallick and *Mineral* Corpufcles affix'd to
and became conjoin'd with them ; either
within, where it was poffible, in their hollows and interftices ; or without, on their
furface and outfides, filling the one, or covering the other : And all this in different
degrees and proportions, according to the
different circumftances of each individual
cafe.

All this is prov'd by the fame Obfervations.

P. 179, &c.

LXXXIII. The inward parts of the prefent Earth are very irregular and confufed.
One Region is chiefly *Stony*, another *Sandy*,
a third *Gravelly*. One Country contains
fome certain kinds of *Metals* or *Minerals*,
another quite different ones. Nay the
fame lump or mafs of Earth not feldom
contains the Corpufcles of feveral *Metals*
or *Minerals*, confufedly intermix'd with
one another , and with its own Earthy
parts. All which irregularities, with feveral others that might be obferv'd , even
contrary to the Law of Specifick Gravity
in the placing of the different *Strata* of the
Earth, demonftrate the Original *Fund* or
Promptuary of all this upper Factitious Earth
to have been in a very Wild, Confus'd and
Chaotick condition.

All

Eſſay, paſ-
ſim & p.
175, &c.
Varen.
Geog. l. r.
c. 7. prop.
7.
All this the fore-mention'd, and all other Obſervations of the like nature fully prove.

LXXXIV. The Uppermoſt and Lighteſt
Stratum of Soil or *Garden Mold*, as 'tis call'd;
which is the proper Seminary of the Vegetable Kingdom; is ſince the Deluge very
thick ſpread uſually in the Valleys and
Plains, but very thin on the Ridges or Tops
of Mountains : Which laſt for want thereof are frequently Stony, Rocky, Bare and
Barren.

This, eaſie Obſervations of the ſurface of the
Earth in different places will quickly ſatisfie
us of.

LXXXV. Of the four Ancient Rivers
of Paradiſe two ſtill remain, in ſome meaſure : but the other two do not ; or at leaſt
are ſo chang'd, that the *Moſaick* Deſcription does not agree to them at preſent.

Gen. ii. 10,
11, 12, 13,
14.
This the multitude of unſatisfactory attempts
to diſcover all theſe Rivers, and their courſes;
with an impartial compariſon of the Sacred Hiſtory with the beſt Geographical deſcriptions of
the Regions about *Babylon*, will eaſily convince
an unbyaſs'd Perſon of.

LXXXVI. Thoſe *Metals* and *Minerals*
which the *Moſaick* deſcription of Paradiſe,
Gen. ii. 10,
11, 12, 13,
14. Ezek.
xxviii. 13.
Apoc. xxi.
18, 19, 20.
with xxii.
2.
and its bordering Regions takes ſuch particular notice of, and the Prophets ſo emphatically refer to, are not now met with
ſo plentifully therein.

This muſt be allow'd on the ſame grounds
with the former.

LXXXVII. This Deluge of Waters was

a

a fignal Inſtance of the Divine Vengeance on a Wicked World; and was the effeſt of the Peculiar and Extraordinary Providence of God.

God ſaw that the wickedneſs of man was great in the earth, and that every imagination of the thoughts of his heart was only evil continually. And it repented the Lord that he had made man on the Earth, and it grieved him at his heart. And the Lord ſaid, I will deſtroy man whom I have created from the face of the earth; both man, and beaſt, and the creeping thing, and the fowls of the air; for it repenteth me that I have made them. Gen. vi. 5, 6, 7.

The earth was corrupt before God, and the earth was filled with violence, and God looked upon the earth, and behold it was corrupt; for all fleſh had corrupted his way upon the Earth. And God ſaid unto Noah, the end of all fleſh is come before me, for the earth is filled with violence through them; and behold I will deſtroy them, with the earth. Ver. 11, 12, 13.

Behold I, even I, do bring a flood of waters upon the earth, to deſtroy all fleſh wherein is the breath of life from under heaven; and every thing that is in the earth ſhall dye. Ver. 17.

God ſpared not the old world, but ſaved Noah, *the eighth perſon, a preacher of righteouſneſs; bringing in the flood upon the world of the ungodly.* 2 Pet. ii. 5.

LXXXVIII. Tho' the *Moon* might perhaps undergo ſome ſuch changes at the Deluge as the *Earth* did, yet that Face or *Hemiſphere* which is towards the Earth, and which is alone expos'd to our view, has not acquir'd any ſuch groſs Atmoſphere, or Clouds, as our Earth has now about it, and which are here ſuppos'd to have been acquir'd at the Deluge.

This

This the prefent figure, and large divifions of Sea and Land vifible in the Moon, with her continued and uninterrupted brightnefs, and the appearance of the fame Spots, (without the interpofition of Clouds or Exhalations) perpetually, do fufficiently evince.

LXXXIX. Since the Deluge there neither has been, nor will be, any great and general Changes in the ftate of the World, till that time when a Period is to be put to the prefent Courfe of Nature.

Gen. viii.
21, 22.   *The Lord fmelled a fweet favour, and the Lord faid in his heart, I will not again curfe the ground any more for man's fake; for (or altho') the imagination of man's heart is evil from his youth: Neither will I again fmite any more every thing living as I have done. While the Earth remaineth, feed-time and harveft, and cold and heat, and Summer and winter, and day and night fhall not ceafe.*

And this as to the time paft is abundantly confirm'd by all the Ancient Hiftory and Geography compar'd with the Modern; as is in feve-
Effay, par.   ral particulars well obferv'd by Dr. *Woodward*,
1, & 5.   againft the groundlefs opinions of fome others to the contrary.

CHAP.

CHAP. V.

Phænomena *relating to the General Con-*
flagration. With Conjectures *pertain-*
ing to the fame, and to the fucceeding
period till the Confummation *of all*
things.

XC. **A**S the World once perifhed by
Water, fo it muft by Fire at the
Conclufion of its prefent State.

The heavens and the earth which are now, by the 2 Pet.iii.7.
word of God, are kept in ftore, referved unto fire,
againft the day of judgment, and perdition of ungodly
men.

The heavens fhall pafs away with a great noife, Verfe 10,
and the elements fhall melt with fervent heat ; The
earth alfo, and the works that are therein, fhall be
burnt up.

In the day of God the heavens, being on fire, fhall Verfe 12.
be diffolved, and the elements fhall melt with fervent
heat.

But this is fo fully attefted by the unanimous
confent of Sacred and Prophane Authority, that
I fhall omit other particular Quotations ; and Dr. *Hack-*
only refer the Reader where he may have more *well's* Apo-
ample fatisfaction. logy of
the Pow-
er and
Provi-
dence of
S C H O L I U M. God. l. 4.
c. 13.
Having proceeded thus far upon more certain Theor l. 3.
grounds, and generally allow'd Teftimonies, as c. 3.
to the moft of the foregoing *Phænomena;* I
X might

might here break off, and leave the following *Conjectures* to the same state of Uncertainty they have hitherto been in. But being willing to comply with the Title, and take in all the great and general Changes from first to last; from the primigenial *Chaos*, to the *Consummation* of all things : Being also loth to desert my *Postulatum*, and omit the account of those things which were most exactly agreeable to the Obvious and Literal sense of Scripture, and fully consonant to Reason and Philosophy : Being, lastly, willing however to demonstrate, that tho' these most remote and difficult Texts be taken according to the greatest strictness of the Letter, yet do they contain nothing but what is possible, credible, and rationally accountable from the most undoubted Principles of Philosophy : On all these accounts I shall venture to enumerate, and afterward to account for the following *Conjectures*. In which I do not pretend to be Dogmatical and Positive; nay, nor to declare any firm belief of the same, but shall only propose them as *Conjectures*, and leave them to the free and impartial consideration of the Reader.

XCI. The same Causes which will set the World on Fire, will also cause great and dreadful *Tides* in the *Seas*, and in the *Ocean*; with no less Agitations, Concussions, and *Earthquakes* in the *Air* and *Earth.*

Mat. xxiv. 29.   *The Powers of Heaven shall be shaken.*

Joel. iii. 16.   *The Lord shall roar out of Sion, and utter his voice from Jerusalem, and the heavens and the earth shall shake.*

Luk. xxi. 25, 26. Vid. Theor. l. 3. c. 11.   *The sea and the waves roaring : Mens hearts failing them for fear, and for looking after those things which are coming on the Earth; for the powers of heaven shall be shaken.* XCII.

XCII. The *atmosphere* of the Earth, before the Conflagration begin, will be opprefs'd with *Meteors, Exhalations,* and *Steams;* and thefe in fo dreadful a manner, in fuch prodigious quantities, and with fuch wild confufed Motions and Agitations, That the *Sun* and *Moon* will have the moft frightful and hideous countenances, and their antient fplendour will be intirely obfcur'd ; The *Stars* will feem to fall from Heaven ; and all manner of Horrid Reprefentations will terrifie the Inhabitants of the Earth.

I will fhew wonders in the heavens and in the Joel ii. 30, *earth ; blcod, and fire, and pillars of fmoke. The* 31. *fun fhall be turned into darknefs, and the moon into blood, before the great and terrible day of the Lord come.*

The fun fhall be darkened, and the Moon fhall not Mat xxiv. *give her light, and the ftars fhall fall from heaven,* 29. *and the powers of heaven fhall be fhaken.*

There fhall be figns in the fun, and in the moon, Luk. xxi. *and in the ftars, and upon the Earth diftrefs of Na-* 25, 26. *tions, with perplexity :* —*Mens hearts failing them for fear, and for looking after thofe things which are coming on the earth.*

XCIII. The *Deluge* and *Conflagration* are referr'd, by ancient Tradition, to great Conjunctions of the Heavenly Bodies ; as both depending on, and happening at the fame.

Thus *Seneca* exprefly: *Berofus* (fays he) *who* Nat. *was an Expofitor of* Belus, *affirms, That thefe Revolu-* Quæft. i. *tions depend on the Courfe of the Stars; infomuch that* 3. c. 29. *he doubts not to affign the very times of a Conflagra-tion, and a Deluge : That firft mention'd when all*

X 2   *the*

*the Stars, which have now so different Courses, shall
be in Conjunction in* Cancer : *All of them being so
directly situate with respect to one another, that the
same right line will pass through them all together :
That last mention'd when the same company of Stars
shall be in conjunction in the opposite sign* Capri-
corn.

XCIV. The space between the *Deluge*
and the *Conflagration*, or between the ancient state of the Earth, and its Purgation
by Fire, Renovation, and Restitution again,
is, from ancient Tradition, defin'd and terminated by a certain great and remarkable
year, or *Annual* Revolution of some of the
Heavenly Bodies: And is in probability what
the Ancients so often refer'd to, pretended
particularly to determine, and stil'd The
Great or *Platonick* Year.

Theor. 1.
3. c. 4.

This year is exceeding famous in old Authors;
and not unreasonably apply'd to this matter by
the *Theorist*: Which it will better suit in *this*
than it did in *that Hypothesis*.

XCV. This general *Conflagration* is not
to extend to the intire dissolution or destruction of the Earth, but only to the Alteration, Melioration, and peculiar disposition thereof into a new state, proper to receive those Saints and Martyrs for its Inhabitants, who are at the first Resurrection
to enter, and to live and reign a thousand
years upon it, till the second Resurrection,
the general Judgment, and the final consummation of all things.

The

The Heavens being on fire shall be dissolved, and the elements shall melt with fervent heat. Nevertheless we, according to his promise, look for new heavens, and a new earth, wherein dwelleth Righteousness. 2 Pet. iii. 12, 13.

Behold, I create new heavens, and a new earth, and the former shall not be remembered nor come into mind. Isa.lxv.17.

Verily I say unto you, That ye which followed me, in the regeneration, when the Son of Man shall sit upon the throne of his glory, ye also shall sit on twelve thrones judging the twelve tribes of Israel. And every one that hath forsaken houses, or brethren, or sisters, or father, or mother, or wife, or children, or lands for my names sake, shall receive an hundred fold, now in this time, houses, and brethren, and sisters, and mothers, and children, and lands, with (his present) persecutions, and in the world to come eternal life. Mat. xix. 28, 29. Mar. x. 29, 30. Luke xviii 29. 30.

Of old thou hast laid the foundations of the earth; and the heavens are the work of thy hand: They shall perish, but thou shalt endure; yea all of them shall wax old like a garment; as a vesture shalt thou change them, and they shall be changed. Psa. cii. 25, 26.

I saw thrones, and they sat upon them; and judgment was given unto them: And I saw the Souls of them that were beheaded for the witness of Jesus, and for the word of God, and which had not worshipped the beast, neither his image, neither had received his mark upon their foreheads, or in their hands, and they lived and reigned with Christ a thousand years. But the rest of the dead lived not again until the thousand years were finished: This is the first resurrection. Blessed and holy is he that hath part in the first resurrection; on such the second death hath no power: But they shall be priests of God, and of Christ; and shall reign with him a thousand years,&c. Apoc. xx. 4, &c.

X 3   But

But so much has been said on this head, to omit others, by the *Theorist*, that I shall refer

Theor.l.4. c. 2, 3, 4, 5, 9.

the *Reader* thither, for the other Testimonies of the Holy Scriptures, and the unanimous consent of the most Primitive Fathers : Both which he at large, and to excellent purpose, (some particulars excepted) has insisted on.

XCVI. The state of Nature during the *Millennium* will be very different from that at present, and more agreeable to the *Antediluvian, Primitive*, and *Paradisiacal* ones.

Acts iii. 21.

Whom the heavens must receive until the time of the restitution of all things, which God hath spoken by the mouth of all his holy Prophets since the world began. See more in the *Theory.* Book 4. Chap. 9. and in the proofs of the former Proposition.

XCVII. The Earth in the *Millennium* will be without a Sea, or any large receptacle fill'd with mighty collections and quantities of Waters.

Apoc.xxi. 1

I saw a new heaven, and a new earth ; for the first heaven, and the first earth were passed away, and there was no more sea.

XCVIII. The Earth in the *Millennium* will have no succession of Light and Darkness, Day and Night ; but a perpetual Day.

Apoc.xxi. 25.
Cap. xxii. 5.

The gates of the new Jerusalem shall not be shut at all by day ; for there shall be no night there.

And there shall be no night there.

XCIX. The state of the *Millennium* will not stand in need of, and so probably will be without, the light and presence of the Sun and Moon.

And

And the City had no need of the Sun, neither of the Moon to shine in it. Apoc. xxi. 23.

And they need no candle, neither light of the sun. Cap. xxii. 5.

C. At the conclusion of the *Millennium*, the Final *Judgment* and *Consummation* of all things, The Earth will desert its present Seat and Station in the World, and be no longer found among the Planetary *Chorus*.

I saw a great white throne, and him that sat on it; from whose face the earth and the heavens fled away, and there was found no place for them. Apoc. xx. 11. Theor. 14. c. 10.

———————————————

X 4 BOOK,

BOOK IV.

SOLUTIONS:

OR,

An Account of the foregoing *Phæno-mena* from the Principles of Philo-sophy already laid down.

CHAP. I.

A Solution of the Phænomena *relating to the* Mosaick *Creation, and the origi-nal Constitution of the Earth.*

I. All those particular small Bodies of which our habi-table Earth is now compos'd, were originally in a mixed, confused, fluid, and uncertain Condition; without any order or regularity. It was an *Earth with-out form, and void*; had *darkness* spread over *the face of its Abyss*; and in reality was, what it has been ever stil'd, A perfect *Chaos*.

I. **T**HIS has been already sufficiently ac-counted for, and need not be here a-gain insisted on. *Hypoth.* 1. *præis.*

II. The Formation of this Earth, or the Change of that *Chaos* into an habitable World, was not a meer result
from

from any neceſſary Laws of *Mechaniſm* independently
on the Divine.Power; but was the proper effect of the
Influence and Interpoſition, and all along under the
peculiar Care and Providence of God.

II. 'Tis not very eaſy, I confeſs, in ſuch
mighty Turns and Changes of the World, exactly
to determine how far, and in what particulars,
a ſupernatural or miraculous Interpoſition of
the Divine Power is concern'd; and how far
the Laws of Nature, or Mechanical Powers
ought to be extended. Nay, indeed, 'tis difficult enough, in ſeveral inſtances, to determine
what is the effect of a natural and ordinary,
and what of a ſupernatural and extraordinary
Providence. 'Tis now evident, That *Gravity*,
the moſt mechanical Affection of Bodies, and
which ſeems moſt natural, depends entirely on the
conſtant and efficacious, and, if you will, the
ſupernatural and miraculous Influence of Almighty God. And I do not know whether the
falling of a Stone to the Earth ought not more
truly to be eſteem'd a *ſupernatural Effect*, or a
Miracle, than what we with the greateſt ſurprize
ſhould ſo ſtile, its remaining pendulous in the
open Air; ſince the former requires an *active Influence* in the firſt Cauſe, while the latter ſuppoſes
Non-annihilation only. But beſides this, Tho' we
were able exactly to diſtinguiſh in general the
ordinary Concurrence of God from his extraordinary, yet would the task before us be ſtill ſuf-
ciently difficult. For thoſe Events or Actions
are in Holy Scripture attributed immediately to
the Power and Providence of God, which yet
were to all outward appearance according to the
conſtant courſe of things, and would, abſtract-
edly from ſuch Affirmations of the Holy Books,
have been eſteem'd no more miraculous than
the

*Vid. Lem.
9. cum Co-
roll. prius.
And Bent-
ley, Serm.
7. p. 26,
&c.*

the other common Effects of Nature, or usual
Accidents of Humane Affairs; as those who
have carefully consider'd these matters, especially the Historical and Prophetical Parts of the
Old Testament must be oblig'd to confess. Neither is it unreasonable that all things should in
that manner be ascribed to the Supream Being
on several accounts. 'Tis from him every thing
is ultimately deriv'd: He conserves the Natures,
and continues the Powers of every Creature:
He not only at first produc'd, but perpetually
disposes and makes use of the whole Creation,
and every part thereof, as the Instruments of his
Providence: He foresaw and foreadapted the intire Frame: He determin'd his Co-operation or
Permission to every Action: He so order'd and
appointed the whole System with every individual Branch of it, as to Time, Place, Proportion,
and all other Circumstances, that nothing should
happen unseasonably, unfitly, disproportionate-
ly, or otherwise than the Junctures of Affairs, the
demerits of his reasonable Creatures, and the
wise Intentions of his Providence did require.
In fine, he so previously adjusted and contemper'd the Moral and Natural World to one another, that the Marks and Tokens of his Providence should be in all Ages legible and conspicuous, whatsoever the visible secondary Causes
or Occasions might be. Seeing then this is the
true state of the Case; and that consequently,
Almighty God has so constituted the World that
no Body can tell wherein it differs from one,
where all were solely brought to pass by a miraculous Power; 'tis by no means untrue or improper in the Holy Books to refer all those things
which bare Humane Authors would derive from
second Causes, the constant Course of Nature,
and

and the Circumſtances of Humane Affairs to
the firſt Cauſe, the ultimate Spring and Original
of all; and to call Mens Thoughts (which are
too apt to terminate there) from the apparent
occaſions, to the inviſible God the Creator, Governor, and Diſpoſer of the whole, and the ſole
Object of their Regard and Adoration. This is,
I ſay, a very proper and reaſonable procedure;
this is uſually obſerv'd by the Sacred Penmen,
(who are thereby peculiarly diſtinguiſh'd from
Prophane Authors) and this is of the higheſt
advantage in Morality. But then it muſt be
withal acknowledg'd, That this creates great difficulties in the preſent Caſe, and makes it very
hard in a Philoſophick Attempt of this nature, to
diſtinguiſh between thoſe parts of the *Moſaick*
Creation, which are *Mechanically* to be accounted for, and thoſe in which the miraculous *Energy*
of God Almighty interpos'd it ſelf; which yet,
if ever, is certainly to be allow'd in this caſe,
where a new World was to be form'd, and a
wild *Chaos* reduc'd into a regular, beautiful, and
permanent Syſtem. This being ſaid in general,
to beſpeak the *Reader*'s Candor in the preſent
Caſe, and to forewarn him not to fear the
moſt Mechanical and Philoſophick Account of
this Creation, as if thereby the Holy Scriptures
were ſuperſeded, or the Divine Power and Providence excluded; I come directly to the Point
before us, and ſhall endeavour to determine
what are the Inſtances of the extraordinary
Power and Interpoſition of God in this whole
Affair. That as we ſhall preſently ſee how Orderly, Methodical, and Regular this Formation
was, ſo we may before-hand be duly ſenſible how
Supernatural, Providential, and Divine it was
alſo; and ſo as well, like Chriſtians, contem-
plate

plate and adore the Omnipotent Creator in his *Miraculous*, as we, like Philofophers, fhall attempt to confider and remark his Vicegerent Nature in her *Mechanical* Operations therein. For, notwithftanding what has been above infifted on touching the frequency and propriety of afcribing the Effects of Nature to the Divine Power (the former being indeed nothing, but the latter acting according to fixt and certain Laws); yet, becaufe more has been commonly, and may juftly be fuppos'd the importance of the Texts of Scripture hereto relating; becaufe the Finger of God, or his fupernatural Efficiency, is if ever to be reafonably expected in the Origin of Things, and that in a peculiar and remarkable manner; becaufe fome things done in this Creation are beyond the power of Philofophy and Mechanifm, and no otherwife accountable but by the Infinite Power of God himfelf; becaufe the days of Creation are fignally diftinguifh'd from thofe following, in which God is faid to have refted (when yet his ordinary Concurrence, and the Courfe of Nature was continued without Interruption), and muft therefore be reckon'd fuch, on which he truly exerted a Power different from the other. On all thefe accounts, I freely, and in earneft allow and believe, That there was a peculiar Power, and extraordinary Providence exercis'd by the great Creator of all, in this Primitive Origin of the Sublunary World, or Formation of the Earth which we are going to account for. The particular inftances I fhall give of the fame, without prefuming to exclude all others, are thefe following,

1. The

1. The Creation of the matter of the Univerſe, and particularly of that of the Earth, out of nothing, was without doubt originally the alone and immediate Work of God Almighty. Nature (let what will be meant by that Name) could have no hand in this, from whence at the utmoſt ſhe can but date her own Birth. The production of a real Being out of nothing, or to ſpeak more properly, the primary bringing any real thing into Being, is in the Opinion of all Men, the Effect of no leſs than an Infinite and Omnipotent Deity. I have already owned this to be the import of the firſt words of this Creation we are now upon, *In the beginning God created the Heaven and the Earth.* And I think 'tis here no improper place to declare my Opinion, That conſidering the *Idea* and Nature of God includes *Active Power, Infinite Perfection,* with *Neceſſity* and ſo *Eternity of Exiſtence*; when the *Idea* and Nature of matter ſuppoſes *intire Inactivity, no poſitive Perfection,* and a *bare Poſſibility or Capacity of Exiſtence*; 'tis as abſurd and unreaſonable to attribute Eternity and Neceſſity of Exiſtence to the latter, as 'tis rational and natural to aſcribe thoſe Perfections, with a Power of Creation, to the former. The very *Being* and *Nature,* as well as the *Properties* and *Powers* of Matter being moſt juſtly and moſt philoſophically to be referr'd to the Author of all, the Almighty Creator. And altho' our imagination (a poor, finite, limited, and imperfect Faculty) be unable to have a poſitive *Idea* of the manner of the Production of a real Being at firſt (as indeed 'twere ſufficiently ſtrange, if ſo confin'd a Power of ſo imperfect a Creature ſhould adequately reach the higheſt point of Omnipotence it ſelf); yet ſeeing the Abſurdities following the Eternity, and Self-

Self-fubfiftence of Matter on the other fide are fo enormous ; and the certainty of the proper Creation of Spiritual Beings nobler than Matter, fuch as the Souls of Men are, as great, as 'tis utterly incredible they fhould have been *ab æterno* too (for I take it to be demonftrable that Souls are immaterial:) I think 'tis far more reafonable to reft fatisfied with our former Affertion, That God did truly bring Matter into being at firft, than its Eternity fuppos'd, to make only the Modification and Management thereof the Province of the Almighty: And confequently the firft inftance of a Divine Efficiency with relation to the Subject we are now upon, and the higheft of all other, was the original Production of the Matter of which the Earth was to confift, or the proper Creation of thofe inferior Heavens, and of that Earth which were to be the fole Object of the Divine Operations in the fix days Work. This particular, I confefs, does not fo properly belong to our prefent bufinefs, the Formation of the *Chaos* into a habitable World; but could not well be omitted, either confider'd in it felf, as it bears fo peculiar a Relation to our prefent purpofe; or with refpect to that mifconftruction I might with fome *Readers* have otherwife been liable to. But I proceed;

2. The changing of the Courfe and Orbit of the *Chaos* into that of a Planet (to omit the former *Annual*, and fubfequent *Diurnal* Revolutions, which tho' equally from God, yet do not fo fully belong to this place), or the placing of the Earth in its primitive *Circular* Orbit at its proper diftance, therein to revolve about the *Sun*, was either an inftance of the immediate Power, or at leaft of the peculiar Providence of God.

God. For if we fhould fuppofe, as 'tis poffible to do, that God did not by a miraculous Operation remove the *Chaos* or Comet from its very Eccentrick *Ellipfis* to that Circle in which it now began to revolve; but that he made ufe of the Attraction or Impulfe of fome other Body; yet in this cafe, (without confidering that one of thofe Powers at leaft is nothing but a Divine Energy,) the Lines of each Bodies motion, the quantity of force, the proper diftance from the *Sun* where, and the exact time when it happen'd (to name no other particulars here) muft have been fo precifely and nicely adjufted before-hand by the Prefcience and Providence of the Almighty, that here will be not a much lefs remarkable Demonftration of the *Wifdom, Contrivance, Care,* and *Goodnefs,* than the other immediate Operation would have been of the *Power* of God in the World.

(3.) The Formation of the Seeds of all Animals and Vegetables was originally, I fuppofe the immediate Workmanfhip of God. As far as our Micrometers can help us to difcern the Make and Conftitution of Seeds; thofe of Plants evidently, and by what hitherto appears of Animals too, are no other than the intire Bodies themfelves *in parvo*, and contain every one of the fame Parts and Members with the compleat Bodies themfelves when grown to maturity. When therefore, confequently, all *Generation* is with us nothing, as far as we can find, but *Nutrition* or *Augmentation of Parts*; and that agreeably thereto no Seed has been by any Creature produc'd fince the beginning of things: 'Tis very Juft, and very Philofophical to conclude them to have been originally every one created by God, either out of nothing in the primary

Exiftence

Vid. Bentley, Serm. 4.

Exiftence of things; or out of præexifting Matter, at the *Mofaick* Creation. And indeed fince the Origin of Seeds appears to be hitherto unaccountable by the mechanical Laws of Matter and Motion, 'tis but reafonable to fuppofe them the immediate work of the Author of Nature: which therefore I think the warieft Philofopher may well do in the prefent cafe.

(4.) The Natures, Conditions, Rules and Quantities, of thofe feveral Motions and Powers according to which all Bodies (of the fame general nature in themfelves) are fpecifi'd, diftinguifh'd, and fitted for their feveral ufes, were no otherwife determin'd than by the immediate *Fiat*, Command, Power, and Efficiency of Almighty God. 'Tis to be here confider'd, That tho' the Power of mutual Attraction or Gravitation of Bodies appears to be conftant, and univerfal; nay almoft effential to Matter in the prefent conftitution of the world; (the intire Frame of that Syftem in which we are, if not of all the other Syftems, fo ftrictly depending thereon) yet the other Laws

Utinam cætera Naturæ Phænomena ex principiis mechanicis eodem argumentandi genere derivare liceret. Nam multa me movent ut nonnihil fufpicer ea omnia ex viribus quibufdam pendere poffe, quibus corporum particulæ, per caufas nondum cognitas, vel in fe mutuò impellantur, & fecundum figuras regulares cohærent, vel ab invicem fugantur, & recedunt: quibus viribus ignotis, Philofophi hactenus naturam fruftra tentarunt. Newt. Præf. ad Lector.

of Nature, on which the particular qualities of Bodies depend, feems not to be fo; but mutable in themfelves, and actually chang'd according to the changes in the figure, bignefs, texture, or other conditions of the Bodies or Corpufcles with which they are concern'd. Thus the *Cohæfion* of the parts of Matter, and that in fome with lefs, but in others with the greateft and moft furprizing firmnefs; the *Fermentation* of feveral heterogeneous Particles, when mixt together; the

Magneti on

Magnetism of the Loadſtone, with the various
and very ſtrange *Phænomena* of that wonderful
Foſſil; the *Liquidity* of certain Fluids and Solids; the contrary obſtinate inflexibility and re-
ſiſtance of others; the different *Denſity* of ſeveral collections or maſſes of Fluids, (while yet the
greateſt part of their contained ſpace is Vacuity)
not to be conſiderably increas'd or diminiſh'd,
without the deſtruction of the *ſpecies* : All theſe,
and many other *Phænomena* ſhew, That there are
various Rules and Laws of Matter and Motion
not belonging to all, as that of Gravitation does,
but peculiar to ſome particular conditions thereof; which therefore may be chang'd, without
any damage to the Law of Gravity. In the
impreſſing and ordering of which there is room
for, if not a neceſſity of, introducing the particular and immediate efficacy of the Spirit of
God at firſt, as well as of his continual concurrence and conſervation ever ſince ; When therefore, in a full agreement with the ancient Tra-

Gen. i. 2.
*Vid Loca
de Chao
prius lau-
data.*

ditions, 'tis ſaid by *Moſes,* That *the Spirit of God
moved on the face of the waters.* We may juſtly
underſtand thereby his impreſſing, exciting, or
producing ſuch Motions, Agitations, and Fermentations of the ſeveral Parts ; ſuch particular
Powers of Attraction or Avoidance (beſides the
general one of Gravity) of Concord or Enmity,
of Union or Separation ; and all theſe in ſuch
certain Quantities, on ſuch certain Conditions
of Bodies, and in ſuch certain diſtinct Parts and
Regions of the *Chaos,* as were proper and neceſſary for that particular Courſe and Diſpoſition of
Nature which it ſeem'd good to the Divine Spirit to introduce, and on which this future frame
of things here below was ever after to depend.

(5.) The

(5.) The Ordering of all things fo that in the fpace of fix fucceffive Solar Revolutions the whole Creation fhould be finifh'd, and each diftinct Day's work fhould be confin'd to, and compleated in its own diftinct and proper period, is alfo to be afcrib'd to the particular Providence and Interpofition of God. That every thing followed in its own order and place : As that the Seeds of Vegetables on the Third, thofe of Fifh and Fowl on the Fifth, and thofe of the Terreftrial Animals on the Sixth Day, fhould be every one plac'd in their proper Soil, and fitly difpos'd at their proper time to accompany and correfpond with the fuitable difpofition of external Nature, and juft then to germinate and fructify, when the order and procefs of the other parts of the Creation were ready for, and required the fame. Every thing here does fo fuit together, that the plain footfteps of particular Art and Contrivance are vifible in the whole conduct and management of this matter : Which therefore is not to be deriv'd from meer Mechanical Laws of Brute Matter, but from a Supernatural and Divine Providence.

(6.) But principally, The Creation of our Firft Parents is to be efteem'd the peculiar Operation of the Almighty ; and that whether we regard the Formation of their Bodies, or the Forepaft Creation and After-Infufion of their Souls. 'Tis Evident from the *Mofaick* Hiftory of the Creation, that Our Firft Parents were on the very fame Day in which they were made, in a State of Maturity and Perfection, and capable of all Humane Actions, both of Mind and Body. Now if they, like the other Animals, had been produc'd in the ufual Time and Procefs of Generation, and come to ripenefs of Age and Facul-

ties by degrees afterwards ; That were plainly
impoſſible. This Creation therefore muſt have
been peculiar, and the immediate Effect of a
Divine Power. And this is noleſs agreeable to
Philoſophy, than ſuitable to the Dignity of the
ſubject, and for the Honour of Mankind. It
has been already obſerv'd that the Seeds of
Plants and Animals muſt be allow'd to have
been all the immediate Workmanſhip of God ;
and that they contain every individual Part or
Member of the intire Bodies, *in parvo* ; and that
by conſequence Generation is nothing elſe but
Nutrition or Augmentation. Since therefore God
by his immediate Power, Created the intire Bodies of all Plants and Animals, 'tis by no means
har'd to conceive that he might Create them in
what degree of Maturity and Perfection he
pleas'd, without any manner of infringement of
the Order of Nature then to be eſtabliſh'd : And
if we have reaſon to believe, that the Bodies of
bruit Creatures were created *in parvo*, in a ſmall
State, ſuch as we now call Seeds, and ſo requir'd
a proper Generation, *i.e.* Nutrition and Augmentation of parts (as the *Moſaick* Hiſtory plainly
deſcribes them ; and had it not done ſo, we
could not with any certainty have aſſerted it);
We have ſure equal reaſon to believe, from the
deſcription of the ſame Author in this other caſe,
that the Bodies of our Firſt Parents were Originally created in their Mature Bulk, and State of
Manhood, ſo as immediately to be capable of the
ſame Operations which at any time afterward
they might be thought to be. This Miraculous
Origination of the Bodies of our Firſt Parents is
therefore very rationally aſcribed to the Finger of
God by *Moſes* : And we may juſtly believe that
the Bleſſed Trinity, as 'tis repreſented in the Sacred

cred Hiftory, was peculiarly concern'd in the
Production of that Being which was to bear the
Image of God, and be made capable of fome degree of his Immortality. And then as to the Soul
of Man, 'tis certainly a very diftinct Being from,
and one very much advanced above the Body ;
and therefore if we were forc'd to introduce a Divine Power in the Formation of the latter, we
can do no lefs than that in the Creation and Infufion of the former. And indeed the Dignity
and Faculties of the Human Soul are fo vaftly exalted above all the Material, or merely Animal
Creation, that its Original muft be deriv'd from
the immediate Finger of God in a manner ftill
more peculiar and Divine than all the reft. That
nearer refemblance of the Spiritual Nature, Immortal Condition, Active Powers, and Free,
Rational, and Moral Operations of the Divine
Being it felf, which the Souls of men were to
bear about them, did but require fome peculiar
and extraordinary Conduct in their firft Exiftence,
after-Union with Matter, and Introduction
into the Corporeal World. Agreeably whereto
we may eafily obferve a fignal diftinction in the
Sacred Hiftory, between the formation of all
other Animals, and the Creation of Man. In
the former cafe 'tis only faid, *Let the waters bring*
forth the moving creature that hath life. Let the earth
bring forth the living creature after his kind. But of
the latter the entire Trinity confult : *And God*
faid, Let Us make man in our image, after our like-
nefs. And the Lord God formed man of the duft of
the ground, and breathed into his noftrils the breath of
life, and man became a living foul. As therefore
the feveral parts of the Mofaick Creation before-
mention'd are not to be mechanically attempted,
but look'd upon as the effects of the Extraordi-

Gen. i. 20
Verfe 24.
Verfe 26.
Chap. ii. 7

Y 3

nary

nary and Miraculous Power and Providence of
God, fo more efpecially the Formation of the
Body of Man in its mature ftate, and moft of all
the primary Creation and after-Infufion of the
Rational Human Soul, is to be wholly afcrib'd to
the fame wonderful Interpofition and Efficiency
of the Supreme Being, the Creator of all things,
God blefs'd for evermore. All which taken together and duly confidered, is, I think, a fufficient
and fatisfactory Account of the Propofition before us, and attributes as much to the Miraculous and Immediate Hand of God, as either
Tradition, Reafon, or Scripture, require in the
prefent Cafe.

III. **The Days of Creation, and that of Reft, had their
beginning in the Evening.**

Coroll. 1.
Lem. 70.
& Hypoth.
5. *cum Co-*
roll. 1. *pri-*
us.

III. This has been already accounted for, and
need not here be repeated.

Corollary 1. *This Phænomenon in fome meafure
confirms our* Hypothefis, *that the Primitive Days of
the World were* Years *alfo. For otherwife the fpace of
one fingle fhort Night feems too inconfiderable to have
been taken fuch notice of in this Hiftory; and then, and
ever after, made the firft half of the Natural Day.
But if it were equal to half a Year, it was too confiderable to be omitted, and its memory was very juftly
preferv'd in fucceeding Ages.*

Corollary 2. *We may here begin to take notice of
the Regularity and Methodicalnefs of this Hiftory of the
Creation: Which, tho' it principally intends the giving
an account of the* Vifible Parts of the World, *and how the
ftate of Nature in each Period appeared in the* Day
time; *yet Omits not the foregoing* Night: *which is
very Mechanical and Natural. For in the preceding*
Night

*Night all things were so prepar'd and dispos'd, that the
Work of each Day might, upon its appearance, display
it self; might be exhibited, not in its unseen beginnings,
or secret Workings, not in its previous Causes, and
gradual Procedure, (which was not the Design of this
History) but in that more distinct and perfect condition in which things would in the Day time appear to
the view of a Spectator, and under which chiefly they
were to be describ'd and recorded in this History.*

IV. At the time immediately preceding the Six Days
Creation, the Face of the Abyss, or superior Regions of the *Chaos*, were involv'd in a Thick Darkness.

IV. If we confider what has been already faid of *Lem.* 42,
the Nature of a Comet, or peculiarly of that *At-* &c. and
mofphere which has been before fhewn to have been 57, &c.
the ancient *Chaos*, we ought to reprefent it to our *print.*
felves as containing a Central, Solid, Hot Body,
of about 7000 or 8000 Miles in Diameter; and
befides that, a vaftly large, fluid, heterogeneous
Mafs, or congeries of Bodies, in a very rare, feperate, and expanded condition, whofe Diameter were twelve, or perhaps fifteen times as long
as that of the central Solid, or about 100000
Miles; which is the *Atmofphere* or *Chaos* now to be
confider'd: In which we muft remember was
contain'd both a fmaller quantity of dry, folid, or
earthy Parts, (with a ftill much fmaller of Aery
and Watery) and a much larger quantity of denfe
and heavy Fluids, of which the main bulk of the
Atmofphere was compos'd, all confufedly mix'd,
blended, and jumbled together. In which ftate
the *Theorift's* Firft Figure, excepting the omiffion *Theor. p.* 35.
of the Central Solid, will well enough reprefent
it; and in which ftate we accordingly delineate
it in the following Figure:

Y 4   But

Fig 1   *p*

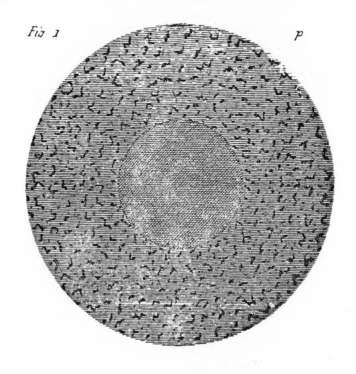

But upon the change of the Comet's Orbit from *Elliptical* to Circular, the Commencing of the *Mofaick* Creation, and the Influence of the Divine Spirit, all things would begin to take their own places, and each fpecies of Bodies rank themfelves into that order, which, according to the law of fpecifick gravity, were due to them. By which method the Mafs of denfe Fluids, which compos'd the main bulk of the intire *Chaos*, being heavier than the Maffes of Earth, Water, and Air, would fink downwards with the greateft force and velocity, and elevate thofe
                                                        Maffe

Masses inclosed among them upwards. Which procedure must therefore distinguish the *Chaos* or *Atmosphere* into two very different and distinct Regions: The lower and larger whereof would be a collection or system of dense and heavy Fluids, or a vast *Abyss* immediately encompassing the central solid Body: The higher and lesser would be a collection, or system of earthy, watery, and aery Parts, confusedly mix'd together, and encompassing the said *Abyss*, in the same manner as that did the central Solid. And this I take to be the state of Darkness, which the Proposition we are upon mentions: And that the *Chaos*, particularly, the Face or upper Regions of it, were at this time in such a dark and caliginous Condition, will easily appear. For all those Opake or Earthy Corpuscles which before rov'd about the immense Regions of the *Atmosphere*, and frequently even then obscur'd the Central Solid to any external Spectator, were now crouded nearer together; and instead of flying up and down in, or possessing an Orb of 40000 or 50000 Miles in thickness, were reduced to a narrower Sphere, and confin'd within a space not perhaps in Diameter above the thousandth part of the former; and must by consequence exclude the Rays of the Sun in anotherguess manner than before. We cannot but observe in our present Air, That the very same Vapours which, when dissipated and scatter'd through the *Atmosphere*, (whose extent yet is not great) freely admit the Rays of the Sun, and afford us clear and lightsome days; when they are collected into Clouds, become opake Masses, and are capable of obscuring the Sky, and rendring it considerably dark to us. In the same manner 'tis easy to suppose, that those Opake and Earthy Masses, which in the those vaster Regions would but in a lefs degree, and in some places, exclude the Beams of the Sun, muft, when collected and crowded clofer together on the furface of the *Abyfs*, exclude them in a degree vaftly furpaffing the former; muft occafion an entire darknefs in all its Regions, and particularly in thofe upper ones, over which they were immediately collected. And if from the former comparifon we eftimate how few Vapours collected into a Cloud with us will caufe no inconfiderable degree of darknefs; and allow, as is but reafonable, a proportionably greater degree of darknefs to a proportionably greater number of Earthy and Opake Corpufcles crowded to gether; we fhall not doubt but all manner of communication with the Heavenly Bodies, and the External World, muft be intirely interrupted; and the leaft imaginable Ray or Beam of Light from the Sun excluded, not only from the loweft, but even all, excepting the very higheft Regions of this fuperior *Chaos*. Which ftate of Nature, belonging to this time, immediately preceding the *Hexameron*, is not amifs reprefented by the *Theorift*'s Second Figure, which is accordingly here delineated.

Theor. p. 56.

V. The

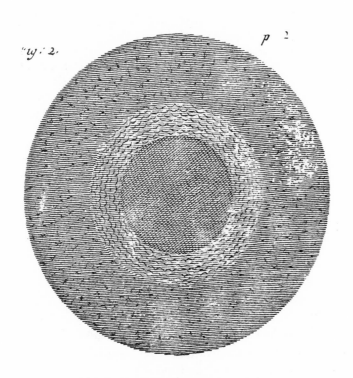

V. The Vifible part of the Firft Day's Work was the Production of Light, or its fucceffive Appearance to all the parts of the Earth ; with the confequent diftinction of Darkness and Light, Night and Day upon the face of it.

V. If we remember in what state we left the *Chaos* in the laft Propofition, and fuffer our thoughts to run naturally along with its fucceeding mutations, we fhall find that the next thing to be here confider'd, (for the Subterraneous Syftem of denfe Fluids, or the great *Abyfs*, not coming directly within the Defign of *Mofes*, is
not

not here to be particularly profecuted any farther) is the Separation of this Upper and *Elementary Chaos,* or Congeries of Earthy, Watery
and Aery Corpufcles, into two fomewhat different Regions; the one a Solid Orb of Earth,
with great quantities of Water in its Pores; the
other an *Atmofphere* in a peculiar fenfe, or Mafs
of the lighteft Earthy, with the reft of the Watery and the Aery Particles, ftill fomewhat confufedly mixt together. For fince this Upper *Chaos,*
(tho' in general much lighter than the *Abyfs* beneath) confifted of parts very Heterogeneous,
and of different fpecifick gravities (the Earthy
being heavier than the Watery, and thofe yet
heavier than the Aery Particles;) 'tis evident,
that in the fame manner as this whole mixed
Mafs was feparated from the heavier *Abyfs* beneath, muft it again feparate and divide it felf into two fuch general Orbs as were juft now mention'd. The *former* confifting of the denfer and
folider parts, fuch as the Earthy, Claiy, Sandy,
Gravelly, Stony *Strata* of the prefent Earth,
with fo many of the Watery Particles as either
being already in thofe Regions muft be inclofed
therein, or could defcend from above, and have
admittance into the Pores thereof: The *latter* of
the lefs Solid, Lighter, and Earthy, with the reft
of the Watery, and the Aery Particles, not yet
fufficiently diftinguifh'd from each other. This
procefs will I fuppofe eafily be allow'd, excepting what relates to the enclofing of the Watery
parts within the Earth; with relation to which,
'tis commonly fuppos'd that becaufe Water is
fpecifically lighter than Earth, it muft in the regular digeftions of a *Chaos,* take the Upper fituation, and cover that higheft Orb, as that
would others of greater gravity than it felf. 'Tis
alfo

alfo commonly imagin'd that the *Mofaick Cofmo-gony* favours fuch an *Hypothefis*, and fuppofes the Waters to have encompafs'd the Globe, and cover'd its furface, till on the third day they were deriv'd into the Seas. Now, as I by no means apprehend any neceffity of underftanding the *Mofaick* Creation in this fenfe; fo I am very fure 'tis contrary to a Philofophick account of the Formation of the *Chaos*; unlefs one of thefe two things were certain, Either that the quantity of Water were fo much greater than that of Earth, that all the Pores and Interftices of the latter could not contain it; or elfe that it was generally elevated into the Air in the form of Vapour, and fuftained there while the Earth fetled and confolidated together, and did not till then defcend and take its own proper place. The *former* of which is neither reconcilable to the *Mofaick* Creation, nor will be afferted by any who knows, even fince the Deluge, how fmall the quantity of Fluids in comparifon to that of the Solids is in the Earth on which we live. And the *latter* is too much to be granted in the prefent cafe by any confidering perfon, who knows that a Comet's Vapours conftitute the main part of that Tail or Mift, which is fometimes equal to a Cylinder, whofe Bafis is 1000000 Miles in Diameter, and its Altitude as far as from the Sun to the Earth, or 54000000 Miles; (as it was in the laft famous Comet in 1681. reprefented in Mr. *Newton's* own Scheme) Let the rarity of the fame be fuppos'd as great as any *Phænomena* fhall require. For to clear this matter by a familiar Inftance or Experiment; Take Sand or Duft, and let them fall gently into a Veffel, till it be near full: Take afterwards fome Water, and pour it alike gently into the fame Veffel: And

And it will foon appear, that, notwithftanding
the greater fpecifick gravity of the Dry and
Earthy, than of the Moift and Watery parts,
(whence one might imagine that the Sand or
Duft would be the loweft, and the Water fwim
uppermoft on the furface of the other, without
mingling therewith) yet will the latter immediately fink downwards, and fo throughly drench
and fatiate the faid Mafs before any will remain
on the top, that its proportion to that of the
Solid parts will be very confiderable. Which
being apply'd to the point before us, will take a-
way all imaginable difficulty in the cafe : It being evident, without this comparifon, that fuch
Watery Particles as were already intermix'd
with the others would remain where they were;
and with this, equally fo, that the reft, which
were above the fame, upon the firft fubfidence of
the Earthy *Strata* would penetrate, pervade and
faturate the fame. So that on this firft *Day* or *Year*
of the Creation, the Earthy and Denfer parts
would take their places loweft, on the furface of
the great Abyfs; would fettle in part into the fame,
and compofe an Orb of Earth ; and in its Interftices and little Cavities all fuch Watery Particles
as were already in this Region, or defcended upon it before its confolidation, would be enclos'd ; and that as far above the furface of the
Abyfs, to which they would be contiguous, as
their quantity could enable them to reach. On
this firft *Day* or *Year* alfo the upper Regions of
the *Chaos*, being now in fome meafure freed from
thefe Earthy and Opake Maffes which before
excluded the fame, and caufed the before-mention'd thick Darknefs; would in fome degree
admit the Rays of the Sun. Now therefore
that glorious Emanation, *Light*, the vifible part
of

of this days Work, would begin to appear on
the face of the Earth: Now would It, by the
Annual Motion, fucceffively illuminate the feveral parts of it: And now would it confequently caufe that natural Diftinction between Darknefs and Light, Night and Day round the whole
Globe, which was to be accounted for in this
Propofition. Which progrefs of the *Chaos,* and
ftate of Nature is well enough exhibited by the
Theorift's third Figure ; which therefore is here Theor. p.
delineated.   38.

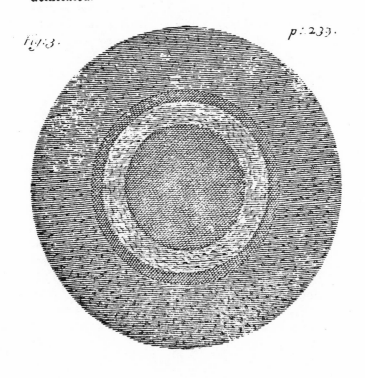

p. 233.

Fig. 3.

Corollary, *Hence we may observe the Justness of the* Mosaick *Creation, and how fitly it begins at the Production of Light ; without taking notice of such prior conditions, and such preparations of the* Chaos *which have been before explain'd, and were in order of Nature previous to this days Work. For this account reaching only to the Visible World, and the Visible Effects in it ; and keeping still within the bounds of sense, and of common observation, could not better be accommodated to the truth of things, and the capacities of all, than by such a Procedure. The Ancient condition of the* Chaos *in former Ages was no way here concern'd, and so was intirely to be omitted. The State of Darkness which immediately preceded the Six Days Work, and which, with relation thereto, was necessary to be mention'd, made a very proper introduction, and so very fitly was to be hinted at by way of Preface thereto. Both which cases are accordingly by* Moses *taken care of. And so the first Period was the Production of Light, the Admission of the Rays of the Sun, and the Origin of Day and Night depending thereon ; as the Method and Decorum of things, with the apprehensions of the People, did both very naturally require. For since in this Sacred History of the Origin of things, not only the Visible World, and the Visible parts of it were singly concern'd ; But principally the Effects to be enumerated were such as requir'd the Light and Heat of the Sun, the one to be View'd, the other to be Produced by ; and without the latter could no more have Been at all, than been Conspicuous without the former ; 'Twas very suitable, and very natural in the first place to introduce the Cause or Instrument, and afterwards in the succeeding Periods, to recount the Effects thereof in the World : First to acquaint us that the Light and Heat of the Sun were in some measure admitted into the upper Regions of the* Chaos,

and

*and then to relate thofe remarkable confequences there-
of which the fucceeding Periods of the Creation exhibited on the face of the Earth. Which Order of Nature, and Succeffion of Things, is accordingly very
prudently and fitly obferv'd, and kept pace with, in
this Sacred Hiftory.*

VI. The vifible part of the Second Day's Work was the
Elevation of the *Air*, with all its contained Vapours ;
the fpreading it for an *Expanfum* above the Earth, and
the diftinction thence arifing of Superior and Inferior
Waters : The former confifting of thofe Vapours ,
rais'd and fuftain'd by the Air; The latter of fuch as
either were inclos'd in the Pores, Interftices and Bowels
of the Earth, or lay upon the Surface thereof.

VI. When at the Conclufion of the former
Day the Heat of the Sun began confiderably to
penetrate the Superior Regions of the *Chaos*,
and the two different Orbs, the Solider Earthy,
and the Fluider Aery Maffes, began to be pretty
well diftinguifhed, the fame things would proceed ftill on this fucceeding Day. The Lower
Earthy *Strata* would be fettling fomewhat clofer
together ; the Watery parts would fubfide, and
faturate their inward Pores and Vacuities, and
the *Atmofphere* would free it felf more and more
from the heavieft and moft Opake Corpufcles,
and thereby become in a greater degree tenuious,
pure, and clear than before. Whereupon by
that time the Night or firft half of this Second
Day or *Year* was over, and the Sun arofe, The
Light and Heat of that Luminary, would more
freely and deeply penetrate the Atmofphere,
and become very fenfible in thefe Upper or Aery
Regions. Which being fuppos'd, the proper
Effect which were to be next expected muft be,
that vaft quantities of Vapours would be elevated into, and there fuftained by the now better

Z   purified

purified Air; while in the mean time all the
Earthy Corpufcles which were uncapable of
rarefaction, and with them all fuch Watery Particles as were fo near the Earth that the Sun's
Power could not fufficiently reach them, were
ftill finking downwards and increafing the craffitude and bulk of the Solid Earth, and of its
included Waters. From all which 'tis eafie
to account for the Particulars of this Day's
Work. The *Expanfum* or Firmament which
was this day fpread out above the Earth was
plainly the *Air*, now truly fo called, as being freed from moft of its Earthy mixtures. The
Superior Waters, All thofe which in the form of
Vapour a half years heat of the Sun, with the
continual affiftance of the Central Heat, could
elevate, and the Air fuftain. The *Inferior Waters*,
thofe which were not elevated, but remain'd
below, all that fell down with, were enclofed
in, funk into, and, if you will, lay upon the
Orb of Earth beneath. And when it is particularly faid by *Mofes* that 'twas this *Expanfum*
or Firmament which was to divide the Superior
from the Inferior Waters, that is exactly agreeable to the nature of things, and fuitable to this
account : It being the *Air* which truly and properly fuftain'd all thofe Vapours, as now it does
the Clouds, above the Earth; and was thereby
the means of feparating them from their Fellows
in the Bowels, or on the furface thereof. Which
ftate of the *Chaos*, or Progrefs of the Creation, is
Theor. p. well reprefented in the *Theorift's* fourth Figure ;
39. which here follows.

Corollary

Fig. 4.

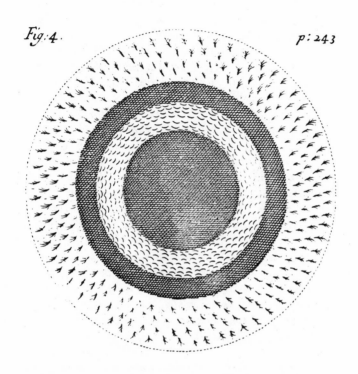

p: 243

Corollary 1. Hence appears a sufficient Reason why in this Six Days Creation one intire Day is allow'd to the Formation of the Air, and the distinguishing the Vapours in the same, from those beneath; which has hitherto-seem'd somewhat strange and disproportionate. 'Tis certain this Work requir'd as long a time, and was of as great importance as any other whatsoever: All that Water which the Earth was to have in its Air, or upon its Surface, till the Deluge, being, 'tis probable, intirely owing to this day's elevation of them. For had they not been thus buoy'd up and sustain'd on high, they must have sunk down-

Z 2   ward

ward, and so been inclosed in the Bowels of the Earth, without possibility of redemption; and have rendred the Antediluvian *World more like to a dry and barren* Wilderness, *than, what it was to exceed, a juicy fruitful and habitable* Canaan.

Coroll. 2. *Hence arises a new confirmation that the* Days *of the Creation were* Years *also. For seeing the quantity of Water which was preserv'd above ground, and fill'd all the Seas before the Deluge, was no greater than was this Second* Day *elevated into Vapour; had this* Day *been no longer than one of ours at present, the foremention'd quantity would have been so far from saturing the Earth, supplying the Rivers, and filling all the Seas, that every day it would be wholly exhal'd afterwards, and suffer the intire Vegetable and Animal Kingdoms to perish for want of moisture. All which, in the* Hypothesis *we here take, is wholly avoided, and a very fit and suitable proportion of Waters preserv'd above for all the necessities of the Earth, with its Productions and Inhabitants. And this consideration affords one very good reason why the commencing of the* Diurnal Rotation *was defer'd till after the Formation of the Earth was over; there being an evident necessity thereof in order to the providing Water sufficient for the needs of those Creatures for whose sake the whole Creation was ordain'd and perform'd. In which procedure plain tokens of the* Divine Wisdom *cannot but be very conspicuous and observable to us.*

VII. The visible parts of the Third Day's Works were two; the former, the Collection of the inferior Waters, or such as were now under the Heaven, into the Seas, with the consequent appearance of the dry Land; the latter, the production of Vegetables out of that Ground so lately become dry.

VII. In order to the Apprehending of the *double* operation of this Day, we muſt call to mind what ſtate the Orb of Earth was in by this time. We have ſeen already that it had been ſetling together, and fixing it ſelf on the ſurface of the *Abyſs* from the very beginning of the Creation; and we ought to ſuppoſe that in the ſpace of two years it was not only become wholly diſtinct from the *Abyſs* below, and the *Atmoſphere* above it, but that it was ſetled and conſolidated together, and its *Strata* grown firm and compacted. We muſt farther obſerve, that by reaſon of its Columns, different Denſity, and Specifick Gravity, (atteſted to, *a priori* from the *Chaos's*, and *a poſteriori* from the internal Earth's *Phænomena*,) it was ſetled into the Abyſs in different degrees, and thereby became of an unequal ſurface diſtinguiſh'd into Mountains, Plains and Valleys. Which things being ſuppos'd and conſider'd, the two Works of this *Day* or *Year* of the Creation, which are of themſelves very different, will be eaſily underſtood and reconcil'd. For when at Sun-ſet, or the concluſion of the laſt Day, we left the Air by half a Years Power of the Sun crowded with Vapours to a prodigious degree; upon the coming on of this Third Day, and in its Night or former half, the ſaid vaſt quantities of Vapours muſt needs deſcend, and ſo by degrees muſt leave the Air pretty free, and take their places on the Surface of the Earth; altering thereby their own denomination, and becoming of *Upper* or *Cæleſtial*, *Lower* or *Terreſtrial* Waters. Indeed if we do but allow the effect to be in any meaſure anſwerable to the time, we ſhall grant that in the half year of Night, which is the former part of this Third Period of the Creation, the main Body of the

Vid. Lem. 78. cum Coroll. & Hypoth. 2 prius.

Vapours muſt have not only deſcended down upon the Earth, but, by reaſon of the inequality of its Surface, and the Solidity withal, have run down from the higher and more extant parts, by the Declivities and Hollows, into the loweſt Valleys, and moſt depreſſed Regions of all; muſt in theſe places have compos'd Seas and Lakes every where throughout the Surface of the Earth; and ſo by that time the light appear'd and the Sun's riſing began the latter part of this Day, the intire face of the Globe, which was juſt before cover'd as it were with the deſcending Waters, muſt be diſtinguiſh'd into overflow'd Valleys, and extant Continents, into *Seas* and *Dry-land,* that very Work of this Day we were in the firſt place to enquire about. *The waters under the heavens were* now *gathered together into* their reſpective and diſtinct *places, and the dry land appear'd* and became fit for the Production of the Vegetable Kingdom. Which therefore moſt naturally leads us to the ſecond branch of this Day's Work. For when this part hitherto was compleated on the Night or former half of this Day (which the Abſence of the Sun ſo long together rendred peculiarly and ſolely fit to permit and procure the deſcent of the Vapours); and when at the ſame time the Dry Land was now diſtinguiſh'd from the Seas, and juſt become (in the utmoſt degree) moiſt and juicy; upon the Sun Riſing, or coming on of the Day-time, 'twas of all other the moſt fit and convenient Seaſon for the Germination of the Seeds of Vegetables, and the growth of Trees, Shrubs, Plants and Herbs out of the Earth. The Soil, Satur'd and Fatned by the foregoing half Year's deſcent of Vapours, was now like the Ἰλὺς that fruitful Seminary of the Vegetable and Animal

productions

productions of Primitive Nature, so much celebrated by all Antiquity. An intire half year of
the Sun's presence together, was a time as proper
and as natural for such a purpose as could possibly be desir'd. And when there was this half
Year of Day to spare in this Period of the Creation, after one Work was compleated ; and the
same was so very fitly prepar'd and dispos'd for
the production of Vegetables ; 'tis no wonder
that this above all the other Divisions has a double
Task, and that the Seas and Dry Land were distinguish'd, and the Vegetables produc'd on the
same *Day* or *Year* of the Creation ; according
as from the *Mosaick* History the present Proposition asserts. And if we allow for the defect
of the inequalities of the outward Surface, too
small to be therein consider'd ; and suppose the
Atmosphere somewhat clearer than before ; the
former figure will still serve well enough, and
represent the progress and state of the Earth at
the conclusion of this *Third Day.*

Theor. 1.
J. p. 42.
& l. 2. c. 7.

Theor. p.
39. & su-
pra.

Corollary 1. *When according to our present accounts of these matters, this is the only day of the
Creation to which a double work, and that the one
quite different from the other, ought to be ascrib'd,
and is ascrib'd by* Moses ; *The* Night *being peculiarly fit for the former, and the* Day *for the latter operation ; which could happen on none of the other Periods; This exactness of correspondence ought to be
esteem'd an Evidence of the literal sense of the Writer, and of his accommodation to the nature of things;
and a very considerable confirmation of those* Hypotheses *on which it so naturally depends.*

Coroll. 2. *Hence arises a* Confirmation *of what
was before asserted that the* Antediluvian Earth *had
only lesser Lakes and Seas, not a vast Ocean. For
when the quantity of Waters belonging to the Earth*

Phænom.
43. prius.

Z 4   *and*

and Air at first, was no more than was elevated in one half year, and at once sustain'd by the Air; no one will imagine it sufficient to fill the intire Ocean alone, if there had been neither lesser Seas, nor Rivers to be supply'd therewith. And so, vice versâ, *It having been prov'd by other Arguments, that there was no Ocean, but only lesser Seas, before the Flood, This Account which affords sufficient quantity of Water for the latter, but not for the former, is thereby not a little confirm'd.*

Coroll. 3. *Tho' the Heat and Influence of the Sun was on this Third Day very great, yet was his Body not yet Visible. For since at his Rising the Earth and lowest Regions of the Air were very full of moisture, while the higher Regions were very clear and bright; the force of his heat would be so great as to elevate considerable quantities of Vapours on a sudden, and thereby (e're the lowest Air had deposited its Vapours, and rendred it self transparent) the Sun would anew hide himself in a thick Mist, and so prevent his own becoming conspicuous, which otherwise 'tis not improbable he might this Day have been.*

VIII. The Fourth Day's Work was the Placing the Heavenly Bodies, Sun, Moon, and Stars, in the Expansion or Firmament, i. e. The rendring them Visible and Conspicuous on the Face of the Earth: Together with their several Assignations to their respective Offices there.

VIII. Altho' the Light of the Sun penetrated the *atmosphere* in some sort the first Day, and in the succeeding ones had very considerable influence upon it; yet is it by no means to be suppos'd that his Body was Visible all that while. Tho' we every day enjoy much more Light and Heat from the Sun than the Primitive Earth could, for a considerable space, be suppos'd to have done, yet 'tis but sometimes that the Air

is

is fo clear as to render his Body difcernible by
us. A very few Clouds or Vapours gather'd together in our Air are able, we fee, to hinder fuch
a profpect for Weeks, if not Months together ;
while yet at the fame time we are fufficiently
fenfible of his Force and Influence in the conftant productions of Nature. Which things being duly confider'd, and the vaftnefs and denfity of the *Upper Chaos* allow'd for, 'twill be but
reafonable to afford a great fpace, even after the
firft penetration of Light, for the intire clearing
of the *Atmofphere,* and the diftinct view of the
Sun s Body by a Spectator on the Surface of
the Earth. I fuppofe no one will think the
two firft *Days* or *Years* of the Creation too long
for fuch a work ; or if any one does, the particular work and ftate of the *Atmofphere* on
the fecond Day will prevent the moft probable
part of fuch a furmife, and fhew the impoffibility of the Sun's Appearance at that time,
And the fame reafon will in a fufficient, tho a
lefs degree, prevent any juft Expectations on the
third Day, as was obferv'd in the laft *Corollary.*
But now upon the coming on of this *fourth Day,*
and the *Sun's* defcent and abode below the Horizon for an intire half year, thofe Vapours which
were rais'd the day before muft fall downwards,
and fo before the approach of the Morning leave
the Air in the greateft clearnefs and purity imaginable, and permit the *Moon* firft, then the *Stars,*
and afterward, upon the coming on of the Day,
the *Sun* himfelf moft plainly to appear and be
confpicuous on the Face of the Earth. This *fourth
Day* is therefore the very time when, acording to
this Account, and the Sacred Hiftory both, thefe
Heavenly Bodies, which were in being before,
but fo as to be wholly Strangers to a Spectator on
Earth,

Earth, were rendred vifible, and expos'd to the view of all who fhould be fuppos'd to be there at the fame time. They now were in the Sacred Stile, *placed in the Firmament of Heaven, gave Light upon the Earth*; began to *rule* plainly and vifibly *over the Day, and over the Night, and to divide the Light from the Darknefs*; as ever fince they have continued to do. And now the inanimate World, or the Earth, Air, Seas, and all their Vegetable Productions are compleat; and the Tradition of thofe *Chinefes* who inhabit *Formofa*, and other Iflands, appears well-grounded, and exactly true, who hold, That the World, when firft created, was without Form or Shape; but by one of their Deities was brought to its full Perfection in four Years. Which Progrefs of the Creation, and State of Nature is exactly reprefented by the *Theorift*'s fifth and laft Figure; which therefore here follows,

Atlas Chin. Part 2. p. 46. Apud War. Geolog. p. 58.

Theor. p. 41.

IX. The

Fig:5.

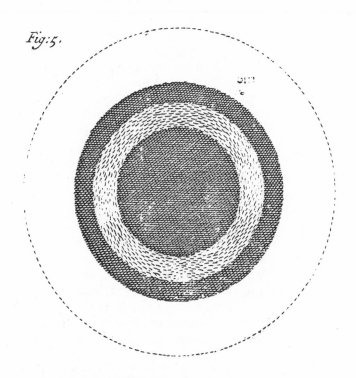

IX. The fifth Day's Work was the Production of the Fiſh and Fowl out of the Waters; with the Benediction beſtow'd on them in order to their Propagation.

IX. The Terraqueous Globe being now become habitable both to the ſwimming and volatil Animals; and the Air clear, and ſo penetrable by that compleat Heat of the *Sun*, which was requiſite to the Generation of ſuch Creatures; 'tis a very proper time for their Introduction. Which was accordingly done upon this fifth *Day* or *Year* of the Creation. Thoſe Seeds, or little Bodies of Fiſh and Fowl which were contain'd in the Water,

(or

(or moiſt fruitful 'Ιλὺς of kin to it) were now expos'd to the kindly warmth of the *Sun*, and the
conſtant ſupply of a moſt gentle and equal Heat
from beneath; they were neither diſturbed by
the ſudden alteration of the Temperature of the
Air from the violence of Winds, or by the Agitations of the Tide (which was both very ſmall,
in theſe ſmall Seas; and by reaſon of the abſence of the *Diurnal Rotation*, imperceptibly eaſy,
gentle, and gradual;) theſe Seeds, I ſay, when
invigorated with the Divine Benediction, became now prolifick; and in this fifth Day's time
a numerous Off-ſpring of the ſwimming and volatil Kinds aroſe, whereby the two fluid Elements, Water and Air became repleniſh'd with
thoſe firſt Pairs, which by the Benediction they
ſtraightway receiv'd, were enabled to become
the original of all of the ſame Kinds, which
ever were to be the Inhabitants of thoſe Regions
afterwards. Which time and procedure is no leſs
agreeable to the State of the World in our *Hypotheſis*, than 'tis to the expreſs Affirmations of
Moſes, who makes Fiſh and Fowl the ſole Product of the fifth *Day* or *Year* of the Creation.

X. The Sixth Day's Work was the Production of all the
  Terreſtrial or Dry-land Animals; and that in a different
  manner. For the Brute Beaſts were produc'd out of the
  Earth, as the Fiſh and Fowl had been before out of the
  Waters; but after that the Body of *Adam* was form'd
  of the Duſt of the Ground; who by the Breath of
  Life breath'd into him in a peculiar manner, became a
  Living Soul. Some time after which, on the ſame
  day, he was caſt into a deep Sleep, and *Eve* was form'd
  out of a Rib taken from his ſide. Together with ſeveral other things, of which a more particular account
  has been already given on another occaſion.

X. The

X. The Earth being now grown more Solid,
Compact, and Dry, its Surface diftinguifh'd into Sea and Dry-land, each of which were ftor'd
in fome fort with Inhabitants and Vegetables,
the Air being fully clear, and fit for Refpiration,
and the other Difpofitions of External Nature
being equally fubfervient to this, as well as it had
been before to the laft day's Productions; 'twas
a proper Seafon for the Generation of the *Dry-
land Animals,* and the Introduction of the nobleft
of them, *Man*; which accordingly were the firft
Works, on this fixth *Day* or *Year* of the Creation. Any more particular account of which,
or of the following Works is not fo directly the
defign of this *Theory*, and fo fhall not be here
farther infifted on. We may only take notice
of two things; the one is the peculiar *Manner*; the other the peculiar *Time* for the Creation of Man. As to the former, Tho' 'tis granted that all the other Day's Works mention'd by
Mofes were brought to pafs in a natural way by
proper and fuitable Inftruments, and a mechanical Procefs, as we have feen through the whole
Series of the foregoing Creation; yet 'tis evident, as has been already obferv'd, That an immediate and miraculous Power was exercis'd in
the formation of the Body, and Infufion of the
Soul of Man, as well as in fome other particular Cafes belonging to this Origin of Things.
In plain terms, I take it to be evident, That
that fame Λόγος Θεάνθρωπος, our Bleffed Mediator, who was afterward very frequently converfant on Earth, appear'd in a humane Form to
the Patriarchs, gave the Law in a vifible Glory,
and with an audible Voice on Mount *Sinai*,
guided the *Iraelites* perfonally in a Pillar of Fire,
and of a Cloud through the Wildernefs, inhabited

Solut. 2.
prius.
Vid John
i 18. and
v 37 and
vi.45,46.
Matth xi.
27. 1 John
iv. 12.
Rom i.20.
Col. i 15.
1 Tim. i.
17. and 6.
15, 16
with Exod
3. and 19.

ted between the *Cherubins* in the Holy of Holies, and took the peculiar Stile, Titles, Attributes, Adoration, and incommunicable Name of the God of *Ifrael,* and at laft was Incarnate, liv'd a true Man amongft us, died for us, and afcended into Heaven, makes ftill Interceffion for us with the Father, and will come to Judge the World in Righteoufnefs at the laft Day: That this very fame Divine Perfon was actually and vifibly, in a humane Shape, converfant on Earth, and was truly and really employ'd in this Creation of the World (and particularly in this peculiar Formation of Man) fo frequently afcribed to him in the Holy Scriptures. It being both unfit and impoffible for the Divine Nature it felf, or at leaft that of the Father, to be fo much, and in fuch a manner concern'd with the Corporeal World, and the finful Race of Mankind, as we find here and every where this *Divine Perfon,* our Bleffed Mediator, to have been; as the Texts quoted a little above compar'd together do I think fully prove. Seeing therefore our Saviour Chrift, God-man, was perfonally prefent, and actually employ'd in this Primitive Creation of the World: Seeing Man was to be a Creature intirely different from all the reft, a Being compounded of a Spiritual and Immortal Soul, and of a Material and Corruptible Body: Seeing in both thefe he was to be made in the likenefs of that Divine Perfon, who created him, and be conftituted his Deputy and Vicegerent among the Creatures here below; 'twas but reafonable there fhould be as great a diftinction in his Original, as was to be in his Nature and Faculties, his Office and Dignity, his Capacities and Happinefs from the other parts of the vifible Creation; and by confequence,

that

that peculiar Interpofition of God himfelf in the
Formation of the Body, and Infufion of the
Soul of our firft Parents, fo particularly obfervab-
ble in the *Mofaick* Hiftory, is both very agreeable to the Nature of things, very fuitable to the
Wifdom of God, and very reconcilable to the
moft Philofophick Accounts of this Origin of
the World; and withal a remarkable token of
the Dignity of Human Nature, of the diftinction between his Soul and Body, and of the
great Condefcenfion and Love of God towards
us, and fo the moft highly worthy of our confideration. Neither is the other circumftance the
peculiar *Time* of the Creation of Man to be
pafs'd over without a proper Reflection on it.
'Twere eafy to fhew, That none of the preceding Days were in any degree fo fit for; nay,
moft of them not capable of this Creation and
Introduction of Man. But upon this fixth Period, when every thing which could be fubfervient to him, and advance his felicity, was compleated; he who was to be the Lord of All, and
for whofe fake the whole was fram'd, was brought
into the World. When the *Light* had been pene-
trating into, and clarifying this dark and thick
Atmofphere for more than five compleat *Years* together; when the *Air* was freed from its number-
lefs Vapours, and become pure, clear, and fit for
his Refpiration; when the *Waters*, as well fuperior as interior, were fo difpos'd as to minifter
to his neceffities by Mifts and Dews from the
Heavens, and by Springs and Rivers from the
Earth; when the *Surface of the Earth* was become
dry and folid for his fupport, and was cover'd
over with Trees, Shrubs, Plants, Herbs, Grafs,
and Flowers for his Suftenance and Delight;
when the glorious *Firmament of Heaven*, and the
beautiful

beautiful Syftem of the *Sun*, *Moon*, and *Stars*
were vifible and confpicuous to him, the Objects of
his Contemplation, the Diftinguifhers of his Seafons; by whofe powerful Influences the Earth
was invigorated, and the World rendred a fruitful and ufeful, a lightfome and pleafant Habitation to him; when, laftly, *all forts of Animals* in
the *Seas*, in the *Air*, or on the *Earth*, were fo
difpos'd as to attend, benefit, and pleafe him one
way or other; when, I fay, all thefe things were
by the Care, Beneficence, and Providence of God
prepar'd for the entertainment of this principal
Gueft, then, and not till then, was *Man* created and introduc'd into the World: Then, and
not before was He conftituted the Lord and Governor of the whole, and *all things put in fubje-*
ction under his feet. In which intire procedure
the Wifdom and Goodnefs of the Creator, and
the Dignity and Honour of his principal Creature here below, are equally confulted; and the
greateft occafion imaginable given to our firft Parents, and all their Pofterity of adoring and ce-
lebrating the Divine Bounty to them in the prefent and fucceeding Ages. Which naturally leads
us to the next Propofition.

*Pfalm viii.
6.*

XI. God having thus finifh'd the Works of Creation,
Refted on the Seventh day from the fame; and Sanctified or fet that Day apart for a Sabbath, or Day of
Reft, to be then and afterward obferv'd as a Memorial of his Creation of the World in the fix foregoing,
and his refting or keeping a Sabbath on this Seventh
day. Which Sabbath was reviv'd, or at leaft its Obfervation anew enforc'd on the *Jews*, by the Fourth
Commandment.

XI. Nothing fure could be more fit and proper at this time than the praifing and worfhiping

ping of that Powerful and Munificent Creator, who in the foregoing six Days Productions had so operously and so liberally provided for the well-being and happiness of Mankind. And seeing this intire Fabrick was defign'd for the use and advantage of all succeeding Generations as well as the present, it could not but be reasonable to perpetuate the Memory of this Creation, and devote one Period in seven to the peculiar Worship and Service of that God who was both the Author of the Works themselves, and of this Institution of the Sabbath, to perpetuate the memory of such his six Days of Work, and of this seventh of Rest, to all future Generations. What relates to the Fall of *Adam*, and the intire Moral State of the World, comes not within the compass of this Phylical *Theory*, and so (notwithstanding it naturally enough belongs to this Day, and might, I imagine, be shewn not to be so difficult, as for want of a right understanding thereof, 'tis usually imagin'd to be, and that without receding from the literal, obvious, and usual Sense of Scripture) must be wholly omitted in this place.

> XII. There is a constant and vigorous Heat diffused from the Central towards the superficiary Parts of our Earth.

XII. This has been already accounted for, and need not here be resum'd.

Corollary. *From the consideration of the very long time that the Heat of a Comet's central Solid may endure, 'tis easy to account for that otherwise strange Phænomenon of some of those Bodies, viz. That tho' the Tails of the Comets appear to be no other than Steams of Vapours rarified by the prodigious Heat acquir'd in their approaches to the Sun; yet some at least*

Vid. Lem. 65. & Hypoth. 1. Arg. 7. prius.
Vid. Fig. Comet. A. D. 1680. apud Newt. & nostram. Fig. 1.

A a

laſt of theſe Comets have no inconſiderable ones as they are deſcending towards the Sun, *long before they approach near enough to acquire new ones by a freſh Rarefaction of their Vapours in his Vicinity. For ſince the prodigious Heat acquir'd at the laſt* Perihelion *muſt remain for ſo many thouſands of Years, tho' the Tail which the* Sun's *own Heat rais'd at that time muſt have been either diſperſed through the* Ether, *or by its Gravitation return'd to its old place in the* Atmoſphere; *yet will there ſtill remain a Tail, and its Poſition will be no other than if the* Sun's *own Heat had elevated the ſame. For by what Heat ſoever the Vapours in a Comet's* Atmoſphere *become rarer than the Parts of the* Solar Atmoſphere *in which they are, or ſubject to the Power and Velocity of the* Sun's Rays *elevating the ſame, a Tail muſt be as certainly produc'd as if the* Sun's *own Heat were the occaſion of it. Which Obſervation rightly conſider'd, will afford light to the forementioned* Phænomenon, *and will deſerve the conſideration of* Aſtronomers, *to whom it is ſubmitted.*

XIII. The habitable Earth is founded or ſituate on the Surface of the Waters; or of a deep and vaſt Subterraneous Fluid.

Lem. 71,
&c And
Solut. 5,6,
7. priùs.

XIII. This has been ſufficiently explain'd already, and is obſervable in the foregoing Figures of the four latter periods of the *Moſaick* Creation.

XIV. The interior or intire Conſtitution of the Earth is correſpoudent to that of an *Egg.*

XIV. This is alſo very eaſily obſervable in the ſame Figures: Where (1.) the *Central Solid* is anſwerable to the *Yolk*; which by its fiery Colour, great Quantity, and innermoſt Situation, exactly repreſents the ſame: Where (2.) the
great

great *Abyſs* is analogous to the *White*; whoſe Denſity, Viſcoſity, moderate Fluidity, and middle Poſitition, excellently expreſs the like Qualities of the other: Where (3.) the *upper Orb* or habitable Earth correſponds to the *Shell*, whoſe Lightneſs, Tenuity, Solidity, little inequalities of Surface, and uppermoſt Situation admirably agree to the ſame. 'Tis indeed poſſible to ſuppoſe that the Quantities, ſpecifick Gravities, and Craſſitudes of each Orb (to inſtance in nothing elſe here) may be in the Earth proportionable to their *Analogous* ones in an *Egg*; but becauſe the Similitude is ſo very obvious and full in the foregoing more certain reſpects, and more than ſufficient on thoſe accounts to ſolve the preſent *Phænomenon*; and becauſe a bare poſſibility, or fancied probability cannot deſerve any more nice conſideration; I forbear; and look upon the Coincidences already obſerv'd, not a little ſurprizing and remarkable.

XV. The Primitive Earth had Seas and Dry-land diſtinguiſh'd from each other in great meaſure as the preſent; and thoſe ſituate in the ſame places generally as they ſtill are.

XV. The former part of this has been already ſufficiently explain'd; and of the latter part there can then be no reaſon to make any queſtion; ſince the ſame Earth that was made at firſt, does ſtill, as to its main parts, remain as it was to this Day. *Solut. priùs,*

XVI. The Primitive Earth had Springs, Fountains, Streams, and Rivers, in the ſame manner as the preſent, and uſually in or near the ſame places alſo.

XVI. The Origin of Fountains and Rivers is undoubtedly either from Vapours deſcending

from

from *without* the Surface of the Earth, or from
Steams elevated by the heat *within.* And which
way foever we chufe to folve the prefent, 'twill
alfo ferve to folve the Primitive *Phænomena* here
mention'd. 'Tis only to be obferv'd, That before the upper Earth was chap'd and broken at
the commencing of the *Diurnal Rotation*; and
indeed before the *Strata* became fo firmly confolidated as they afterward were, the fubterraneous Steams would arife, and pafs through the
fame more uniformly, and more eafily, and fo
more equally difpenfe their Waters over every
Part and Region of the Earth, than afterward.

Effay, p.
121, &c.
and p. 152.   Corollary. *If therefore Dr.* Woodward *be right
in afferting, That the Cracks and* Fiffures, *which he
calls* perpendicular *ones, fince the intire Confolidation of the Strata of the Earth, are neceffary to the
Origin of Springs, (and I believe he may have good
grounds for his Opinion) from the Being of fuch
Springs and Fountains after the Confolidation of the
Strata, and before the Flood, 'tis evident, that the
Diurnal Motion did not commence till after the Annual; nay, till after the Formation and Confolidation of the Earth: And fo what on* other *grounds
was before rendred highly probable, will appear nearer
to certainty on* This: *For 'tis plain, If the prefent
Diurnal Motion commenc'd either with the Annual,
or indeed any time before the Formation of the Earth,*
Vid. Lem.
67, 68, 69.
prius. *the Figure of the Chaos, and fo of the Abyfs and
Upper Earth, would originally be that of an Oblate
Sphæroid, as it is now; the Strata would be all coherent, united, and continued, without any Cracks or
perpendicular Fiffures at all; and the Origin of
Springs, on the* Doctor's *Grounds, muft in a natural way be plainly impoffible. Since therefore the
Diurnal Rotations commencing after the Confolidation*

tion of the Strata *gives a Mechanical and Natural Account of the Chaps and* perpendicular Fissures; *since without th? same in the present Case no natural Cause of th:? is by any assigned; since withal 'tis unquestionable that there were Springs and Rivers before the Flood; and since, lastly, it appears that such Fissures were necessary to the being of those Springs and Rivers, 'tis very reasonable, nay, necessary to suppose, that the* Diurnal Rotation *did not commence till after the Formation and Consolidation of the Earth was over; or, which is almost all one, till the Fall of Man, as we formerly asserted.* Hypoth. 3. priùs.

XVII. The Primitive Earth was distinguish'd into Mountains, Plains, and Vallies, in the same manner, generally speaking, and in the same places as the present.

XVII. This has been sufficiently explain'd already, and need not here be reassum'd. And that each of these Seas, Springs with their Rivers, and Mountains, were generally the same, and in the same places as the present, there is no reason to doubt; they being usually the very same individuals then and now, and so unquestionably cannot have chang'd their primary Situations. Lem. 71, &c. and Solut. priùs.

XVIII. The Waters of the Seas in the Primitive Earth were *Salt*, and those of the Rivers *Fresh*, as they are at present, and each, as now, were then stor'd with great plenty of Fish.

XVIII. This has no difficulty in it, seeing our present Seas and Rivers are the very same, or of the same nature; and their several Inhabitants the Spawn or Off-spring of those primitive ones.

XIX. The Seas were agitated with a like *Tide*, or *Flux and Reflux*, as they are at present.

A a 3

XIX. The

Lem. 79.
Coro. Co-
rol. prius.

XIX. The presence of the *Moon* and *Sun* being the cause of the Tides, and those Bodies by consequence being equally dispos'd before, as since the Deluge, to produce them; this Proposition can have no manner of difficulty. Only we may take notice of these two things, (1.) That in the State of Innocence, before the Diurnal Revolution began, the frequency of the Tide must depend on the *Lunar* Period, and happen but twice in each Month, as now it does in somewhat above a days time with us: On which account the increase and decrease of the Waters would be extreamly gentle, leisurely, and gradual, without any imaginable Violence or Precipitation. (2.) That in the whole *Antediluvian* State the Tides were lesser than since, by reason of the smallness of the Seas *then* in comparison of the great Ocean, from whence *now* the most considerable ones are deriv'd. All which yet hinders not, but they might be sensible enough in some Creeks, Bays, and Mouths of Rivers: The peculiar circumstances of those places in *that* as well as in the *present* State, rendring the Tides, the Elevations and Depressions of the Waters *there*, most considerable and violent of all others.

XX. The Productions of the Primitive Earth, as far as we can guess by the remainders of them at the Deluge, differ'd little or nothing from those of the present, either in Figure, Magnitude, Texture of Parts, or any other correspondent respect.

XX. These things seem to depend on two Particulars; *viz.* partly on the primary Bigness, Figure, and Constitution of the constituent, insensible Parts, or Elements of Bodies; and partly on the quantity of Heat made use of in their Production

Production or Coalition. Which being suppos'd, the Proposition will easily be establish'd. For, as to the first, I suppose they remain invariably the same in all Ages, and are by any natural Power unalterable. And as to the last, whatever be to said of the State of Innocence, or the first Ages succeeding, on some peculiar accounts, which I believe might be warmer than at present; yet as to the times here referr'd to, there is no need to suppose any great difference of Heat, either from the *Sun*, or the Central Body: And indeed, all the difference on any accounts to be suppos'd between the Heat before and since the Deluge, must be too inconsiderable to be taken notice of in any such sensible Effects as this Proposition does refer to. For the *Sun's* heat was not above a twenty fifth part greater than 'tis now, and the space of four or five thousand Years makes but a small difference in that of the Central Solid, if at first it were heated any whit near the degree mention'd in the Calculation referr'd to in the Margin. And tho' its real Heat were decreas'd, yet in case its facility of Penetration were increas'd in the same Proportion, the heat on the Face of the Earth would still be equal and invariable. And so by these accounts, the Productions of Nature in all Ages must be pretty equal and agreeable, as this Proposition requires.

Phænom. 23 & 27. prius.

Lem. 65. prius.

Corollary. *Tho' the Lives of the Antediluvians were so much longer than ours at present, yet were they not generally of a more Gygantick Stature than the past or present Generations since have been. In all which Ages, notwithstanding, there have been some of an extraordinary Bigness and Stature, and will be still no doubt in the future Ages to the end of the World.*

A a 4   XXI. The

XXI. The Primitive Earth had such *Metals* and *Minerals* in it, as the present has.

XXI. This is easily accounted for. For since the *Antediluvian*, and the present Earth, are either the very same, as the lower Regions; or at least of the same nature, the Off-spring of a Comets *Atmosphere* (as even that acquir'd Crust at the Deluge was) 'tis no wonder if each of them contain the same *Species* of Bodies within it.

XXII. Arts and Sciences were invented and improved in the first Ages of the World, as well as they since have been.

XXII. There is little need of giving particular Reasons for this. All I shall observe, is, That seeing the Ignorance and Barbarity of the Ages after the Deluge, is the greatest Objection against this Proposition; 'tis avoided in our *Hypothesis.* The insensible, tho' prodigious Change of the State of Nature, and the perishing of all the Monuments of the old Learning or Arts at the Flood, with the want of correspondence in the latter Years to the former Tradition, reducing the few remainders of the former State wholly to seek for their Learning, notwithstanding it might have been cultivated and improv'd to great degree before the Deluge; as therefore in all probability it was.

CHAP. II.

A Solution of the Phænomena *relating to the* Primitive State *of the* Earth.

XXIII. The *Primitive* ftate of the Earth admitted of the primary production of Animals out of the Waters and Dry Ground, which the fubfequent ftates, otherwife than in the ordinary method of Generation, have been uncapable of.

XXIII. 'TIS not to be expected that I fhould here be able to give a full and methodical account of the growth of the *Primitive* Pairs of Animals, and of the feveral difpofitions of the *Primigenial* ftate of Nature fubfervient or contributary thereto. The method of the Generation of Animals is it felf in general fo little known, and the Hiftory of this firft ftage of the World, as well fo fhort in the Sacred Writings, as fo difficult to be, in all its circumftances, now otherwife underftood, that fuch an Attempt might juftly be look'd upon as too rafh a prefumption. All that ought to be expected, and all that I fhall endeavour is this; To fhew, that as far as is known of that Original Earth, its properties were as peculiarly fit for, as thofe oppofite ones of the fucceeding are incapable of, fuch a production of Animals at firft, as this Propofition takes notice of. Which the five following particulars fhall include. (1.) The long and continued fpaces of Day and Night in the *Primitive* ftate did capacitate it for fuch productions; which the quick returns of the fame afterward prohibited.

Hypoth. 3. prius.

prohibited. 'Twill be eafily granted, that in the Generation of Animals there muft be a pretty conftant and continual warmth, without the frequent interpofition of Cold during the moft part of the procefs. Now this the long days of half a year afforded thefe Primary *Embrio's*; which the fhort ones of only twelve fmall hours, and the fudden and frequent returns of equal Nights, has utterly deni'd to any fuch ever fince. (2.) The *Primitive* Earth was moift and juicy enough to fupply nourifhment all the time of the Generation of the *Fœtus*; which after it was once become perfectly Dry and Solid was not again to expected. It was before obferv'd, that upon the defcent of the vaft quantities of Vapours on the Third Day, the ground was fo tender, foft, and full of juices, as very naturally anfwered to what all Antiquity made the fund and promptuary of the rifing Plants and Animals, the famous '*ιλυς*. And as that was but a neceffary qualification of a Soil which was to produce Animals, fo the want of it ever fince takes away all hopes of a like Propagation. (3.) The *Primitive* ftate of the Earth and Air, where the Animals were produc'd, had heat fufficient for that purpofe; which the fubfequent has not. 'Tis evident that a greater heat than the prefent Earth or Ambient Air can afford, is requifite to, and made ufe of in the prefent Generation of Animals (which the Incubation in the Oviparous, and the ftill warmer Pofition of the *Fœtus* in the Viviparous Animals affure us of:) On which account the prefent Earth muft needs be incapable of their production. But that the Heat in the *Primitive* Earth, and particularly where the Animals were produc'd, was much greater, will thus appear.

As

*Solut. *.*
priùs.

As to the Heat from the Central Body ; while the Earth was fomewhat loofe, and pretty freely admitted the afcending fteams, that, would be confiderably greater than after its more intire confolidation, when thefe fteams were thereby fo much confin'd within, or diverted to fome particular conceptacles. Befides, The Production of Animals was near *Paradife*, and I fuppofe no where elfe. Now thofe middle Regions, (of which *Eden*, the Country of *Paradife*, was one) being fituate under the ancient Ecliptick, and prefent Tropick, (of which before) enjoy'd alfo a greater Heat from the fame Central Body by reafon of their greater nearnefs thereto, than fince they or the correfponding parts of the *Torrid Zone* do or can partake of. For when the Earth was then perfectly Sphærical, the middle, and their neighbouring parts were about 10 miles nearer the Central Solid than the fame Regions now are : (They being in that proportion Elevated , and the circumpolar deprefs'd at the commencing of the *Diurnal Rotation*:) Which greater Vicinity of the Central Heat muft certainly have a fuitable effect, and caufe fomewhat warmer Regions thereabouts than they have been ever fince. Moreover, If the real proper heat of the Central Solid be in any confiderable proportion diminifh'd in near 6000 years time, (as in *fome* proportion it muft be) That degree of Heat which it had at firft, was ftill the moft powerful of all other ever fince. But then as to the Solar Heat, (to take no notice of the greater nearnefs of the Sun's Body before the Deluge than fince, as not directly reaching the prefent cafe:) 'Tis evident that Paradife, fituate under or near the very Ecliptick it felf, muft receive the utmoft power

of

Hypoth 4. prius.

Lem. 67, 68. cum coroll. prius.

of the same heat which any part of the Globe
were capable of, which by lying under the Tropick afterward it would not do.   On all which
accounts joyn'd together, 'tis evident that the heat
in the *Primitive* State was much more confiderable, and so much more adapted to the Generation of Animals than that in the subsequent

Phænom.   ever was or can possibly be.   (4.) The *Primi-*
39. priùs.   *tive* state was perfectly still and calm ; free from
all such winds, storms, violent tides, or any the
like hurries and disorders as at present wholly
render the production of Animals impossible :
Which quiet condition, if in some respects it en-
dur'd till the Deluge, yet, as even in those the
Paradisiacal state might have the preheminence ;
so in other, particularly the gentleness of the

Solut. 19.   Tides, it had still the most peculiar advantage ;
priùs.   as was before observed.   (5.) The Equability
of Seasons, and the greater uniformity of the

Phænom.   Air's temperature, which in part remain'd till
36 priùs.   the Deluge, but might be more signal in the *Pa-*
radisiacal state, rendred that Earth as proper, as
the contrary sudden, uncertain, and violent extreams of heat and cold, drought and moisture,
sultry and frosty Weather now, wholly indispose
it, for such a production of Animals.   Which
Prerogatives of the *Primitive* Earth and Air will
certainly demonstrate, if not its intire fitness,
yet sure its less unfitness for such an original
Generation as was here to be accounted for,
and is all, as was before observ'd , that can
justly be requir'd and expected in the present
case.

Solut. 2.   Corollary. *When it has been before allow'd, that*
priùs.   *all Generation is but Nutrition ; and that all Seeds, as*
well of Animals, as of Plants, are the immediate
workmanship of God ; 'Tis evident that this Suppo-
sition

*sition of the Original Production of Animals out of the
Waters and Earth ; according to the plainest letter of
the* Mosaick *History, does by no means derogate
from the Divine Efficiency, and the wonderful Art
and Skill in the Structure of their Bodies ; nor in the
least favour that ungrounded and pernicious opinion of
the* Equivocal *or* Spontaneous *Generation of any of
them.*

Vid. *Bent-
ley,* Serm.
4.

> XXIV. The Conftitution of Man in his *Primitive* State
> was very different from that ever fince the Fall; not
> only as to the Temper and Perfections of his Soul ,
> but as to the Nature and Difpofition of his Body
> alfo.

XXIV. The Book of *Genefis* affords us fo fhort
a Hiftory of this *Primitive* Stage of the World,
and of the Conftitution of Man therein ; and
all other accounts are fo inconfiderable in this
refpect, that a particular account of all things relating to this Propofition is by no means to be
expected. 'Tis in general fufficient, that we
have, from Sacred and Prophane Authority,
evinc'd the ftate of External Nature to have
been mighty different from the prefent; and
that confequently the State of Man, even on
Philofophical Confiderations, ought to be fuppos'd equally different from the prefent alfo.
And 'tis fo highly unreafonable from meer obfervations made now, to pafs a Cenfure on what
was done then ; and from the Frail, Imperfect,
Sinful, and Miferable Condition of Humane
Nature in our Days, to judge of the fame in
its State of Innocence, Perfection and Felicity ;
or from the Circumftances it is in at prefent,
to determine thefe it muft at that time have
been in ; that nothing can be more fo. We
might almoft as well Argue that Angels Eat and
Drink,

Lem 70.
cum Co-
roll. &
Hypoth 3.
prius.

Drink, Sleep and Wake, Work and Reft, becaufe *We* do fo ; or that the *Infant* in the Womb
Sees and Hears, Talks and Difcourfes, Reads
and Writes, becaufe afterward *He* commonly
does the fame things, as that becaufe *We* have
need of Cloathing to cover our Shame, and
have Inflexible, Robuft, and in a certain time
Corruptible Temperaments of Body, therefore
fo had our *Primitive Parents* in the State of Innocency. But to fpeak fomewhat more diftinctly
to thofe two particulars included under this Propofition, (1.) That in the actions relating to
the propagation of the *Species*, there fhould be no
fenfe of Shame, and confequently no occafion
for covering fuch parts as were therein concern'd,
is by no means ftrange, in a ftate of Innocence;
where there was no inclination to any finful
kind or degree of Application, and where all
fuch inferior Appetites were in compleat fub-
jection to the Superior, the Reafon and Con-
fcience of Man.   'Tis rather an evident Token
of our Guilt, a demonftration of the diforder
and pollution of our Nature and Faculties *now*,
that what in permitted circumftances is innocent and natural in it felf, nay neceffary for
the propagation of the *Species*, and the prefervation of Mankind, fhould make us blufh: 'Tis a
plain note of the vilenefs of our *prefent* ftate, a
mark of the bafenefs of our condition *now*, that
what God and Nature have ordain'd for the
continuation of the World, fhould yet inevita-
bly feem to have fomething of Indecency and
Turpitude adhering to it : So far, that meer bafh-
fulnefs and modefty oblige us to conceal and
pafs over in filence all that belongs thereto. It
indeed might more reafonably be made a query,
why the Covering our Nakednefs has been fo
                                          general,

general, and is so necessary *now*, (as it has justly by all Ages and Nations been esteem'd) than why it was otherwise in this *Primitive* state of the World. (2.) That the use of one sort of Food (that of the *Tree of Life*) might be capable of fixing and setling the temper of a humane Body, of rendring it so lasting, that, while its Earthly condition was to continue, it might never be dissolv'd; and that the use of a contrary sort of Food, (That of the *Tree of Knowledge of Good and Evil*) might be capable of so far corrupting and disordering the same, that it would become subject to Sickness, Misery, and Dissolution in a shorter space, is, I think, even by what we at present see, by no means incredible. We cannot but observe how great a change a course of Diet, moderate, wholesome, and agreeable, will make in our present temperament for the better; and on the contrary, how far an intemperate, and immoderate indulgence of our Appetites, either as to the kinds or quantities of our Meats and Drinks, tho' but for a few Weeks or Months, will do the same for the worse; even to the spoiling and destroying of a very good habit of Body, to the depriving men of their healths; nay frequently of their Lives too by a violent Disease. If we therefore, to take the narrowest Supposition, imagine the eating of that pernicious and forbidden Fruit to have been confin'd to one *Day* or *Year* of this *Primitive* State (which yet there is no necessity of doing); 'twill be no harsh or incredible supposal; especially, if we consider what has been said of the present State of Things, and how much more the temper of our first Parents Bodies, and the particular Food on which they fed, might be peculiarly fitted for

the

the fame purpofes; that the intemperate Indulgence of a very peftilent courfe of Diet for fo many Months together might break and pervert the well temper'd Conftitutions of our firft Parents, might render their Bodies liable to fuch Diftempers as in length of time would diffolve and entirely overthrow them; or, in other words, would *render Mankind fickly, miferable, and mortal Creatures for ever after*. Which is, I think, enough to clear the Propofition before us, fo far as a bare *Phyfical Theory* is concern'd therein.

> XXV. The Female was then very different from what fhe is now; particularly fhe was in a ftate of greater Equality with the Male, and little more fubject to Sorrow in the Propagation of Pofterity than he.

XXV. That the original State and Circumftances of the Female, fhould be as they are here reprefented, is fo far from being ftrange, that the contrary ones of that Sex at prefent, were not the occafion thereof known, might much more juftly appear fo. For granting the Equality of Humane Souls in themfelves, 'tis not very eafy to give a good reafon, why that part which one half of Mankind was to bear in the Propagation of it, fhould fubject it to fuch a low Condition, great weaknefs of Nature, and thofe fevere Pains and Agonies which did not at all affect the other; as God and Nature have at prefent made unavoidable. And as to the change of her Name after the Fall, from *Adamah* and *Iffchah* to *Eve* (which latter feems to denote her Capacity *then attain'd* of becoming the Mother of all thofe Generations of Mankind which were afterward to live on the Face of the Earth) it may probably intimate (to omit any other Obfervations that might be made on it) fome change

Gen. v. 2. & ii. 23, 24. with iii. 20.

change in the Method or Circumstances concerning Humane Generation. And if we consider, that *Adam* and *his Wife* were no inconsiderable time in Paradise together, even after the Blessing of Increase and Multiply, before their Fall; and carefully consider the Texts quoted in the Margin, we shall perhaps believe 'tis no improbable conjecture.

Gen. ii. 25 & iii. 7, 10, 11. & iv. 1.

XXVI. The other Terrestrial Animals were in a state of greater Capacities and Operations; nearer approaching to reason and discourse; and partakers of higher degrees of Perfection and Happiness, than they have been ever since.

XXVI. Since the *Primitive* state of External Nature was so exceeding different from the present, as has been already prov'd; the other Terrestrial Animals, as well as Man, ought to be suppos'd of a somewhat proportionably different Temper, Abilities and Actions. Besides, The Divine Providence is concern'd to suit one Being to Another; and to accommodate still the subordinate, to the Superior rank of Creatures in the World: On which account 'tis not strange, that the Bruit Animals were in their Primitive Constitution very much distinguish'd from, and advanced above such as are now upon the Earth; the Diversity with Relation to Mankind, to whom in each Period they were to be subservient, being so very remarkable. For since Mankind upon the Fall degenerated into a Sensual and Bruitish way of Living, the Bruit Creatures themselves would very unwillingly have paid their due homage and submission, had not they in some degree degenerated from their Primitive Dignity at the same time. Which degeneracy suppos'd, a former greater degree of

B b

Affinity,

Abilities, Operations, and Happiness is at the same time suppos'd also. And to strengthen this conjecture, I may venture to Appeal to *anatomy*, whether the present Bodies of Bruits do not appear capable, as far as can be discover'd, of nobler operations than we ever now observe from them. The advantage of even *Mankind* in this respect seeming not very considerable over the *Bruits that perish*.

XXVII. The temper of the Air, where our first Parents liv'd, was warmer, and the Heat greater before the Fall than since.

XXVII. This has been already accounted for in the twenty third Propofition before.

XXVIII. Thofe Regions of the Earth where our first Parents were plac'd, were productive of better and more useful Vegetables with less Labour and Tillage than fince they have been.

XXVIII. That we may account for this Propofition, and that Curfe which was inflicted on the ground at the Fall, in good meafure included therein ; we muft obferve, that the growth of Plants and Vegetables depends on a degree of Heat proportionate to the peculiar temper and exigence of each Species ; and by confequence that, let the number of Seeds in any Soil be never fo many, or their kinds never fo diverfe, yet the Surface of the Earth muft remain bare and barren, until the peculiar Heat of the Seafon and Climate be adapted to them : Now feeing different kinds of Seeds require different degrees of Heat, 'tis only fuch certain kinds of the fame that will at once fhew themfelves, or fpring out of the Earth ; the reft, to which the Heat is not adjufted, lying all the

while

while as Dormant and Dead as if they did not really Exiſt in Nature. Thus we have ſeveral diſtinct Crops of Vegetables in the ſeveral Seaſons of the Year. Thoſe Seeds which the ſmall Heat of *February* and *March* is not able to raiſe, lye ſtill in the Earth till the greater force of the Sun in *April* and *May* excite them. In like manner ſeveral others, which are too craſs and unpliable for the moderate warmth of the Spring, are by the yet greater intenſeneſs of the Heat in *June*, *July*, and *Auguſt*, rais'd from their Seats, and oblig'd to ſhoot forth and diſplay themſelves. Nay, when in the Months of *September* and *October* the Sun's Power is diminiſh'd, and its Heat but about equivalent to that of *March* and *April*, it again ſuits the Plants which were *then* in Seaſon; ſo that they many of them ſpring up afreſh in *theſe* Months, and flouriſh over anew, as before they did in *thoſe*; as Dr. *Woodward* Eſſay, p. very well diſcourſes upon this occaſion. In like 167, &c. manner we may alſo conſider this matter with relation to the different Climates and Zones of the Earth, and their quite different Crops of Plants, according to thoſe different degrees of Heat made uſe of in their Vegetation. When therefore we obſerve in the ſame Country a various Crop and Order of Vegetables every Year, according to the various Power of Heat in each Seaſon; (a different Face of the Earth being gradually viſible from *February* till *July*, in proportion to the gradual increaſe of Heat all that ſpace;) we cannot tell, in caſe the Heat increas'd ſtill to a greater intenſeneſs afterward, but a new and unſeen Face of things might appear; and many unheard of kinds of Vegetables might put forth, and expoſe themſelves to our Obſervation, even in the preſent State and Age of the World.

But as to the *Primitive* World, wherein all
the Seeds of thofe Vegetables which God O-
riginally Created were frefh and vegetous,
and wherein there was a much greater Heat
than fince has been to invigorate and produce
them; 'tis very reafonable, and very agreeable
to Nature to fuppofe, that many forts of Trees,
Plants, Herbs, and Flowers, which the colder
temper of the fubfequent Earth were unable to
excite and produce, were then every Year rais'd,
and became the principal Recreation and Suftenance of our firft Parents in the ftate of Innocency. 'Tis very probable they might never
fee fuch a Poor, Jejune, and Degenerate State of
the Vegetable Kingdom as we fince have done,
till their unhappy Fall occafion'd the Introduction of that miferable condition of all things
which has ever fince continued among us. Thus
as one Country or Climate, becaufe of its
greater Coldnefs, is now the Seminary of feveral Vegetables which the warmer Regions are
either perfect Strangers to, or advance to a
greater degree of perfection; So upon the degeneracy of the *Primæval* State into the *prefent*,
and the mighty Abatement of the Ancient Heat
(taken together with the worfe Juices and other
effects of that Abatement contributary perhaps
to the fame thing) 'tis natural to allow that feveral fuch Vegetables (fuppofe *Thorns* and *Thiftles*)
which were before either perfect ftrangers to,
or had been advanc'd to a greater degree of
Perfection by the Juices and Warmth of Paradife, became the conftant and troublefome Heir-
looms there; to the no little regret of our firft
Parents; who till then had only feen and enjoy'd the better Set of the *Primigenial* Vegetables.
And if we confider withal, that a main intention

tion of the Toil, Tillage and Manure of the
Husbandman, seems to be design'd to Inspirit
and Envigorate the too Cold and Unactive Soil
with Warm and Active Particles, we shall not
be unwilling to grant, that those Labours of the
Husbandman, on this, as well as on several
other accounts which might be mention'd, must
have been in the *Primitive* state very facile and
easie, in comparison of those which are necessary
in the *present* state.

SCHOLIUM.

'Twill be here, I imagin, not improper to re-
mind the Reader once for all of the Nature
and Effects of that extraordinary *Change*, which
the Fall of Man, and the Consequent Curse of
God brought upon the Earth : That he may
with the greater ease, of his own accord, view
and compare the States of External Nature before and after the Fall one with another, and
with those things which the Propositions we are
now upon do assert concerning them. 'Tis evident then, from what has been before laid down
hereto relating, that the Primitive state of things
before the Fall was thus. The Earth, being
newly form'd, was scarcely as yet intirely consolidated, and so pretty uniformly pervious to
the warm Steams ascending from beneath. Its
Figure was perfectly Spherical, and its *Strata* or
Layers by consequence were even, continued,
and join'd; and so the Central Heat, being equally distant from all the parts of the Earth's Surface, did very equally diffuse it self, and equally
affect all the Climates of the Globe. The Soil

B b 3

or

or Uppermoſt *Stratum* of the Earth was newly
moiſten'd by the deſcent of the Waters, before
they compos'd the Seas on the Third Day of
the Creation, and by the plenty of Moiſture
which it ſtill receiv'd every Night. The Air
was perfectly Clear, Homogeneous, Tranſparent,
and Sufce, tree of the utmoſt Power of the Solar
Heat. The Seaſons were equable, or gently
and gradually diſtinguiſh'd from one another,
by the Riſing, Setting, Deſcending and Aſcending Sun, without any quick Interpoſitions of
Day and Night to diſturb them. The *Torrid
Zone* of the Earth, as I may call thoſe Regions
near the Solar Cedſe, was very much Expos'd
to the Sun, and very much warm'd withal by
its Vicinage to the Central Solid. The *Moon*
in twelve Revolutions equally meaſur'd out the
Year, and caus'd the moſt gentle, eaſie, and gradual Tides imaginable. This, with all its natural Conſequents, was the State of the *Primitive*
World. But as ſoon as Man had ſinn'd and
render'd that happy State too good for him, or
indeed rendred himſelf wholly incapable thereof: And as ſoon as God Almighty had pro-
nounced a Curſe on the Ground, and its Productions, preſently the Earth began a new and
ſtrange Motion, and revolv'd from Weſt to
Eaſt on its own *Axis*: A ſingle Νυχθήμερον, or
Revolution of Night and Day, either immediately or by degrees, (according as the preſent
Velocity of the *Diurnal Rotation* was ſuddenly or
gradually acquir'd) returned frequently, and
became no longer than 24 ſhort Hours; while
the *Annual* Motion, perform'd on a different
Axis, diſtinguiſh'd the Seaſons, and in Conjunction with the *Diurnal*, deſcrib'd the Equator,
and the Tropicks; and by the acceſs and receſs
of

of the Sun from the laft named Circles, caus'd it to vifit the feveral Regions enclos'd thereby. The Face of the Earth was really diftinguifh'd into *Zones*, by the Tropicks and Polar Circles, truly divided from one another; with refpect whereto the particular Regions of the Earth chang'd their Situation ; the Equator being that Circle with regard whereto they were now to be determin'd, as they had been before with regard to the Ecliptick ; and fo that Paradife which was before at the middle, became the Northern boundary of the *Torrid* Zone. The Figure of the Earth, which was before truly Spherical, degenerated into an *Oblate Sphæroid* ; the *Torrid Zone* rifing about 10 Miles upward, and the *Frigid* one fubfiding as much downwards. The *Compages* of the Upper Earth, and of its *Strata*, became thereby chap'd, broken and divided, and fo carried up the warm Steams from beneath, to particular Conceptacles and *Volcano's*, which before ferv'd in a more equal and uniform manner to heat and invigorate the intire Earth, and its productions. The Tides, laftly, became frequenter, and fo more fudden and violent than before. Which fhort Summary or Scheme of the States of Nature in our *Hypothefis* before and after the Fall, ought to be all along born in mind, and reflected on, in order to the paffing a right judgment on the accounts of thofe *Phænomena*, in the Solution whereof we are now engag'd : And which otherwife might feem very odd and unaccountable to the Reader. Which being thus difpatch'd, I proceed :

XXIX. The *Primitive* Earth was not equally Paradifiacal all over. The Garden of *Eden* or Paradife being a peculiarly fruitful and happy foil, and particularly furnifh'd with all the neceffaries and delights of an

innocent

innocent and blessed life, above the other Regions of the Earth.

XXIX. That all the *Primitive* Earth could not be equally Paradisiacal, and enjoy the same Priviledges and Conveniences beyond the Present, is easily prov'd. For seeing one of its principal causes of Fertility, and other Prerogatives, was the greater degree of Heat at the Paradisiacal Regions; The Climates near the Solar Course being alone capable of such greater Heat, must be alone capable of its Effects also ; and consequently, we are to confine our enquiries for the Garden of *Eden* to the Countries not very remote from the Ancient Ecliptick. Now that some peculiar Spot or Region thereabouts might, beyond all the rest, be Fertile, Pleasant and Paradisiacal, 'tis not difficult to suppose. At the present there is a mighty variety in Countries in the very same Hemisphere, Climate, and Parallel. The particular Prerogatives of one Region beyond another do not intirely depend on the Sun, or the Vicinage of the Central Heat : But partly on the Nature and Temper of the Soil ; the kinds of Vegetables and Fossils thereto belonging ; the number, qualities, and conflux of Rivers ; the firmness or looseness of the inferior *Strata*, hindring, or freelier permitting the ascent of the Subterraneous Steams, Juices, and *Effluvia*: From the coincidence of which, and of other such things, in a peculiar and advantagious manner, order'd and dispos'd on purpose by the Divine Providence at the *Mosaick* Creation, the extraordinary pleasantness and felicity of this Earthly Paradise, or Garden of Pleasure, is I suppose to be deduced: and which being consider'd, will, I believe, be sufficient to give satisfaction in the Proposition before us.

XXX. The

XXX. The place of Paradise was where the united Rivers *Tigris* and *Euphrates* divided themselves into four Streams, *Pison*, *Gihon*, *Tigris*, and *Euphrates*.

XXX. This Situation of Paradise has been already confider'd, and need not here be reaffum'd. Only we may obferve, That no Scruples would ever have been rais'd about this Matter, in cafe the foremention'd Rivers had ftill been vifible, their Courfe ftill agreeable to the *Mofaick* Defcription, and the Metals and Minerals mention'd of the adjoyning Countries had been as evidently there to be found in *ours*, as they appear to have been in thofe *Primitive* Times. Seeing therefore the following *Theory* will fo clearly affign the Caufe of fuch Diverfity, that every *Reader* will be oblig'd to grant it much harder to have accounted for the *Phænomena of Paradife*, confiftently with the other *Phænomena of Nature*, if all things were now as they were at firft, than almoft any other of the *Antediluvian* World : I may juftly hope that this fo difputed a Queftion of the Situation of the Garden of *Eden*, or Primitive Paradife, to thofe who embrace the other parts of the *Theory*, will remain no longer fo, but be as fix'd and undoubted, within at leaft the limits of that *Hypothefis* here referr'd to, as any other Country or Region with the fame exactnefs determin'd by Geography.

Hypoth. 4. priùs.

XXXI. The Earth in its *Primitive* State had only an *Annual Motion* about the *Sun* : But fince it has a *Diurnal Rotation* upon its own *Axis* alfo : Whereby a vaft difference arifes in the feveral States of the World.

XXXI. This has been at large explain'd and prov'd already.

Lem. 50, & Hypoth. 3. priùs.

XXXII. Upon

XXXII. Upon the firſt commencing of this *Diurnal Rotation* after the Fall, its *Axis* was oblique to the Plain of the Ecliprick as it ſtill is: or in other words, the preſent Viciſſitudes of Seaſons, *Spring*, *Summer*, *Autumn*, and *Winter*, ariſing from the *Sun's* acceſs to, and receſs from the *Tropicks*, have been ever ſince the Fall of Man.

XXXII. This has in ſome meaſure been inſiſted on already in the *Hypotheſis* laſt mention'd, and needs no other direct and poſitive proof than the preſent Obliquity of the Earth's *Axis*: It being evident, that without a miraculous Power, the ſame Situation or Inclination which it had originally, would and muſt invariably remain for all ſucceeding Ages.

Newt. p. 187.

C H A P. III.

A Solution of the Phænomena *relating to the* Antediluvian *State of the Earth.*

XXXIII. The Inhabitants of the Earth were before the Flood vaſtly more numerous than the preſent Earth either actually does, or perhaps is capable to maintain and ſupply.

XXXIII. THIS Propoſition will not appear ſtrange, if we conſider, (1.) The much greater fertility of the *Antediluvian* Earth, to be preſently accounted for; whereby it was capable of maintaining a much greater number of Inhabitants than the preſent, even on the ſame ſpace of Ground. (2.) The Earth was more equally habitable all over before, than ſince the Deluge. For

For before the acquisition of those heterogeneous mixtures, which the Deluge occasion'd, and which I take to be the Causes of all our violent and pernicious Heat and Cold in the *Torrid* and *Frigid Zones* of our Earth; 'tis probable the Earth was pretty equally habitable all over, by reason of the Vicinage of the Central Heat to the *Polar* Regions, and the more direct Exposition of the middle Regions to that of the *Sun.* I do not mean that the *Frigid Zones* were equally hot with the *Torrid*; but that the Heat in the one, and the Cold in the other, were more kindly; and the excesses of each much less considerable than at present, since the Introduction of the beforemention'd Mixtures, and particularly of such Sulphureous and Nitrous *Effluvia*, as are now, I believe, become Calorifick and Frigorifick Particles in our Air, the main occasions of the violence and pernicious Qualities of the Heat and Cold thereof, and the most affecting to our Senses of all other. So that 'tis probable, before the Acquisition of these *adventitious* Masses, the *Antediluvian* Air was every where sufficiently temperate to permit the comfortable Habitation of Mankind on all parts of the Globe; and the *Antediluvian* Earth was by consequence capable of many more Inhabitants than the present is, or can be; as every one will readily grant, who considers how few Inhabitants, in comparison, three of the five Zones of our present Earth do maintain. (3.) The dry Land or habitable Earth it self was, by reason of the absence of the intire Ocean, full as large and capacious again as the present: For the Ocean, I think, takes up now at the least one half of the intire Globe; but then afforded as large, spacious, and habitable Countries, as the other parts of the Earth.

(4.) The

(4.) The Mountains which are now generally bare and barren, were before the Deluge, so far as they were supply'd with Water, as fruitful as the Plains or Vallies; and by reason of a larger Surface, were capable of maintaining rather more Animals than the Plains, on which they stand, would otherwise have been: The present defect of a fruitful Soil being owing to the Deluge; and there being no good reason, that I know of, to be assign'd why, on a primary Formation, and in a calm and still State of the Air, the higher Parts of the Earth should not be cover'd with a fruitful Soil or Mold, as well as the level or lower adjoyning to them. All which Accounts taken together, will, I think, give reasonable Foundation for such vast numbers of Inhabitants, as according to the Computation of this Proposition, the *Antediluvian* World was replenish'd withal.

Corollary 1. *Since by very reasonable Computations of the numbers of the Inhabitants of the Earth at the Deluge, according to the* Hebrew *Chronology, they appear to have been sufficient abundantly to replenish the intire Globe, and as many as in reason the same could sustain;* The Septuagints *addition of near six hundred Years in this Period of the World to the* Hebrew *Accounts, is so far from clearing Difficulties thereto relating, that it rather increases the same, and enforces the allowance of more Inhabitants at the Deluge, than we can well tell where they could live and be maintain'd.*

Coroll. 2. *Since according to the* Hebrew *Chronology from the Deluge till the time of* Abraham's *going into* Canaan, *was the intire space of* 427 *Years, and the Lives of Men during that interval were in a mean three hundred Years long; 'tis easy on the Grounds proceeded upon in this* Phænomenon's *Calculations,*

lations, to prove, *That there is no need to recede from that Account, or introduce the additional Years of the* Septuagint *in this Period, to produce the greatest Numbers of Men which in that, or the immediately succeeding Ages, any Authentick Histories of those Ancient Times do require us to suppose.*

Coroll. 3. *The Deluge which destroy'd the whole Race of Mankind (those only in the* Ark *excepted) could not possibly be confin'd to one or more certain Regions of the Earth, but was, without question, truly Universal.*

Coroll. 4. *Seeing it appears, That Mankind has a gradual increase, and that in somewhat more than four thousand Years, our Continent of* Europe, Asia, *and* Africa, *has been so entirely Peopled from the Sons of* Noah; *and seeing withal* America *is much less in extent, and, I suppose, generally speaking, was never so. full of People: In case we suppose that Famines, Wars, Pestilences, and all such sad destroyers of Mankind have equally afflicted the several Continents of the Earth, Some light might be afforded to the Peopling of* America, *and about what Age since the Deluge, the* American's *past first from this Continent thither; which a more nice enquiry into the Particulars here to be consider'd might assist us in.*

XXXIV. *The Brut Animals, whether belonging to the Water or Land, were proportionably at least, more in number before the Flood than they are since.*

XXXIV. *That part of this Proposition which concerns the Dry-land Animals, is sufficiently accounted for, by what has been discours'd under the last Head, which equally belongs to them as to Mankind: And if we extend the other part concerning the Fishes, to the Seas then in Being, and their comparative Plenitude, there will need no additional Solution. It being not to be supposed* pos'd that the absolute numbers of Fish before the Deluge, should be greater than at present, as the case was of the Dry-land Animals; because the latter being universally destroy'd, (those in the Ark alone excepted) were to begin their Propagation anew; but the former not being so, did but increase their still numerous Individuals, and must thereby soon recover and surpass their former Multitude, as will easily be allow'd on a little consideration of this Matter.

Corollary. *Hence arises a strong Confirmation of what is on other grounds already asserted, That there were only smaller Lakes and Seas, but no great Ocean before the Deluge. For since it appears by this* Phænomenon, *that the Waters of the* Antediluvian *Earth were much more replenish'd, nay, crouded with Fish than now they are; and since there was no general Destruction of them, as there was of Dry-land Animals at the Deluge; had there been as great a Compass, or as vast an Ocean for their Reception then, as at present there is, the numbers now in every part of the Ocean or Seas, ought to be vastly greater than they then were, as being all the Off-spring of those which every where surviv'd the Deluge, and which have propagated themselves for more than four thousand Years since the same; which being disagreeable to the Observations referr'd to in this* Phænomenon, *is little less than a Demonstration of the falshood of that* Hypothesis *on which 'tis built, or a full Attestation to our Assertion, that there were only smaller Lakes and Seas, but no great Ocean before the Deluge.*

XXXV. The *Antediluvian* Earth was much more fruitful than the present; and the multitude of its vegetable Productions much greater.

XXXV. Before

XXXV. Before I come directly to solve this and the following Propositions, I must premise, that 'tis usually unreasonable to ask, why such *Phænomena* belong'd to the *Antediluvian* World : They being commonly but the natural and regular Properties of an Original Earth, newly form'd out of a *Chaos*; such as one should rationally expect in a World newly come out of the Hands of its Creator, and fitted for the Convenience and Fruition of noble Creatures; such as the generality of our fellow Planets, (especially our next Neighbour, the *Moon*) as far as we can observe, appear to have had at first; and hitherto retain'd. All that can in reason be desir'd, is this, To give a plain and intelligible Account of those opposite *Phænomena* of the Earth, which we *now* are sensible of, and by what means the Deluge could occasion the same. Which therefore shall be frequently the business of the succeeding Solutions. And as to the present case, the decrease of the Fertility of the Earth at the Deluge, these Causes are assignable, (1.) The decrease of the *Sun*'s Heat by the greater distance of the Earth from him since, than before the Deluge. It has been before prov'd, that till the Deluge, the Earth's Orbit was Circular, and the *Radius* of that Circle very little longer than the nearest distance at the *Perihelion* now: So, that when the Heat of the *Sun* is as the density of his Rays, or *reciprocally* as the Squares of the Earth's distance from him : If instead of the present *Ellipsis* we take, for Calculations sake, as we ought, a Circle in the middle between the nearest and farthest distance, we shall find that the *Sun*'s Heat on the Earth in general before the Deluge, was to its present Heat as almost a hundred to ninety six, or a twentieth part

part of his intire Heat greater before than since
the fame, which is by no means inconsiderable
in the Case before us. (2.) The Heat of the
Central Body was considerably damp'd and obstructed, both by the Waters of the Deluge
themselves, acquir'd from abroad, and now contain'd in the Pores and Caverns of the Earth
under us; and by that Sediment of them which
now composes that upper Cruft of Earth we dwell
upon, and which being fetled and consolidated
on the Superficies of the Ancient Earth would
prove a great hindrance to the ascending Steams,
not to be overcome but by degrees, and in
length of time afterwards. From both which
Causes very a notable Damp would be put to the
Influence of the Central Heat, on which as well
as on the *Sun's*, the Fertility of every Soil does
in part depend. (3.) The upper Earth, or fruitful Soil it self, the main Fund and Promptuary
of the vegetable Kingdom, is now very inconsiderable in quantity, if compar'd with that of the
Primitive or *Antediluvian* Earth. For when this
last mention'd was the intire product of the Ancient *Chaos* at the original Formation of the
Earth, and the first, what only was afforded from
a small part of such a *Chaos*, the Comet's *Atmosphere*, and by the Storms born off the Tops of
Mountains at the Deluge, while the old Soil
lies buried under the Sediment or Cruft on which
we live; 'tis no wonder that our fertile *Stratum*
is now thinner spread, and so the Productions
less copious in the present, than they were in the
Antediluvian State of Things. And this, tho' we
suppose the Soil from the Comet, or from the
Tops of the Mountains, to be as good in it self,
and to have remain'd as pure and unmix'd with
any heterogeneous Matter in this confusion of
                                                    things

things at the Deluge, as it would at the regular
Formation of the Earth at firſt; which yet is
by no means ſuppoſable; and the contrary to
which being allow d for, will ſtill farther afford
us a reaſon of the preſent Aſſertion. So that
ſince the preſent Soil is both much worſe in Quality, and much leſs in Quantity than the old
one; and ſince the Heat, whether of the *Sun* or
Central Solid is ſo much leſſen d at the Deluge,
which things include the main Cauſes of Fertility; 'tis no wonder that the *preſent* Earth is nothing near ſo fruitful and luxuriant in her Productions, as the *Antediluvian* was.

    XXXVI. The Temperature of the *Antediluvian* Air was
more equable as to its different Climates, and its different Seaſons; without ſuch exceſſive and ſudden Heat
and Cold; without the ſcorching of a *Torrid Zone*, and
of burning *Summers*; or the freezing of the *Frigid Zones*,
and of piercing *Winters*: and without ſuch ſudden and
violent changes in the Climates or Seaſons from one extreme to another, as the preſent Air; to our Sorrow,
is ſubject to.

    XXXVI. Seeing the primary State here men-
tion'd, is but a proper reſult from the firſt Formation of the Earth; all that need be accounted
for, is the Alteration at the Deluge.   1.) The
mighty difference of Climates, eſpecially of
the *Torrid* and *Frigid Zones*, is, I ſuppoſe, owing
not wholly to the *Sun's* Heat, or the Nature of
the Air it ſelf, but partly to thoſe Calorifick and
Frigorifick Mixtures, which are uncertainly contain d therein. Meer Heat and Cold are very
different things from that Pothery and Sultry,
that Froſty and Congealing Weather, which al-
ternately in *Summer* and *Winter*, at the *Line* and
the *Poles* we uſually now feel. Theſe Effects
ſeem plainly deriv'd from Nitrous or Sulphu-

reous,

reous, or other the like Steams exhaled into,
mixed with, and suſtained by that thick and
groſs *Atmoſphere* which now encompaſſes the
Earth. All which, I mean as well the groſs
Atmoſphere it ſelf, as thoſe its Heterogeneous Mixtures, are a very natural Off-ſpring of the Deluge, according to the preſent Account thereof.
For ſeeing we at that time paſs'd clear through
the *Chaotick Atmoſphere* of a Comet, and through
the Tail deriv'd from it, we muſt needs bear off,
and acquire vaſt quantities of ſuch heterogeneous
and indigeſted Maſſes, as our Air now contains
in it; whence thoſe Effects here mention'd
would naturally proceed. 'Tis probable the original Air was too pure, rare, and thin, to ſuſtain
any groſs and earthy Particles, tho' they had
been left in it at the firſt; and ſo its Heat both
for kind and degree, was no other than the proper Place and Influence of the *Sun* could require: And 'twas *thus* ſure more uniform through
the ſeveral Climates of the Earth than *now* it
is; when our Air in the *Torrid Zone*, being full of
Sulphureous and Sultry, and in the *Frigid* ones
of Nitrous and Freezing *Effluvia* or Exhalations,
the violence of an unkindly in Heat the one,
and of the like unkindly Cold in the other, are
ſo ſenſible, and ſo pernicious, as all experience
atteſts them now to be. (2.) The uncertainty
of our Seaſons, with the ſudden and unexpected
changes in the Temper of our Air, are on the
ſame accounts equally viſible with the former.
For the Temper of the Air ſince the Deluge,
eſpecially with regard to our Senſations, not re-
ſulting from the external Heat only, but from
the Kinds and Quantities of its heterogeneous
and adventitious Mixtures, will not now depend
on the Seaſon of the Year alone, but on the

veering

veering of the Wind, and its uncertain removal
of the Air and its Steams from one Region to
another. Thus if in *Summer* the *North* Wind
chance to blow any long time together, 'twill
bring along with the Air fo great quantities of
the Cold, Freezing, Nitrous Steams, as may
quite overcome the *Sun's* Heat, and caufe a very
cold Seafon of a fudden; if the *South* Wind do
the like in the *Winter*, the contrary Effect will
follow, and we fhall have a warm Seafon when
Froft and Snow were more naturally to be expected. Thus, accordingly, frequent experience fhews the *Sun* to be fo little mafter of the
Seafons of the Year, that fometimes *January* and
July for feveral Days are hardly diftinguifhable.
It fometimes happens, that we have this Day a
Froft, the next proves fo warm, that the former
Cold is forgotten, till perhaps the fucceeding
Night puts us more affectingly in mind of it
again. Nay, in a very few Hours fpace a fultry
and a freezing Air not feldom do fucceed each
other, to the great harm and mifery of Mankind,
and of all their fellow Animals in our prefent
State; from which therefore we have good reafon to believe our happier Progenitors before the
Deluge were intirely free. (3.) That our Sea
fons are fo extream in their feveral Kinds, is eafy
to be hence accounted for alfo. For were there
no fulphureous or calorifick Steams in the Air, all
pothery and fultry Weather, and fuch fort of
Heat as chiefly affects our Bodies, would be quite
avoided, and the great increafe thereof after the
Summer Solftice, which arifes, 'tis probable, in
part from the Airs retention of one days Heat,
till the next augments it again, would in good
meafure ceafe among us. And the like is to be
faid of the Cold in *Winter*, in all the refpects

before-

before-mention'd. The original of all which Effects being so easily deducible from the present Account of the Deluge, 'tis no question but the *Antediluvians* might, to their comfort, be wholly Strangers to them. Their Climates were not of so very different Temper; their Seasons leisurely and gradual, intirely following the Solar Course; And their *Summers* and *Winters* not so mighty different; at the most in the single Proportion of the *Sun's* Presence or Absence, Direct or Oblique Situation. In this equable State the *Polar* Inhabitants might with little danger cut the *Line*, and the *Ethiopians* visit the *Frigid Zones*. In this condition of the World, the peculiar Air of every Country went not far from home, to disturb that of others: A few Days never made any sensible Alteration in the temperature of the Air; and all that an intire *Spring* or *Autumn* could do, would still leave the same pretty equable, to be sure very tolerable. On all which, and several other consequential Accounts, we have but too much reason to envy the Ancient Happiness of our Forefathers, and to be sensible of that fatal and destructive *Catastrophe*, which the wickedness of Mankind brought upon themselves, and all their Posterity to this very Day, at the Deluge we are now speaking of.

XXXVII. The Constitution of the *Antediluvian* Air was Thin, Pure, Subtile and Homogeneous, without such gross Steams, Exhalations, Nitrosulphureous, or other Heterogeneous Mixtures, as occasion Coruscations, Meteors, Thunder, Lightning, with Contagious and Pestilential Infections in our present Air; and have so very pernicious and fatal (tho' almost insensible) Effects in the World since the Deluge.

XXXVII. The

XXXVII. The confideration of the foregoing *Solution* is fufficient to clear the prefent *Phænomenon* alfo; to which therefore the *Reader* is referr'd.

> XXXVIII. The *Antediluvian* Air had no large, grofs Maffes of Vapours or Clouds, hanging for long feafons in the fame. It had no great round drops of Rain, defcending in multitudes together, which we call Showers: But the Ground was watered by gentle Mifts or Vapours afcending in the Day, and defcending, in great meafure, again in the fucceeding Night.

XXXVIII. This is alfo eafily underftood from what has been already faid. So rare, thin, pure, and fubtile an Air as the *Antediluvian* was, would fcarce fuftain fuch grofs and heavy Maffes, as the Clouds are: It would not precipitate the fuperior Vapours upon the inferior in fuch quantities, and with fuch violence, as is neceffary to the Production of great round fenfible Drops of Rain: It had no grofs Streams to retain Heat after the caufe of it was gone, and the *Sun* fet; and fo the Vapours which were rais'd in the Day, would defcend again in the Night, with the greateft regularity and gentlenefs. In all which refpects the different Nature, Craffitude, and irregular Compofition of our prefent grofs *Atmofphere*, acquir'd at the Deluge from the Comet's, in which fuch Opake Maffes, as the Clouds, are frequently to be obferv'd, muft naturally admit and require thofe contrary Effects, which the prefent Propofition takes notice of, and were to be here accounted for.

> XXXIX. The *Antediluvian* Air was free from violent Winds, Storms, and Agitations, with all their Effects on the Earth and Seas, which we cannot but now be fufficiently fenfible of.

XXXIX. Thefe

XXXIX. Thefe *Phænomena* are fuch proper confequents of a Primitive Formation, and the original of thofe oppofite ones ever fince the Deluge fo naturally thence to be deriv'd, that there is no reafon to imagine them to have been before. A Comet's *Atmofphere* is a very *ftormy Fluid*, wherein Maffes of Opake Matter are continually hurled about, all manner of ways, in a very uncertain and violent manner. Seeing therefore we acquir'd at the Deluge fo great a quantity of the fame *Atmofphere*, of which ours is now in part compos'd, 'tis impoffible to expect any other State of things than fuch as this *Phænomenon* mentions, and was to be here accounted for.

Corollary. *Hence it appears, That the* Wind of the

Gen. iii. 8. Margin.

Day, *of which* Mofes *makes mention at the Fall of Man, was not a conftant* Phænomenon *of the Earth, but peculiar to that time. And this is very agreeable to the* Hypothefis *before laid down of the commencement of the* Diurnal Rotation *at the very Day here mention'd; according to which, a Wind muft neceffarily arife at that point of Time, tho' there were none before or after, till the Deluge. On that beginning of the* Diurnal Rotation. (1.) *The* Equatorial *Regions would be elevated, the* Polar *deprefs'd, the* Orb of Earth *would be chap'd and broken, and warm Steams burft out at the Fiffures thereby produc'd; all which could fcarce happen without fome Agitation of the Air. But,* (2.) *What is more certain and more confiderable, when the* Terraqueous Globe *began on a fudden to revolve from* Weft *to* Eaft, *the Air could not prefently accompany it, and fo muft caufe a Wind from* Eaft *to* Weft; *till receiving by degrees the Impreffion, it kept at laft equal pace therewith, and refting refpectively, caufed a conftant Calm afterwards. Which Wind being therefore (from the Earth's Velocity there) greateft towards the* Equator *and* Tropicks,

picks, *near the latter of which was the place of Paradise, would be considerable enough, especially in a state otherwise still and calm, to be taken notice of by the Sacred History; and be a kind of Relick or Footstep of the then Commencement of that* Diurnal Rotation, *which is so necessary to account for it, and has been from other Arguments already prov'd in its proper place.*

XL. The *Antediluvian* Air had no *Rain-bow*; as the present so frequently has.

XL. This is easily accountable from what has been already said. For, (1.) The descent of the Vapours necessary to it was usually, if not only in the Night when the absence of the *Sun* rendred its appearance impossible. (2.) The descending Vapours compos'd only a gentle Mist, not sensible round Drops of Rain, as we have before seen, on which yet the *Rain-bow* entirely depends; as those who understand the Nature and Generation thereof will easily confess. So that tho' the *Sun* were above the Horizon at the fall of the Vapours, the appearance of the *Rain-bow* was not to be expected. (3.) Were the Vapours that fell compos'd of sensible round Drops, and fell in the day-time, and this in sufficient Quantities, yet for want of a Wind which might drive them together on one side, and thereby clear the Air on the other, for the free admission of the Rays of Light, a *Rain-bow* were seldom or never to be suppos'd before the Deluge; all which circumstances being now quite otherwise, give us clear reasons for the present frequent appearance of that beautiful and remarkable *Phænomenon*, tho' till the Deluge, it was a perfect Stranger to the World.

C c 4   XLI. The

XLI. The *Antediluvians* might only eat Vegetables; but the Ufe of Flefh after the Flood was freely allow'd alfo.

XLI. That a State of Nature as to the Air, Earth, Fruits, and other circumftances fo very different from ours at prefent, fhould require a fuitable difference in the Food and Suftenance of Mankind, is very reafonable to believe. But be-fides, (1.) When the Lives of Animals were na-turally fo long, (as in correfpondence to Man-kind is fairly to be fuppos d) before the Deluge; 'tis not improbable that God Almighty would not permit them to be taken away on any other cccafion than that of Sacrifice or Oblation to himfelf. (2.) Perhaps in the tender and even Condition of the *Antediluvians*, the eating of Flefh would have fpoil'd their Tempers, and fhortened their Lives; fuch Food being, I fup-pofe, fitter for our grofs and fhort-liv d State fince the Flood, than that refin'd and lafting one before it. (3.) Perhaps the *Antediluvian* Ve-getables were more juicy, nourifhing, and whol-fome, not only than Flefh, but than themfelves have fince been; which the better and more fertile Soil out of which they grew then, gives fome reafon to conjecture. And whether they had not then fome Vegetables which we have not now, may deferve the confideration of fuch as fearch after their remains in the Bowels of the Earth: The fame care of the Vegetable, as of the Animal Kingdom not appearing in the Sa-cred Hiftory relating to the Deluge. However, (4.) If we obferve that even at this day, the warm Seafons and Countries are lefs difpos'd to the eating of Flefh than the cold ones; and re-member that the *Antediluvian* Air was in fome
degree

degree warmer than the prefent, we fhall not be
wholly to feek for a particular reafon of this *Phæ-*
nomenon.

> XLII. The Lives of the *Antediluvians* were more univer-
> fally equal, and vaftly longer than ours now are : Men
> before the Flood frequently approaching near to a thou-
> fand, which almoft none now do to a hundred years
> of Age.

XLII. Tho' feveral other things might here
deferve to be confider'd, yet I fhall only infift
upon the difference between the *Antediluvian*
Air, and that fince the Flood, to give an account of this Propofition. The confideration of
the Pure, Unmixed, Equable, and Gentle Conftitution of the former ; compar'd with the
Grofs, Thick, Hetorogeneous, Mutable, and Violent Condition of the latter, of it felf affording
a fufficient Solution of this difficulty. That Air
which is drawn in every breath; whofe included Particles, 'tis probable, infinuate themfelves
continually into our Blood, and the other Fluids
of our Bodies; and on which all experience
fhews humane Life and Health exceedingly to
depend ; being at the Deluge chang'd from a
Rare and Thin, to a Thick and Grofs Confift-
ence ; from an equability or gradual and gentle
warmth and coolnefs of Temperature, to ex-
tremity of Heat and Cold; and that with the
moft fudden and irregular fteps from one to
another ; from True and Pure Air, or an Homogeneous Elaftical Fluid, to a mix'd and confufed *Compofitum* or *Atmofphere,* wherein all forts
of *Effluvia,* Sulphureous, Nitrous, Mineral and
Metallick, *&c.* are contain'd. Which circumftances, if there were no other, will, I imagine,
give a fatisfactory account of the mighty difference

rence as to the point of Longævity between the *Antediluvians* and thofe which ever fince have dwelt on the Face of the Earth. We may obtain fome fmall and partial refemblance of it in a perfon who had liv'd many years upon the top of a high Mountain, above the Clouds and Steams of our Earth, and whofe temperament of Body was peculiarly difpos'd for fo Pure, Thin, and Undifturb'd an *Æther* as there he enjoy'd; and afterward were confin'd to the moft Foggy, Marfhy, and Stinking part of the Hundreds in *Effex*, or of the Boggs in *Ireland*. What Effect in Point of Life and Health fuch a Change muft have on the Perfon before-mention'd, 'tis not difficult to imagine: And as eafie, on a like comparifon of the *Antediluvian Æther*, and the prefent *Atmofphere* to account for the Propofition before us; and fhew as well why men dye at all uncertain Periods of Years, and have while they live a Precarious State of Health, with frequent ficknefses; as why none reach any whit near the long Ages of thofe that before the Deluge continued in Health and Security for near a thoufand Years.

XLIII. Tho' the *Antediluvian* Earth was not deftitute of leffer Seas and Lakes, every where difpers'd on the Surface thereof; yet had it no *Ocean*, or large receptacle of Waters, feparating one Continent from another, and covering fo large a portion of it, as the prefent Earth has.

XLIII. From the Original Formation of the Earth above defcrib'd, and its unequal fubfidence into the *Abyfs* beneath, while in the mean time vaft quantities of Vapours were fuftain'd above, and afterwards let fall upon the Earth, its Surface would be unequal; its loweft Valleys fill'd with
Water;

Water; and a truly *Terraqueous Globe* would
arife. But thefe two plain Reafons may be affigned why any great Ocean were not to be expected at the fame time. (1.) So Vaft and
Deep a Valley as the Ocean implies, is not in
reafon to be deriv'd from fuch a regular formation of the Earth from a *Chaos*, as we have
above defcrib'd. No good reafon being affignable, why in fuch a confufed mixture as we call
a *Chaos*, the parts fhould be fo ftrangely difpos'd,
that on one fide, all the Upper Orb for fome
fcores of Degrees, and fome thoufands of Miles
together, fhould be Denfer and Heavier than
the reft, and by its finking deepeft into the
Abyfs, produce the vaft Channel of the Ocean;
while on another fide the fame Orb, for as many Degrees and Miles, fhould be univerfally
Rare and Light enough to be very much extant,
and compofe a mighty Continent, as the cafe
is in our prefent Earth. Tho' the *atmofphere* of
a Comet, be fo truly Heterogeneous, and its
Opake or Earthy Maffes fo unequally fcatter'd
abroad on the different fides thereof, as even,
fetting afide the inequality of the Denfity and
Specifick Gravity of the feveral Columns, might
compofe an Orb of different Thicknefs or Craffitude, and fo caufe an unequal Orb on the
Face of the *Abyfs*, like that we before fuppos'd
it originally to have been; Yet fo mighty an
inequality, as the prefent Divifion of the Earth
into an Ocean and Continents muft fuppofe, is
by no means to be allow'd in the Primitive *Chaos*;
nor would I fuppofe by any be afferted, if the
Generation of thofe grand Divifions of our
Globe were otherwife accountable: which on
our Principles being fo eafily done, as will foon
appear, no reafon can plead here for their *Primi-*
tive

tive Introduction. And sure thofe Agitation and Motions of Parts vifible in fome fort now in Comets *Atmospheres,* and to be however granted in the digeftion of its parts at firft, muft fure mix and jumble the parts together to a degree fufficient to prevent fo ftrange an inequality, as the Original Exiftence of the Ocean and Continents muft needs imply. However (2.) The quantity of Water preferv'd above ground was little or nothing more, as we have fhew'd, than the Heat of the Sun and Central Solid was able to elevate, and the Air at once to fuftain, during half a years fpace; the day time of the fecond Period of the Creation : Which how infufficient it muft have been to the filling of the great Ocean, is eafily underftood. Which things confider'd, the Abfence of the Ocean, as well as the Exiftence of Seas, is very eafily accountable in the *Antediluvian* World.

CHAP. IV.

A Solution of the Phænomena *relating to the* Univerfal Deluge, *and its Effects upon the Earth.*

XLIV. In the Seventeenth Century from the Creation, there happen'd a moft extraordinary and prodigious Deluge of Waters upon the Earth.

XLIV. WHatever difficulties may hitherto have rendred this moft Noted *Cataftrophe* of the Old World, that it was *deftroy'd by Waters,* very hard, if not wholly inexplicable

explicable without an Omnipotent Power, and
Miraculous Interpofition; fince the Theory of Vid. Fig.
Comets, with their *Atmofpheres* and *Tails* is dif- 1, & 4,
cover'd, they muft vanifh of their own accord. & 7.
For if we confider that a Comet is no other
than a *Chaos* ; including the very fame Bodies,
and Parts, of which our own Earth is compos'd ;
that the outward Regions of its *Atmofphere* are
plain Vapours, or fuch a fort of Mift as we frequently fee with us; and the *Tail* a column of
the fame Vapours, rarified and expanded to a
greater degree, as the Vapours which in the
cleareft Days or Nights our Air contains at prefent, are ; and that withal fuch a Comet is capable of paffing fo clofe by the Body of the
Earth as to invelve it in its *Atmofphere* and *Tail*
a confiderable time, and leave prodigious quantities of the fame Condenfed and Expanded Vapours upon its Surface ; we fhall eafily fee that a
Deluge of Waters is by no means an impoffible
thing ; and in particular that fuch an individual
Deluge as to the Time, Quantity, and Circumftances which *Mofes* defcribes, is no more fo,
but fully accountable. that it *might* be, nay almoft demonftrable that it really *was.* All which
the *Solutions* following will I think give an eafie
and mechanical account of.

XLV This prodigious Deluge of Waters was mainly occafion'd by a moft extraordinary and violent Rain, for
the fpace of forty Days, and as many Nights, without
intermiffion.

XLV. When the Earth paffed clear through
the *Atmofphere* and *Tail* of the Comet, in which
it would remain for about 10 or 12 hours (as
from the Velocity of the Earth, and the Craffitude of the faid *Tail* on Calculation does appear)

it muſt acquire, from the violence of the Column of Vapours deſcend towards the Sun, im-
peded by the Earth's Interpoſition and Reception
of the ſame ; and from the Attractive Power of
the Earth it ſelf withal, enforcing more to deſcend ; it muſt, I ſay, acquire upon its Surface
immenſe quantities of the Vapours before mention'd.   A great part of which being in a very
Rare and Expanded condition, after their Primary Fall, would be immediately mounted upward into the Air, and afterward deſcend in
violent and outragious Rains upon the Face of
the Earth.   All thoſe Vapours which were rarer
and lighter than that Air which is immediately
contiguous to the Earth, muſt certainly aſcend
to ſuch a height therein, where its Denſity and
Specifick Gravity were correſpondent (as far as
that Croud of their fellow Vapours, with which
the Air was oppreſs'd would give leave ;) And ſo
afterwards, as they cool'd, thicken'd, and collected together, like our preſent Vapours muſt deſcend in moſt prodigious Showers of Rain for a
long time afterwards, and very naturally occaſion
that forty Days and forty Nights Rain mention'd
in the Propoſition before us.

> XLVI. This vaſt quantity of Waters was not deriv'd
> from the Earth or Seas, as Rains conſtantly now are ;
> but from ſome other Superior and Cœleſtial Original.

XLVI. This is already evident from what has
been juſt now ſaid : The ſource of all theſe
Rains being one of thoſe Superior or Cœleſtial
Bodies which we call *Comets* ; or more peculiarly the *Atmoſphere* and *Tail* thereof.

> XLVII. This vaſt Fall of Waters, or forty Days Rain,
> began on the fifth day of the Week, or *Thurſday* the
>   twenty

twenty seventh day of *November*, being the seventeenth day of the second Month from the *Autumnal Equinox*; (corresponding this Year 1696. to the twenty-eighth day of *October*.)

XLVII. This has been already explain'd in effect, in the *Hypothesis* hereto relating; where it was prov'd that a Comet on that very day here nam'd pass'd by the Earth; and by consequence began those Rains which for the succeeding forty days space continued without any Interruption. — Hypoth. 10. priùs,

XLVIII. The other main cause of the Deluge, was the breaking up the Fountains of the great *Abyss*, or causing such Chaps and Fissures in the upper Earth, as might permit the Waters contain'd in the Bowels of it when violently press'd and squeez'd upwards, to ascend, and so add to the quantity of those which the Rains produced.

XLVIII. This has in part been explain'd in the *Lemmata* hereto relating; and will be more fully understood from the Figure there also refer'd to. For Let a d b c represent the Earth, moving along the Ecliptick G H, from G towards H. 'Tis evident that the Figure of the Earth before the approach of the Comet, as far as 'tis here concern'd, was Sphærical. But now, let us suppose the Comet b i D h (as it was descending towards its *Perihelion*, along its *Trajectory* E F, from E towards F) to approach very near, and arrive at the nearest Position, represented in the Figure. 'Tis evident that this presence of the Comet would cause a double Tide, as well in the Seas above, as in the *Abyss* below; the former of which being less considerable in it self, and not to our present purpose, need not be taken any farther notice of: But the — Lem. 82, 83. priùs, Fig 7.

the latter would be vaftly great, (fuppofe feven
or eight Miles high above its former Pofition)
would produce mighty Effects on the Orb above
it, and fo deferves a nicer confideration in this
place. As foon therefore as the Comet came
pretty near, (as fuppofe within the *Moon's* diftance)
this double Tide would begin to rife, and increafe
all the time of its approach, till the Comet was
neareft of all, as in the Figure. And then thefe
Tides, or double Protuberances of the *Abyfs*,
would be at their utmoft height. So that the
Surface of the *Abyfs*, and of its incumbent Orb
of Earth, would put on that *Elliptick*, or rather
truly and exactly *Oval* Figure, under which 'tis
here reprefented. Now, 'tis certain, that this
Sphæroid Surface of the *Abyfs* is larger than its former *Sphærical* one ; 'tis alfo certain, that the Orb
of Earth which refted on this *Abyfs*, muft be
oblig'd to follow its Figure, and accommodate it
felf to this large *Oval* ; which being impoffible
for it to do while it remain'd Solid , continued,
and conjoyn'd, it muft of neceffity enlarge it
felf, and by the violent force of the encreafing
Surface of the *Abyfs* be ftretch'd, crack'd, broken,
and have innumerable *Fiffures* made quite through
it, from the upper to the under Surface thereof,
nearly *perpendicular* to the fame Surfaces. So
that this Orb of Earth which originally, in its
primary formation, was Sphærical ; its inward
Compages or *Strata* even, conjoin'd, and continual ; which had afterward, at the commencing
of the *Diurnal Rotation*, been chang'd into an
Oblate Sphæroid, and at the fame time been thereby broken, chap'd, and disjointed ; by that time
its wounds had been well healed, and it was in
fome meafure fetled, and fix'd in fuch a condition, receiv'd this new Difruption at the Deluge,

Vid.
Schol.
poft Hy-
poth. 10.
priùs.

Lem. 82.
priùs.

luge. Its old Fiffures were open'd, and the
Fountains of the *Abyfs* (moft Naturally and
Emphatically fo ftil'd, according to Dr. *Wood-*
ward's Account of the Origin of Fountains)
broken up; and fufficient Gaps made for a
Communication between the *Abyfs* below, and
the Surface of the Earth above the fame, if any
occafion fhould be given for the Afcent of the
former, or Defcent of any thing from the latter.
And here 'tis to be noted, that thefe Chaps and
Fiffures, tho' they were never fo many or fo
open, could not of themfelves raife any Subterraneous Waters, nor contribute one jot to
the drowning of the Earth. The Upper Orb
was long ago fetled, and funk as far into the
Abyfs as the Law of *Hydroftaticks* requir'd ; and
whether 'twere intire or broken, would caufe no
new preffure; and no more than maintain its
prior fituation on the Face of the Deep. Thefe
Fiffures had been at leaft as open and extended
in their Original Generation, when the *Diurnal*
Rotation began, as at this time, and yet was
there no danger of a Deluge. So that tho' this
breaking up of the Fountains of the Deep was
a prerequifite condition, and abfolutely neceffary to the Afcent of the Subterraneous Waters,
yet was it not the proper and direct caufe or
efficient thereof : *That* is to be deriv'd from
another original, and is as follows. As foon as
the prefence of the Comet had produc'd thofe
vaft Tides, or double elevation and depreffion
of the *Abyfs*, and thereby disjointed the Earth,
and caus'd the before-mention'd patent holes or
breaches quite through the Body of it, the Fall
of Waters began, and quickly cover'd the Earth,
and crouded the Air with vaft quantities thereof: Which Waters being adventitious or addi-

Vid Effay
Pa. 124,
&c. and
Pa. 152.

D d   tional

rional ones, and of a prodigious weight withal, muſt preſs downward with a mighty force, and endeavour to ſink the Orb of Earth deeper into the *Abyſs*, according as the intire weight of each column of Earth, and its incumbent Waters together, agreeably to the Law of *Hydroſtaticks*, did now require. And had the Earth, as it was in its firſt ſubſiding into the *Abyſs*, been looſe, ſeparate, and unfix'd, ſo as to admit the *Abyſs* between its parts, and ſuffer a gentle ſubſidence of the Columns of Earth in the requiſite proportion, we could ſcarce have expected any Elevation of the Subterraneous Waters. But the *Strata* of the Earth were long ago ſetled, faſtened, and conſolidated together, and ſo could not admit of ſuch a farther immerſion into the fluid. On which account the new and vaſt preſſure of the Orb of Earth upon the *Abyſs* would certainly force it upward, or any way, whereſoever there were a paſſage for it : To which therefore the Breaches, Holes, and *Fiſſures* ſo newly generated, or rather open'd afreſh by the violence of the Tides in the *Abyſs* beneath, would be very ready and natural Outlets; through which it would Aſcend with a mighty force, and carry up before it whatever was in its way, whether Fluid or Solid, whether 'twere Earth or Water. And ſeeing, as we before ſaw, the Lower Regions of the Earth were full of Water, pervading and repleniſhing the Pores and Interſtices thereof; which Waters on the opening of the *Fiſſures* would from all ſides ouze into, and fill up the Inferiour parts of the ſame, and reſt upon the Face of the *Abyſs*; the *Denſe Fluid* of the *Abyſs*, in its violent Aſcent through the *Fiſſures*, would carry before it, and throw out at the tops of the ſaid *Fiſſures* great quantities

Lem. 75, 76. prius. (margin)

Solut. 6 prius. (margin)

ties of the fame; and if its force were any where fufficient, would caft it felf alfo out at the fame paffages; and by both or either ways would mightily add to the quantity of the Waters already on the Face of the Earth, and become a frefh and a prodigious augmentation of that Deluge, which began already to overwhelm and deftroy the Inhabitants thereof. For the better apprehenfion of this matter, let us imagine the following Experiment were made. Suppofe a *Cylinder* of Stone or Marble fitted fo exactly to a hollow *Cylindrical* Veffel, that it may juft Afcend or Defcend freely within it : Let the *Cylinder* of Stone or Marble have fmall holes bored quite through it, parallel to the *Axis* thereof : Let the Veffel be fill'd half full of Water; and the *Cylinder*, as gently as you pleafe, be put into the Veffel, till it touch the Water : Let then each of the holes through the *Cylinder* be fill'd in part with Oyl, or any other Fluid lighter than the Water, to Swim upon the Surface thereof : Things being thus provided, you have the very cafe of the Deluge before you; and what effects you here, in a leffer degree, will obferve, are but the reprefentations of thofe great and remarkable ones of which we are now fpeaking. For as the weight of the *Cylinder* preffing upon the Surface of the Water would fqueeze the Oyl upon its Surface through the holes, and caft it out thereat with fome violence, and caft it felf too out at the fame paffages if the holes were not too high, in comparifon to the quantity of the intire preffure upon the Surface of the Water; juft fo the Weight of the Columns of Earth, augmented by the additional Waters of the Comet, would fqueeze and prefs upon the Surface of the *Abyfs*; which being a

Fluid

Newt p.
270, &c.

Fluid Mass, and incapable of sustaining a pressure in one part, without equally communicating it to all the rest, any way whatsoever; must burst out wherever such pressure was wanting, and throw it self up the *Fissures*; carrying up before it, and throwing out upon the Earth those Waters which (like Oyl on the Water in the Experiment) lay upon its Surface, and for the altitude perhaps of some Miles cover'd the same; and thereby mightily increasing the greatness of the Deluge, and having a main stroke in that destruction which it brought upon the Earth. All which, I think, gives us a clear, easie, and mechanical account of this (hitherto inexplicable) *Secondary* Cause of the Deluge, the breaking up the Fountains of the Great Deep, and thereat the elevating the Subterraneous Waters, and bringing them out upon the Face of the Earth.

Corollary 1. *These Chaps or* Fissures *at the Deluge would commonly be the same with those at the commencing of the* Diurnal Rotation. *It being easier to break the* Compages *of the Earth where it had once been broken already, and was never united well again, than in other places where it was intire and continued: And those parts which sustain'd the rather greater force at the former Convulsion, would at least as well sustain this, of which we are now speaking, and preserve their former continuity still, as they did before the Flood.*

Coroll. 2. *Hence if these* Fissures *are the occasion and source of* Fountains, *as* Dr. Woodward *very probably asserts, The* Antediluvian *and* Postdiluvian *Springs must be generally the very same; as arising from the same Originals; so far as the mutations at the Earth's Surface to be afterward explain'd would permit and allow in the case.*

Coroll. 3.

Coroll. 3. *Since we have before shew'd, that the Mountainous Columns of the Earth are the loosest, the least compacted, and least solid of all others, The Earth would be the most subject to the Fissures and Breaches in those parts, and the generality of Springs and Rivers would now proceed from thence: Unless the peculiar Stony, or other firm Compages of the same prevented the Effects here mention'd, as sometimes perhaps might happen in the present case.*

Coroll. 4. *Hence 'tis evident, that there was no great Ocean, but only smaller Lakes and Seas, before the Flood. For otherwise the Tide or Flux of the Ocean would have been so great and violent, as to have superseded almost all the designs of the ensuing Deluge, and have withal extremely endanger'd, if not certainly destroy'd, the Ark, and all those Creatures which were entring into it: Which the small Tides in the small Lakes and Seas would not at all affect, or disturb.*

XLIX. All these Fountains of the great Deep were broken up on the very first day of the Deluge, or the very first day when the Rains began.

XLIX. This is very easily understood from the space of time that the Comet was near the Earth. For the duration of this Disruption, or breaking of the Orb of Earth, occasion'd by the nearness of the Comet, must be commensurate thereto; which, tho' we should take in all the space it was nearer than the Moon, could not possibly, as is easie to Calculate, amount to Nine Hours; which is indeed much more than need be allow'd; and is yet sufficiently within that Days space which this *Phænomenon*, if occasion were, could allow us to suppose; and so fully satisfies the same.

D d 3 L. Yet

L. Yet the very same day, *Noah*, his Family, and all the Animals entred into the *Ark*.

L. Tho' 'tis otherwise not a little strange that the entry into the Ark should be defer'd till this Day; yet 'tis clear and easie on the present *Hypothesis*. For as to the Fountains of the great Deep, which were broken up this Day, thereby the Earth and its Contents were only gradually and insensibly elevated; but no other disturbance given to *Noah* in his Entry into the Ark at the same time. The *Fissures* indeed were now made, but till the weight of the Waters from the Comet could operate, no Water would from thence arise to disturb him. And tho they had, yet unless there were some of the great Fissures or Spouts just where he was, no interruption could this day be given him therefrom. As to the Rains themselves, tho' they all fell first upon the Earth nearly within the compass of this Day, and so must cause a most prodigious destruction and confusion upon the Earth where they so fell; yet the peculiar situation of Mount *Caucasus*, on or near which the Ark was, did secure it; this day, tho' so outragious and destructive a one to the Inhabitants of the other parts of the Globe, was yet here fair and calm, as at other times: Which is thus demonstrated. 'Tis evident that Mount *Caucasus* is situate pretty near the Center of our *Northern Continent;* or indeed some 20 or 25 degrees *North of* from the same; that is, as will hereafter appear, pretty near the Point b, or somewhat below it towards c: Which Mountain *Caucasus* was directly expos'd therefore to the Comet at its nearest distance, represented in the Figure. When the Comet therefore was

moving

Solut 65. infrà Fig. 7.

moving from E to F, fo foon as the Earth came
within its *Atmofphere* and *Tail*, a *Cylindrical* Column of Vapours would be intercepted, and
bore off by the Earth in its paffage, whofe Bafis
were fomewhat larger than a great Circle on the
Earth, and whofe Direction or *Axis*, from the
compound Motion of the Comet and of the
Earth, were at about 45 degrees of Inclination
with the Ecliptick or parallel to c d, the leffer *Axis*
of the Earth. That is, the firft fall of the Vapours would affect one *Hemifphere* of the Earth at
a time, that, namely, which were properly expos'd
to their defcent ; and the other would be not at
all affected therewith, till the Earth's *Diurnal
Rotation* by degrees expos'd the other parts in
like manner, and brought every one at laft within the verge of that *Hemifphere* on which was
the firft and moft violent defcent of the Vapours.
Now this *Hemifphere* would be reprefented in the
Figure by a d b ; and the oppofite one, which
intirely efcap'd at the fame time by a c b. So
that feeing the Ark, or Mount *Caucafus*, was
below the Point b ; and by the Diurnal Rotation quickly got farther within the fair *Hemifphere* ; it would remain in the fame during all
the time of this firft violent Fall of the Waters,
and have a calm and quiet day for the entry into the Ark ; while the other Regions of the
Globe were fubject to fo violent a Storm, and
fuch fury of defcending Vapours as no Age paft
or future had been, or were to be expofed to.
This place could only be capable of fome falling
Vapours three or four hours after Sun-fet, in
cafe the Earth were not at that time got clear
of the Tail of the Comet, in which it had been
all the preceding day : And confequently, *Noah*
had as fair and calm a time of entring into the

Ark,

Ark, with all his Family, and the other Animals,
as could be desir'd; when no other parts of the
Globe, but those agreeing in such a peculiar
situation with him, could have permitted the
same. Which is, I think, not a meer *Satisfactory,*
but a very *Surprizing* account of the present
Proposition.

Corollary 1. *Hence the time of the breaking open
of the Fountains of the Deep, and of the beginning of
the Rains, very nearly coincident therewith, is determin'd; and that, agreeably to the* Mosaick History,
much nearer than to a Day; *(with which exactness
we have hitherto contented our selves in the case)
And indeed almost to an* Hour. *For seeing all the
Fountains of the great Deep were broken up on this
day; seeing the forty days Rain began on the same
day; seeing* Noah, *with all his Family, and all the
other Creatures entred on this self-same day into the
Ark; all which certainly require very near an intire
day; and yet seem very incompatible; there is no
other way but to assert, that tho' the breaking up of the
Fountains of the Great Deep, and the Fall of the Waters, were coincident, and upon the same day with
the Entry into the Ark, as the Text most expresly
asserts; yet the place where the Ark was, escap'd the
effects of the same till the Evening; and while the rest
of the Earth was abiding the fury of the same, enjoy'd so calm, fair, and undisturb'd a day, as permitted their regular and orderly going into the Ark
before the Waters overtook them. So that the Deluge
must, according to the Sacred History, have commenc'd
in the Morning, and yet not reach'd the particular
place where* Noah *was till the Evening, or the coming on of the ensuing Night: Which how exactly the
present Hypothesis is correspondent to, I shall leave
the Reader to judge from what has been said under
this last Proposition; according to which 'tis plain,*
that

that the Comet paſs'd by the Earth, broke up the Fountains of the Deep, and began the forty days Rains
after Sun-riſing, about Eight or Nine a Clock in the
Morning; from which time till Eight or Nine a Clock
at Night, and long after Sun-ſet, tho' the Waters
fell with the greateſt violence on the Earth, yet they
affeƈted a ſingle Hemiſphere at a time only, into
which the Diurnal Rotation did not all that while
convert the Regions near the Ark; and this moſt nicely
and wonderfully correſponds to the greateſt accuracy of
the preſent caſe, and of the Moſaick Hiſtory. So
that now we may, agreeably both to the Sacred Hiſtory, and the Calculations from the preſent Hypotheſis, aſſert, that the Deluge began at the Meridian
of Mount Caucaſus on Thurſday the twenty ſeventh
day of November, in the year of the Julian Period,
2365, between Eight and Nine a Clock in the Morning. Which exaƈtneſs of Solution, wherein not only
the Day, but almoſt Hour aſſign'd from the Moſaick
Hiſtory is correſpondent to the preſent Hypotheſis,
how remarkable an Atteſtation it is to the ſame, and
how full a confirmation of the moſt accurate Verity of
the Moſaick Hiſtory, I need not remark: Such re-
fleƈtions when Juſt, being very Natural with every
careful Reader.

Corollary 2. Here is an inſtance of the peculiar
Providence of God in the Preſervation of the Ark, by
ordering the Situation ſo as to eſcape the Violence of
the thick Vapours in their firſt precipitate fall, which
otherwiſe muſt probably have daſh'd it to pieces. For
conſidering their Velocity of Motion, which indeed was
incredible, no leſs than eight hundred Miles in the
ſpace of a Minute; 'tis not eaſy to ſuppoſe, that any
Building could ſuſtain and preſerve it ſelf under the
violence thereof; which we ſee the Ark, by the peculiar place of its Situation, twenty or twenty five degrees
North-Eaſt from the Center of our Northern Continent,

nent, was wonderfully secured from, while the other Regions of the Earth were expos'ed thereto, and in great measure, 'tis probable, destroy'd thereby.

Coroll. 3. Hence 'tis evident, That the place of the Ark before assign'd, at Mount Caucasus, was its true one, and not any Mountain in or near Armenia. For had it been there seated, it had been expos'd to the violence of the falling Vapours, and instead of a quiet entry into the Ark on this first day of the Deluge, the Ark it self, with all the Creatures that were to be preserv'd in it, would have utterly perish'd in the very beginning thereof.

Coroll. 4. Hence the reason may easily be given, why the History of the Deluge takes no notice of this passing by of the Comet; viz. because none of those who surviv'd the Deluge, could see or perceive the same. For at the time of the approach of the Comet at first, both the latter end of the Night-season, when all were asleep; and the Mists, which according to the Nature of the Antediluvian Air, were probably then upon the Earth, and obscur'd the Face of the Heavens, hindred any prospect of this dreadful Body. And soon after the Morning came, they were actually involv'd in the Atmosphere of the Comet, and so in its Tail presently after, which would only appear a strange and unusual Mist or Cloud at a distance, wholly depriving them of the distinct view of the Comet it self, and leaving them utterly ignorant of the true occasion of the following Catastrophe, unless any intimation should have been given them thereof by a Divine Revelation.

LI. Tho' the first and most violent Rains continued without intermission but forty Days, yet after some time the Rains began again, and ceased not till the seventeenth Day of the seventh Month, or a hundred and fifty Days after the Deluge began.

LI. It

LI. It has been already obferv'd, That the Comet would involve the Earth in its *Tail* a fecond time, about fifty four or fifty five Days after its firft paffing by, as well as it did before; as 'tis alfo reprefented in the Figure. Which being fuppos'd, the Earth muft receive a new ftock of Vapours as before; and the Rains which had intermitted for fourteen or fifteen Days, muft begin again. The differences between the former and latter Rains would be, (1.) Thefe latter Vapours proceeding from the *Tail*, whereas the former did principally from the much denfer *Atmofphere* of the Comet, would be lefs copious, and lefs violent than the other, and caufe a gentler Rain. (2.) Thefe Vapours being newly rarified by the prodigious Heat at the *Perihelion*, and rais'd thereby to a mighty height in the *Tail*, from their greater rarity and lightnefs, higher afcent in our Air confequent thereupon, and longer time thence neceffary to their cooling and defcent in Rains upon the Earth, would be much longer in falling, and produce a continual Rain of many more days than the former did. Both which are exactly agreeable to the *Mofaick* Hiftory; whence it appears, that the firft Rains had the principal ftroke in the Deluge; and that if this fecondary Rain commenc'd at the time here affign'd, it muft have continued 95 or 96 days; which is confiderably more than double the number of thofe 40, within which the former Rains were confin'd.

Ccroll. 1.
Schol.
poft Hypoth. 10.
priùs.
Fig. 1.

LII. This fecond, and lefs remarkable Rain was deriv'd from fuch a caufe as the former was.

LII. This is fufficiently evident already, fince the fame Comet afforded the matter for both Rains equally. LIII.

LIII. Tho' the Fountains of the great Deep were broken up, and the forty days Rain began at the same time; yet is there a very observable mention of a threefold growth, or distinct augmentation of the Waters, as if it were on three several accounts, and at three several times.

LIII. This is particularly correspondent to the present *Hypothesis*; wherein (1.) The principal Rain of 40 days; 2.) The Eruption and Ascent of the Subterraneous Waters, occasion'd by their weight and pressure; (3. The lesser Rain of 95 or 96 days, were both different in themselves, and in their time of commencing, and caus'd a distinct augmentation of the Waters, agreeably to the greatest nicety of this Proposition.

LIV. The Waters of the Deluge increas'd by degrees till their utmost height; and then decreas'd by degrees till they were clearly gone off the Face of the Earth.

LIV. This is evident as to the increase of the Deluge, by what has been already said; and will equally be so of its decrease, when we come to it hereafter.

LV. The Waters of the Deluge were Still, Calm, free from Commotions, Storms, Winds, and Tempests, of all sorts, during the whole time in which the *Ark* was afloat upon them.

Phænom.
39. præs.

LV. It has already appear'd, that there were no Storms, Tempests, or other violent Commotions in the *Antediluvian* Air till the Deluge; and that during the space here referr'd to, none would arise, 'tis but reasonable to allow. For as to the first and principal Rain, it was so constant, so downright, and so uninterrupted, that no little commotion in the Air could have place; or if it

had

had, could difturb it; which is commonly the cafe of long and fetled Rains with us at this day. As to the Subterraneous Waters, afcending with fome violence, they were confin'd to feveral particular places, and not univerfal ; and though they might caufe fome commotions at the bottom of the Waters, yet might the furface of the fame, and the Air, be fufficiently calm and undifturb'd. But as to the third Caufe of the Deluge, It muft be granted, agreeably to what has been before obferv'd, That the defcending Vapours would not be merely fuch, but mix'd with many heterogenerous Particles of all forts, Sulphur, Brimftone, Niter, Coal, Mineral *Effluvia*, Metallick Steams, and the like, which the prodigious heat at the *Perihelion* had diffolv'd and elevated into the Tail of the Comet : From the confufed mixture, irregular fermentations, and difagreeing motions of all which, 'tis probable the preternatural and violent commotions in the *Atmofphere* then, and fince, are mainly to be deduc'd. So that affoon as the latter 94 or 95 days Rains were almoft over ; affoon as thefe rarified Corpufcles were defcended into the lower and narrower Regions of the Air ; and being crouded clofer, were, by the greater heat there predominant, put into fuch irregular fermentations as they were already difpofed for ; 'Tis natural to fuppofe that Winds, and Storms of all forts, and thofe in a very extraordinary manner, would arife, and caufe the moft fenfible and extream perturbations of the Waters (now covering to a vaft depth the face of the whole Earth) that could eafily be conceiv'd : Of which the following Propofition will give farther occafion to difcourfe.

Coroll. 3.
Lem. 65.
prius.

LVI Yet during the Deluge there were both Winds and Storms of all forts in a very violent manner.

J. VI. Seeing

LVI. Seeing, as we juft now faw, that at the end of the latter Rains the greateft Storms poffible were to be expected ; and feeing yet the *Ark*, which had been afloat fo long, and was fo ftill (the Waters being now at the very higheft) was incapable of abiding a ftormy Sea, as we prov'd under the former *Phænomenon*; there at firft view appears the greateft danger imaginable, of its perifhing in the future immoderate and extraordinary Commotions. And this danger is increafed by this Reflection ; That as probably it had been afloat during the moft part of the 150 days, while the Waters were gradually and gently augmenting ; fo one would imagine ought it to be, for at leaft as many days, during the at leaft as gentle and gradual decreafe of the fame afterwards : *i. e.* The *Ark* ought to have been as long afloat in the ftormy, as it had been in the calm part of the Deluge. But this difficulty, which is to appearance fo entirely infoluble, will foon vanifh, if we confider that the *Ark* refted upon *Caucafus*, the *then* higheft Mountain in the world. For feeing the Waters prevailed above the fame Mountain 15 Cubits only, a great part of which depth of Water would be drawn by the *Ark* it felf ; upon the very firft ceafing of the Rains from above, and of the Waters from the *Abyfs* beneath, which permitted the leaft fubfiding and diminution of the Deluge, the *Ark* muft immediately reft upon the ground , and thereby fecure it felf from the impending Storms. And that accordingly it did fo, at the time affign'd, on the conclufion of the 150 days, or the very fame individual day when the Wind began , is particularly and exprefly obferv'd and affirm'd by *Mofes* : Which being a very remarkable coincidence, exactly agreeable to the prefent *Hypothefis*,

Vid. Solu. 59. infrà.

Gen. vii. 20.

as

as well as to the Sacred Hiftory, and of very
confiderable Importance, I fhall fet down the
words at large, as follows:

The waters prevailed upon the Earth an hundred Gen. vii.
and fifty days (viz. from the feventeenth of the fe- ult. & viii.
cond, to the feventeenth of the feventh Month). 1, 2, 3, 4.
And God remembred Noah, *and every living thing,
and all the Cattel that was with him in the Ark:
And God made a wind to pafs over the earth, and
the waters affwaged. The fountains alfo of the deep,
and the windows of heaven were ftopped, and the rain
from heaven was reftrained. And the waters returned from off the earth continually: and after the
end of the hundred and fifty days, the waters were
abated. And the ark refted in the feventh month, on
the feventeenth day of the month, upon the mountains
of* Ararat.

Corollary. *Hence 'tis obvious to remark the wonderful Providence of God for the Prefervation of the
Ark, and the fole Remains of the old World therein
contain'd, in ordering all circumftances, fo, that it was
afloat juft all the calm Seafon of the Deluge, but as
foon as ever any tempeftuous Weather arofe, was fafe
landed on the top of* Caucafus.

> LVII. This Deluge of Waters was univerfal in its extent
> and effect; reaching to all the parts of the Earth, and
> deftroying all the Land-Animals on the intire Surface
> thereof; thofe only excepted which were with *Noah* in
> the Ark.

LVII. This might juftly have been made a
Corollary of the next Propofition, (for if the Waters in any one Region, much more a compleat
Hemifphere, exceeded the tops of the higheft
Mountains, it would certainly diffufe it felf and
overflow the other alfo): But being capable in
the prefent *Hypothefis* of a feparate Proof, deferves

ferves a diftinct Confideration. Now of the feveral Caufes of the Deluge, thofe Vapours which
were deriv'd from the Comet's Tail, both at the
firft and fecond paffage of the Earth through the
entire Column thereof, by reafon of the Earth's
Mora, or abiding therein about 12 hours, or a fe-
mi-revolution, and the fall of the Vapours on an
entire Hemifphere at the fame time, would affect the whole Earth , and though not exactly
equally, yet pretty univerfally make a Deluge
in all the Regions of the Globe. The fubterraneous Waters, being the proper effect of the
weight of the other, would alfo be as univerfal
as they, and that every where, generally fpeaking , in the fame proportion. Tis true, the
Waters which were derived from the Atmofphere
of the Comet (the principal Source of the 40
days Rain) were not wholly fo univerfal as the
former *at firft,* by reafon of the fhorter *Mora* or
abiding of the Earth therein (though even
much above half of the Earth's entire furface
would hence be immediately affected): But if
we confider the Velocity of the Earth's *Diurnal
Rotation ,* and that the Mafs of newly acquir'd
Vapours was not at firft partaker of the fame,
but by degrees to receive the impreffion thereof,
we fhall with eafe apprehend, that a few of the
firft Rotations would wind or wrap thefe, as
well as the other Vapours, quite round the Earth,
and thereby caufe a very equal diftribution of
them all in the *Atmofphere,* and at laft render
the Rains very evenly Univerfal. To which
uniform diftribution the Nature of the Air it
felf, as at prefent it I fuppofe does, might contribute : Such an *Elaftical Fluid* as the Air fcarce
fuffering a lafting Denfity or Croud of Vapours
in one Region, without communicating fome

part

part to the others adjoining ; that fo a kind of *Equilibrium* in the weight, craffitude, and denfity of its feveral Columns may be preferv'd through the whole. So that at laft, the Deluge muft have been Univerfal, becaufe every one of the Caufes thereof appear to have been truly fo.

> LVIII. The Waters at their utmoft height were fifteen Cubits above the higheft Mountains, or three Miles at the leaft perpendicular above the common Surface of the Plains and Seas.

LVIII. In order to make fome eftimate of the quantity of Water which this *Hypothefis* affords us, let us fuppofe that the one half came from the Comet, or the Rains ; and the other half from the Subterraneous Water : (Tho' 'tis nor impoffible that much the greater part might arife from the latter :) Let us alfo fuppofe, that the tenth part of the reft arofe from the *Tail* of the Comet, at both the times of its enclofing the Earth ; and the other nine from its *Atmof-phere* ; (tho' 'tis poffible that a much lefs propor-tion ought to be deriv'd from the former) 'Tis evident from the Velocity of Comets, at the di-ftance from the Sun here to be confider'd, and the ufual Craffitude or Diameter cf the Tails thereof, that the Earth would be near half a day, or 12 hours each time within the limits thereof ; and by confequence that it would intercept and receive upon it felf a *Cylindrical* Column of Va-pour, whofe *Bafis* were equal to that of a great Circle on the Earth, and whofe *Altitude* were about 75000 Miles. If we therefore did but know the proper denfity of the Vapour compo-fing the Tail of the Comet, or what proportion it bears to that of Water, 'twere eafie to reduce this matter to Calculation, and very nearly to

determine

determine the quantity enquired after. That the Tail of a Comet, especially at any considerable distance from the Comet it self, is exceeding rare, is evident, by the vastness of its extent, and the distinct appearance of the fixt Stars quite through the immense Crassitude of its entire Column. Let us, for computation's sake, suppose that the Density of Water to that of this Expanded Column of Vapour is as 340000 to one; or, which is all one, (since Water is to our Air in Density as 850 to one) that the Density of our Air, is to the Density of this Column of Vapour, as 4000 to one, (which degree of rareness if it be not enough at a great distance from the Comet, as at the second passage; yet I suppose may be more than sufficient at the very Region adjoining thereto, as at the first passage; and so upon the whole no unreasonable *Hypothesis*:) So that if we divide the Altitude of this *Cylindrical* Column of (750000 Miles, or) 3750000000 Feet by 340000 (37500 by 34) we shall have a Column of Water equal thereto. By which Calculation the quantity of Water acquir'd at each time of the passage through the Tail, would equal a *Cylinder*, whose *Basis* were a great Circle on the Earth, as above; and whose Altitude were 1103 Feet: Which quantity being twice acquir'd, must be doubled; and then will amount to a *Cylinder* whose *Basis* were the same as above, and whose Altitude were double the others, or 2206 Feet. Now *Archimedes* has demonstrated, that the intire Superficies of a Sphere or Globe is four times as large as the *Area* of one of its great Circles. And by consequence the Column of Vapour before-mention'd, when converted into Rain Water, and spread upon the Face of the Earth, would cover the Globe intirely

ly round (had there been no Dryland or Mountains extant above the Surface of the Plains and
Seas) a quarter of the height laſt aſſign'd, or
541½ Feet every way: Which being ſuppos'd,
and what was at the firſt *Poſtulated* of the *Atmoſphere's quota,* the whole Water afforded by the
Comet will cover the Earth intirely to the perpendicular height of the 541c½ Feet. To which
add, by the Original *Poſtulatum,* the equal quantity aſcending from the Bowels of the Earth, the
Total amounts to 10821 Feet; or above two Miles
perpendicular Altitude: Which, when allowance
is made for thoſe large ſpaces taken up by the
extant Dry Land and Mountains, will approach
very near that three Miles perpendicular height
requir'd by the preſent *Phænomenon.*

Corollary. *If the ſeveral particulars requiſite to
the nice adjuſtment of theſe Computations were more
exactly enquir'd into, ſome light on the preſent Hypotheſis, might be afforded to the Denſity of the Atmoſ-*
pheres *and* Tails *of Comets, which is hitherto undeter-
min'd; the conſideration of which matter muſt be refer'd to* Aſtronomers.

> LIX. Whatever be the height of the Mountain *Caucaſus,*
> whereon the *Ark* reſted, *now*; it was *at that time* the
> higheſt in the whole World.

LIX. If we conſult the Figure here refer'd to, Fig. 7.
we ſhall eaſily apprehend the Reaſon of this,
otherwiſe, ſtrange *Phænomenon.* For ſeeing this
Mountain was the higheſt in *Aſia,* or the middle
Regions of our Continent; and ſeeing withal
that intire Continent, and chiefly the middle
Regions thereof, were elevated by the greateſt
protuberance of the *Abyſs* d b c above any other
correſpondent parts of the whole Globe; the ab-
ſolute or intire height of this Mountain ariſes

not

not only from its proper Altitude above the
neighbouring Plains, but also from the Elevation
of the whole Continent, or peculiarly of its
middle Regions above the Ancient Surface of
the Seas; so that by this advantage of situation,
it was at the time here concern'd higher not only than its Neighbours, which its own Elevation
was sufficient for, but than any other on the Face
of the whole Earth : Some of which otherwise
it could, I believe, by no means have pretended
to match, much less to out-do in Altitude. Now
altho the presence of the Comet which produc'd
these Tides in the *Abyss*, and elevated the intire
Continents above their ancient level, did not remain after the Disruption of the Fountains of the
Deep on the first day of the Deluge; yet the
Effect thereof, the Elevation of the Continents
above their ancient Level, would not so soon, nay
would scarce ever intirely cease. We know by
common observation, that if a Solid or Setled
Mass of Bodies be torn or pull'd in pieces, 'tis not
easie to put every thing into its place, and reduce the whole to the same fixed Position, and
within the same fixed limits, it had before. If a
solid compacted mound of Earth were once
shatter'd and divided, were levell'd and remov'd,
tho' afterward every individual Dust of the former Earth were laid together again upon the very same Plot and Compass, yet would it not be
immediately confin'd within its ancient dimen-
sions ; its Height would be at first considerably
greater than before ; and tho' that in length of
time would be by degrees diminish'd, by the gradual setling and crouding together of the parts,
and so some approaches would be made thereby
towards its ancient density, and lesser elevation ;
yet neither would be intirely attain'd ; in any
mo-

moderate fpace of time at leaft. And this is the very cafe before us. That Oval Figure which the Orb of Earth was ftretch'd to at the Deluge, would remain for a confiderable time, and be many years in fetling fo clofe together, that it might afterward remain fixt and firm for the following generations ; before which time 'tis evident, that the Regions near the Center of our Northern or Larger Continent, were 'the higheft, and thofe at 90 degrees diftance every where the loweft ; and by confequence at the time of the *Arks* refting, the Mountain *Caucafus,* near the Center of the *Northern* Continent, was elevated above the reft, and particularly above the *Pike of Teneriff,* which feems to be at prefent the higheft of all others. And thus that *terrible Phænomenon* is folv'd, which the Reverend Mr. *Warren* was fo puzzled with, that even on the allowance of fo much Miracle as the *creation* of the Waters of the Deluge, and *Annihilation* of the fame afterward, yet cou'd he not account for the Letter of *Mofes* without a forc'd and un-grounded Suppofition, to the fame purpofe with the Propofition before us. As you will find him, and not without reafon, very *emphatically* expref-fing himfelf on this occafion.

Geolog. p. 329, 330. and De-fence, p. 171, 172.

Corollary 1. *Here is a vifible inftance of the Divine Providence for the prefervation of the Remains of the Old World, by ordering the building of the Ark near that which would be the higheft Mountain in the World ; that fo upon the very firft ceafing of the Rains, and the beginning of the Winds and Storms, it might immediately be fafe on the top thereof.*

Coroll. 2. *The fame careful and wife providence is confpicuous in the fo accurately adjufting all the cir-cumftances of the Deluge, that tho' it fhould be high enough to deftroy the whole ftock of the Dry-land*

E e 3

Animals ;

Animals; *and yet but just so much above the Mountain* Caucasus, *as permitted the* Ark *to rest at the very first decrease of the Waters, and the commencing perturbations of the Air, and the Waves necessarily ensuing; which otherwise must still have destroy'd it, notwithstanding the advantage of its situation before observ'd.*

Coroll. 3. *Supposing the Truth of our first* Postulatum, *of the Verity of the Letter of the* Mosaick *History; as certain as is the greater height of the* Pike of Teneriff, *or of any other Mountain in the World, above that of* Caucasus Now; (*of which I suppose no body makes any question*) *so certain is it* (*bating unknown causes, and a miraculous Power, as is always in such cases to be suppos'd*) *that a Comet was the cause of the* Mosaick *Deluge. For 'tis certain, by the plainest deduction from the express words of Scripture, that the Mountain on which the* Ark *rested was at that time the highest in the World. 'Tis therefore certain, that the Continent or Basis on which Mount* Caucasus *stands, was elevated higher at the Deluge than 'tis at present: and 'tis also certain, that no Body or Mass of Bodies in the whole World can elevate or depress a Continent of the Earth, but such as are capable of approaching the same; or in other words, but Comets; and consequently a Comet* did *approach near the Earth at the time assigned, and* was *the cause of the Deluge. Which Chain or Connexion I take to be so strong, that I believe it will not be possible to evade its force; and so what on other arguments has been already establish'd, is fully confirm'd by this.*

Coroll. 4. *'Tis equally demonstrable, that the Upper Orb or Habitable Earth is founded on a Subterraneous* Fluid, *denser and heavier than it self: This circumstance being absolutely necessary to account for the* Phænomenon *we are now upon. For if the internal Regions of the Globe were firm and solid* (*as is commonly suppos'd*;

suppos'd ; tho' wholly gratis, *and without ground :*) *Tho' the Comet had pass'd by, yet there could have been no elevation of any Continent, and the Proposition before us must still have remain'd Insoluble.*

LX. As the Fountains of the great Deep were broken up at the very same time that the first Rains began, so were they stopp'd the very same time that the last Rains ended ; on the seventeenth day of the seventh Month.

LX. Tho' I cannot say that the Account of the Deluge, now given, can determine to a Day the time of the Subterraneous Waters ceasing to spout forth (this *stoppage of the Fountains of the Deep* in *Moses*) yet 'tis evident, that the time defin'd by the History is very agreeable to that which from the consideration of the thing it self one should naturally pitch upon. For since the Ascent of the Subterraneous Waters depended on the Waters produc'd by the Rains, as on the beginning of those Rains it began to ascend, on the continuance thereof continued to do the like, so at the ceasing, probably enough might it cease also; as this Proposition assures us it really did.

LXI. The abatement and decrease of the Waters of the Deluge was first by a Wind which dried up some. And secondly, by their descent through those Fissures, Chaps, and Breaches, at which part of them had before ascended into the Bowels of the Earth, which received the rest. To which latter also the Wind, by hurrying the Waters up and down, and so promoting their lighting into the before-mention'd Fissures, was very much subservient.

LXI. In order to the giving a satisfactory account of this Proposition, and of the draining the Waters of the Deluge off the Surface of the Earth (which to some has seem'd almost as difficult to solve as their first Introduction); It must first be

E e 4   granted,

granted that the Air could receive and fuftain but
very inconfiderable quantities, in comparifon of
the intire Mafs which lay upon the Earth; yet
fome it might, and would naturally do; which
accordingly both the *Wind* here mentioned, and
the *Sun* alfo took away, and turn'd into Vapour
immediately after the ceafing of the latter Rains.
But as to all the reft, there is no imaginable place
for their Reception, or whither their natural
Gravity oblig'd them to retreat to, excepting the
Bowels of the Earth; which muft therefore be diftinctly confider'd in this place. Now we may remember, from what has been formerly faid, that
the quantity of Solids, or earthy Parts in the upper
Orbs primary Formation, was very much greater
than that of Fluids, or watery Parts; and confequently, that the inward Regions of the Earth being generally dry and porous, were capable of
receiving mighty quantities of Waters without
any fwelling, without any alteration of the external Figure, or vifible Bulk. And indeed, if we
allow, as we ought, any confiderable Craffitude
to this upper Orb, its interior Regions might eafily
contain a much greater quantity of Waters than
what was upon the Earth at the Deluge; efpecially when fo great a part of them was before
there, and would only fill up their old places
again. So that all the difficulty is now reduc'd
to this, By what Pipes, Canals, or Paffages, thefe
Waters could be convey'd into the Bowels of the
Earth? Which in truth can admit of no difpute,
nothing fure being to be conceiv'd more natural *Inlets* to thefe Waters, than thofe very *perpendicular Fiffures* which were the *Outlets* to fo great
a part of them before. As foon therefore as the
Waters ceas'd to afcend upwards through thofe
Breaches, they muft to be fure defcend downwards

Lem. 78.
cum Co-
roll. & So-
lut. 6.
præfis.

wards by the fame; and this defcent is more natural than the *prior* afcent could be efteem'd to
be; which was a force upon them, compelling
them againft their Natures to arife upwards,
when this retreat into the fame Interftices is no
other than their cwn proper Gravity requir'd,
and inclin'd them to. The cafe here is in part
like that of a *Sive*, firft by force prefs'd down into a Veffel of Water, till it were fill'd therewith,
and then fuffer'd to emerge again; where through
the very fame Holes at which the Waters afcended into, they afterward defcended out of the
Sive again, and retreated into their own Element as before. All that in particular deferves
here to be farther noted, is, the Intereft of the
Wind, or of the Agitations of the Waters (*goings
and returnings* in the *Hebrew* Phrafe) made mention of in this Propofition. And thefe Commotions are in truth very ufeful, and very neceffary
affiftants to the draining of the Waters from off
the Earth. For when the moft part of the Fiffures were in the Mountains, 'twould have been
a difficult thing to clear the Vallies and lower
Grounds, had there been a perfect Calm, and
every Collection of Waters remain'd quietly in its
own place. But when the Waters were fo violently agitated and hurried from one place to
another, they would thereby very frequently light
into the *Fiffures*, and Breaches, and fo defcend
as well as the reft into the heart of the Earth;
very agreeable to the Affertion of this Propofition.

Corollary 1. *Seeing the moft of the Fiffures were in
the Mountains, the decreafe and going off of the Waters would be greateft at firft, while the generality of
the Mountains were under water, and lefs and gentler
afterwards.*

Coroll.

Coroll. 2. *Several low Countries now bordering on the Seas, might for many Years after the Deluge be under Water, which by the defcent of more of the Waters into the Bowels of the Earth, might become Dryland afterward; and by their fmoothnefs and equability fhew their once having lain under, and been made fo plain by the Waters. Inftances of which are now very obfervable in the World: In particular, thofe parts of* Cambridgefhire *and* Lincolnfhire *which border on the* German Ocean, *appear very evidently to have originally been in the fame cafe, as any careful Obferver will eafily pronounce.*

> LXII. The dry Land, or habitable Part of the Globe, is fince the Deluge divided into two vaft Continents, almoft oppofite to one another, and feparated by a great Ocean interpos'd between them.

Fig. 7.

LXII. The Figure in which the Comet left the Earth, and which it would in fome meafure retain ever after, was, as may be feen in the Figure, an Oval or *Oblong Sphæroid*, whofe longer *Axis* a b would determine the higheft extant Parts of the Earth; and whofe fhorter *Axis* c d, by a Revolution about the Center perpendicularly to the longer *Axis*, would alike determine the loweft or moft deprefs'd Parts thereof. When therefore as many Waters were run down into the Earth as the Apertures could receive; all that remain'd (excepting the ancient leffer Seas fomewhat augmented every where) muft be found in the loweft Vallies, or near the fhorter *Axis*'s Revolution, all round the Globe, compofing a mighty Ocean; while the two elevated Regions, near the two ends of the longer *Axis*, were extant above the Waters, and compos'd thofe two oppofite Continents of the Earth, made mention of in this Propofition.

Corollary

Corollary 1. *'Tis probable that* America *is intirely separated from our Continent by the interpos'd Ocean, without any Neck of Land, by which it has been by many imagin'd to communicate with* Tartary.

Coroll. 2. America *was peopled from this Continent some Ages after the Deluge by Navigation. For seeing there is no Communication between us and them by Land; seeing also the Ancient Inhabitants of it perish'd intirely at the Deluge (as the Testimony of the Sacred Scriptures, the consideration of their lesser Numbers, and the impossibility of any Preservation of Men by an Ark any where but at the Mountain* Caucasus, *the highest Hill near the Center of the highest Continent in the World, appearing from what has been said, do conspire to demonstrate). 'Tis evident they must have been repeopled by Sea, from this Continent.*

Coroll. 3. *Navigation, tho' it was not before the Flood, or till then very inconsiderable; yet is not so wholly new and late in the World, as some imagine. Which Observation is very agreeable with the Sacred Records, which intimate no less than three Years Voyages in the days of* Solomon; *and with* Herodotus, *who mentions a Voyage through the* Red-Sea *round* Africa, *and so through the* Straights of Gibraltar *into the* Mediterranean *in the days of* Neco.

1 Kings x. 22. 2 Chron. ix. 21. L. 4. c. 42, 43.

LXIII. One of these *Continents* is considerably larger than the other.

LXIII. Since in all Tides, and so in those Protuberances which occasion'd the present Continents, that which respects the Body producing the same, is larger than its opposite one; 'tis evident, so it ought to be here, and the Continent situate about the Point b, considerably larger than the opposit. one about a, agreeably to this Proposition.

Coroll.

Corollary. *In this posture of the Abyss, and its incumbent Orb, the Earth is correspondent to the Egg, its ancient Symbol and Representative, not only in its inward and intire Constitution, but in some measure in its external Figure also; the resemblance between them becoming by this means in a manner Universal.*

LXIV. The larger Continent lies most part on the *North-side* of the Equator; and the smaller, most part on the *South*.

LXIV. The Position of the Continents depended mainly on the time of the year when the Comet passed by. For since the Comet descended in the Plain of the *Ecliptick* from the Regions almost opposite to the *Sun*, and came to its nearest distance about 130 degrees onward from the Point in the *Ecliptick* opposite to the *Sun*, before which, and yet scarce till after the Comet were past 90 degrees, or the Periphery of the *Ecliptick*, would the Tides be great enough to burst the Orb of Earth, and fix the Centers of the Continents; By considering the place of the *Earth* in the *Ecliptick*, and counting about 100 degrees onward, one may determine the Latitude of the Point on the Earth directly expos'd to the Comet's Body, and by consequence of its opposite Point also; about which Points the two Continents lay. Now the Earth being about the middle of *Taurus* to an eye at the *Sun* (which I always in such cases suppose), at the time of the passing by of the Comet, about the middle of the second Month from the *Autumnal Equinox*, the latter part of *Leo* (being 100 degrees onward from the Point opposite to the *Sun*) will nearly determine the Latitude of the larger Continent d b c, as by consequence will the latter part of *Aquarius* that of the smaller d a c: On which accounts 'tis evident, that the larger must be mostly on the *North*, and the smaller mostly on the *South-side* of the Equator.   LXV. The

LXV. The Middle or Center of the *North Continent* is about fixteen or eighteen degrees of *Northern* Latitude; and that of the *South* about fixteen or eighteen degrees of *Southern* Latitude.

LXV. This Propofition (which more nicely determines that Pofition of the Continents which the laft more generally afferted) is thus demonftrated. Each Continent muft retain that Pofition which it had when its Compages was burft by the Elevation of the *Abyfs*. Now the burfting of the Orb is to be fuppos'd before the Comets neareft diftance; and by confequence the Centers of the two Continents a and b ought to have the Latitude of the Points about 90, or rather nearer an 100 degrees onward beyond that oppofite to the *Sun*, or beyond the *Sun* it felf. So that the Center of the *Northern* Continent, near the *South-Eaft* point of *Arabia*, and of the *Southern*, near the Source of the vaft River *De la Plata*, ought to be about the fame Latitude with the 20th degree of *Leo*, and of *Aquarius*, or near 16 degrees, the former of *Northern*, the latter of *Southern* Latitude, as this Propofition afferts them really to be.

Corollary 1. *If therefore we were to determine the time of the Year of the Comet's paffing by the Earth, or the commencing of the Deluge, from the Pofition of the Centers of our two oppofite Continents, which depend thereon, we ought to affign it near the middle of the fecond Month, from the* Autumnal Equinox, *agreeably to the time already fixt both from the Sacred Hiftory, and the Calculations of* Aftronomy *at the tenth* Hypothefis *foregoing.*

Coroll. 2. *Hence all thofe Corollaries to the third and fourth Argument of the faid tenth* Hypothefis *are mightily confirm'd: To which I refer the* Reader *for their fecond perufal; the importance of their Subjects well-deferving the fame at his hands.* Coroll.

Coroll. 3. *Hence perhaps we may derive the occa-*
fion of that ancient, current, and much infifted-on Tra-
dition concerning the high or elevated fituation of Para-
dife; which is fo very much attefted to by Antiquity,
and yet fo very ftrange and obfcure in it felf. For fince
Paradife, as has been already prov'd, was very near
that point where the Center of our Continent is, the
Eaft *or* Southeaft *Border of* Arabia: *And fince*
withal, as we have fhewn, the fame Regions were by
the Comet at the Deluge elevated more than any others
on the intire Globe; and fince, laftly, it would for a long
time retain in good meafure fuch its moft rais'd fitua-
tion, and continue higher than any other correfpondent
parts of the Earth; this appears a rational Occafion or
Foundation of that celebrated Tradition here refer'd to:
Which otherwife how to give any tolerable account of,
upon any folid Principles, I confefs I am, and have al-
ways been wholly to feek.

LXVI. Seeing the Motion of the Comet about
its neareft Pofition was much more confiderable
than the *Diurnal* one of the Earth; and feeing
withal the greater and higher protuberance would
arrive at a fufficient force to burft its incumbent
Orb or Continent fomewhat fooner than the
leffer and lower; it will follow that the Point b
would not be juft oppofite to the Point a, but nearer the place q in the Figure. By which means the
diftance from q by c to a would be greater than
from the fame q by d to a; or from the Center
of the greater Continent to that of the leffer
South-eaftward, than *South-weftward* : Exactly as
this Propofition requires.

LXVII. Neither

LXVII. Neither of the *Continents* is terminated by a round or even circular Circumference: but mighty Creeks, Bays, and Seas running into them; and as mighty Peninfula's, Promontories, and Rocks jetting out from them, render the whole very unequal and irregular.

LXVII. If the Surface of the Earth before the Deluge had been even and fmooth, without Mountains and Valleys, and their Confequents, Seas and Dry Land, the paffing by of the Comet muft indeed, as before, have certainly caus'd a diftincti-on of the two Continents, and muft have interpos'd an Ocean between them; but then thefe two circumftances would have obtain'd alfo, firft, that all the Waters of the intire Globe would have left the Continents, and folely compos'd an Ocean; and fecondly, That the Termination or Boundaries of the Ocean and the Continents would have been circular, round, and even on every fide. But fince the Surface of the Earth was uneven, irregular, and diftinguifh'd every where into Mountains, Plains and Valleys, into Seas and Dry Land, the prefent Terraqueous Globe, with thofe inequalities of the Termination of each Continent mention'd in this Propofition, is a moft eafie and natural, nay plainly neceffary refult of this great Mutation at the Deluge.

Coroll. 1. *Hence 'tis farther evident, that the Surface of the* Antediluvian *Earth was not plain and even, but had thofe diftinctions of Mountains and Valleys, Seas and Dry Land, which from other Arguments has been before eftablifh'd.*

Coroll. 2. *Hence therefore it appears (what fhould have been before obferv'd) that all the Earth might be Planted and Peopled before the Deluge, tho' Navigation were then either not at all, or not confiderably known: There being no Ocean or feparate Continents; and fcarce any fuch thing as an Ifland, or Country but what with eafe might be gone to by Land.* **LXVIII.**

LXVII. The depth of that *Ocean* which feparates thefe two *Continents*, is ufually greateft fartheft from, and leaft neareft to either of the fame *Continents* ; there being a gradual defcent from the *Continents* to the middle of the *Ocean*, which is the deepeft of all.

LXVIII. The reafon of this gradual declivity towards the middle of the Ocean, is very plain from the Figure hereto belonging. For fince the Earth's Surface became in fome degree an Oval, or *oblong Sphæroid*, 'tis neceffary that there fhould be (as far as the other irregularities of the Globe would permit) a defcent from the ends of the longer *Axis* b and a, to thofe of the fhorter c and d in their intire circumvolution, which gives a moft obvious account of the prefent *Phænomenon*.

LXIX. The greateft part of the *Iſlands* of the Globe are fituate at fmall diftances from the Edges of the great *Continents*; very few appearing near the middle of the Main *Ocean*.

LXIX. Since Iflands are only fuch high Regions as would be extant above the Surface of the Waters, tho' they cover'd the Neighbouring parts ; and fince the Ocean, as we have now fhewn, was deepeft in the middle between the two Continents ; 'tis plain that, *Cæteris paribus*, the higher Regions would more frequently be extant near the Continents, than about the middle of the faid Ocean ; as this Propofition afferts.

LXX. The Ages of Men decreas'd about one half prefently after the Deluge ; and in the fucceeding eight hundred or nine hundred Years, were gradually reduced to that ftandard at which they have ftood ever fince.

LXX. The firft part of this is already fufficiently accounted for in that Propofition, where the caufes

of

of the change in the duration of Mens lives at the
Flood were in general enquir'd into. But the
reasons of the gradual Decay in the succeeding
Ages are here to be assign'd. Now here 'tis not
impossible that the considerably long lives of the
first *Postdiluvian* Patriarchs might in part depend
on the vigorous Constitution of their Fathers, not
to be *immediately* impair'd to the utmost, or destroy'd in their Posterity, till by degrees, and in
length of time it was effected. But besides, 'tis to be
consider'd, which I take to be the principal thing,
that seeing the corrupted *Atmosphere*, with the pernicious Steams arising from the newly acquir'd
Chaotick Crust, or Sediment of the Waters, and
their unhappy Effects on the Fruits, as well as living Creatures upon the Earth, must be allow'd
the occasion and cause of the shortning of Humane Life; such Regions as were freest from, or
most elevated above the said Sediment, or *Chaotick
Atmosphere*, must have chiefly continued as they
were before, and so the ancient Longevity would
chiefly be preserv'd therein. Which being suppos'd, and what has been already advanc'd
withal consider'd, this Proposition will be easy,
plain, and natural; and a peculiar Attestation of
the present *Hypothesis*. For seeing *Noah* and the
Ark were landed on *Caucasus*, the most elevated
Region of the Earth, and freest from the Sediment of the Waters, as well as the grossness of
the *Chaotick Atmosphere* below, that place would
scarce differ for a good while from the *Antediluvian* State of things, and the lives of Animals
would retain very near their ancient Duration;
which accordingly we find was really done. *Noah*
survived the Deluge no less than 350 Years, and
compleated 950 in the whole (somewhat beyond
the moderate proportion of the *Antediluvians*

them-

themselves, as the Table will easily shew). But
run by reason both of the descent of his Posterity into the Plains, and lower Grounds, and
principally by the gradual subsidence of those
Regions themselves into the gross *Atmosphere* below, they became gradually liable to those Dif-
eases, and that shortness of Life, which we before shew'd to have been the sad Effects thereof,
and to which all Mankind has since been subject.

Corollary 1. *Mankind increased vastly more soon
after the Deluge than in these latter ages of the World.
For whereas a Country is 280 Years now in doubling
its Inhabitants, had the same rate held ever since the
Deluge, Mankind at this day would not have reach'd
the number of two hundred thousand Souls; which
yet is esteem'd to be between three and four hundred
Millions, or near two thousand times as many as the
said number, deducible from the present rate of the Increase of Mankind. So that 'tis evident, That the
Antediluvian* Fruitfulness, *and numerous Stock of
Inhabitants (which are also themselves hereby fully
establish'd) must have prevail'd,* servata propor-
tione, *among the Primitive* Posdiluvians *for some
Centuries, or else no account were to be given of the
present numbers of Men upon the Face of the Earth;
whereby the Verity of this Proposition, the Veracity
of* Moses *therein, the great importance thereof, and
the necessity of the present* Solution, *and of that*
Theory *on which it is built, are mightily confirm'd.*

Coroll. 2. *Hence we may nearly determine the
Ages of Men for the first eight or nine hundred
Years after the Deluge, from the length of their Lives
given. Thus* Job, *who appears to have liv'd at the
least between two and three hundred Years, must
have been contemporary with some of the Patriarchs
between*

Coa. xi. 1.

Grount. p.
59, 85, 86.

Job 42.
16.

between Heber *and* Abraham, *to whom that Duration of Humane Life belong'd ; and thus we may examine and determine the Ages of the moſt Ancient King's mention'd in Prophane Hiſtories, from the like Duration of their Lives or Reigns , as the following* Corollary *will more particularly obſerve.*

Coroll. 3. *Neither the* Egyptian Dynaſties, *nor the* Aſſyrian Monarchy, *could be coeval with the firſt ſeven or eight hundred Years after the Deluge, none of their Kings Reigns ſet down by Chronologers reaching that number of Years which the length of Humane Life at that time requir'd ; nay, nor any other than Kings now may, and do arrive at in theſe latter Ages of the World.*

Coroll. 4. *The* Antediluvian *and* Poſtdiluvian *Years mention'd in Scripture were true Years of twelve, not fictitious ones of one Month apiece, as ſome, that they might reduce the Age of the firſt Patriarchs to the ſhort term of Life ſince uſually attain'd to, have been willing to ſurmiſe. This fancy is ſtrangely abſurd , and contrary to the Sacred Hiſtory, and in particular irreconcilable with this Propoſition. For had the ancient Years been* Lunar, *of one Month, and the latter* Solar *of a twelve, by which the ſame Duration of Humane Life had been differently meaſur'd; the numbers of Years which Men liv'd, muſt have alter'd in the Proportion of twelve to one of a ſudden, at ſuch a change in the Year referr'd to, and not gradually and gently, as 'tis here evident they did.*

LXXI. Our upper Earth for a conſiderable depth, even as far as we commonly penetrate into it, is *Factitious ,* or newly acquir'd at the Deluge : The ancient one being covered by freſh *Strata* or *Layers* of Earth at that time, and thereby ſpoil'd or deſtroy'd as to the uſe and advantage of Mankind.

LXXI. 'Tis

LXXI. 'Tis not to be suppos'd, that the Waters of the Deluge were merely the pure Element of Water, sincere and unmix'd. What came from the Comet's *Atmosphere*, must partake of its earthly heterogeneous Mixtures; and what was squeez'd up from beneath, must carry up much Dirt and earthy Matter along with it. Besides which, as soon as the stormy Weather began, the soak'd and loosen'd Tops of Mountains would easily, by the Winds and Waves together, be wash'd off, or carried away into the Mass of Waters, and increase the impurity and earthy mixtures thereof. On all which accounts the Waters of the Deluge would be a very impure, thick, and muddy Fluid, and afford such a quantity of earthy Matter as would bear some considerable Proportion to that of the Water it self. Now this earthy Matter being heavier than the Water, would by degrees settle downwards, and compose first a mighty thick, dirty, muddy Fluid in the lower Regions of the Waters, and at last a plain earthy Sediment at the bottom of them; which would at once spoil and bury the old Surface of the Ground, and become a new Crust or Cover on the face thereof. Now, that we may see whether this Sediment or Crust could be so thick and considerable as this *Phænomenon* requires, let us suppose, as before, the perpendicular height of the Waters of the Deluge to have been three Miles above the common Surface of the Plains and Seas, and the thirtieth part only of the intire Fluid on the Face of the Earth to have been earthy Parts fit to compose the Sediment or Crust beforemention'd. Let us also remember what has been already observ'd from Mr. *Newton*, That Earth is

at least three times as dense and heavy as Water;

ter; fo that the thirtieth part in quantity of Matter, would only take up the ninetieth part of the whole fpace, either in the Waters, or when 'twas fetled down by it felf, and became a new Cruft or Orb upon the Earth. If we then divide 15000, the number of Feet in the whole height of the Waters, (not here to allow for the fpaces poffefs'd by the extant Parts of the Earth) by 90, (1500 by 9) the quotient will fhew the the Craffitude or Thicknefs of this Sediment or Cruft covering the Face of the Earth, *viz.* $166\frac{2}{3}$ Feet, one place taken with another indifferently. Which quantity fully accounts for the Propofition we are upon, and agrees with the Obfervations made in the Bowels of our prefent Earth to as great accuracy as one could defire or expect.

Corollary 1. *Hence it appears, That the Earth was generally uninhabitable for feveral years after the Flood: This new factitious Sediment of the Waters requiring no little fpace of time ere it would be fully fetled, its Strata confolidated, its Surface become hard and dry, and its Vegetables fprung out of it; before which time 'twere uninhabitable by Man, and the other Dry-land Animals.*

Coroll. 2. *Hence we may fee the Care and Wifdom of Divine Providence for the Prefervation and Maintenance of* Noah, *and of all the Creatures in the* Ark, *after their coming out of the fame again; by ordering all things fo, that the* Ark *fhould reft on the higheft Mountain in the World, and that the Waters fhould fo little furpafs the fame, that the Sediment thereof could neither fpoil the Fruits of the Ground, nor render the Surface uninhabitable, as it did on the other Regions of the Earth. For fince the quantity of the Sediment would generally be proportionable every where to the perpendicular height of the Waters over*

the

the Surface of the Ground below; tho' it would cover all the other Regions of the whole Earth, yet on this highest of all Mountains, (cover'd but a few Days, or perhaps Hours, with any Waters, and they never above fifteen Cubits perpendicular height) the quantity of the Sediment would here be perfectly inconsiderable, and the Earth would not be at all alter'd from what it was before, nor its Vegetables hurt by this Universal Deluge. So that this, and this was the spot of Ground capable of receiving the Ark, and of sustaining the Creatures therein, till afterwards the rest of the Earth became fit for their Descent and Habitation. To this spot therefore, by such a wonderful adjustment of all the requisite Circumstances of the Deluge, preserv'd and distinguish'd from all the rest of the World, the Divine Providence did conduct the Ark; and on this was laid the Foundation of the present Race of Mankind, and of all those Terrestrial Animals, which are now on the Face of the whole Earth; which otherwise had perish'd at their Exit out of the Ark, notwithstanding their wonderful Preservation therein during the Rage of the Deluge.

Coroll. 3. Hence we may easily understand whence Gen. viii. 11. the Olive-branch was brought by the Dove to Noah. For when the Trees adjoining to the Ark, or on the neighbouring Tops of the Hills had suffer'd small damage by the Flood, and had since the clearing of the Waters enjoy'd almost the whole Spring, and half the Summer; they must be as flourishing, and full of as many new and tender Sprouts as ever; one of which might therefore be easily broken off by the Dove, and brought to Noah in her Mouth; which new, dry, and firm Sprout or Branch, being a clear evidence, that the Waters were not only gone, and the Ground dry a great while before, but that the Earth was full, as formerly, fit for the Production

of

of its wonted Trees and Fruits, must exceedingly tend to the Satisfaction of Noah, and the Confirmation of his Faith and Hope in an entire Deliverance, and in the future Renovation of the World.

LXXII. This *Fictitious Craft* is univerfal, upon the Tops of the generality of the Mountains, as well as in the Plains and Vallies; and that in all the known Climates and Regions of the World.

LXXII. This is a neceffary confequent from the Univerfality of the Deluge already accounted for. And tho the generality of the Mountains would ufually have a thinner Sediment or Cruft than the Plains or Vallies, in proportion to the leffer height of the Waters over each of them refpectively; yet they being at the Deluge much inferior to the height of *Caucafus*, muft be generally cover'd with the fame Cruft (unlefs the Storms and Waves wafh'd it down again after its firft fetling upon any of them) as the Obfervations fhew they really now are.

Corollary 1. 'Tis hence evident, even abftractedly from the Sacred Hiftory, that there has formerly been an Univerfal Deluge, much higher than the generality of the Mountains. So that hereafter, fince the fo ufeful Obfervations of Naturalifts, and principally of Dr. Woodward hereto relating, we need not endeavour to fecure the Credit and Veracity of the Mofaick Hiftory of the Deluge by Ancient Records, and the univerfal Atteftation of Antiquity; (which Teftimonies yet are too evident and numerous to be denied) but may from our own Eyes, at the neighbouring Mines and Coal-Pits, fatisfy our felves of the exact truth of this part of the Sacred Volume, which has been fo much excepted againft by ill-difpo'ed Perfons. So wonderful is the Method of the Divine Wif-

F f 4 *dom*

*d.m in its feaſonable Atteſtations afforded to the Sa-
cred Scriptures! That not only the* Very Day, *as we
have ſeen, when the Flood began, aſſign'd by* Moſes
*may ſtill, after more than four thouſand years, be
prov'd from* Aſtronomy *to have been the true one;
which the Learned are chiefly capable of judging of,
and being primarily influenc'd by: But the Reality
and Univerſality of the Deluge it ſelf is demonſtrable
from ſuch common and eaſie Obſervations, in all parts
of the World, at the Neighbouring Mines or Coal-pits,
that the Vulgar and Moſt Illiterate may be Eye-wit-
neſſes of the certain Effects of it, and ſo fully convinc'd of the fidelity of the Sacred Hiſtorian therein.*

Vid. Bent-
ley's Serm.
4. P. 34, 35.

Coroll. 2. *'Tis no wonder that none of the* Antediluvian *Cities, Towns, Buildings, or other Remains
are any where to be met with ſince the Deluge: They
being all generally buried perhaps above two hundred
foot deep in the Earth, by the Sediment of the Waters.*

LXXIII. The Parts of the preſent upper *Strata* were, at
the time of the Waters covering the Earth, looſe, ſeparate, divided, and floated in the Waters among one
another uncertainly.

LXXIII. This Propoſition needs no farther
Explication; being already plain in what has
been already ſaid.

LXXIV. All this Heterogeneous Maſs, thus floating in
the Waters, by degrees deſcended downwards, and
ſubſided to the Bottom, pretty nearly according to the
Law of Specifick Gravity; and there compos'd thoſe
ſeveral *Strata* or *Layers*, of which our preſent upper
Earth does conſiſt.

LXXIV. This Propoſition is as eaſie as the former; and included in what has been already ſaid.

LXXV. Vaſt multitudes of Fiſhes, belonging both to the
Seas and Rivers, periſh'd at the Deluge; and their
          Shells

Shells were buried among the other Bodies or Maſſes which ſubſided down, and compos'd the *Layers* of our upper Earth.

LXXV. Where ſo Heterogeneous a Maſs of Corpuſcles were diſpers d every where through the Waters, and towards the bottom, eſpecially at the latter end of their ſubſidence, render'd the ſame very thick and muddy, 'tis natural to ſuppoſe, that multitudes of Fiſhes, partly ſtiſled with the Spiſſitude and groſsneſs of the *Fluid*, (ſcarce there deſerving that name;) and partly poiſon'd with the kinds of ſome of thoſe Corpuſcles which they took in together with their Nouriſhment therein, would be deſtroy'd and periſh in the Waters : Which being granted, the reſt ſo eaſily follows as not to need any farther Explication.

LXXVI. The ſame Law of Specifick Gravity which was obſerv'd in the reſt of the Maſs, was alſo obſerv'd in the ſubſidence of the Shells of Fiſhes ; they then ſinking together with, and accordingly being now found encloſ'd among thoſe *strata* or Bodies which are nearly of their own Specifick Gravities : The heavier Shells being conſequently ſtill encloſ'd among the heavier *Strata*, and the lighter Shells among the lighter *Strata*, in the Bowels of our preſent Earth.

LXXVI. This *Phænomenon* is ſo natural and neceſſary, conſidering the gradual increaſe of the thickneſs of the groſs Sediment downward, and the equal ſubjection of Shells to the Law of Specifick Gravity with all other Bodies, that I ſhall not inſiſt any farther upon it.

Corollary. *This ſingle* Phænomenon *of the Shell's of Fiſh inclos'd in the moſt Solid Bodies, as Stone and Marble, and that all over the World, according to their ſeveral Specifick Gravities, at great depths within the Bowels of the Earth; which is ſo ſtrange in it ſelf,*

*self, so surprizing to the Spectators, and so unac-
countable without the most unusual and precarious Miracles be introduc'd, on any other principles; and yet
so easily and naturally solv'd in the* Hypothesis *before
us; is a strong, I had almost said an Invincible Argument for the verity thereof; and as undeniable as
a Physical assertion is capable of: That is, 'Tis (as far
as we can in reason pronounce) without a Miracle,*
certainly true.

> LXXVII. The *Strata* of *Marble*, of *Stone*, and of all other
> solid Bodies, attained their solidity as soon as the *sand*,
> or other matter whereof they consist, was arriv'd at
> the bottom, and well settled there. And all those
> *Strata* which are solid at this day, have been so ever
> since that time.

LXXVII. Seeing this upper Cruft or Sediment
was compos'd in great part of the Earthy Corpufcles or Masses of a *Chaos*, as well as the Primitive Earth was at the *Mosaick* Creation: The
very same reasons assignable for the coalescence
and consolidation of the former, are equally to
be suppos'd in the present case, and render it
equally reasonable with the other. And if the
Dense Fluid, or any parts or steams from that
were instrumental to the Original Union of parts
at the Primary Formation of the Earth, tis
probable there was no want of it at the Deluge;
The *Atmosphere* of the Comet, and the Fountains
of the Deep, being both capable of supplying
sufficient quantities, among the larger plenty of
their Watery and Earthy Masses; as is plain
from what has been already said. Neither in
case some of it were acquir'd by the means afore-
mention'd, is it to be expected that we ought to
see it still on the Face of the Earth, as we do
the Ocean. For seeing this *Dense Fluid* is much
heavier

heavier than Water or Earth, it would be at the
very bottom of all, and so either be inclosed in
the Pores and Caverns at the bottom of the Sediment, or transform'd into a different Body by
its composition with the Earthy parts it was enclos d withal, and did consolidate.

LXXVIII Thefe *Strata* of *Stone*, of *Chalk*, of *Cole*, of
Earth, or whatever matter they confifted of, lying thus
each upon other, appear now as if they had at firft been
parallel, continued, and not interrupted : But as if,
after some time th v had been diflocated and broken
on all fides of the Globe, had been elevated in fome,
and deprefs'd in other places ; from whence the Fiffures
and Breaches, the Cavern and *Grotto's*, with many
other irregularities within and upon our prefent Earth,
feem to be deriv'd.

LXXVIII. When the Sediment fetled down
gradually upon the Surface of the Ancient Earth,
it would compofe *Strata* or *Layers* as even, continued, and parallel as one could defire, and as
the faid Surface did permit. And had the faid
Surface been fix'd and unalterable, this evennefs
and parallelifm, this uniformity and continuity
of the *Strata* would have remain'd unalterable
alfo to this day. But fince, as we have formerly fhewn, the intire Orb of Earth was at the beginning of the Deluge crack'd, chap'd, and broken; and for many years afterwards would by
degrees fettle and compofe it felf towards its former figure and rotundity again ; tho' the Series
and Connexion of the *Strata* might before they
were confolidated, be as regular as you can imagine, yet when the *Bafis* or Foundation on
which they refted, and the Surface on which they
were fpread fail'd by degrees, in feveral places,
and proportions, by the rifing of fome Columns
upwards, and the fetling of others downwards,
this

this Upper Orb or Cruft, where the Strata were not become intirely Solid, like Stone and Marble, muft follow in great part the fate of the other, and be diflocated, elevated, or deprefs'd in correfpondence to that whereon it refted: And have thereby a Set of Chaps and Fiſures directly overagainft thofe which were before in the Ancient Earth. But as for fuch places where the new Strata were become Stony or Solid, and incapable of a compliance with the under Earth, by the fettling downward or elevation of its immediate Baſis the Primitive Earth, thofe Caverns and Grotto's, thofe Caves and Hollows which appear within the Earth, or its Mountains, would naturally arife ; while the Solid Strata, like Beams or Arches, fuftain'd the impending Columns, notwithftanding the finking and failure of their immediate Foundations ; by which Caufes the Surface and Upper Regions of the Earth would become very uneven, and full of fmall irregularities, fuch as the prefent Phænomenon aſſures us of.

Corollary 1. *Hence we fee a plain Reafon why Mountainous and Stony Countries are only or principally Hollow and Cavernous: Some leſſer Mountains being perhaps occafion'd by the fubfidence of the neighbouring Columns, and the Caverns they enclofe thereby produc'd; and the Solidity of the* Strata *being the proper Caufe of fuch Caverns in other Cafes: Of which the fofter, more looſe, and pliable Earth was accordingly incapable.*

Corollary 2. *Tho' the Ancient Earth were fetled, and become uneven in the fame degree, and in the fame places as the prefent is ; and that before the confolidation of the new Sediment ; yet the* Series *of the feveral* Strata *one under another on each fide of any* Fiſſure, *would in fome meaſure correfpond to one another,*

ther, as if the confimilar Strata *had once been united, and had afterwards been broken and funk down unequally ; as is manifeft from the confimilar fituation and fubfidence of the confimular Corpufcles ; whereby the like order and craffitude of each* Stratum *might be ftill preferv'd, tho' not fo exactly, as if the fuftaining Surface had been even and fmooth when the Sediment compos'd thofe* Strata, *and the Fiffures had afterward been made through both Orbs at once, and caus'd fuch inequality.*

Coroll. 3. *Hence would arife mighty and numerous Receptacles of Water within the Earth, efpecially in the Mountainous parts thereof. For ufually where a folid* Stratum *fuftain'd the Earth above, while the parts beneath funk lower, and thereby produc'd a Cavern, the Waters would ouze and flow into it from all quarters, and caufe a conflux or inclofed Sea of Waters in the Bowels of the Earth: Which Cavities might fometimes communicate with one another, or with the Ocean ; and fometimes contain Reftagnant Waters, without any outlet : All which are very agreeable to the prefent* Phænomena *of the Earth.*

Coroll. 4. *Hence appears the Reafon of the raging of Earthquakes in Mountainous Countreys, and of the burfting forth and continuation of* Volcano's *there. For thefe Caverns, which we have obferv'd the Mountainous Countreys to be mainly liable to, are fit to receive and contain together Nitrous and Explofive, Sulphureous and Inflammable fteams, in great quantities ; and withal to admit the Air to fan, and affift that Explofion or Inflammation, which feems to be the occafion of thofe dreadful* Phænomena *in our prefent Earth.*

Coroll. 5. *If therefore there be no other Caverns than thofe accounted for juft now, and taking date from the Deluge; 'tis very probable there were few or no* Volcano's *or Earthquakes, fo much depending on them, before the Flood.* Coroll. 6.

Coroll. 6. In case what has been, or might farther be said, be not found sufficient to account for some observations made, concerning the inward parts of our Earth; but Dr. Woodward's Hypothesis of the Dissolution of the before united Strata, by a general Earthquake, or the explosive force of the Steams of Heat ascending from the Central parts, be found necessary; such a supposition will by no means disagree with the present Theory. For when the Subterraneous ascending Steams were every way stop'd, and their ordinary course from the Central to the Superficiary Parts obstructed, by the new Sediment or Crust growing fast and solid, and in some places Stony and Impenetrable; they would be every where preternaturally assembled, especially in the cracks, breaches and fissures of the Ancient Earth, in greater quantities than usual, and so might by a sudden Rarefaction, or Explosion, burst through the Upper Crust, and cause all those Fissures, little Hills, Caverns, Grotto's, and Inequalities which Dr. Woodward's Observations require, and this Proposition takes notice of. In this case therefore the particular and distinct consideration of the Phænomena, must determine and arbitrate between the former more natural and gentle, and this latter more violent and extraordinary method of accounting for the present face of Nature upon and within the Earth.

LXXIX. Great numbers of Trees, and other Vegetables, were also, at this subsidence of the Mass aforesaid, buried in the Bowels of the Earth: And such very often as will not grow in the places where they are lodg'd: Many of which are pretty intire and perfect, and to be distinctly seen and consider'd to this very day.

Solut. 56. pius.

LXXIX. Seeing the latter part of the Deluge, after the seventeenth day of the seventh Month, or the twenty seventh day of *March* with us at present, prefent, was very Windy, Stormy, and Tempeftuous; the moft Extant and Mountainous parts of the Earth would be mightily expos'd to the fury both of the Winds and Waves : Which confequently would tear up, or wafh away the loofe and unfolid Upper Earth, with all its Furniture of Trees and Plants; and not feldom carry them great diftances from their former Seats. Now thefe Vegetables, if no *Earthy Metallick* or *Mineral* Maffes adher'd to them, being, bulk for bulk, lighter than the Earthy Sediment, would fettle down laft of all, and would lye upon the Surface of the Earth, and there rot away and difappear. But if confiderable quantities of the heavieft *Strata*, or of *Metallick* or *Mineral* Matter, as would fometimes happen, adher'd to them, they would fink lower, and be inclofed in the Bowels of the Earth, either near to, or far from the place of their own growth, according as the Billows and Storms happen'd to difpofe of them. All which Changes and Diflocations of the Soil and furface with their Fruits and Plants, might leave once fertile Countries Bare and Barren; and lodge fuch Vegetables in others, which of themfelves, before the new Sediment, much more fince the fame, were wholly incapable of fuch productions; according to the exigency of the Propofition before us.

LXXX. It appears from all the tokens and circumftances which are ftill obfervable about them, That all thefe Vegetables were torn away from their ancient Seats in the Spring time, in or about the Month of May.

LXXX. When we have already prov'd, that the Windy and Stormy Weather which tore up thefe Vegetables, did not begin till the feventeenth

Solut. 56. plus.

teenth day of the feventh Month from the Autumnal Equinox; anfwering to our *March* the
twenty feventh now; and when it appears that the
higher any Mountain or Continent was, the lefs
while, and in a lefs degree would the Waters
prevail upon it; and fo little fometimes as not
wholly to deftroy the growing Vegetables, at this
due time of the Year; 'tis evident that whether
the Sediment were newly fetled, and had enclos d them or not, fo many as were torn up
from thefe higheft parts of the Earth muſt be in
that forwardnefs as the Months fucceeding the
beginning of the Storms (*April, May* and *June*)
ufually bring them to, very agreeably to the
Propofition before us. And that we have rightly
fuppos'd thefe *Foſſil Plants* to have been fuch as
grew on the elevated parts of the Earth only,
(how far diftant foever the fury of the Waves and
Storms may have lodg'd them) and fo to have
been torn up by the Storms in the affigned manner, appears both by the heaps in which they are
frequently found crouded together, and by the
kinds of Plants thus buried in the Earth: Of which
latter, (tho' his opinion, according to his own *Hypothefis* be, that all forts were originally lodg'd in
the Earth, tho' fome be fince periſh'd) Dr. *Woodward*'s words are (in his kind and free Letter, in
anfwer to my Queries about them) *The Foſſil
Plants are very numerous and various, and fome
of them intire, and well preferv'd. I have met
with many of the fame Species with thofe now
growing on our Hills, Woods, Meadows, Heaths, &c.
But none of the Water-Plants; I mean fuch as are
peculiar to Lakes, Rivers, and the Sea.* Which
Teſtimony is a peculiar Confirmation of the
prefent *Hypothefis.*

Corollary:

Corollary. *Hence the Ancient Years beginning at the* Autumnal Equinox, *and the consequent commencing of the Deluge, the seventeenth Day of the second Month from thence, and not from the Spring, is evidenc'd by this very Observation which Dr.* Woodward, *the Author thereof, suppofes wou'd prove the contrary. So that the time of the Deluge's commencing affign'd by our* Hypothefis, *appears at laft to be confirm'd both by the* Scriptures, *by the* Ancients, *by* Aftronomy , *by* Geography, *and by* Natural Obfervation ; *and is confequently by fo very remarkable a Concurrence and Correfpondence of 'em all, put beyond any reafonable Doubt or Scruple.*

LXXXI. All the *Metals* and *Minerals* among the *Strata* of our upper Earth, owe their prefent Frame and Order to the Deluge ; being repos'd therein during the time of the Waters covering the Earth, or during the Subfidence of the before-mention'd Mafs.

LXXXI. This can have no difficulty in it, feeing our upper Earth is *factitious*, and compos'd of the forefaid Sediment of the Waters of the Deluge ; which including the Corpufcles of *Metals* and *Minerals*, as weal as others, wou'd alike afford every one thofe places which they have ever fince poffefs'd.

LXXXII. Thefe *Metals* and *Minerals* appear differently in the Earth, according to the different manners of their firft Lodgment: For fometimes they are in loofe and fmall Particles, uncertainly inclos'd among fuch Maffes as they chanc'd to fall down withall : At other times, fome of their Corpufcles happening to occur and meet together, affix'd to each other ; and feveral convening, uniting, and combining into one Mafs, form'd thofe *Metallic* and *Mineral Balls* or *Nodules* which are now found in the Earth. And according as the Corpufcles chanc'd to be all of a kind, or otherwife, fo the Mafs were more or lefs fimple, pure, and homogeneous : And according as o-

ther

ther Bodies, Bones, Teeth, Shells of Fish, or the like, happen'd to come in their way, these Metalick and Mineral Corpuscles affix'd to, and became conjoyn'd with 'em: either within, where it was possible, in their Hollows and Interstices ; or without, on their Surface and Outsides ; filling the one, or covering the other. And all this in different Degrees and Proportions, according to the different Circumstances of each individual Case.

LXXXII. All these things are but proper Effects of such a common Subsidence of all these Masses and Corpuscles together in the *Chaotick* Sediment as is above-mention'd : And no longer or more particular Account is necessary, or can be satisfactory, till Dr. *Woodward's* larger Work (which we in time hope for) affords us the Observations more nicely and particularly than we yet have them. To which, therefore, the Inquisitive Reader must be refer'd in this and the like Cases.

LXXXIII. The inward parts of the present Earth are very irregular and confus'd : One Region is chiefly Stony, another Sandy, a third Gravelly : One Country contains some certain kind, of Metals and Minerals ; another contains quite different Ones : Nay the same Lump or Mass of Earth not seldom contains the Corpuscles of several Metals or Minerals confusedly intermixt one with another, and with its own Earthy Parts. All which Irregularities, with several others that might be obferv'd, even contrary to the Law of specifick Gravity , in the placing of the different *Strata* of the Earth, demonstrates the original Fund or Promptuary of all this upper factitious Earth, to have been in a very wild, confus'd, and *Chaotick* Condition.

LXXXIII. Seeing the Sediment of the Waters was compos'd of what Earthy Matter was uncertainly brought up out of the inner Earth, and of what a true and proper *Chaos* afforded, these

thefe *Phænomena* are as natural and accountable
therefrom, as on any other mechanical *Hypothefis*, they muft appear ftrange, perplexing, and
inexplicable to Philofophick Minds.

> LXXXIV. The uppermoft and lighteft *Stratum* of Soil
> or *Garden-Mold*, as 'tis call'd, which is the proper
> Seminary of the Vegetable Kingdom, is fince the De-
> luge very thick fpread ufually in the Valleys and
> Plains, but very thin on the Ridges and Tops of
> Mountains : Which laft for want thereof are fre-
> quently ftony, rocky, bare, and barren.

LXXXIV. Two plain reafons are to be given for this *Phænomenon* ; (1.) The quantity of
Water, and its Sediment ; and by confequence
of Soil or fertile Earth was lefs over the Mountains than over the Plains and Valleys. (2.) After the Subfidence of the Sediment, and before
its entire Confolidation, the Tops of Mountains were moft expos'd to the fury of the
Winds and Storms ; which wou'd therefore
more eafily bear away that lighteft and leaft
united *Stratum* which lay uppermoft in thofe
bleak places, than in the more retir'd and
skreen'd Plains and Valleys ; and by diminifhing the Soil in the former, and thereby augmenting it in the latter places, moft eafily
make all things correfpond in this Propofition.

> LXXXV. Of the four ancient Rivers of Paradife, two
> ftill remain in fome meafure ; but the other two
> do not ; or at the leaft are fo chang'd that the Mo-
> faick Defcription does not agree to them at pre-
> fent.

LXXXV. That the great Rivers wou'd ftill
retain in great meafure their old Courfes, has
been obferv'd already ; and feeing the Foun-

tains, and the general inequalities of the Earth, on which their Origin and Channels depend, were the same generally before as since the Deluge, there can be no doubt thereof. As to the change, with reference to the other two Rivers. If the Gulph of *Perfia* were anciently free from Waters, and were no other than the very Country of *Eden*; and if the very Entrance of that Gulph into the *Perfian* Sea were the *Garden of Eden*, or *Paradife*, as has been before afferted, there can be no difficulty in the cafe : The Channels of thefe Rivers, and indeed of their Fellow-Branches too after their laft Partition, being now under Water, and not to be enquir'd after. But tho' we fhou'd allow that *Paradife* was where 'tis generally placed, near *Babylon*, and upon the Continent, yet will there be no wonder at the difappearance of thefe two Rivers, which, with their Fellows, are bury'd to a fufficient depth under the Sediment we have been fpeaking fo much of before ; and fo no more to be enquir'd after in this than in the former Cafe.

> LXXXVI. Thofe *Metals* and *Minerals* which the *Mo-
faick Defcription of *Paradife*, and of its bordering
Regions, takes fuch particular notice of, and the
Prophets fo emphatically refer to, are not now met
with fo plentifully therein.

LXXXVI. The prefent upper Earth being, as we have feen, *factitious*, and a new Cruft fince the Flood covering over the ancient Surface thereof, thofe Primitive Treafures muft lie too deep in the Bowels of the prefent Earth, to be eafily approach'd by us, and fo are entirely loft as to the ufe or enjoyment of Mankind.

LXXXVII.

LXXXVII. This Deluge of Waters was a fign alinftance of the Divine Vengeance on a wicked World, and was the effect of the peculiar and extraordinary Providence of God.

LXXXVII. Tho' the paffing by of a Comet, and all thofe Effects of it in the drowning of the World, of which we have fo largely difcours'd hitherto, be not to be ftil'd in the common ufe of the Word *Miraculous*; (tho' in no very improper Senfe, all fuch Events may have *that* Appellation, of which before) yet is there the greateft reafon in the World to attribute this mighty *Turn* and *Cataftrophe* of Nature, to the Divine Providence, and the immediate, voluntary, actual, interpofition of God ; and that in thefe enfuing Particulars, and on thefe following Accounts ; which I fhall be the fhorter upon, as having in the place fore-mention'd explain'd my Mind fomewhat largely about things of this Nature. (1.) The Bodies made ufe of in this and the like Changes of Nature, are originally the Creatures of God, and continually preferv'd by Him ; and fo what they are inftrumental in, ought moft juftly to be afcrib'd to the principal Caufe, the great Creator and Confervator of 'em all. (2.) All thofe Powers of Attraction or Gravitation, &c. and thofe Laws of Motion by which thefe Bodies are capable of producing fuch Effects, a e alike owing to the Divine Operation, Appointment, and Efficacy, both in their primitive Impreffion, and continual Energy ; and fo ftill the Effects themfelves are to be afcrib'd to a Divine Original. (3.) That particular Conftitution of the Earth on the Face of the fluid Abyfs, and other fuch Difpofitions,

Vid. Solut. 2. præis.

G g 3   where-

whereby it became subject to a universal Deluge, were also the Consequents of the Divine Power and Providence in the formation of the Earth. (4.) That peculiar Situation or Constitution of the Orbits and Motions of Comets, whereby they, by reason of their passing thro the Planetary System each Revolution are fit to cause such great Mutations in it, was the Effect of the particular Order and Disposition of God, in the primary frame of the Universe. (5.) The Coincidence of the Plain of a Comet's Orbit with that of the Ecliptick, can have no other Foundation in Nature, than a like design d and contriv'd Appointment of God. (6.) The way of the Comet's Motion from East to West, contrary to that of the Planets, by which the Particulars of the Deluge were in good Measure provided for, cou'd also be nothing but the Effect of the same Design and Providence of God. (7.) The so nice and exact adjustment of the Motions of both the Comet and the Earth; that the former shou'd pass just so near, and impart such a certain quantity of Waters, and not more or less than wou d drown the World, and just cover the highest Mountain, and yet reach no farther; in short, as wou'd secure the *Ark* for future Generations, and yet not leave one dry-land Animal besides alive; this exactness is a most peculiar and strange Effect of the most wise and sagacious Providence of God in this mighty Revolution. But (8.) Lastly, (to omit repeating some things before observ'd as we pass'd along) The precise time of the passing by of the Comet, and thereby of destroying the World, is, in the most peculiar manner, and highest degree, the result of

the

the Divine Providence. That exactly at a time which was fit and proper, and in an Age that juftly deferv'd fo great a Judgment, the Comet fhou'd come by, and over-whelm the World, is very remarkably and extraordinarily the Finger of God himfelf. That Omnifcient Being, who forefaw when the degeneracy of Human Nature wou'd be arriv'd at an *unfufferable* degree of Wickednefs, the Iniquities of the World wou'd be compleatly *full*; and when confequently his Vengeance ought to fall upon them, prædifpofed and preadapted the Orbits and Motions of both the Comet and the Earth, fo that at that very time, and only at that time, the former fhou'd pafs clofe by the latter, and bring that dreadful Punifhment upon them. Had not God Almighty on purpofe thus adjufted the Moments and Courfes of each, 'twere infinite odds that fuch a Conjunction or Coincidence of a Comet and a Planet, wou'd never have happen'd during the whole fpace, between the Creation and Conflagration of this World; much more at fuch a critical Point of time when Mankind, by their *unparallel'd* Wickednefs were deferving of, and only difpos'd for this *unparallel'd* Vengeance, no lefs than almoft an *utter Excifion.*

And this I take to be the Secret of the Divine Providence in the Government of the World, and that whereby the Rewards and Punifhments of God's Mercy and Juftice are diftributed to his Rational Creatures, without any difturbance of the fetled Courfe of Nature, or a miraculous interpofition on every Occafion. Our Imperfection is fuch, that we can only act *pro re nata*, can never know before-hand the Behaviour or Actions of Men;

neith

neither can we forefee what Circumftances
and Conjunctures will happen at any certain
time hereafter ; and fo we cannot provide for
future Events, nor prædifpofe things in fuch a
manner that every one fhall be dealt with, or
every thing done no otherwife than if we
were then alive and prefent, we fhou'd think
proper and reafonable, and fhou'd actually do.
But in the Divine Operation 'tis quite otherwife : God's Præfcience enables him to act after a more fublime manner ; and by a conftant
Courfe of Nature, and Chain of Mechanical
Caufes, to do every thing fo as it fhall not be
diftinguifhable from a particular Interpofition of
his Power, nor be otherwife than on fuch a
particular Interpofition wou'd have been
brought to pafs. He who has created all
things, and given them their feveral Powers
and Faculties, forefees the Effects of 'em all :
At once looks through the intire Train of future
Caufes, Actions, and Events, and fees at what
Periods, and in what manner twill be neceffary and expedient to bring about any changes,
beftow any Mercies, or inflict any Punifhments
on the World : Which being unqueftionably
true, 'tis evident he can as well provide and
prædifpofe natural Caufes for thofe Mutations,
Mercies, or Judgments before-hand ; he can as
eafily put the Machin into fuch Motions as
fhall, without a neceffity of his mending or
correcting it, correfpond to all thefe forefeen
Events or Action, as make way for fuch Alterations afterward by giving a random force
to the whole : And when thefe two ways are
equally poffible, I need not fay which is
moft agreeable to the Divine Perfections, and
moft worthy of God. So that when the Univerfal

verfal Courfe of Nature, with all the Powers
and Effects thereof, were at firft deriv'd from,
and are continually upheld by God; and
when nothing falls out any otherwife, or at
any other time, than was determin'd by Divine Appointment in the Primitive Formation
of the Univerfe: To affign *Phyfical* and *Mechanical* caufes for the Deluge, or fuch mighty
Judgments of God upon the Wicked, is fo far
from taking away the Divine Providence therein, that it fuppofes and demonftrates its Intereft in a more Noble, Wife, and Divine
manner than the bringing in a miraculous
Power wou'd do. Let us fuppofe a *Fulmen*
or Thunderbolt originally, and on purpofe,
put into fuch a Motion, as without any farther
Interpofition of Prov'dence, wou'd direct it to
the Head of a Blafphemer; and whilft he was
curfing his Maker, ftrike him dead upon the
Spot; which the Præfcience and Power of
God fhew to be equally poffible with a prefent Miracle: I think fuch a violent Death
wou'd be as properly *extraordinary*, and a *Divine Judgment*, as any other whatfoever:
Which I take to have been the very cafe of
the Deluge, which I am here peculiarly
concern'd about. Nature is God's Confticu-
tion, and ever fubfervient to him; and the
ftate of the *Natural* is always accommodated
to that of the *Moral* World. What is done
by Nature, and fecond Caufes, is moft properly done by God at laft, who is ultimately and really almoft all we can mean by
thofe Names.

Corollary. *What has been here faid upon this
Occafion, if rightly underftood and appl'd to all
other Cafes, would clear our Minds from many*

of

of thofe Perplexities about the Divine Providence which are ready to difturb 'em. For Inftance: We pray to God for fruitful Seafons, for Health, for Peace, for the Succefs of our Endeavours, for a Bleffing on our Food and Phyfick, and deprecate the contrary Miferies from us. Yet at the fame time we fee the Seafons depend on the fettled Courfe of the Sun, or other natural and neceffary Caufes; we find our Health or Sicknefs to be the proper Effects of our Diet and Regiment; we obferve Peace and War fubject to the Intrigues of Princes, and the plain Refults of vifible Conjunctures in Humane Affairs; we know that Worldly Prudence and Cunning has a main Stroke in the Succefs of Mens Labours; we feel the advantagious Effects of fome Food and Phyfick, and have Reafon to believe the fame does very much refult from the Goodnefs of the Druggs, the Fitnefs of the Proportion, the Difpofition of the Body, and the Skill of the Phyfician, and can frequently give a plain and mechanical Reafon of the different Operations of all thofe things; neither do we hope for the Exercife of a miraculous *Power in thefe or the like Cafes. The Confideration and Comparifon of all thefe things together frequently puzzles the Minds of good Men, efpecially thofe that are more Contemplative and Philofophical, and makes 'em wonder what Intereft our Devotions, or what Advantage our Prayers can have. Second Caufes will work according to their Natures, let Mens Supplications be never fo importunate: And to expect a Miracle in anfwer to every Petition, is more than the moft Religious dare pretend to. This* Dilemma *has had a contrary Effect upon the Minds of Men, while the* Philofopher *was in Danger of doubting of the Succefs, and fo ready to grow cold in his Devotions, and the more unthinking, yet not lefs religious* Man'

re'

rejected the Confideration of the Manner, or the
Operation of second Caufes, and more wifely look'd
up only to God, and imagin'd him immediately concern'd in every Occurrence, and on that Principle
doubted not the Effect of his Prayers. But 'tis, methinks. evident that neither of thefe were exactly in
the Right ; and equally fo, that the due Confideration of what has been above-faid, would prevent
the Dilemma, and take away all reafonable Scruple. 'Tis true that Natural Caufes will operate as
ufual : 'Tis alfo true that Miracles are not ordinari-
ly to be expected : But withal 'tis as true that the
fame all-wife Creator, who appointed that conftant
Courfe of Nature, forefaw at the fame time all thofe
Difpofitions of Men, and in particular thofe Devotions of his Worfhippers, to which fuitable Rewards
were to be provided, and fuitable Anfwers returned ; and therefore has fo order'd the Series of Natural Caufes, as to make that very Provifion for the
fame which otherwife he would have done by the miraculous Interpofition of his Providence ; and which
therefore is equally to be afcrib'd to him with
the greateft Wonders. 'Tis true, the Frame of Nature is now conftant and fettled : But 'tis true alfo that it was fo fettled on the Profpect of the moral Behaviour, and in Correfpondence to the good
or bad Actions of Mankind, forefeen and præfuppo-
fed in the Primitive Conftitution of all ; and by
Confequence whatever Benefits or Afflictions the conftant Courfe of Nature and fecond Caufes bring to
us, are equally capable to be the Matter of our
Prayers or Deprecations of our Humiliation or Gratitude before God, as the immediate Effects of a
miraculous Power ; and the Divine Providence no
lefs to be acknowledg'd and addrefs'd to in the former
than in the latter Cafe : But becaufe our Imperfection is fo great that the Confideration of the
Pri-

Priority *of the* future Actions, *Men to the* Præfcience of God *in the Order of Nature; and the Dependence of the latter on the* former, *is too high for
our Comprehenfion, and tho' demonftrable by, yet in-
fcrutable to the Reafon of Mankind; and becaufe we
are therefore ftill ready to conceive what is fore-
known by God to be neceffary and inevitable ; let the
moral Behaviour of M:n be as it will : Becaufe
I fay this* Præfcience *of God is too Divine a thing
to be eafily penetrated and aply'd by us to all Occafions. I confefs 'tis the moft obvious and the moft
prudent, as well as the moft Scriptural Way to keep
within our Faculties, and alway to fuppofe an immediate Exerting of a new Power in every new
Turn in the World, and without the troublefome
Inquifition into the Nature and Defign of the Primitive Conftitution of the Material World, to refer
all things to an immediate Providence: Into which
every one muft ultimately and originally be refolv'd, and which has as well and as congruoufly
taken care of all Events, as if fuch a miraculous Efficiency were really concern'd on every
individual Occafion. Which whole Matter thus
explain'd may be of Ufe to thofe who through
the not underftanding the Method of the Divine
Providence, and its Confiftency with an uninterrupted Courfe of Nature, have perplex'd their own
Minds, and endanger'd their Religion : Which pernicious fcruples true Philofophy, when rightly underftood, is the only Means of difpelling and preventing. Nothing being more true or momentous
than this, that 'Tis as ever our Ignorance or Miftakes only, that fully the Providence of
God, or diminifh our Religious Affections to
him.*

LXXXVIII.

LXXXVIII. Tho' the Moon might perhaps undergo some such Changes at the Deluge as the Earth ; yet that Face or Hemisphere which is towards the Earth, and which is alone expos'd to our View, has not acquir'd any such gross Atmosphere or Clouds, as our Earth has now about it, and which are here suppos'd to have been acquir'd at the Deluge.

LXXXVIII. Seing the *Moon* appears to be of a Constitution so like that of the Earth, and seeing she is so near a Neighbour and constant Companion thereof, she seems at first Sight liable to the same *Cataftrophe* with the Earth at the Deluge. But that we may confider how far the Comet could affect her, we muft remember that at the firft Paffage of the Comet, Her Situation feems almoft dipos'd to convey her juft after the Earth along that large void *Cylindrical* Space, whofe Vapours the Earth had intercepted, and born away before it, as by comparing the 2*d* and 4*th* Figures is eafie to underftand. Befides, tho' fhe caught her Share of the Vapours from the Atmofphere and Tail of the Comet, yet her Mountains are fo much higher, compar'd with thofe on Earth, that at the moft only an inconfiderable Inundation of Waters on one Hemifphere, not an univerfal Deluge were to be suppos'd : For, laftly, by Reafon of the Slownefs of her Diurnal Revolution thofe Vapours Lem. 39 prius which were caught by one Hemifphere (and indeed by very little more than one at the utmoft) would fall near the fame Places in Rain, which they at firft fell upon when Vapour ; and ftill affect little more than a fingle Hemifphere thereof. So that the moft that can be fuppos'd of the *Moon's* Deluge, is, that the lower Grounds on one Hemifphere fhou'd be overflow'd ; especially if we except the fecond Paffage through the

the Tail of the Comet after its *Perihelium* : For it
muſt be confeſs'd that thoſe ſecondary and leſs
principal Rains of about 9 Days Continuance,
which we before obſerv'd the Earth to have been
liable to, muſt needs be allow'd to have affected the
Moon alſo ; and ſeeing from them the Impurities
and Commotions of our Atmoſphere appear to
have been deriv'd, it ſeems at firſt View neceſſary
that the Moon ſhould have acquir'd ſuch a groſs
Atmoſphere, ſuch Clouds and Meteors as we ſaw
the Earth did at the ſame time ; which looks
very unlike to her *Phænomena,* or the latter Part
of this Propoſition we are now upon. But this
Difficulty which at firſt ſight ſeems ſo formida-
ble, will intirely vaniſh if we obſerve the then
Poſition of the Moon, and thence conſider
which Hemiſphere would be affected therewith.

Coral. 5.
Schol.
poſt Hy-
poth. 12.
priùs.
For (as we before in Part obſerv'd) the Moon
wanted but two or three Days of the New,
when ſhe with the Earth paſs'd the ſecond time
thro' the Tail of the Comet ; and by Conſequence the Vapours aſcending from the Sun fell
pretty exactly upon that Hemiſphere of the
Moon, which is never expos'd to the Earth ; without Affecting that which we can obſerve, and
with which we are alone concern'd. In a Word,
in this ſecond Paſſage, the Moon ought to have
acquir'd a groſs Atmoſphere on the oppoſite Hemiſphere and its bordering Parts, the Limb of
her Body, while the viſible Hemiſphere retain-
ed its ancient Purity and Clearneſs : The latter
Part of which is known to be true ; and if
Bp. *Wilk.*
New
World.
Lib. 1.
Prop. 10.
the Reader conſults the Right Reverend and
Learned Author quoted in the Margent, he
may ſee reaſon to eſteem the other very probable
alſo ; which is, I think, abundantly ſufficient
to clear this Matter.

LXXXIX.

requisite conditions for a general Conflagration would be the consequents of this Passage of the ascending Comet, is plain and evident: For (1.) on the Approach of the Comet, a vast Tide would arise in the great Abyss; and by the new, more considerable, and more violent Elevations thereof into the Protuberances, and the *Sphæroid* Surface of the whole, the old *Fissures* and Breaches would be open'd again, and not a few new ones generated; not only, as at the Deluge, in the Mountainous or more loose Columns, extant above the Surface of the Waters of the Globe; but in all Parts, and under the Seas and Ocean, as well as in other places; which *Fissures* must immediately swallow up the main Mass or Bulk of the Waters upon the Face of the Ground, and send 'em to their Fellow-Waters in the Bowels of the Earth; which was the first and principal ftep towards a general Conflagration. And then (2.) the Vapours acquir'd from the Comet's Atmosphere, which at the Deluge were, by reason of their long absence from the Sun in the remote Regions beyond *Saturn*, pretty cool; at this time must be suppos'd, by reason of their so late and near approach to the Sun about the *Perihelion*, exceeding hot and burning; and that to so extraordinary a degree, that nothing but the *Idea* of the Mouth of a *Volcano*, just belching out immense quantities of liquid and burning Streams, or Torrents of fiery Matter, can in any measure be suitable to the Violence thereof. Imagine, therefore, the Earth to pass through the very middle of this Atmosphere, for 7000 or 8000 Miles together, and to bear off with it a *Cylindrical* Column

the cof,

LXXXIX. Since the Deluge there neither has been, nor will be any great and general Changes in the State of the World, till the time when a Period is to be put to the prefent Courfe of Nature.

LXXXIX. Seeing we know no other Natural Caufes that can produce any great and general Changes in our Sublunary World, but fuch Bodies as can approach to the Earth, or, in other Words, but Comets; and feeing withal, the next Approach of the Comet, will, in probability, bring the prefent State of things to a Conclufion, and *Burn* the World; of which prefently: 'Tis evident the Earth is fecure enough all the intermediate fpace: And as hitherto we accordingly find it has been, fo we need not fear but it will be, preferv'd till the foremention'd *Conflagration.*

CHAP.

CHAP. V.

Phænomena *relating to the* General Conflagration: *with* Conjectures *pertaining to the same; and to the succeeding Period, till the* Consummation *of all things.*

XC. **A**S the World once perish'd by *Water*, so it must by *Fire* at the Conclusion of its present State.

XC. As we have given an Account of the *Universal Deluge* from the Approach of a Comet in its descent towards the Sun; so will it not be difficult to account for the *General Conflagration* from the like Approach of a Comet in its ascent from the Sun. For 'tis evident from what has been already explain'd, that in case a Comet pass'd behind the Earth, tho' it were in its Descent, yet if it came near enough, and were it self big enough, it wou'd so much retard the Earth's annual Motion, and oblige it to revolve in an *Ellipsis* so near to the Sun in its *Perihelion*, that the Sun it self wou'd scorch and burn, dissolve and destroy it in the most prodigious degree; and this Combustion being renew'd every Revolution, wou'd render the Earth a perfect *Chaos* again, and change it from a Planet to a Comet for ever after. 'Tis evident *this* is a sufficient cause of a general Conflagration with a Witness; and

and such an one as wou'd inti
Make of the present, and the p
future World. On which last a
allow the following *Phænomena*,
introduce *this*, at this Period h
see whether a Conflagration of
ctive, and more refining Nature,
expected, and may not be account
here let it be observ'd, that the
of it self seems sufficient to burn
solve the upper Earth, (as thos
Dr. *Woodward*, know the Power an
of the same now, and its aston
and terrible Effects in Earthquak
of *Volcano's*, and other *Phænomena* o
ture, ought to allow) if thes
were by any means remov'd; I n
ters of the Seas and Ocean, and
of the Air: For 'tis the vast qua
ters of the Earth, and the Col
middle Region of the Air every wh
whole Air in the Frigid *Zones*, 1
Vapours *cold down* again, which
into 'em never so *hot*, which fe
prevent the effects of the Subterra
and to hinder the Conflagration o
If therefore the passing by of a C
pable of emptying the Seas and
of rendring the Air, and its cond
Surface of the Earth extreamly
flam'd, no more, I suppose, will
to a general Conflagration: Or i
Assistance be afforded by the Pre
Comet, it will be *ex abundanti*, an
tribute still the more certainly, an
suddenly, to kindle such a fatal i
dreadful a Combustion. Now that

H h

thereof, whose *Bafis* were somewhat larger than a great Circle on the Earth, and whose Altitude were the Number of Miles juft now mention'd; and then tell me whether the Air, and its adjoining uppermoft Region of the Earth, will not be fufficiently hot and fcorching; which was the other Step to the general Conflagration. Befides all which, what quantities of this fiery Exhalation, or Torrent of melted liquid Matter wou'd run down the *Fiffures* into the Bowels of the Earth, and by joining with the central hot Steams already there, invigorate them, and accelerate the direful Inflammation; and what piercing and fcorching fiery Corpufcles the central Body it felf during its vicinity, wou'd alfo fend out; and what an additional Power wou'd thereby be afforded the prevailing Heat, I need not fay. Upon the whole, I may appeal to the Reader, if the concurrence of all thefe external Caufes, to fay nothing here of any internal Difpofitions in the Earth it felf thereto, do not appear abundantly fufficient within a little time to fet the World on Fire, and bring on that terrible Conflagration which both Sacred and Profane Teftimonies confpire to forewarn us of; and fo whether the *Theory of Comets* does not afford us almoft as commenfurate and compleat an Account of the *laft burning*, as it already has done of the *ancient drowning* of the Earth.

XCI. The fame Caufes which will fet the World on Fire, will alfo caufe great and dreadful Tides in the Seas and Ocean; with no lefs Agitations, Concuffions, and Earthquakes in the Air and Earth.

XCI. Seeing the Eruption of the central
Heat, (the caufe, 'tis probable, of all our
Earthquakes) the prefence of a Comet, (the
caufe once already of the moft prodigious Tides
that ever were) and the enflam'd *Chaos*, or
fcorch'd Atmofphere of the Comet, (a fmaller part of which occafion'd all our Tempefts,
our Meteors, our Thunder and Lightning ever
fince the Deluge) will all concur at once,
ard with joint Forces confpire together; nothing in the World can be fuppos'd more terrible, nor more exactly correfpondent to the
Phænomenon before us.

XCII. The Atmofphere of the Earth, before the Conflagration begin, will be opprefs'd with Meteors,
Exhalations, and Steams ; and thefe in fo dreadful a
manner, in fuch prodigious quantities, and with
fuch wild confufed Motions and Agitations, that
the Sun and Moon will have the moft frightful
and hideous Countenances, and their ancient Splen-
dor will be intirely obfcur'd : The Stars will feem
to fall from Heaven ; and all manner of horrid Reprefentations will terrifie the Inhabitants of the
Earth.

XCII. Thofe who confider how a Comets
Atmofphere appears to us after its *Perihelion*,
and what large quantities of its newly fcorch'd
Maffes our Air muft be clog'd and burthen'd
withal, will expect no other effects than thofe
here mention'd; and will eafily believe that all
fuch horrible Appearances wou'd enfue , and
that in the moft amazing Degree, and extravagant Inftances poffible. The *Theorift's* Reprefentation of this Matter will be, generally fpeaking, but a fair and juft *Idea* thereof.

Theor
l. 3 c. 11

XCIII.

LXXXIX. Since the Deluge there neither has been, nor will be any great and general Changes in the State of the World , till the time when a Period is to be put to the prefent Courfe of Nature.

LXXXIX. Seeing we know no other Natural Caufes that can produce any great and general Changes in our Sublunary World, but fuch Bodies as can approach to the Earth, or, in other Words, but Comets; and feeing withal, the next Approach of the Comet, will, in probability, bring the prefent State of things to a Conclufion , and *Burn* the World ; of which prefently : 'Tis evident the Earth is fecure enough all the intermediate fpace : And as hitherto we accordingly find it has been, fo we need not fear but it will be, preferv'd till the foremention'd *Conflagration.*

CHAP.

C H A P. V.

Phænomena *relating to the* General Conflagration: *with* Conjectures *pertaining to the same; and to the succeeding* Period , *till the* Consummation *of all things.*

XC. **A**S the World once perish'd by *Water*, so it must by *Fire* at the Conclusion of its present State.

XC. As we have given an Account of the *Universal Deluge* from the Approach of a Comet in its descent towards the Sun; so will it not be difficult to account for the *General Conflagration* from the like Approach of a Comet in its ascent from the Sun. For 'tis evident from what has been already explain'd, that in case a Comet pass'd behind the Earth, tho' it were in its Descent, yet if it came near enough, and were it self big enough, it wou'd so much retard the Earth's annual Motion, and oblige it to revolve in an *Ellipsis* so near to the Sun in its *Perihelion*, that the Sun it self wou'd scorch and burn, dissolve and destroy it in the most prodigious degree; and this Combustion being renew'd every Revolution, wou'd render the Earth a perfect *Chaos* again, and change it from a Planet to a Comet for ever after. 'Tis evident *this* is a sufficient cause of a general Conflagration with a Witness;
and

and such an one as wou'd intirely ruine the
Make of the present, and the poſſibility of a
future World. On which laſt account, if we
allow the following *Phænomena*, we muſt not
introduce *this*, at this Period however; but
ſee whether a Conflagration of a leſs deſtructive, and more refining Nature, be not to be
expected, and may not be accounted for. And
here let it be obſerv'd, that the Central Heat
of it ſelf ſeems ſufficient to burn up, and dif-
ſolve the upper Earth, (as thoſe who, with
Dr. *Woodward*, know the Power and Vehemence
of the ſame now, and its aſtoniſhing Force,
and terrible Effects in Earthquakes, Eruptions
of *Volcano's*, and other *Phænomena* of preſent Nature, ought to allow) if theſe two things
were by any means remov'd; I mean the *Waters* of the Seas and Ocean, and the *Coldneſs*
of the Air: For 'tis the vaſt quantity of Waters of the Earth, and the Coldneſs of the
middle Region of the Air every where, and of the
whole Air in the Frigid *Zones*, returning the
Vapours *cold down* again, which were ſent *up*
into 'em never ſo *hot*, which ſeems ſtill to
prevent the effects of the Subterraneous Heat,
and to hinder the Conflagration of the Earth.
If therefore the paſſing by of a Comet be capable of emptying the Seas and Ocean, and
of rendring the Air, and its contiguous upper
Surface of the Earth extreamly hot and in-
flam'd, no more, I ſuppoſe, will be neceſſary
to a general Conflagration: Or if any more
Aſſiſtance be afforded by the Preſence of the
Comet, it will be *ex abundanti*, and only contribute ſtill the more certainly, and the more
ſuddenly, to kindle ſuch a fatal Fire, and ſo
dreadful a Combuſtion. Now that both thoſe

requiſite

requisite conditions for a general Conflagration wou'd be the confequents of this Passage of the afcending Comet, is plain and evident: For (1.) on the Approach of the Comet, a vaſt Tide wou'd arife in the great Abyſs; and by the new, more confiderable, and more violent Elevations thereof into the Protuberances, and the *Sphæroid* Surface of the whole, the old *Fiſſures* and Breaches wou'd be open'd again, and not a few new ones generated; not only, as at the Deluge, in the Mountainous or mo e loofe Columns, extant above the Surface of the Waters of the Globe; but in all Parts, and under the Seas and Ocean, as well as in other places; which *Fiſſures* muſt immediately fwallow up the main Mafs or Bulk of the Waters upon the Face of the Ground, and fend 'em to their Fellow-Waters in the Bowels of the Earth; which was the firſt and principal ſtep towards a general Conflagration. And then (2.) the Vapours acquir'd from the Comet's Atmofphere, which at the Deluge were, by reafon of their long abfence from the Sun in the remote Regions beyond *Saturn*, pretty cool; at this time muſt be fuppos'd, by reafon of their fo late and near approach to the Sun about the *Perihelion*, exceeding hot and burning; and that to fo extraordinary a degree, that nothing but the *Idea* of the Mouth of a *Volcano*, juſt belching out immenfe quantities of liquid and burning Streams, or Torrents of fiery Matter, can in any meafure be fuitable to the Violence thereof. Imagine, therefore, the Earth to pafs through the very middle of this Atmofphere, for 7000 or 8000 Miles together, and to bear off with it a *Cylindrical* Column the cof, thereof, whofe *Bafis* were fomewhat larger than a great Circle on the Earth, and whofe Altitude were the Number of Miles juft now mention'd; and then tell me whether the Air, and its adjoining uppermoft Region of the Earth, will not be fufficiently hot and fcorching; which was the other Step to the general Conflagration. Befides all which, what quantities of this fiery Exhalation, or Torrent of melted liquid Matter wou'd run down the *Fiffures* into the Bowels of the Earth, and by joining with the central hot Steams already there, invigorate them, and accelerate the direful Inflammation; and what piercing and fcorching fiery Corpufcles the central Body it felf during its vicinity, wou'd alfo fend out; and what an additional Power wou'd thereby be afforded the prevailing Heat, I need not fay. Upon the whole, I may appeal to the Reader, if the concurrence of all thefe external Caufes, to fay nothing here of any internal Difpofitions in the Earth it felf thereto, do not appear abundantly fufficient within a little time to fet the World on Fire, and bring on that terrible Conflagration which both Sacred and Profane Teftimonies confpire to forewarn us of; and fo whether the *Theory of Comets* does not afford us almoft as commenfurate and compleat an Account of the *laft burning*, as it already has done of the *ancient drowning* of the Earth.

XCI. The fame Caufes which will fet the World on Fire, will alfo caufe great and dreadful Tides in the Seas and Ocean; with no lefs Agitations, Concuffions, and Earthquakes in the Air and Earth.

XCI. Seeing the Eruption of the central Heat, (the caufe, 'tis probable, of all our Earthquakes) the prefence of a Comet, (the caufe once already of the moft prodigious Tides that ever were) and the enflam'd *Chaos*, or fcorch'd Atmofphere of the Comet, (a fmaller part of which occafion'd all our Tempefts, our Meteors, our Thunder and Lightning ever fince the Deluge) will all concur at once, and with joint Forces confpire together; nothing in the World can be fuppos'd more terrible, nor more exactly correfpondent to the *Phænomenon* before us.

> XCII. The Atmofphere of the Earth, before the Con-
> flagration begin, will be oppreſs'd with Meteors,
> Exhalations, and Steams; and thefe in fo dreadful a
> manner, in fuch prodigious quantities, and with
> fuch wi'd confuſed Motions and Agitations, that
> the Sun and Moon will have the moft frightful
> and hideous Countenances, and their ancient Splen-
> dor will be intirely obfcur'd: The Stars will feem
> to fall from Heaven; and all manner of horrid Re-
> prefentations will terrifie the Inhabitants of the
> Earth.

XCII. Thofe who confider how a Comet's Atmofphere appears to us after its *Perihelion*, and what large quantities of its newly fcorch'd Maſſes our Air muft be clog'd and burthen'd withal, will expect no other effects than thofe here mention'd; and will eafily believe that all fuch horrible Appearances wou'd enfue, and that in the moft amazing Degree, and extravagant Inftances poffible. The *Theorift*'s Reprefentation of this Matter will be, generally fpeaking, but a fair and juft *Idea* thereof.

Theor
l. 3. c. 11

XCIII.

XCIII. The Deluge and Conflagration are referr'd by ancient Tradition to great Conjunctions of the Heavenly Bodies, as both depending on, and happening at the fame.

XCIII. In our Accounts of the Deluge and Conflagration, there is a *notable* conjunction of the Heavenly Bodies indeed; not fuch an Imaginary one as the *Aftrologers* fo ridiculoufly make a ftir about; the bare Pofition of two or more of the Celeftial Bodies in or near the fame ftreight Line, from the Eye of the Spectator, while they are at the moft remote Diftances from one another; which is a poor jejune thing indeed: But a real one with a Witnefs; when three of the Heavenly Bodies, the Earth, the Moon, and the Comet, not only are in an Aftrological *Heliocentrick* Conjunction, or only feem to an Eye in the Sun to be conjoyn'd together, but are really fo near as to have the mightyeft effects and Influences on one another poffible; which we have fufficiently fhewn in the prefent *Theory*, and which does peculiarly correfpond to the *Phænomenon* before us.

Corollary. 'Tis not *improbable but the ancient Tradition, that the Deluge and Conflagration fome way depended on certain remarkable Conjunctions of the Heavenly Bodies, mif-underftood, and afterward precarioufly and widely mif-apply'd, might give occafion and rife to* Aftrology; *or that mighty quoil and pother fo many in all ages have made about the* Conjunctions, Oppofitions, *and* Afpects *of the Heavenly Bodies, and the* Judiciary *predictions therefrom; which even the Improvements of folid Philofophy in our Age have not been able yet to banifh wholly from among us; the occafion whereof is otherwife exceeding dark and unaccountable.*

XCIV.

XCIV. The fpace between the Deluge and the Conflagration ; or between the ancient State of the
Earth and its Purgation by Fire, Renovation, and
Reftitution again, is from ancient Tradition defin'd
and terminated by a certain great and remarkable
Year, or *Annual* Revolution of fome of the Heavenly
Bodies ; and is in probability what the Ancients
fo often referr'd to, pretended particularly to determine, and call'd the *Great* or *Platonick* Year.

XCIV. If we allow, as we ought, that in
all probability the fame Comet that brought
on the Deluge will bring on the Conflagration ; and that the fame Comet has not return'd, nor is to return, till the Conflagration; this matter is eafie, and the correfpondence accurate and remarkable : For this fingle
Revolution is truly an *Annual* one, and as proper a Year with regard to the Comet, as that
of our Earth is with refpect to us ; and fo
may moft juftly and naturally fuit the *Great* or
Platonick Year, taken notice of in the Propofition before us.

XCV. This general Conflagration is not to extend to
the future Annihilation or Deftruction of the Earth ;
but only to the Alteration, Melioration, and peculiar Difpofition thereof into a new State, proper to
receive the fame Saints and Martyrs for its Inhabitants,
who are of the firft Refurrection to enter, and to live
and reign a thoufand Years upon it, till the fecond
Refurrection, the general Judgment, and the final
Confummation of all things.

Lava, or
our Ha-
rel, place. XCVI. Seeing the *Abyfs* confifts of a denfe
and compact *Fluid*, not capable of any Rarefaction or Diffolution by the moft violent Heat
imaginable, 'tis evident that the caufes here affign'd can only extend to the upper Orb, or
habitable Earth, without any farther Progrefs.

So

So that the effect of this Conflagration will be the reduction of this upper Earth, and its Atmosphere, into a confus'd, mixt, and *Chaotick* State; much such an one as was before obferv'd to have preceded the Original Formation of it. So that as the Heat decreafes, 'tis but reafonable to expect a kind of Reiteration of the *Mofaick* fix Days Creation, or a Renovation of the Primitive State of the Earth; to the Defcription of which therefore I muft refer the Reader.

XCVI. The State of Nature duing this *Millennium* will be very different from that at prefent, and more agreeable to the *Antediluvian, Primitive*, and *Paradifiacal* ones.

XCVI. This is apparent from the conclufion of the former *Solution*.

XCVII. The Earth in the *Millennium* will be without a Sea, or an large Receptacle fill'd with mighty Collections and Quantities of Water.

XCVII. The Primitive Seas depended on two things; the former, the concurrence of the Central and Solar Heat for an intire half Year together, in the Elevation of fufficient quantities of Vapours: The latter, the Earth's contiderable folidity attain'd before the defcent of the fame Vapours which were to compofe the Seas, of which we are fpeaking: So that if either of thefe be wanting in this reiterated Formation of the Earth, tis evident the Effect muft fail, and the *Globe* be no longer a *Terraqueous* one after the Conflagration. Now the next Propofition but one, afferting the probability of the intire abfence of the Sun, muft infer

Solut. 6. & 7. prius.

H h 4 an

an equal probability of the entire Abfence of Seas alfo, accoiding as this Propofition afferts.

XCVIII The Earth in the *Millennium* will have no Succeffion of Light and Darknefs, Day and Night; but a perpetual Day.

XCVIII. In cafe the Earth's *Diurnal Rotation*, upon which thefe Viciffitudes depend, was retarded fo as to be only exactly equal and commenfurate to its *Annual Motion*, (as the cafe in the *Moon's Diurnal* and *Menftrual* Revolutions is at prefent, as we have before obferv'd) the Earth wou'd conftantly expofe the fame Hemifphere to the Sun, (as the Moon does now to the Earth) and all fucceffion of Day and Night for ever ceafe; the one half of the Globe enjoying a perpetual Day, while the other was involv'd in Darknefs, or excluded all advantages from him, and thereby enduring a continual Night, fo far as natural Caufes are here to be confider'd. And that this Retardation of the Earth's *Diurnal Rotation* (even without a recurring to the miraculous Power of its firft Author) is accountable from that paffing by of a Comet, which we affign for the occafion of the Conflagration, is very eafe and obvious: For in cafe its Afcent and Paffage by be on the Laft fide, or before the Earth; and in cafe it approach fo near as to rub againft it, 'tis evident fuch an Impulfe is contrary to the courfe of the *Diurnal Rotation*, and is therefore capable (the Proportions of every thing being adjufted by Divine Providence) of putting fuch a ftop to the fame as is neceffary to the prefent *Phænomenon*, and fo may put a Period to that conftant Succeffion of Light and Dark-

Lem. 33. prius.

Darkness, Day and Night, which has obtain'd
ever since the Fall of Man; and withal distinguish the Surface of the Earth into two quite different and contrary Hemispheres; near the *Vertex* of one of which the Sun it self, and
near that of the other, its opposite Point in the
Heavens, will be always situate.

Corollary. *Seeing such a rub of the Comet wou'd
affect the* Annual Motion *of the Earth as well as
the* Diurnal, *'tis possible it might retard the former as well as the latter, and reduce the* Elliptical
Course *and Orbit of the Earth, to its ancient Circular
one again.*

> XCIX. The State of the *Millennium* will not stand in
> need of, and so probably will be without, the Light
> and Presence of the *Sun* and *Moon.*

XCIX. Seeing the Earth wou'd be on the foregoing Supposition distinguish'd into two quite
different Hemispheres, the one of which wou'd
be wholly destitute of the Light and presence of the *Sun,* and, as far as appears by
St. *John,* supply'd by a Supernatural Light, fixt
and permanent above its *Horizon,* 'tis clear that
the first Branch of this Proposition is accountable thereby, as far as this Physical *Theory* is
concern'd therein. And as to the *Moon,* seeing 'twas only a signal and peculiar Providence
that caus'd her equal acceleration, and consequent
accompanying the Earth at the former passing
by of the Comet; and that no such Providence
is again to be expected; 'tis evident that that
Rub or Stoppage of the *Earth's Annual Motion,*
which retards the same, and does not retard
the *Moon's* also, will separate these Planets,
and procure their Orbits, Courses, and Periods to be quite different from one another's
ever

ever after ; according to the greateſt rigour of
the preſent Propoſition.

> C. At the Concluſion of the *Millennium* , the *Final
> Judgment*, and the *Conſummation* of all things, the
> Earth will deſert its preſent Seat and Station in
> the World, and be no longer found among the
> *Planetary Chorus.*

C. If any Comet inſtead of paſſing by, or
gently rubbing the Earth, hit directly againſt
it, in its Courſe either towards or from the
Sun, it muſt deſert its ancient Station , and
move in a quite different *Elliptick* Orbit ; and
ſo of a Planet become again a Comet, for the
future Ages of the World.

COROLLARIES

FROM THE

WHOLE.

I. SEing the *new and ſolid Improvements of Philoſophy do all along give ſo rational Accounts
of thoſe Ancient* Theorems, *which have been propagated down from the eldeſt Ages, without being then
either underſtood, or intelligible to their Propagators ;
'tis reaſonable to truſt and rely on ſuch* Ancient
Traditions, *not only Sacred, but prophane alſo, in
theſe or any other parallel Caſes ; they being in all
probability the moſt valuable Remains, and moſt venerable*

nerable *Truths which the primitive Parents of the World deliver'd down to their Posterity in succeeding Generations.*

II. *Seeing most of these Ancient* Theorems *are very much beyond the distinct Knowledge of those who deliver them; contrary to the common Opinion of Mankind, judging usually by sensible Appearances; and in themselves, considering the low State of Natural Knowledge at the same times, were highly improbable, if not utterly incredible to inquisitive Minds: and indeed several of them relating to the* Chaos, *the* Creation, *the* primary Constitution and State of *the* World, *and the* Deluge *it self, impossible to be discover'd without Supernatural Revelation; and yet seeing, after all, they do now appear as agreeable to Reason, and the most solid Mechanical Philosophy, as any new Discoveries, built on the exactest Observations of present Nature whatsoever;* 'Tis apparent that these Ancient Accounts, *especially those contain'd in the* Holy Scriptures, *were not originally deriv'd from the Natural Skill and Observation of the first Authors, or any other meerly Humane Means, but from the immediate and Supernatural Revelation of God Almighty; who was therefore much more conversant with Mankind in the first, than he has been in these last Ages of the* World; *as the* Old Testament-History *assures us.*

III. *The Measure of our present Knowledge ought not to be esteem'd the* Κριτήριον *or Test of Truth; or to be oppos'd to the Accounts receiv'd from Profane Antiquity, much less to the inspir'd Writings. For notwithstanding that several Particulars relating to the Eldest Condition of the World, and its great* Catastrophe's, *examin'd and compar'd with so much*
Phi-

Philosophy as was till lately known, were plainly un-accountable, and, naturally speaking, impossible; yet we see, now Nature is more fully, more certainly, and more substantially understood, that the same things approve themselves to be plain, easie, and rational.

IV. *'Tis therefore Folly in the highest degree, to reject the Truth, or Divine Authority of the Holy Scriptures, because we cannot give our Minds particular Satisfaction as to the* manner, *nay or even* possibility *of some things therein asserted. Since we have seen so many of those things which seem'd the most incredible in the whole Bible, and gave the greatest Scruple and Scandal to* Philosophick *Minds, so fully and particularly attested, and next to demonstrated from certain Principles of* Astronomy *and* Natural Knowledge; *'tis but reasonable to expect, in due time, a like Solution of the other Difficulties. 'Tis but just sure to depend upon the* Veracity *of those Holy Writers in other Assertions, whose* Fidelity *is so intirely established in these hitherto equally unaccountable ones.*

V. *The* Obvious, Plain, *or* Literal Sense *of the Sacred Scriptures, ought not, without great Reason, to be eluded or laid aside: Several of those very Places which seem'd very much to require the same hitherto, appearing now to the minutest Circumstances, true and rational, according to the strictest and most Literal Interpretations of them.*

VI. *We may be under an Obligation to believe such things on the Authority of the Holy Scriptures, as are properly* Mysteries; *that is, though not really Contradictory, yet plainly Unaccountable to our*

(pre-

(prefent degree of) *Knowledge and Reafon. Thus
the Sacred Hiftories of the* Original Conftitution, *and great* Cataftrophe's *of the World have
been in the paft Ages the Objects of the Faith of* Jews
and Chriftians, *though the Divine Providence had
not afforded fo much Light as that they cou'd o-
otherwife fatisfie themfelves in the Credibility of
them, till the new Improvements in* Philofophy.
*And this is but juft and reafonable; for fure the
Ignorance or Incapacity of the Creature does by no
means afford fufficient Ground for Incredulity, or
juftifie Men in their rejecting Divine Revelation,
and impeaching the Veracity or Providence of the
Creator.*

VII. *Seeing the Natural and the Moral World
are alike fubject to the Divine Providence, and
that the fame Author has indited thofe Writings
which relate to both; the Difcovery of the* Verity
*of the Holy Scriptures in the moft difficult Points
relating to the* one, *ought to make us entirely fecure of the like* Verity *of the fame Scriptures relating to the* other, *notwithftanding any Difficulties ftill remaining about 'em : As the wife, proportionate, and Harmonious Order and Regularity of the*
Natural *World, where no Freedom of the Creature Interpofes, and gives any occafion for Diforder, juftly obliges us to believe the moft wife and
equal Methods of Providence to be equally exercis'd about the* Moral *one alfo; although the In-
tricacies arifing from the abufe of the Liberty of
Will in Rational Creatures, render them hitherto
more obfcure to us in the latter Cafe than in the
former : So certainly the Eftablifhment of the* Verity *of the Scriptures in the moft harfh and difficult Affertions touching the* Natural *World, (the
proper Cafe in which the Improvement of Philofophy*

was

was likely to afford means for our Determination)
ought to assure us of the like Verity of the same Scriptures in the other Points, more peculiarly the Subjects of Divine Revelation, less capable of affording any other means of Satisfaction, and yet more directly the Design, Scope, and Drift of the Sacred Writers, and the Concern of Divine Providence than the other.

Τῷ δὲ Βασιλεῖ τῶν Αἰώνων Ἀφθάρτῳ, Ἀοράτῳ, Μόνῳ Σοφῷ Θεῷ Τιμὴ καὶ Δόξα εἰς τὰς Αἰῶνας τῶν Αἰώνων. ΑΜΗΝ.

A POST-

A

POSTSCRIPT.

SINCE the finishing of the fore-going *Theory*, I met, a few Days since, with a very good Book just publish'd, call'd, *A Conference with a Theist*; By the Reverend and Learned Dr. *Nichols*; wherein I found him making considerable use of an *Essay* of Sir *William Petty's*, concerning the *Multiplication of Mankind*, and the *Growth of the City of London*; and perceiving thence that *Learned Gentleman* to have there made use of 360 Years, as the Mean or equal Standard for the doubling of Mankind in the present Age; when I had, by Mistake, pitch'd upon 280, from a Book which 'tis suppos'd the same *author* was concern'd in before. I hereupon procur'd this latter Book it self, and set my self to the consideration thereof, and particularly as to what more immediately concern'd my self, and those Calculations I had superstructed upon a somewhat different *Hypothesis*. By which means I found that this last, and therefore more Authentick *Essay* had not only on very good Grounds fixt 360 Years for the ordinary middle rate of the doubling Mankind with us atprefent, but had withal remark'd such very different Extreams on either hand sometimes obsetv'd, and still more different ones very

ry

ry poffible to be obferv'd in the World, as gave great Light to feveral things contain'd in the Holy Scriptures, and particularly to fome, infifted on in the foregoing *Theory*, and fo was very well worthy of a careful Confideration. Thus it has feem'd very ftrange to fome, that in 215 Years, the ╌ Perfons defcended of *Jacob* fhou'd amount to fo many as by the Calculation above has been made appear they really did. But now if we confider what Sir *William Petty* proves, that the increafe of Mankind has been actually from 120 to 1200 Years in doubling; and may fairly be from 10 to 1200, according to the prefent Obfervations; and withal confider that the Lives of Men *then*, generally fpeaking, were more than fix times as long as the middle duration of ours *now*; and fo on account of more numerous Pofterity, and Co-exiftence, there is to be about eighteen times as many as the fame Number, at the fame Rate of Propagation, wou'd produce with us: If, I fay, we confider thefe things, we fhall be foon fatisfy'd with the Sacred Hiftory in this otherwife furprizing Narration, and not at all think it ftrange that the Children of *Ifrael* doubl'd themfelves in fourteen Years, till the *Exodus* out of *Ægypt*, or the After-Reduction of the Period of Human Life, to the prefent Standard, before their Entrance into the Land of *Canaan*, feeing 'tis not fo incredible as the doubling of any Family or Nation in twenty Years now with us wou'd appear to be; which no one can fay to be otherwife than very reafonable, and what does not unfrequently happen in thefe latter Ages of the World, for many Generations together. But what is more to my prefent purpofe, and the main Occafion of this

Poft-

Ibid.

Phænom. 33. cum 70 prius.

Poſtſcript (beſides the rectifying my own miſtakes, and that ſmall difference which it has occaſion'd in my Calculations, which the Candid
Reader will eaſily pardon and amend) is an Obſervation I have made on occaſion of my lighting upon this laſt *Eſſay* of Sir *William Petty*,
whereby at once this Matter, of the Multiplication of Mankind in the paſt Ages, may be in
good meaſure determin'd; and Sir *William's* miſtake touching the different Proportions thereof
in the different Periods of the World ſince
Moſes's time, may be corrected, to the great Illu-
ſtration of the Sacred, as well as Prophane Accounts of the ancient Ages of the World. And
the Obſervation is this, That Mankind, as far
as we have means of enquiry, have generally
ſpeaking increaſed in one and the ſame given
Proportion, and doubled themſelves in 360
Years in all the paſt Ages of the World, ſince
the fixing of the preſent Period of Humane
Life. The truth of which Obſervation I thus
prove. 'Tis evident that the moſt ancient Age
of the World, capable of being compar'd with
the preſent, was that of *Moſes*, when the
Lives of Men were reduc'd to Seventy or Eighty
Years, their preſent Standard; and that therefore the ſucceding Period of Four hundred and
ſeventy nine Years, from the *Exodus* out of *Egypt*,
till the building of *Solomon's* Temple, was the
firſt conſiderable enough for our preſent purpoſe. 'Tis alſo evident, That the Hiſtory of
the *Jews*, or the Sacred Hiſtory, is the only
one *ancient* enough, and *certain* enough to be
introduc'd, and depended on in the preſent caſe.
Nay, indeed, 'tis evident that the *Jews* from
their Union together, and their Diſtinction

*Vid. Phæ-
nom. 33,
cum 70,
priùs.*

I i   from

from the neighbour Nations, as well as the accuracy of their Genealogies and Numbers frequently recorded in Scripture, are alone capable of affording any full and uncontefted inftances of this Matter. 'Tis, laftly, evident in particular, That the numbers of the Children of *Ifrael* were exactly taken, and are as exactly recorded at the beginning, and a little before the end of the foremention'd Period, as we fhall fee prefently. So that we have here the faireft opportunity poffible of clearing this matter, and of comparing the moft ancient, with the lateft increafe of Mankind; the doing of which will eftablifh the truth of that Obfervation I am now upon, beyond reafonable contradiction; which I thus attempt. At the

Exod. xii. 37. Numb. i. 1, 2, 18, 20, 45, 46, 47, 49.

Exodus of the Children of *Ifrael* out of *Egypt*, the number of the *men on foot, befides children, was* about *fix hundred thoufand*. More exactly, a little above a year afterwards, the number of the Males of *Ifrael above twenty years old, all that were able to go forth to war*, were (befides the *Levites*) Six hundred and three thoufand, five hundred and fifty. Now the number of the years between thefe Accounts of the People, and that towards the Conclufion of the Reign of *David*, was about 472 or 473, as Chronologers very well know. Say then, by the Golden Rule, if 360 Years double the People, or produce 1200000, how many, by a proportionable increafe, will 473 Years produce? The Product whereof is 1576666; which therefore, according to the foremention'd rate, ought to be the number of the *Ifraelites* at the time when *David* numbred them 473 Years afterwards. Now the number of the *Ifraelites* taken by *Joab* was exprefly

exprefly *eight hundred thoufand valiant men that*   2 Sam.
drew the Sword. Befides which, there were   xxiv. 9.
twelve Companies of 24000 men a-piece, already numbred and enroll'd, to wait by Turns
on the King in the twelve Months of the Year: 1 Chron.
Which are 288000. So that the Total of the   xxvii. 1.
Men of *All Ifreal* was 1088000, or, in a round
number, 1100000 *Men*, as 'tis exprefly in the
Book of *Chronicles.* To which add the Men of   1 Chron.
Judah 470000. or, including, as ufual, the   xxi. 5.
fmall Tribe of *Benjamin*, (which, befides *Levi*,   Ibid.
came not into the former Sum:) about 500000.
according to the exprefs words of the Book of
Samuel. And fo at laft the *Total* Sum is 1600000,   2 Sam.
or more nicely 1588000, which is wonderfully   xxiv. 9.
near the former fum of 15-6666 produc'd by the
Arithmetical Calculation above, and highly worthy of our regard and admiration. 'Tis true, the
Ifraelites rather decreas'd in the Wildernefs; and
at the end of the firft thirty eight or thirty nine
years, (by reafon of the cutting off the intire   Numb.
murmuring Generation e're the youngeft of   xxvi. 51,
them were fifty nine years old) were not quite   64,65.
fo many as at the time of their firft numbring
when they came out of *Egypt.* But then as
this will be an excepted cafe, and the remaining 434 years within a fmall matter will ftil anfwer the affigned Proportion; fo indeed this
deftruction was not greater than ought to be
fuppos'd oft-times to happen; and fuch as both
has formerly, and does at this day frequently
happen in the World; on the allowance of
which, the Period of 360 Years was determined : And therefore ought not to be diftinctly
confider'd in the prefent cafe. We may therefore, upon the whole matter, very reafonably

     deter-

determine, that, excepting what disturbance extraordinary and uncommon Wars, Famines, Plagues, and such other Merciless destroyers of Mankind have given thereto, Mankind have generally increas'd in the same determinate Proportion, and doubled themselves in three hunderd and sixty years, for more than three thousand years, from the Time of *Moses*, till the present Age; as was to be prov'd. Which Observation thus establish'd, what Light it might afford *Ancient History*, and the *Holy Scriptures*, as well as the present *Theory*, 'tis not my business here to enquire: But I shall refer the same to the careful Consideration of the Reader.

FINIS.

Books Printed for Benj. Tooke.

CUr*fus Mathematicus*: Mathematical Sciences in Nine Books : comprehending Arithmetick, Geometry, Cofmogràphy, Aftronomy, Navigation, Trigonometry, with the Defcription, Conftruction and Ufe of Geometrical and Nautical Inftruments, and the Doctrine of Triangles applied to Practice in Menfurations of all Kinds. By *William Leybourn*, Philomath. *Fol.*

Fables of *Æfop*, and other Eminent Mythologifts, with Morals and Reflections. By Sir *Roger L'Eftrange. Fol.*

A Catalogue of Books printed in *England* fince the dreadful Fire of *London* in 1666. to the end of *Michaelmas* Term 1695. With an Abftract of the General Bills of Mortality fince 1660. And the Titles of all the Claffick Authors, *Cum Notis Variorum*, and thofe for the ufe of the *Dauphin. Fol.*

Dioptrica Nova: A Treatife of Dioptricks. In Two Parts. Wherein the various Effects and Appearances of Spherick-Glaffes, both Convex and Concave, Single and Combined in Telefcopes and Microfcopes. Together with their Ufefulnefs in many Concerns of Humane Life, are explained. By *William Molyneux* of *Dublin*, Efq; Fellow of the Royal Society. *Quarto.*

Two Sermons preach'd before the Condemn'd Criminals at *Newgate*, 1695. By *B. Crooke*, M. A. Rector of St. *Michael Woodftreet, London. Quarto.*

A Collection

A Collection of some Papers, writ upon several Occasions, concerning Clipt and Counterfeit Money, and Trade, so far as it relates to the Exportation of Bullion. By Dr. *Hugh Chamberlain.* *Quarto.*

Prælectiones Academicæ in Schola Historices Camdeniana. Auctore Henrico Dodwello. Octavo.

Two Letters written to a Gentleman of Note, guilty of Common Swearing. To which is added a third Letter to another Gentleman in the Commission of the Peace, exciting him to the Performance of his part in executing the late Act against Prophane Cursing and Swearing. *Twelves.*

ERRATA.

Pag. 1. lin. 4. read agreeably. p. 5. l. 11. r. World. p. 7. l. 5. r. are.
p. 10. l. 24. r denotes. p. 24. l. 5. r. had. p. 33. l. 4. r. Phænomena. p. 47. l. 16. r. direct. p. 56. l. 3. r. scarce. p. 77. l. 15. r. receding. p. 89. l. 20. dele and. p. 31. l. 10. r. 1 year 322 days. l. 11.
12 years or more nicely 4332 days. l. 12. 30 years more nicely 10759 days. p. 30. l. 2. r. are. p. 60. 29. at the end add
[will be I suppose] p. 93. l. 22. r. Hypothesis. p. 101. l. 5.
must have been. p. 138. l. 2. r. But if that were as. p. 142. l. 23.
r. months [immediately succeeding one another.] p. 149. l. 10.
r. demonstrate. p. 159. l. 5. r. were. p. 175. l. 2. r. Phænomena.
p. 176. l. penult. marg. r. 107. p. 211. l. 1. r. Atmosphere. p. 221.
l. 23. r. with the course, &c. p. 225. l. 29. r. deem. p. 230. l. 17.
after [and] add [that Account]. p. 231. marg. r. Hypoth. 1.
p. 234. l. 23. r. Hexaemeron. p. 236. l. 17. r. And lightest
Earthy. p. 246, & 252. r. Iæus. p. 252. l. 6. r. nor. p. 290. l. 25.
r. Heat in. p. 300. l. 1. r. Agitations.

History of Geology

An Arno Press Collection

Association of American Geologists and Naturalists. **Reports of the First, Second, and Third Meetings of the Association of American Geologists and Naturalists, at Philadelphia, in 1840 and 1841, and at Boston in 1842. 1843**

Bakewell, Robert. **An Introduction to Geology. 1833**

Buckland, William. **Reliquiae Diluvianae:** Or, Observations on the Organic Remains Contained in Caves, Fissures, and Diluvial Gravel. 1823

Clarke, John M[ason]. **James Hall of Albany:** Geologist and Palaeontologist, 1811-1898. 1923

Cleaveland, Parker. **An Elementary Treatise on Mineralogy and Geology. 1816**

Clinton, DeWitt. **An Introductory Discourse:** Delivered Before the Literary and Philosophical Society of New-York on the Fourth of May, 1814. 1815

Conybeare, W. D. and William Phillips. **Outlines of the Geology of England and Wales. 1822**

Cuvier, [Georges]. **Essay on the Theory of the Earth.** Translated by Robert Kerr. 1817

Davison, Charles. **The Founders of Seismology. 1927**

Gilbert, G[rove] K[arl]. **Report on the Geology of the Henry Mountains. 1877**

Greenough, G[eorge] B[ellas]. **A Critical Examination of the First Principles of Geology. 1819**

Hooke, Robert. **Lectures and Discourses of Earthquakes and Subterraneous Eruptions. 1705**

Kirwan, Richard. **Geological Essays. 1799**

Lambrecht, K. and W. and A. Quenstedt. **Palaeontologi:** Catalogus Bio-Bibliographicus. 1938

Lyell, Charles. **Charles Lyell on North American Geology.** Edited by Hubert C. Skinner. 1977

Lyell, Charles. **Travels in North America in the Years 1841-2.**
Two vols. in one. 1845

Marcou, Jules. **Jules Marcou on the Taconic System in North America.**
Edited by Hubert C. Skinner. 1977

Mariotte, [Edmé]. **The Motion of Water and Other Fluids.** Translated
by J. T. Desaguliers. 1718

Merrill, George P., editor. **Contributions to a History of American
State Geological and Natural History Surveys.** 1920

Miller, Hugh. **The Old Red Sandstone.** 1857

Moore, N[athaniel] F. **Ancient Mineralogy.** 1834

[Murray, John]. **A Comparative View of the Huttonian and Neptunian
Systems of Geology.** 1802

Parkinson, James. **Organic Remains of a Former World.** Three vols.
1833

Phillips, John. **Memoirs of William Smith, LL.D.** 1844

Phillips, William. **An Outline of Mineralogy and Geology.** 1816

Ray, John. **Three Physico-Theological Discourses.** 1713

Scrope, G[eorge] Poulett. **The Geology and Extinct Volcanos of
Central France.** 1858

Sherley, Thomas. **A Philosophical Essay.** 1672

Thomassy, [Marie Joseph] R[aymond]. **Géologie pratique de la
Louisiane.** 1860

Warren, Erasmus. **Geologia:** Or a Discourse Concerning the Earth
Before the Deluge. 1690

Webster, John. **Metallographia:** Or, an History of Metals. 1671

Whiston, William. **A New Theory of the Earth.** 1696

White, George W. **Essays on History of Geology.** 1977

Whitehurst, John. **An Inquiry into the Original State and Formation
of the Earth.** 1786

Woodward, Horace B. **History of Geology.** 1911

Woodward, Horace B. **The History of the Geological Society of London.**
1907

Woodward, John. **An Essay Toward a Natural History of the Earth.**
1695